White Flight

POLITICS AND SOCIETY IN TWENTIETH-CENTURY AMERICA

Series Editors: William Chafe, Gary Gerstle, Linda Gordon, and Julian Zelizer

A list of titles in this series appears at the back of the book.

White Flight

ATLANTA AND THE MAKING OF MODERN CONSERVATISM

Kevin M. Kruse

PRINCETON UNIVERSITY PRESS
PRINCETON AND OXFORD

Library of Congress Cataloging-in-Publication Data
Kruse, Kevin Michael, 1972–
White flight : Atlanta and the making of modern conservatism / Kevin M. Kruse.
p. cm. — (Politics and society in twentieth-century America)
Includes bibliographical references and index.
ISBN 13:978-0-691-09260-7 (cloth : alk. paper)
ISBN 10:0-691-09260-5 (cloth : alk. paper)
1. Atlanta (Ga.)—Race relations. 2. African Americans—Segregation—Georgia—
Atlanta—History—20th century. 3. Atlanta (Ga.)—Politics and government—20th
century. 4. Conservatism—Georgia—Atlanta—History—20th century.
5. Whites—Georgia—Atlanta—Migrations—20th century. 6. Whites—Georgia—
Atlanta—Politics and government—20th century. 7. Government, Resistance to—
Atlanta—History—20th century. I. Title. II. Series.

F294.A89A233 2005
305.8'009758231—dc22   2004062468

British Library Cataloging-in-Publication Data is available

This book has been composed in Sabon

Printed on acid-free paper. ∞

pup.princeton.edu

Printed in the United States of America

10 9 8 7 6 5 4 3 2

for Lindsay

Contents

List of Illustrations

Acknowledgments

THIS BOOK would not have been possible without the inspiration and support of colleagues, friends, and family. There are not enough pages here to thank them properly or enough time to express the depths of my debt to them all.

First, I must thank the three academic communities I have been lucky to call home. As an undergraduate at the University of North Carolina at Chapel Hill, I had the good fortune to learn from Kenneth Janken, John Kasson, and Harry Watson. My thesis adviser there, William Leuchtenburg, showed me at an early stage that a good historian pays attention not just to detail but to his students as well. Then, as a graduate student at Cornell, I thankfully found many more scholars in his mold: Tim Borstelmann, Michael Kammen, Mary Beth Norton, and Dan Usner, to name just a few. As I began my dissertation, my thesis committee, Dick Polenberg, Bob Harris, and Isabel Hull, provided intellectual stimulation, warm encouragement, and thoughtful advice. I especially wish to thank Dick Polenberg, my graduate adviser, whose incisive questions and suggestions improved the project considerably. And though he had no "official" role in the crafting of the dissertation, Nick Salvatore blessed me (and it) with innumerable bits of advice, words of encouragement, and an unflagging spirit of good humor and sharp wit. Finally, as a junior faculty member at Princeton, I have been lucky to have so many colleagues who are both rich with insight and generous with their time. In one form or another, the entire Department of History—faculty, staff, graduate and undergraduate students—has helped make me a better historian and this a better book. But for the time they have spent reading my work and sharing their thoughts with me, I owe a special debt to Jeremy Adelman, Molly Greene, Dirk Hartog, Drew Isenberg, Bill Jordan, Steve Kotkin, Liz Lunbeck, Gyan Prakash, Dan Rodgers, Marc Rodriguez, Nell Painter, Peter Silver, Chris Stansell, Bob Tignor, and Sean Wilentz. Together, the department and the university have provided me with a model environment for intellectual growth and academic production.

Outside of those institutions, countless other scholars have helped this project as well. Sections of the manuscript have been presented as papers at annual meetings of the American Historical Association, the Organization of American Historians, the History of Education Society, and the Southern Historical Association, as well as at smaller conferences, workshops, and invited lectures at the University of Cambridge, the University of Georgia, the University of Oxford, the University of Pennsylvania, Princeton University, Saint Louis University Law School, and the University of Sussex. Many thanks to the warm and receptive audiences at these events and, of course, to the scholars who served as chairs or offered comments: Liz Cohen, Jane Dailey, Pete Daniel, Eddie Glaude, Arnold Hirsch, Yasuhiro Katagiri, Valinda Littlefield, Wendy Plotkin, Bryant Simon, Tom Sugrue, Mark Tushnet, and Wayne Urban. At a later stage, in February 2004, a conference on new themes in suburban history at Princeton let me exchange thoughts with, and learn from, an impressive collection of scholars: Betsy Blackmar, Sheryll Cashin, David Freund, Gerald Frug, Gary Gerstle, Jim Goodman, Arnold Hirsch, Matt Lassiter, Margaret O'Mara, Steve Macedo, Becky Nicolaides, Adam Rome, Robert Self, Peter Siskind, Tom Sugrue, and Andy Wiese. My thinking on what I've come to call the "politics of suburban secession" developed from the wonderful discussions of that weekend.

For additional conversations and insights that shaped the book in important ways, I must also thank Tony Badger, Tomiko Brown-Nagin, Dan Carter, Bill Chafe, Mary Dudziak, Adam Fairclough, Jim Goodman, Linda Gordon, Michael Klarman, Wendell Pritchett, Tom Sugrue, and Stephen Tuck. In particular, Jim Patterson, Matt Lassiter, and Clive Webb deserve special thanks for their close reading of several chapters, while Liz Cohen has earned my endless gratitude for providing a thoughtful and encouraging review of the entire manuscript. Cliff Kuhn served double duty, not only helping me navigate the archives in Atlanta, but also putting his encyclopedic knowledge of the city to work in a close reading of the dissertation. My greatest academic debt goes to Gary Gerstle, who expressed confidence in the project's possibilities at an early stage and did more to aid in its realization than I ever might have hoped. His careful readings of the text and advice for revisions have been invaluable. Moreover, Gary and his fellow series editors provided a wonderful home for the manuscript, while my editor Brigitta van Rheinberg and the staff at Princeton University Press did a tremendous job transforming it into a book.

Portions of this research appeared, in somewhat different form, in two essays previously published by the author: "The Fight for 'Freedom of Association': Segregationist Rights and Resistance in Atlanta," in *Massive Resistance: Southern Opposition to the Second Reconstruction*, Clive Webb, ed. (Oxford University Press, 2005) and "The Politics of Race and Public Space: Desegregation, Privatization and the Tax Revolt in Atlanta," *Journal of Urban History* (September 2005). I would like to thank Oxford University Press and the *Journal of Urban History* for permission to reprint this material.

Many institutions and individuals made the research for this book possible. Financial support from several sources was indispensable. At Cornell, a Sage Fellowship, a Mellon Dissertation Fellowship, and an Ihlder Fellowship from the Department of History all supported this work as a dissertation. At Princeton, assistance from the University Committee on Research, the Dean of the Faculty, and the Department of History subsidized several return trips to Atlanta. Through their generosity, the benefactors who funded the David L. Rike University Preceptorship in History have also afforded me a generous budget for research. The Spencer Foundation, finally, provided grant money that enabled a crucial semester's leave from teaching, during which I was able to complete the manuscript.

As any historian can attest, archivists can make or break a project. This dissertation owes a great deal to the resourcefulness and helpfulness of a good number of archivists, librarians, and staff members in and around the city of Atlanta. The Special Collections and Microfilm staffs at Emory University deserve special praise for making months of research there an unbelievably productive and pleasant time. Likewise, Helen Matthews and the staff of the Atlanta History Center deserve thanks for their unflagging support. Cliff Kuhn and the other researchers responsible for the Georgia Government Documentation Project at Georgia State University have compiled an impressive collection of oral histories which have enriched this project, and many others, to no end. I owe similar debts to the archivists at Atlanta University, the staff of the Atlanta Public School Archives, the record keepers of the Fulton County Superior Court, and the archivists at the National Archives depository in East Point, Georgia, particularly Gary Fulton. For help in securing photographs and publication permissions for the finished book, I must thank Naomi Nelson of Emory University, Pam Prouty of the *Atlanta Journal-Constitution*, and Betsy Rix of the Atlanta History Center. And for his beautiful maps, many thanks to cartographer David Deis.

The two years I lived in the wonderful city of Atlanta were made even happier by the presence of so many good friends who helped me understand the city and, just as important, helped pull me out of the archives on a regular basis: Mike Haslam, Matt Monroe, Jame and Jessica Lathren, Nathan and Chris Seay, Kelly Teasley, and Maggie White. Above all, Dave and Jen Haslam and, in later stages, Tim Sobon opened their homes to me on countless occasions for short and long stays in Atlanta. I can't thank them enough. From long distance, meanwhile, others kept my spirits up: Kevin Brennan, John Lee, Stuart Nichols, Shirley Paddock, John Pijanowski, Dan and Maria Smith, Pete Smith, and Sandro Vitaglione. In the last stages of this project, friends from New York and New Jersey have offered much-needed encouragement and welcome distractions from the last stages of editing: Jason and Jen Calloway, Eric Greenhut, Clea

Karlstrom and Steve Selwood, Adam and Jayne Olsen, Todd Miller, Jake and Cory Raiton, Steve Raizes, Pranay Reddy, Dave Sacks, David and Sara Schivell, Kurt Schliemann and Kathleen Lancaster, Colleen Schwartz, Jon Schwartz, Sheraz Shere, Alan Singer and Cynthia Lawton-Singer. And whenever my energy was low, I could always count on Andre Benjamin, Antwan Patton, Ahmir-Khalib Thompson, Tariq Trotter, Thom Yorke, and company for motivation.

As always, my incredible family managed to keep me going throughout this project. My sisters, Amy and Lisa, and my brother, Eric, have always been there to lift my spirits when I needed it and to put me in my place when I needed that. Their spouses, Jim Hubbuch, Jeff Carter, and Shala Kruse, have not only given me a great deal of encouragement, but four nieces and a nephew too. My in-laws, Lorne and Marg Hamilton, have always made me feel like a son instead of a son-in-law, and Marlo and Chris Gaddis have welcomed me into their family as well. My own parents, Mike and Mary Jean Kruse, have given me so much I don't know where to begin. They were the first and most important teachers in my life. They have been a shining example of love and commitment, of dedication and perseverance through adversity. For those lessons and more, I can't thank them enough. Most of all, I owe my greatest debt to my wife and best friend, Lindsay. She has read every word, listened to every headache, and heard every anecdote more times than she could have cared to do. She has put up with my absence when the writing was going well and, worse, my presence when it was not. The dedication page of this book was given to her as a gift for our first wedding anniversary, the "paper" anniversary. Every other page reflects the dedication she has always shown me.

—Jersey City, New Jersey, August 2004

White Flight

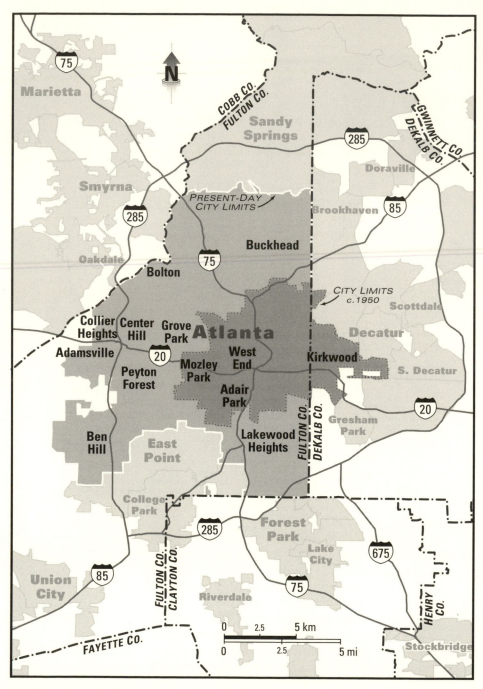

1.1 Overview map of Atlanta

Introduction

IN THE STORIES spun by its supporters, Atlanta had accomplished the unthinkable. Their city was moving forward, they boasted, not just in its bank accounts and business ledgers, but in the ways the races were learning to live and even thrive together. While the rest of the South spent the postwar decades resisting desegregation with a defiant and often ugly program of "massive resistance," Atlanta faced the challenges of the civil rights era with maturity and moderation. During these decades, the city had emerged as a shining example for the New South, a place where economic progress and racial progressivism went hand in hand. This was, to be sure, not an empty boast. By the end of the 1950s these supporters could point with pride to a litany of sites that the city had desegregated, from public spaces like the buses, airport, libraries, and golf courses to countless private neighborhoods in between. When Atlanta successfully desegregated its public schools in 1961, even national observers paused to marvel at all the city had accomplished. The city found countless admirers across the country, from the press to the president of the United States, but it was ultimately its own Mayor William Hartsfield who coined the lasting motto. "Atlanta," he bragged to anyone in earshot, "is the City Too Busy to Hate."[1]

Just a year later, this image came crashing down. The trouble surfaced in an unlikely place, a quiet, middle-class subdivision of brick ranch houses and loblolly pines called Peyton Forest. And the trouble started in an unlikely way, as city construction crews built a pair of roadblocks on Peyton and Harlan Roads. The barriers seemed to have no significance. They were simply wooden beams which had been painted black and white, bolted to steel I-beams, and sunk into the pavement. But their significance lay in their location. As all Atlantans understood, the roadblocks stood at the precise fault line between black and white sections of the city. Over the previous two decades, black Atlantans had escaped the overcrowded inner city and purchased more and more homes in neighborhoods to the west; during the same period, white Atlantans to the south had grown increasingly alarmed as those areas "went colored." The roadblocks were meant to keep these two communities apart and at peace, but they had the opposite effect. Indeed, the barricades immediately attracted intense national and even international attention. Civil rights activists surrounded the racial "buffer zone" with picket lines, while wire photos carried the images across the globe, sparking an unprecedented public relations nightmare. "We Want No Warsaw Ghetto," read one picket. Another denounced "Atlanta's Image: A Berlin Wall." Civil rights organizations announced they would launch a boycott against area merchants unless the barriers were removed, and two lawsuits were immediately filed in local courts. Mayor Ivan Allen Jr., who had recently replaced Hartsfield in office, had expected some backlash but was stunned by its intensity. From retirement, his predecessor offered a bit of belated advice: "Never make a mistake they can take a picture of."[2]

As the national press denounced the "Atlanta Wall," local whites embraced the roadblocks as their salvation. The day after the crews sealed off their streets, residents wrapped the barricades in Christmas paper and ribbon; beneath the words "Road Closed," someone added, "Thank the Lord!" Meanwhile, a powerful organization of white homeowners, the Southwest Citizens Association, sought to explain white residents' perspective. President Virgil Copeland, a Lockheed employee, told reporters that the barricades were simply a response to the "vicious, block-busting tactics being used by Negro realtors." Carlton Owens, an engineer at Atlantic Steel and a member of Southwest Citizens' board of directors, noted that several residents had said they were going to "sell and get out" if something concrete were not done "to stabilize the situation." "The barricades were erected for that purpose," Copeland added, "and we think they will do it. All we want to do is to keep our homes." Barbara Ryckeley, an officer with Southwest Citizens, pointed out that not just Peyton Forest but all of white Atlanta was "endangered" by black expansion. "If the whites could just win once," she explained, "they would have some hope for holding out. I think the whole city of Atlanta is at stake. You realize that every time Negroes replace whites about eighty-five percent of the whites move out of the city?"[3]

As much as they embraced the "Peyton Wall," these whites worried it would not be enough. Two weeks later, their fears came true. Sources reported that blacks were closing deals on three homes on Lynhurst Drive, immediately west of the Peyton Forest neighborhood. According to alarmist press coverage, the sales represented a deliberate attempt to break through the roadblocks—a "flank attack" on the all-white neighborhood. "If those barricades hadn't been put up," an unnamed "Negro leader" was quoted as saying, "I don't think Lynhurst would have been bothered." As white residents expressed outrage, black real-estate agents claimed the story had been concocted by Southwest Citizens. Soon, this war of words escalated into a pitched battle. Late one Friday night in February, "parties unknown" descended on the Harlan Road barricade, pulled the I-beams out of the ground, sawed the timbers in half, and tossed the scraps into a nearby creek. The next morning, stunned residents grabbed saws and hand tools, chopped down nearby brush and trees, dragged the debris into the street and added a few dozen heavy stones for good measure. That night, the raiders returned and set fire to the new barricade. Once firefighters subdued the blaze, Mayor Allen announced that the city would rebuild the barricades, deploring the fact that "any group has seen fit to take the law into their own hands." Early Monday morning, construction crews sunk new beams into the scorched asphalt, attaching steel rails this time to prevent further fires. Just to make sure, small groups of robed Klansmen stood guard at the barricades on Monday and Tuesday night. Patrolling the street, they held aloft signs: "Whites Have Rights, Too."[4]

In spite of the movement to insure its permanence, the "Peyton Wall" was short-lived. Local courts quickly ruled against the roadblocks and the mayor, relieved to find a way out of the public relations nightmare, had them immediately removed. But as the barricades were destroyed, so was whites' confidence in the neighborhood. In less than a month, most homes in Peyton Forest—including that of Virgil Copeland, the head of the homeowners' resistance movement—were listed for sale with black real-estate agents. "When the barricades came down, everything collapsed," he told a reporter. "It's all over out there for us." Indeed, by the end of July 1963 all but fifteen white families had sold their homes to black buyers and abandoned the neighborhood. They were not simply fleeing Peyton Forest, Copeland pointed out, but the city itself. "We are trying to find some area outside the city limits where we can buy homes and get away from the problem" of desegregation, he noted. "Everybody I know is definitely leaving the city of Atlanta."[5]

The "Peyton Wall" incident, as famous as it was fleeting, was only the most public eruption of the much larger phenomenon of white flight. That year alone, the beleaguered mayor noted, City Hall had been confronted with 52 separate cases of "racial transition," incidents in which whites fled from neighborhoods as blacks bought homes there. And although the information never appeared in Atlanta's positive press coverage, a steady stream of white flight had in fact been underway for nearly a decade. During the five years before the 1962 Peyton Forest panic, for instance, nearly 30,000 whites had abandoned the city. Afterward, the numbers only grew larger. In 1960 the total white population of Atlanta stood at barely more than 300,000. Over the course of that decade, roughly 60,000 whites fled from Atlanta. During the 1970s, another 100,000 would leave as well. "The City Too Busy to Hate," the skeptics noted, had become "The City Too Busy *Moving* to Hate."[6]

This book explores the causes and course of white flight, with Atlanta serving as its vantage point. Although it represented one of the largest, most significant, and most transformative social movements in postwar America, white flight has never been studied in depth or detail. Indeed, the scant attention it has received has only been as a causal factor for other concerns, such as the decline of central cities and the rise of suburbia. This study, however, seeks to explore not simply the effects of white flight, but the experience. While many have assumed that white flight was little more than a literal movement of the white population, this book argues that it represented a much more important transformation in the political ideology of those involved. Because of their confrontation with the civil rights movement, white southern conservatives were forced to abandon their traditional, populist, and often starkly racist demagoguery and instead craft a new conservatism predicated on a language of rights, freedoms, and individualism. This modern conservatism proved to be both subtler and stronger than the politics that preceded it and helped southern conservatives dominate the Republican Party and, through it, national politics as well. White flight, in the end, was more than a physical relocation. It was a political revolution.

In order to understand white flight with precision, we first need to understand the whites who were involved. As a starting point, therefore, this study seeks to reconstruct the world of segregationists, without relying on familiar stereotypes. In the traditional narrative, white resistance to desegregation has generally been framed as yet another southern lost cause. In the wake of the Supreme Court's ruling against desegregation in *Brown*, this story goes, southern politicians on the national scene denounced the decision in no uncertain terms, while their counterparts in state politics passed a wide array of legislation to prevent desegregation at home. This campaign of political resistance was reinforced on a second front, as segregationist organizations employed extralegal and illegal methods to enforce conformity among whites and inspire fear among blacks. At the forefront of this movement, the powerful White Citizens' Councils used economic reprisals to intimidate those who dared to challenge the racial status quo. Although the Councils did not advocate violence, their endorsement of resistance encouraged cruder acts of intimidation and terrorism. The Ku Klux Klan soon rode again in the South, and a wave of murder, assault, and arson followed in its wake. For a time, these assorted groups succeeded in their campaign against desegregation. But in the end, the determined activism of the civil rights movement and, in time, the intervention of the federal government overcame the resistance of these die-hard segregationists. By the mid-1960s, with black children enrolled in once-white schools across the South and major pieces of civil rights legislation passed at the national level, this narrative concludes, the forces of massive resistance had been soundly defeated.[7] Recent revisions to this traditional narrative have only concluded that massive resistance was perhaps even more of a failure than originally thought. According to this argument, segregationist brutality and lawlessness only elicited the nation's sympathies for the civil rights movement and inspired the intervention of the federal government. Massive resistance not only failed to save segregation, this theory holds, but actually helped speed its demise.[8]

As compelling as this traditional interpretation of massive resistance has been, it suffers from a focus that stresses the words and deeds of top-level politicians over the lived realities of everyday whites. This approach dates back more than three decades, when historian Numan Bartley firmly entrenched such a top-down political perspective in his seminal study of massive resistance.[9] The studies that followed in his wake have largely fleshed out the original framework, detailing the different components of white political resistance. Some scholars have offered close studies of the careers of segregationist politicians,[10] while others have chronicled the growth of the white supremacist organizations that acted as their unofficial allies.[11] Still others have conducted thorough studies of the southern communities that served as the central stages in this political drama.[12] Ironically, because of their reliance on this top-down political perspective, such studies have actually missed some of the most important political changes that occurred at the grass roots during these years. At the top levels of southern politics, massive resistance stood as a campaign that accepted no alteration in the racial status quo and allowed no room for accommodation with change. In the famous phrasing of Alabama governor George Wallace, this stance became cemented as a defiant promise: "Segregation now! Segregation tomorrow! Segregation forever!" Indeed, Wallace's career represents a repeated series of such stances, ranging from his promise never again to be "out-niggered" in politics to his defiant "stand in the schoolhouse door."[13] Looking back on white opposition to desegregation, many historians have seized upon the promises and posings of such politicians and assumed that segregationist resistance was precisely the all-or-nothing proposition that its boldest defenders made it out to be. Rendering judgment on the movement's success, these observers have simply compared the promises to preserve the racial status quo of 1954 with the realities of desegregation a decade later. Judged by such standards, the conclusion was clear: massive resistance failed.

This study, however, argues that white resistance to desegregation was never as immobile or monolithic as its practitioners and chroniclers would have us believe. Indeed, segregationists could be incredibly innovative in the strategies and tactics they used to confront the civil rights movement. In recent work on the late nineteenth- and early twentieth-century South, several historians have argued that the system of racial segregation was never a fixed entity, but rather a fluid relationship in which blacks and whites constantly adjusted to meet changing circumstances.[14] If the southern system of racial subjugation is understood as responsive to change during its era of dominance, it naturally follows that segregationist ideology and strategy did not remain inert when the system confronted, in the form of the civil rights movement, a threat to its very existence. And, as this story makes clear, the original goals of massive resistance were, in fact, frequently revisited and revised as the struggle to defend the "southern way of life" stretched on. While national politicians waged a reactionary struggle in the courts and Congress to preserve the old system of de jure segregation, those at the local level were discovering a number of ways in which they could preserve and, indeed, perfect the realities of racial segregation outside the realm of law and politics. Ultimately, the mass migration of whites from cities to the suburbs proved to be the most successful segregationist response to the moral demands of the civil rights movement and the legal authority of the courts. Although the suburbs were just as segregated as the city—and, truthfully, often more so—white residents succeeded in convincing the courts, the nation, and even themselves that this phenomenon represented de facto segregation, something that stemmed not from the race-conscious actions of residents but instead from less offensive issues like class stratification and postwar sprawl. To be sure, on the surface, the world of white suburbia looked little like the world of white supremacy. But these worlds did have much in common— from the remarkably similar levels of racial, social, and political homogeneity to their shared ideologies that stressed individual rights over communal responsibilities, privatization over public welfare, and "free enterprise" above everything else. By withdrawing to the suburbs and recreating its world there, the politics of massive resistance continued to thrive for decades after its supposed death.

If we shift our attention away from politicians and focus on the lives of ordinary segregationists, the flexibility and continuity of white resistance becomes clear. Exploring the ever-shifting terrain of race relations and conservative politics at the grass roots, this study finds inspiration in the work of many others. In recent years, for instance, a new generation of scholarship on the civil rights movement has moved beyond simply recounting the words and deeds of prominent civil rights leaders to delve instead into the hopes and beliefs of ordinary African Americans. As a result, our understanding of that movement has been enriched by a better appreciation of the social texture of the African American community.[15] Building on such work, new studies in southern history have likewise sought to move beyond a superficial understanding of segregationists and instead root the actions of ordinary whites in a deeper social and cultural analysis.[16] At the same time, other historians have chronicled the course of modern conservatism in areas outside the South, taking their subjects seriously and thereby reconstructing their world and worldview as they themselves understood them.[17] This book draws on the insights and interpretations of such works, seeking to treat its subjects with the same degree of seriousness.

If we truly seek to understand segregationists—not to excuse or absolve them, but to understand them—then we must first understand how they understood themselves. Until now, because of the tendency to focus on the reactionary leaders of massive resistance, segregationists have largely been understood simply as the opposition to the civil rights movement. They have been framed as a group focused solely on suppressing the rights of others, whether that be the larger cause of "civil rights" or any number of individual entitlements, such as the rights of blacks to vote, assemble, speak, protest, or own property. Segregationists, of course, did stand against those things, and often with bloody and brutal consequences. But, like all people, they did not think of themselves in terms of what they opposed but rather in terms of what they supported. The conventional wisdom has held that they were only fighting *against* the rights of others. But, in their own minds, segregationists were instead fighting *for* rights of their own—such as the "right" to select their neighbors, their employees, and their children's classmates, the "right" to do as they pleased with their private property and personal businesses, and, perhaps most important, the "right" to remain free from what they saw as dangerous encroachments by the federal government. To be sure, all of these positive "rights" were grounded in a negative system of discrimination and racism. In the minds of segregationists, however, such rights existed all the same. Indeed, from their perspective, it was clearly they who defended individual freedom, while the "so-called civil rights activists" aligned themselves with a powerful central state, demanded increased governmental regulation of local affairs, and waged a sustained assault on the individual economic, social, and political prerogatives of others. The true goal of desegregation, these white southerners insisted, was not to end the system of racial oppression in the South, but to install a new system that oppressed them instead. As this study demonstrates, southern whites fundamentally understood their support of segregation as a defense of their own liberties, rather than a denial of others'.[18]

Understanding segregationists in such a light illuminates the links between massive resistance and modern conservatism. Those responsible for the rise of the New Right have long denied any connection between these two strands of American conservatism. In 1984, for instance, noted conservative activist Paul Weyrich asserted that the leadership of the New Right "bears no resemblance to the reactionary Southern icons of the past."[19] Despite such claims, several historians and journalists have repeatedly linked the New Right with the Old South. Much like the traditional narrative of massive resistance, their interpretation has generally relied on a top-down explanation of political transformation predicated on the presidential campaigns of Strom Thurmond, Barry Goldwater, George Wallace, Richard Nixon, and Ronald Reagan. Focusing largely on closed-door strategy sessions and stump speeches of such conservative politicians, these studies have paid particular attention to their use of the "racially coded language" first developed by segregationists like George Wallace to appeal to white voters in national campaigns. Some of the more famous instances, such as Ronald Reagan's anecdote about the apocryphal Chicago "welfare queen" and George H. W. Bush's notorious Willie Horton advertisement, seemed less-than-subtle appeals to racist assumptions about black criminality and shiftlessness. While this study does not discount the importance of such language and imagery, it argues that the connections between the Old South and New Right run much deeper than mere rhetorical appeals to racism.[20]

This study advances a new perspective on the connections between southern segregationists and modern conservatives. Although it touches on the conventional political narrative that has contributed to our understanding of the origins of the New Right, it has a rather different dynamic. Instead of focusing on the ways in which national politicians sought to exploit the anger and alienation of white voters, this study focuses on those whites themselves. The conventional framework, with its attention on the highest levels of national campaigns, largely neglects the important transformations taking place at the grass roots. More problematic, because it focuses only on the more famous flashpoints in presidential politics, this narrative inexplicably skips past the years between the Dixiecrat rebellion of 1948 and the Goldwater campaign of 1964. Because racial conservatism was not a central issue in the intervening elections, the creation narrative of modern conservatism has overlooked that era entirely. But during the decade and a half between the collapse of the Dixiecrats and the rise of the Goldwater Republicans came one of the most turbulent and transformative eras in southern history. The vast bulk of the civil rights movement and the white resistance it inspired unfolded in the late 1940s, 1950s, and early 1960s. During that period the entire southern landscape was reshaped. Southern politics was no exception.

In the end, this work demonstrates that the struggle over segregation thoroughly reshaped southern conservatism. Traditional conservative elements, such as hostility to the federal government and faith in free enterprise, underwent fundamental transformations. At the same time, segregationist resistance inspired the creation of new conservative causes, such as tuition vouchers, the tax revolt, and the privatazation of public services. Until now, the origins of those phenomena have been located in the suburban areas of the South and Southwest, a region since christened the "Sunbelt."[21] In recent years, scholars have explored that landscape to explain the rise of the "tax revolt" in the late 1970s,[22] the trend toward isolation in exclusive "gated communities" in the 1980s,[23] and the attendant privatization of public services thereafter, ranging from the establishment of private security forces to the campaign for tuition vouchers for private education.[24] While this scholarship generally assumed that such conservative trends emerged from an established suburban Sunbelt in the late 1970s and 1980s, this book argues, to the contrary, that those trends were already apparent before the rise of the suburbs, inside cities such as Atlanta, as early as the 1950s.

In locating the origins of these phenomena in urban, and not suburban, politics, this book considers the origins of the conservative "counterrevolution" in their proper environment. Problematically, some accounts often start their stories only after the white suburbs had become an accomplished fact. And by solely examining the conservative political outlook in that overwhelmingly white and predominantly upper-middle-class environment, these observers have often failed to appreciate the importance of race and class in the formation of this new conservative ideology. Inside such a homogeneous setting, it is perhaps easy to understand how some have accepted without question the claims of some conservative activists that their movement was—and still is—"color-blind" and unassociated with class politics.[25] Indeed, in the suburbs, with no other colors in sight and no other classes in contention, such claims seem plausible. How could modern conservatism be shaped by forces that weren't there? But, as this study shows, when the conservative politics of the Sunbelt is correctly situated in the crucible of urban politics, surrounded by different races, multiple classes, and competing social interests, it can be seen in a rather different light.

Indeed, a community-level approach helps illuminate the realities of white resistance to desegregation in a number of ways. First, such a perspective best brings into focus the complex relationships between people and places, which are always their clearest at the local level. Only by restricting the scope of a study to a specific setting and a finite time can otherwise unwieldy issues—racism, segregation, backlash, and "white flight"—be dissected and discussed in any meaningful detail. Second, this work employs a community-level approach to demonstrate the interconnected nature of different stages of white resistance. Too often, civil rights histories have focused on a single aspect of the story, such as school desegregation or the sit-ins, without acknowledging that all these struggles were closely intertwined in the minds of whites and blacks alike.[26] As this book demonstrates, white resistance to desegregation was much more complex than previously understood. Chronicling the course of segregationist activity, in a single city, in a single era, allows for patterns of individual involvement, cycles of protest and politics, and an overall evolution of segregationist thought and conservative ideology to come into focus.

In examining these issues inside the urban environment, this study adopts an approach used by urban historians in recent years to explore postwar race relations in northern cities, particularly Chicago and Detroit. Like those histories, this work discovers an interconnected web of racial, social, and economic conflicts inside Atlanta's city limits that suggests that the "urban crisis" was a phenomenon that stretched far beyond the industrial Northeast. In the struggles over race and residence, for instance, Atlanta closely resembles those cities. The familiar language of homeowners' rights and community protection resurfaces in white neighborhoods here, as does the pattern of violence visited upon all those who challenged them. The common themes shared by the homeowners' movements of the urban North and the segregationist resistance of the urban South suggest that the white backlash that surfaced in later years was not, as many assumed at the time, a southern product imported to the North. Instead, white flight was a phenomenon that developed in cities throughout the nation, with the commonalities and cross-regional connections only becoming clear in retrospect.[27]

While this study sees more similarities than differences in the urban struggles of the North and South, it does find such differences. Unlike northern studies, which uncovered large amounts of "hidden violence" sparked by residential conflicts and chronicled a successful white resistance to racial change, this study demonstrates, almost counterintuitively, that whites in this segregated city were generally less violent in their resistance and less successful than their counterparts in the urban North. The relative failure of racists in Atlanta was not due to their lack of commitment to the cause, but because the black population they challenged was both larger and stronger than those in the North. In terms of percentages, Atlanta's black population outpaced that of most northern cities: in 1940, for instance, blacks represented 35 percent of Atlanta's population, but just 8 and 9 percent in Chicago and Detroit, respectively. By the 1970s, as the disparities in racial percentages narrowed, these metropolitan areas looked more alike—with black political power rising in the cities and conservative white suburbs growing around them. But the paths taken by northern and southern cities to that common destination had decidedly different origins. In cities of the postwar South, the larger demographic presence of African Americans meant that both the pressure for racial residential transition and the political clout of the black community were much stronger than in the North. As a result, southern whites were confronted with a pace of residential racial change that came much earlier, faster, and stronger than their northern counterparts.[28]

Readers familiar with the Rust Belt narrative will find other differences in the Sunbelt. For one, the relative lack of heavy industry in Atlanta and most other southern cities dictated a different pattern of postwar change, especially in regard to race. In northern cities, the predominance of heavy industry helped move race relations in both progressive and reactionary directions. At first, the rise of biracial unions served as an early impetus for desegregation not simply on the shop floor but throughout the city. But as hard times fell on northern cities, the consequences of economic decline and deindustrialization—massive layoffs, plant closings, and industrial relocation to the suburbs—not only fueled white flight, but also served to splinter the unions and, in the process, the entire liberal-labor political alliance. But in the South, with a few notable exceptions, the postwar urban struggle centered not on deindustrialization but desegregation.[29] Again, this represented a key difference. In most northern cities, court-ordered desegregation had no direct impact until the early 1970s, when the Supreme Court considered—albeit briefly—the implementation of metropolitan-wide remedies such as cross-district busing. When busing became an issue in nonsouthern cities like Denver, Detroit, and Boston, it had a tremendous impact on white flight and urban decay. But until then, school desegregation played virtually no role. In the South, however, desegregation, especially in the schools, had tremendous influence during the 1950s and 1960s in reshaping cities and the course of white resistance within them. Desegregation of neighborhood schools impacted surrounding neighborhoods, of course, convincing white residents to sell their homes and leading community institutions to pull up roots. The process worked in reverse as well, as racial residential change often prompted the transfer of public schools and other public spaces from white to black hands. The changes that deindustrialization made to the physical landscape of Rust Belt cities have been widely recognized, but this study argues that desegregation had just as significant an impact on the structures and spaces of the urban and suburban Sunbelt.

On the surface, Atlanta may seem an odd focal point for examining the ways in which white resistance reshaped the urban environment, social relations, and political ideology of the South. For contemporaries, Atlanta always seemed an exception to the segregationist rule, a city that presented a moderate image and contributed much to the civil rights movement. Central figures in the African American struggle for equality, such as W.E.B. Du Bois, James Weldon Johnson, Walter White, Martin Luther King Sr., Martin Luther King Jr., Ralph Abernathy, Whitney Young, Julian Bond, John Lewis, Andrew Young, and Vernon Jordan, all lived inside its limits at one time or another. Likewise, key civil rights agencies, such as the Commission on Interracial Cooperation, the Southern Regional Council (SRC), the Southern Christian Leadership Conference (SCLC), and the Student Non-Violent Coordinating Committee (SNCC), all called Atlanta home. So too did the South's premier cluster of black colleges, Atlanta University, and the region's best-known hub of black economic activity, Auburn Avenue. There was, perhaps, no clearer source of African American strength in the modern South than Atlanta.[30]

This is all true. But as Atlanta emerged as the center of civil rights activity, it still remained the site of sustained segregationist resistance. Some of the most brutal incidents of Jim Crow violence occurred inside Atlanta, including a notoriously bloody race riot in 1906 and the infamous lynching of Leo Frank in 1913. In the 1920s and 1930s, the Ku Klux Klan located its national headquarters on prestigious Peachtree Street; after the Second World War, a revived version of the hooded order held its ceremonial rebirth just outside the city's limits. (One historian of the Klan has gone so far as to anoint Atlanta "its holy city.") Aside from the several incarnations of that organization, other white supremacist groups have anchored themselves in Atlanta as well, including the country's first neo-Nazi organization. During the civil rights era, a number of the South's leading segregationists called Atlanta their home, including Eugene and Herman Talmadge, Marvin Griffin, Calvin Craig, and Lester Maddox. Tellingly, when segregationists waged legal challenges against the 1964 Civil Rights Act, two of the three cases came from Atlanta.[31]

Given the central historical importance of Atlanta, for both civil rights activists and segregationists alike, the lack of scholarship on its changes during the civil rights era is surprising, to say the least. Recently, fine work has been done on race relations in the first half of the century,[32] but the historiography on the postwar era remains thin. What scant scholarship does exist has been dominated by a paradigm stressing the centrality of the "community power structure" above all else. Now commonplace, the phrase was originally coined to describe Atlanta, a city long controlled by a moderate coalition of businessmen and boosterish politicians.[33] In studies centered on this power structure, the course of civil rights has usually been addressed, but only in relation to the main concern of mainstream politics. After World War II, African Americans emerged as a crucial part of the coalition that controlled the city, and, as such, these scholars have had to explain their rise to prominence and their role as the "junior partner" in a reformulated power structure.[34] But black Atlantans operating outside—or even against—the dominant political coalition have received little attention in these works.[35] In the past decade, additional works on the civil rights era have appeared,[36] but little change has been made to the "community power structure" approach created a half century ago. Black radicals are still marginalized. Meanwhile, the great numbers of white working-class and middle-class segregationists aligned on the other side of the racial divide have received no attention at all.[37]

   This book seeks to change that approach, shifting the focus to those whites who found themselves outside the mainstream of the moderate coalition and who, in time, moved themselves outside the city as well. A focus on the resistance of such whites, predominantly of the working and middle classes, should not be misinterpreted as a simplistic claim that they alone were racist while other whites were not. In the end, virtually all whites reacted to the course of civil rights change with some degree of opposition and distancing. For working-class whites, the confrontation came in the late 1940s and early 1950s, as their neighborhoods emerged as the focal point in the city's struggles over residential desegregation. With middle-class whites, however, the conflict only surfaced in the second half of the 1950s, as residential desegregation spread into their neighborhoods and, more important, as the public spaces they frequented—parks, bus lines, and the public schools in particular—came under the mandate of court-ordered desegregation. Upper-class whites, meanwhile, stuck by the moderate coalition until the early 1960s, when civil rights activists targeted both their public lives, as the sit-ins focused on the businesses they owned, and their private lives, as civil rights leaders questioned their commitment to integration in light of the segregated world in which they lived and played. *How* whites reacted to desegregation thus emerges as a constant. As this study shows, class differences merely determined *where* and *when* they did so.

   The story that follows takes place in the city and suburbs of Atlanta but has connections to the country as a whole. It has such connections not simply because the local struggle over segregation spread across the region and sought resolution in national politics, but because the issues that stood at the center of that struggle also stood at the center of the postwar national debate: the demise of white supremacy and the rise of white suburbia; the fragmentation of old liberal coalitions and the construction of new conservative ones; the contested relationship between the federal government and state and local entities; the debates over the public realm and the private; the struggle over the distribution of money and the sharing of power; the competing claims to basic rights and responsibilities of citizenship; and, of course, conflicts rooted in divisions of generation, class, and, above all, race. All these issues spread far beyond the city limits of Atlanta and into every corner of the country. In the end, then, this is not simply an Atlanta story or a southern story. It is, instead, an American story.

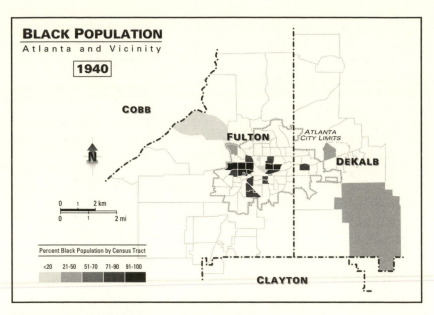

Map 1.2 Black population, Atlanta and vicinity, 1940

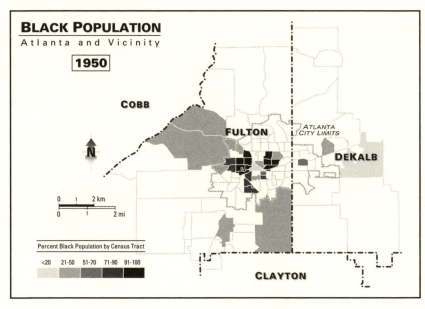

Map 1.3 Black population, Atlanta and vicinity, 1950

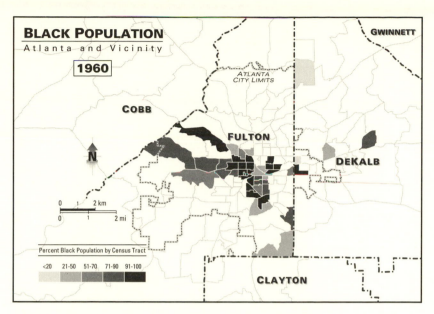

Map 1.4 Black population, Atlanta and vicinity, 1960

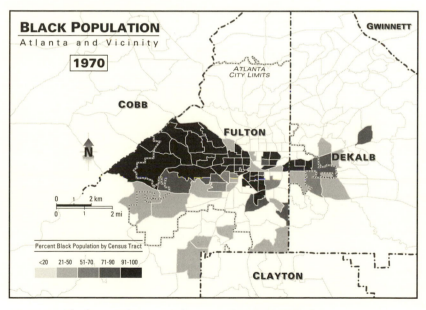

Map 1.5 Black population, Atlanta and vicinity, 1970

CHAPTER ONE

"The City Too Busy to Hate": Atlanta and the Politics of Progress

THE STORY OF Atlanta's struggles with segregation was centered, oddly enough, on neither the crusade of civil rights activists nor the reactionary resistance of segregationists. Instead, the tale balanced on the moderate coalition that controlled the city in the postwar era. During those decades, an unlikely collection of moderate white politicians, elite businessmen, and African American leaders dictated the pace of racial change. Seeing the successes of "the city too busy to hate," visitors arriving in Atlanta were stunned by the differences they saw between it and other cities in the Deep South. Repeatedly, they found themselves reduced to what became a common litany of questions. How did Atlanta do it? How did the white elites take control of local politics in a city and state so dominated by other classes of whites? How did they come to find common cause with a racial minority oppressed throughout the rest of the region? How did blacks, meanwhile, overcome the significant legal and political obstacles in their way to become a central political power inside Atlanta? And once both groups had succeeded, how—and why—did they join forces?

While such questions about Atlanta's leaders were asked and answered countless times, those posing them rarely came away with much in the way of details. Floyd Hunter, a sociology graduate student from the University of North Carolina, was determined to dig deeper. In a stroke of luck, for both Hunter and those who sought insight into the true patterns of political power in Atlanta, he secured an audience in late 1950 with a man who had not only all the answers but a willingness to share them. Hughes Spalding, senior partner in Atlanta's most prestigious law firm, welcomed the student to his offices and, to Hunter's astonishment, proceeded to lead him through a frank and detailed blueprint of the highest levels of politics and society in Atlanta. "You fellows who make these surveys most of the time do not get 'under the crust,' " Spalding told his stunned guest. "I'm going to take you under the crust." Over the next hour, the lawyer discussed in candid detail the inner workings of the coalition that ran the city. As Hunter took notes, Spalding traced the behind-the-scenes networks linking city hall and the Atlanta Chamber of Commerce, tracking the ways in which the city's political and business elites worked together to keep both races in Atlanta prosperous and at peace.[1]

Walking away from the session, Hunter searched for a way to describe all he had learned. In the end, he found himself forced to coin a new phrase, one that would change the ways sociologists, historians, and political scientists thought about local government. Atlanta, he decided, was ruled by a "community power structure." Actually, as Hunter soon discovered, the city had two power structures, not one. The white elite was not the only game in town. "I find that it will be necessary to run a separate study in the Negro community," he informed his thesis adviser. "There is a power structure there that cannot be overlooked, and follows, as far as I can see at this point, much the same pattern as the white." And so, just as Hunter traveled to Spalding's offices to learn about the white elite, so too did he visit the corridors of power in black Atlanta to understand its dynamics. Through his travels between black and white Atlanta, Hunter uncovered the secrets of the city's moderate coalition. In the wake of World War II, these two elites, white and black, had worked together to create something in the city that stood apart from the more familiar politics of white supremacy surrounding Atlanta: a political system that saw racial progressivism and economic progress as inseparable.[2]

The close cooperation of Atlanta's elites did not mean that racism or racial politics did not exist inside the city. Far from it, in fact. When Hunter asked Hughes Spalding to name some of the "major issues before the Atlanta community," the attorney answered, "I will give you one— segregation. You can slice that one in two and have two [issues] if you want to, or if you want four, cut it four ways." Segregation overshadowed everything, he suggested. And yet, even if the blacks and whites of Atlanta found themselves focused on the racial lines between them, they managed to work across those lines, not simply for their own self-interest but for the common good of the city as well. Ultimately, the story of Atlanta's moderate coalition signaled a departure from a traditional southern politics dominated by white supremacy and rural interests. It represented, instead, a bold model that held that progress in race relations would create progress in economic growth, too. As Hunter and countless others recognized, this was something new.[3]

Georgia and the "Rule of the Rustics"

For the first half of the twentieth century, Georgia was dominated by the politics of rural racism. In the decades after Reconstruction, the state steadily robbed blacks of their hard-won right to vote. The first stage of disfranchisement came in 1877, when the legislature installed a cumulative poll tax. Most freedmen, along with many poor whites, proved unable or unwilling to pay all their back taxes. By 1900 only one out of every ten eligible blacks remained on the rolls. That same year, hoping to rid themselves of that remnant of voters as well, the state Democratic Party began to bar blacks from its primaries. With the Populists in disarray and Republicans reduced to numbers of no consequence, a whites-only Democratic primary effectively removed black voters from the political process altogether. As an added precaution, the state assembly pushed through a constitutional amendment in 1908 to establish the additional burdens of a grandfather clause, literacy test, and property qualification. Taken together, this coordinated attack on black Georgians erased their presence from state politics for decades to come.[4]

As Georgia undermined black voters through disfranchisement and discrimination, it likewise weakened urban voters through the "county unit" system. Under this scheme, installed in 1917, statewide and congressional contests were determined not by the popular vote, but through an arcane electoral arithmetic instead. Originally, each county in Georgia was granted twice as many unit votes as it had members in the lower house of the legislature. The eight most populous counties received six votes each; the next largest thirty took four votes apiece; and the remaining 122 counties each had two. In elections, the candidate with a plurality of votes in a county took all of its votes. When the system was first installed, the distribution of unit votes roughly corresponded to that of the state's population. The allotments were not tied to population shifts, however, but instead remained fixed. As urban populations grew and rural ones shrank, the county unit system thus ensured that smaller counties wielded wildly disproportionate political power. (In 1946, for instance, 14,092 votes from Atlanta's Fulton County carried precisely the same weight as 132 votes from rural Chattahoochee County.) Because of this imbalance, candidates in statewide races simply ignored the cities and concentrated on the four- and two-unit counties of the countryside. As a result, Georgia politics embodied, in the apt phrase of political scientist V. O. Key Jr., the "Rule of the Rustics."[5]

The disfranchisement of blacks and the county unit system ensured that Georgia's politics would be dominated by the forces of rural racism for decades. More than anyone else, Eugene Talmadge embodied that world. A consummate campaigner, the "wild man from Sugar Creek" appeared in all but one statewide Democratic primary in the years between 1926 and 1946. Famous for his fiery stump speeches, Talmadge proved incredibly popular among poverty-stricken whites in the countryside. As he liked to brag, "The poor dirt farmer ain't got but three friends on this earth: God Almighty, Sears Roebuck, and Gene Talmadge." The key to his popularity was his stress on white supremacy. "I was raised among niggers and I understand them," he told crowds from the stump. "I want to see them treated fairly and I want to see them have justice in the courts. But I want

Figure 1.1 A massive rally for Governor Eugene Talmadge in rural Georgia. Elected governor four times and commissioner of agriculture three more, Talmadge was an incredibly popular figure with rural white voters.

to deal with the nigger this way; he must come to my back door, take off his hat, and say, 'Yes, sir.' " This raw racism won Talmadge the overwhelming support of rural whites, which, through the county unit system, won him elections. By 1940 Gene Talmadge had been elected governor three times and commissioner of agriculture three more.[6]

With the dawn of the 1940s, Talmadge and the politics of rural racism seemed permanently cemented in the state. "By the World War II years," historian Numan Bartley has observed, "Georgia's segregated social system had hardened into a rigid caste structure accepted by virtually all whites and substantial numbers of blacks as the ordained and proper way of doing things." Even the unwieldy county unit system had assumed a sense of permanence. In the words of Herman Talmadge, Eugene's son and heir apparent, the system represented a time-honored tradition dating "back before the Christian era when people had similar tribe representation." It was, he hinted, the way things were meant to be. Together, the two institutions protected Talmadge and his associates so thoroughly that in 1949 a shrewd observer of the state boiled Georgia's politics down to one term—"Talmadgism."[7]

During that same decade, however, serious threats to "Talmadgism" emerged. First, when the legislature rewrote the state constitution in 1945, Georgia did away with its poll tax. Though out of office, Talmadge actually endorsed the repeal, on the grounds that the poll tax prevented poor whites from voting. He assured his supporters that blacks would not return to the polls because they "don't care to vote anyway, unless they are encouraged by some communistic elements." Talmadge's successor in office, the otherwise progressive Governor Ellis Arnall, agreed. There was "no danger" that blacks would take part in Georgia's politics, he announced, as long as the state Democratic Party maintained its whites-only primary. That bulwark of segregation, however, was also coming under fire. The first shots came in April 1944, when the United States Supreme Court ruled in *Smith v. Allwright* that the white primary held by Texas Democrats was unconstitutional. Cutting through the segregationist fiction that such primaries were "private" functions and therefore not subject to federal election law, the Court asserted that the primary represented an essential part of the political process and therefore had to be held to the same standards as a general election. Immediately after the ruling, black Georgians mobilized to challenge their state's white primary as well. That July, several blacks, who were already registered, tried to participate in the primary but were turned away at the polls. One of them, the Reverend Primus King of Columbus, filed a federal suit in response. Ruling on the case in October 1945, the U.S. District Court in Atlanta simply applied the Texas precedent and invalidated Georgia's white primary. The ruling was affirmed on appeal in March 1946, and the Supreme Court refused to review the matter in April. Thus, within a year's time, both the poll tax and white primary had been struck down.[8]

Suddenly, after more than forty years of obstruction, Georgia's black population found political roads open again. The National Association for the Advancement of Colored People (NAACP), whose lawyers had led the charge against the white primary, watched its membership in Georgia surge to some 13,000 strong. Black voters' leagues sprang up across the state, and registration drives began in earnest. By the summer of 1946 more than 100,000 African Americans had registered, just in time to vote in the upcoming gubernatorial primary. This turn of events horrified Georgia's segregationists, and none more so than Gene Talmadge. Running once again for governor, Talmadge made the court decisions and blacks' response to them a central theme of the campaign. Speaking at a Ku Klux Klan rally in Atlanta, his son Herman asked, "Why should Nigras butt in and tell white people who should be elected in a white primary?" His father felt the same way and predicted the turn of events would lead to the end of white supremacy in the state. "With the white primary out of the way," he told a Greensboro audience, "negroes will vote in numbers and repeal our laws requiring [segregation] in schools, hotels, and on trains—even those which prohibit intermarriage." In his mind, the situation was serious but the solution simple. Asked how they might keep blacks away from the polls, Talmadge picked up a scrap of paper and wrote on it a single word: "Pistols."[9]

Some of Talmadge's supporters took the suggestion seriously. In the south Georgia town of Fitzgerald, for instance, signs were tacked onto black churches with a warning: "The First Nigger Who Votes in Georgia Will Be a Dead Nigger." In spite of such threats, many black Georgians showed up at the polls anyway. Rural whites still outnumbered them, however, and Talmadge emerged with his fourth gubernatorial win. (Once again, the county unit system proved crucial to Talmadge's success. He lost the popular vote to opponent James Carmichael, 297,245 to 313,389, but dominated the county unit vote, 242 to 146.) Talmadge's success spurred segregationists to make good on their earlier threats. In western Taylor County, for instance, a black World War II veteran who dared to vote in the primary was dragged from his home and shot to death by four whites. Afterward, a sign was posted on a nearby black church: "The First Nigger to Vote Will Never Vote Again." The ugliest incident, however, came in Walton County, midway between Atlanta and Athens. Hundreds of blacks had turned out to vote there, and segregationist resentment soon reached a fever pitch. "The sight of that long line of niggers waiting to vote put the finishing touches on it," one white man remembered. Shortly after the primary, when word got out about a scuffle between a black tenant and a white landowner, a white mob responded by gunning down the man, his wife, and another married couple in an open field. According to reports, one body was found riddled with 180 bullets. "This thing's got to be done to keep Mister Nigger in his place," explained a local. "Since the state said he could vote, there ain't been any holding him. . . . Gene told us what was happening, and what he was going to do about it. I'm sure proud he was elected."[10]

With his election to a fourth term, Talmadge demonstrated the power of the politics of rural racism for the state and, indeed, the nation. To the dismay of his supporters, however, this chosen son of segregation passed away in an Atlanta cancer ward before he could take office. What followed was a convoluted and controversial succession crisis, known ever after as the "Three Governors" affair. Through the early months of 1947, outgoing governor Ellis Arnall, incoming lieutenant governor Melvin Thompson, and Herman Talmadge, the leading write-in candidate, all claimed rights to the governor's office. In the end, after a good deal of legal wrangling and even some physical confrontations in the statehouse, the office went to the moderate Thompson. Undaunted, Herman Talmadge reclaimed the position in a special election two years later. And with his return, the "rule of the rustics" would continue in state politics for the better part of the next two decades.[11]

ATLANTA AND THE POLITICS OF PROGRESS: THE POWER STRUCTURES

As Georgia's politics drifted further and further under the control of the Talmadge organization, the political scene in Atlanta moved in precisely the opposite direction. This was hardly surprising, since the town was home to the two groups that regularly served as targets in Gene Talmadge's stump speeches—blacks and urban moderates. Long scapegoated under the politics of rural racism, these two constituencies rebelled against the state machine in the 1930s and 1940s and forged a new political system that placed them, and not Talmadge's poor whites, at the center of power.

At the state level, segregationist politics drew strength from the county unit system, which gave poor whites a preponderance of power. Inside Atlanta, working-class whites had long drawn power from a different arrangement—the ward system. For the early decades of the century, city government consisted of a weak mayor and a powerful city council, whose members were elected not on a citywide basis but by individual wards. As a result, councilmen remained closely tied to the white working-class politics of the city. Nearly half of Atlanta's registered voters belonged to trade unions and they marshaled their numbers well. They helped elect a printer, James G. Woodward, as their mayor four times between 1900 and 1916 and installed other blue-collar whites in lower positions. By the 1930s, however, the ward system found itself under steady assault. When a 1929 graft investigation ended in the conviction of six councilmen, the corruption in city politics started to sour more and more voters on the system. The Depression, in turn, further weakened ward operations, as funds for local campaigns and kickbacks dried up along with the city's finances.[12]

The biggest blow to ward politics, however, was the election of Mayor William Berry Hartsfield in 1936. A strong and shrewd politician, Bill Hartsfield was able to rise above the constraints of the "weak mayor" system and emerge as the city's political powerhouse. With the exception of a single term, he remained in the mayor's office, and at the center of Atlanta's political life, until his retirement in 1962. Throughout his long career, Hartsfield relied on a combination of hard work and hucksterism to make his way. The son of a tinsmith, unable to afford a legal education, he wrote to the deans of prominent law schools, asked for their recommendations on readings, and taught himself. (His alma mater, he later

Figure 1.2 William Berry Hartsfield, mayor of Atlanta. With the exception of a single two-year term, Mayor Hartsfield led the city from 1937 until his retirement in 1962. An ardent booster of Atlanta and the politics of progress, Hartsfield coined the city's nickname as "the City Too Busy to Hate."

said without shame, was the Atlanta Public Library.) From there he quickly entered the world of Atlanta politics. Colorful and bold from the start, Hartsfield made the promotion of his city—and, by extension, himself—his top priority. During his years as an alderman, for example, he helped transform the old railroad town into a national center for air transportation. With what would become his habitual flair for the dramatic, Hartsfield first secured a federal airmail route for the city and then publicized his coup by personally riding along with the first delivery to New York. As mayor, Hartsfield became an even bigger booster for his city. When the film *Gone with the Wind* premiered in 1939, for instance, he made sure the first showing was at Loew's Grand Theater on Peachtree Street. Even with Vivian Leigh and Clark Gable in attendance, Hartsfield still stood at center stage, occupying his natural role as ringmaster.[13]

As he played up his public image, Hartsfield also worked behind the scenes to undercut the strength of his rivals in the ward organizations. When he first took office, for instance, the mayor tightly restricted city spending with a new budget law. The patronage system on which aldermen and city councilmen depended soon dried up. Then, in 1939, Hartsfield and his allies in the Chamber of Commerce moved quickly to create a civil service system, robbing the precinct politicians of their appointment power, too. Meanwhile, the mayor and his new departmental heads eliminated nearly two hundred positions in city government and tightened their control over the remaining employees. By the end of the 1930s the ward organizations of the city were fading fast and, with them, the political clout of the city's white working class.[14]

Without the old precinct politics to rally voters, Bill Hartsfield relied instead on a positive public image. In this regard, the mayor was helped immensely by Ralph McGill, the outspoken editor of the *Atlanta Constitution*. McGill had taken charge of the morning paper in 1938, just a year after Hartsfield gained control of city hall. He arrived with a similar splash. On his first day in office, for instance, McGill required that the word "Negro" receive the courtesy of a capital "N." Although he thought of himself as a moderate, McGill would gradually emerge as one of the most liberal and best-known voices of his native South. His political evolution was somewhat slow in coming, but McGill was always an ardent booster of Atlanta and, because of that, a strong supporter of his mayor. In 1953, when McGill wrote a long piece on Hartsfield for the *Saturday Evening Post*, the title captured perfectly McGill's pride in the mayor and the mayor's pride in his city: "You'd Think He Owns Atlanta."[15]

In truth, the men who *did* own Atlanta supported Hartsfield as well. Early in his career, the mayor used his reputation as a reformer to secure the financial and personal support of Atlanta's most influential businessmen. Chief among these was Robert Woodruff. As head of the Coca-Cola Company, Woodruff controlled the city's pride and joy, a business that was then already worth nearly a half billion dollars. But Coca-Cola was only the beginning of Woodruff's power. He also served on the boards of General Electric and the Southern Railway and presided over the powerful Trust Company of Georgia. He held considerable sway at Emory University as well, since he had personally underwritten the medical school and helped establish the research laboratory that would become the Centers for Disease Control. Needless to say, Woodruff cast an enormous shadow. "When he gets an idea," Hughes Spalding noted, "you can depend on it, others will get the idea." Mills Lane, a powerful banker in his own right, agreed: "He was the only man in Atlanta who could snap his fingers and everybody would genuflect."[16]

Together, Bob Woodruff and Bill Hartsfield quickly formed a close working relationship. When the young mayor took office in 1937, the financially strapped city was paying its employees with scrip. At Hartsfield's request, Woodruff stepped forward not only to guarantee the payroll but to refinance the city as well. From then on, the pair remained inseparable. Woodruff's financial muscle and personal support allowed

Hartsfield to emerge as a formidable politician; in return, Hartsfield promoted Woodruff's interests as he promoted the city's. He hawked Coke without end, using it to christen new planes at the airport and toast dignitaries as well. Without hesitation or embarrassment, Hartsfield called himself the mayor of "Coca-Cola City." He reverently referred to Woodruff as "my number one friend on Earth" and prominently displayed his picture in the mayor's office. "I never made a major decision," Hartsfield later admitted, "that I didn't consult Bob Woodruff."[17]

With Woodruff solidly behind the mayor, other businessmen quickly added their support as well. As attorney Harold Sheats remembered, Hartsfield had "a kitchen cabinet of businessmen who advised him." Besides Woodruff and his associates, it included heads of the major banks, Citizens & Southern and First National; executives of major family businesses, such as Rich's Department Store and the Ivan Allen office supply chain; and top men at utilities like the Georgia Power Company and the main railroads. Together, this close alliance of big businessmen and moderate politicians formed an urban elite that was quite unique for its time and place—the "community power structure" of Floyd Hunter's notes. An incredibly close-knit group of friends, neighbors, and business partners from the city's posh Northside, the power structure shared a common history. "Almost all of us had been born and raised within a mile or two of each other," remembered Ivan Allen Jr., a member of the group who would succeed Hartsfield as Atlanta's mayor from 1962 to 1970. "We had gone to the same schools, to the same churches, to the same golf courses, to the same summer camps. We had dated the same girls. We had played within our group, married within our group, partied within our group, and worked within our group." Members of the power structure not only shared a common past and present; they shared a common vision of the future. In Allen's telling, they were "dedicated to the betterment of Atlanta as much as a Boy Scout troop is dedicated to fresh milk and clean air."[18]

Meanwhile, another group of accomplished professionals—college professors and ministers, contractors and real-estate men, insurance executives and bankers—lived and worked together in the finer black neighborhoods of the city with a sense of community and common purpose quite like that of their white counterparts. The center of their power was the short stretch of black businesses on Auburn Avenue. Many knew the street as "Sweet Auburn" because, as one leader later explained, money was sweet. Indeed, there was an abundance of money in the city's black community. By 1945 the black-owned businesses of Atlanta could boast of a combined worth nearing $30 million. The financial strength of Auburn Avenue derived, in no small part, from the work of two unlikely candidates—an ex-slave from rural Georgia and a Texas migrant with a sixth-grade education.

Alonzo Herndon had spent the first seven years of his life as a slave and, as he put it, he "was very near it for twenty years more." Moving to Atlanta, he established an elegant chain of barbershops for an elite white clientele. In 1905, with the profits from that venture, Herndon founded the Atlanta Life Insurance Company. At the time of his death two decades later, the former slave left behind an estate worth a million dollars and a company that had become a financial powerhouse. By the 1940s Atlanta Life had $12 million in assets and fifteen hundred employees, with operations in nine states and an impressive headquarters on Auburn Avenue. Equally important for the growth of Sweet Auburn was Heman Perry. The son of a Texas grocer, Perry learned the insurance trade and founded Standard Life in 1911. Over the next dozen years, he launched a bank, the Citizens Trust Company, and a wide array of "service" organizations for black customers, ranging from a laundry and pharmacy to an engineering firm and fuel corporation. Although Perry personally fell from financial grace in the late 1920s, many of his former employees went on to rebuild the black business community from the ruins. Citizens Trust, for instance, was resurrected and restructured so well that it soon became the first black-owned bank in the Federal Reserve System. At the same time, more of Perry's men founded the Mutual Federal Savings & Loan Association. In time, these two institutions, along with nearby Atlanta Life, would form such a formidable financial center that *Fortune* magazine would christen Auburn Avenue "the richest Negro street in the world."[19]

In terms of politics, meanwhile, the main power broker among Atlanta's blacks was John Wesley Dobbs, a Post Office Republican, and proud member of the Prince Hall Masons. Often called "the Grand," after his masonic title, Dobbs also held an honorific title as "the mayor of Auburn Avenue." Indeed, if Bill Hartsfield had a single counterpart in the black community, it was Dobbs, a man as colorful, controversial, and proud as the mayor himself. He was so well known by his fellow postal workers that Hartsfield once wagered he could mail a letter to "John Wesley Dobbs, U.S.A." from Europe and it would find its way to Auburn Avenue. It did. Returning the flattery years later, Dobbs saw to it that a similar letter to "William B. Hartsfield, U.S.A." made its way from the continent to the mayor's office at City Hall. (Although Dobbs would not live to see it, his grandson, Maynard Jackson Jr., would in time occupy that same office, as Atlanta's first black mayor.) If the "mayor of Auburn Avenue" had a rival for that title, it was Austin Walden. Leader of the city's black Democrats and president of the local NAACP from 1924 to 1936, Walden was recognized as one of the best black attorneys in the South. Armed with a law degree from the University of Michigan, he had long challenged discrimination in Georgia's courts. For decades, Walden and

Dobbs—sometimes at odds, but frequently together—dominated the political dialogue of black Atlanta. That dialogue, in turn, reached the larger community through the pages of the *Atlanta Daily World*, the South's only daily black newspaper. W. A. Scott had established the paper in 1928; after he was gunned down by an unknown assailant in 1934, his younger brother, C. A. Scott, continued to publish the paper. An active participant in the local NAACP and Democratic politics, Scott ensured that political activity on Auburn Avenue received persistent and positive coverage.[20]

Unlike its white counterpart, the black power structure of Atlanta included more than just politicians and businessmen. Auburn Avenue was also home to the city's most prominent black Baptist churches, Ebenezer and Wheat Street. In 1931 Ebenezer's pastor, the Reverend A. D. Williams, passed away, and he left his congregation in the hands of his son-in-law, a rugged sharecropper's son by the name of Martin Luther King Sr. In 1937 a similar generational change occurred at Wheat Street when the congregation replaced its pastor with the Reverend William Holmes Borders, a preacher's son from rural Georgia who had gone on to earn degrees from white colleges in the North. Though often rivals, Holmes and King together pushed their congregations out of their traditional complacency and toward a confrontation with white supremacy. At the same time, the two ministers closely linked their houses of worship with the financial houses of Auburn Avenue. King, for instance, encouraged local insurance agents to become members of the congregation. As they made rounds for Atlanta Life, they could collect contributions for Ebenezer; in turn, they would find a host of new clients in the church. Likewise, Borders remembered how he and other black ministers helped strengthen Citizens Trust by placing their collection money there. "They put in deposit that Monday morning," he recalled. "And the people, seeing their preacher deposit God's money from the churches in Citizens Trust, put their money into it and helped to put it over."[21]

As important as Auburn Avenue was for black Atlantans, there was an even older hub of activity at Atlanta University on the city's west side. Founded in the aftermath of the Civil War, Atlanta University soon claimed esteemed faculty such as John Hope and W.E.B. Du Bois and notable alumni like Walter White and James Weldon Johnson. Withdrawn from the world of white supremacy, the campus was, in Johnson's memories, "a spot fresh and beautiful, a rest for the eyes from what surrounded it, a green island in a dull red sea." By the 1940s the original Atlanta University had merged with four black colleges—Morehouse, Spelman, Morris Brown, and Clark—and the Gammon Theological Seminary to form the Atlanta University Center. As it grew in size, the center became an even greater source of strength for black Atlantans. "Atlanta University was an oasis," remembered Clarence Bacote, a professor of history there. "You could live here, at any of these schools, and not suffer the injustices that the person who had to make his living in the city did. You didn't have to face Jim Crow, you had your own group right out here." While Du Bois had once complained that Atlanta University was an isolated "ivory tower of race," it soon emerged as an active force in the black community at large.[22]

Indeed, the educators of Atlanta University often worked closely with activists from the city's burgeoning civil rights community. The NAACP, of course, had a long relationship with Atlanta. In 1909 Du Bois helped found the organization; in 1917 Walter White founded the local branch, before moving on to lead the national office. Beyond those famous names, however, the local branch made significant gains in the campaigns for voter registration and school equalization. Likewise, the Atlanta Urban League, founded in 1919 in the offices of Heman Perry, led the charge for better housing and fair employment. Under the able leadership of Grace Towns Hamilton and Robert Thompson, the league forged close ties with the businessmen of Auburn Avenue along the way. And, as with the NAACP, one of its local leaders, Whitney M. Young Jr., would later move on to head the national organization.[23]

By the 1930s, then, a new generation of black leaders had emerged in Atlanta. From the businesses of Sweet Auburn and the campuses of Atlanta University, they found financial and intellectual independence, as well as a great deal of pride. In the pulpits of Wheat Street and Ebenezer, they heard ministers who encouraged them to stand up for their rights, and on the streets outside, they had political players like John Wesley Dobbs and Austin Walden who could show them how to do just that. Under the auspices of civil rights organizations, they could leave behind personal rivalries and work together for the betterment of the larger community. Together, they formed a formidable power structure of their own, one that would work closely with the more prominent white power structure toward their common goals.

RISE OF THE MODERATE COALITION

The first, important step toward the creation of the moderate coalition was the reclamation of the vote by black Atlantans. Through the early decades of the century, a small core of black voters had remained registered in Atlanta. Although the white primary had shut them out of most contests, the state's electoral rules allowed them to participate in special elections, such as bond referenda or the failed attempt to recall Mayor James L. Key in 1932. In these years, black leaders were able to seize a few chances to marshal their small "bloc vote" at the polls and bargain with the city for better services or improved schools. Although they made the most of these opportunities, the elections were simply too infrequent and the number of black voters too few to press for any consistent change.[24]

With a new generation of black leaders emerging in the 1930s, however, voter registration quickly became a concerted community effort. Early in the decade, citizenship schools were established to educate blacks about politics and their right to vote. The fluid movement of the schools—held first at Atlanta University, then hosted by the local NAACP, and finally housed at the churches—stood as testament to the new ways that black leaders were working together. Political activity showed a similar coordination. In 1935, for instance, the Reverend Martin Luther King Sr. led a large march to city hall as part of a campaign for voting rights. The next year, John Wesley Dobbs and others founded the Atlanta Civic and Political League, which had the goal of registering ten thousand voters. The group fell short of that goal but continued its registration efforts all the same. "We always thought that it was time for us to get blacks prepared for the ballot," explained Clarence Bacote, "because we never knew when the Supreme Court might overturn the white primary. When that happened, we'd have a representative number on the books." And numbers, black leaders knew, were what mattered in Atlanta. In the early 1940s they had asked Mayor Hartsfield for more street lights in their neighborhoods. He refused: "Come back and see me when you have 10,000 votes." In spite of his bluntness, Hartsfield recognized that such a day was fast approaching. When the Supreme Court struck down the Texas white primary in 1944, for instance, he understood the ruling's implications for his city and his career. "What the courts have done is give the black man in Atlanta the ballot," he confided to his chief of police. "And for your information, the ballot is a front ticket for any-damn-wheres he wants to sit, if he knows how to use it. And Atlanta Negroes know how to use it."[25]

Before the courts could apply the white primary ruling to Georgia, another chance for black political mobilization surfaced when Congressman Robert Ramspeck unexpectedly resigned from office. Instead of simply appointing a caretaker successor, Governor Arnall called for a special election for February 1946. Because it functioned under state guidelines, and not the rules of the Democratic Party, the election was not "protected" by the rules of the white primary. Recognizing the rare opportunity, the NAACP, the Atlanta Civic and Political League, the *Atlanta Daily World*, and local churches and social organizations joined together to launch a massive registration campaign. As a result, Atlanta's blacks more than doubled their strength in the district, from 3,000 to 6,876. Surveying the field, black leaders decided to support the candidacy of Helen Douglas Mankin. A representative of Fulton County in the General Assembly, Mankin already had the backing of a number of liberal groups and organized labor. "Her attitude on the race problem was fair," Bacote recalled, "and she was willing to talk to us." On the night before the election, after the final radio broadcast and after the white newspapers had gone to press, they spread the word: "Vote for the woman." And they did. When the polls closed the next day and every precinct except one had reported, Mankin's opponent held a thin lead of 156 ballots. The final precinct, which would determine the race, turned out to be Precinct B in the predominantly black Third Ward. Of the 1,040 votes cast there, less than twenty went to Mankin's rival, giving her the election by a margin of more than 800 votes. Local observers pinned the victory on the black "bloc vote." The *Atlanta Journal* noted that the "totals swung decidedly in favor of Mrs. Mankin when Three-B reported," adding pointedly that 2,173 blacks were registered to vote there, but only 10 whites. The national press stressed the role of black voters, too. *Newsweek* headlined its coverage "Georgia's Black Ballots," while *Time* was even more direct. Beneath a picture of a grinning Helen Mankin ran a simple caption: "The Negro vote did it."[26]

Thus, Atlanta's black community already had a running start when the courts officially struck down Georgia's white primary in April 1946. Inspired by the decision and their past successes, black leaders established a bipartisan All Citizens Registration Committee to strengthen their presence at the polls. As chairman Clarence Bacote remembered, the registration drive represented "a community effort." The committee itself was composed of rival political leaders, Dobbs and Walden; civil rights activists, such as Grace Towns Hamilton and Robert Thompson of the Urban League; and a variety of businessmen. Citizens Trust and Atlanta Life helped fund the drive, the *Daily World* gave it nonstop coverage, and black churches and colleges contributed to its organization. The turnout was stunning. Within three hours on May 1, for instance, 678 black Atlantans registered at the Butler Street YMCA; the next day, within another three hours, 750 more were added to the rolls at a local housing project; and during a third three-hour period the following day, another 955 signed up at a funeral home. By the end of the two-month drive, the committee had more than tripled the number of blacks registered in the city, to a grand total of 21,244. Less than a year before, blacks had been essentially shut out of Atlanta's politics. Suddenly, they composed more than a quarter of its electorate.[27]

Armed with the vote, Atlanta's black community now had the power to demand better services from the city. In its eyes, a particular problem was the use of police in black neighborhoods. In the words of Herbert Jenkins, chief of police from 1947 to 1972, most white officers "didn't want to spend a lot of time" in black neighborhoods. And on the rare occasions that white patrolmen did appear there, they often caused as much trouble as they solved. As Jenkins remembered, "at one time most of the members of the police department were members of the Ku Klux Klan" who relished the chance to put black Atlantans in their "place." Hoping to solve the problems caused by both the absence and presence of white policemen, black leaders had long pressed for the commission of black patrolmen. Before they had the votes, however, their requests were brushed aside. "I remember quite distinctly," Rev. Borders recalled, "going to Mayor Hartsfield and asking him for black police. And he told us, without the slightest blinking of an eye, that we'd get black police about as soon as we'd get deacons in the [white] First Baptist Church." The revolution in registration changed all that, however. When black leaders returned with the same demand in 1947, Hartsfield simply asked, "How many do you want?"[28]

After months of political maneuvering and preparation, eight black patrolmen joined the force in March 1948. But their employment came with a host of restrictions. Keeping with the customs of segregation, they operated out of a separate station, on a separate watch, and solely in the city's black neighborhoods, where they were not allowed to arrest whites. More problematic, their presence on the force met with hostility from white officers. (Much of this was directed at Chief Jenkins, whom some officers dared to call "nigger lover" to his face. The chief responded by busting one of his harshest critics, the head of the police union, and sending him out to walk a foot patrol in a notoriously tough black neighborhood.) For black Atlantans, of course, the sight of black men in uniform elicited a decidedly different reaction. On their first day of patrol, hundreds turned out to see the patrolmen walk the beat. Mayor Hartsfield and Chief Jenkins were there in person, looking on with disbelief as black crowds filled the sidewalks, first watching in silence but soon shouting with joy. As the police patrol turned into a celebratory parade, Bill Hartsfield seized the opportunity and followed right along. Desegregation, he saw, could make for great politics.[29]

To consolidate the political power of black Atlanta, Republican John Wesley Dobbs and Democrat Austin Walden put their partisan differences aside and formed the Atlanta Negro Voters League (ANVL) in 1949. Members of the group would be free to vote for their party's candidates in national elections, but in local races they promised to support the "most desirable" Democratic candidate. Black voters—roughly a fourth of the electorate—would now vote as one, making the black community a powerful swing vote between competing factions. "This concentration of strength was recognized by the city fathers," Clarence Bacote later remembered. "No longer was it political suicide for a candidate for public office to openly seek the Negro vote."[30]

In the 1949 mayoral race, Bill Hartsfield and his main challenger, Fulton County Commissioner Charlie Brown, both reached for that vote. ANVL leaders eventually sided with Hartsfield, who pointed to his recent improvements and made specific promises for the future—more black police, a black fire station, additional parks and public projects in black neighborhoods, and so forth.[31] Unwilling to concede the black vote, the Brown campaign tried to undermine the arrangement. On the night before the election, a doctored list of league endorsements appeared in black neighborhoods, this time with Charlie Brown chosen for mayor.[32] While that served as testament to the new interest of white politicians in black votes, so did Hartsfield's response. He contacted the editors of the *Atlanta Daily World* to denounce the list as a forgery and even sent a sound truck to patrol "those sections where negro citizens vote, for the purpose of notifying them of a false, fraudulent and forged ticket distributed in the late hours of last night."[33] His counterattack worked. In the primary, Hartsfield won with the slimmest possible majority—50.1 percent of the vote—over Brown and two other candidates. A change of just 102 ballots would have forced a runoff. The key to Hartsfield's narrow victory, it seemed, was the solid support of black voters. In three predominantly black districts, for instance, the mayor trounced his challenger by a margin of 3,704 to 658.[34]

After this election, a new political calculus ruled Atlanta. The old allies, business leaders and Bill Hartsfield, realized that they could not maintain control of the city on their own. Instead, a new political coalition would be needed, with blacks supplying a key source of strength at the polls. Just a decade before, such an alliance between the city's privileged white elite and Jim-Crowed black community might have seemed unthinkable. But with the political changes of the postwar era, the two groups realized that they had much in common. Together, they would dominate Atlanta's politics for the next two decades.

THE COALITION IN ACTION

For their own reasons, both halves of the new coalition supported a progressive politics centered on economic growth, civic pride, and—to the surprise of outside observers—a moderate pace of racial change. Black Atlantans pressed for desegregation for obvious reasons. Affluent whites, meanwhile, acquiesced to limited changes in hopes of presenting a positive public image for themselves, their city, and, most important, their business interests.

When it came to handling racial issues, the mayor found himself walking a tightrope between the two groups. Personally, Bill Hartsfield was as much a segregationist as most southern whites of his era. But he was a political realist and quickly put his personal prejudices aside in order to secure black votes. The changes in Hartsfield's racial attitudes were striking. As late as 1944, for instance, he had asked Congressman Martin Dies, head of the House Committee on Un-American Activities, to investigate the NAACP. Hartsfield had no proof of the organization's "subversive activities," but he believed it was behind many of the "professional white agitators" who were "stirring up racial questions in the South." After the creation of his new coalition, however, Hartsfield took a decidedly different tone. In 1951 the NAACP not only held its national convention in Atlanta but found the mayor presiding over opening ceremonies "as warmly as if it had been a meeting of the National Association of Manufacturers." Such actions in the segregated South were, of course, not without risks. A few months after the NAACP convention, segregationists began circulating a number of photos. One showed Hartsfield on stage with the civil rights leaders; another depicted interracial couples dancing. For years thereafter, opponents denounced him as "the NAACP candidate."[35] In truth, however, Hartsfield was not so much concerned with the cause of civil rights as he was with the continuation of his political career. "I knew Negroes were going to vote," he remembered, "and I decided they might as well vote for me." As Hartsfield understood the coalition, blacks were not equal partners with the white elite but rather a resource to be tapped by that elite. "Shortly after leaving office," noted Harold Martin, an Atlanta reporter and early biographer of the mayor, "he was heard to say, privately, that he knew how to 'use' the Negro, but was able successfully to avoid letting the Negro 'use' him."[36]

In his private racism and paternalism, Hartsfield simply echoed the attitudes of his business allies. As Floyd Hunter found in his study of Atlanta's "power structure," many businessmen who appeared racially progressive in public were decidedly less so in private. "I'm a true friend of the Negro," one man told him, "and will be, as long as he keeps his place." Like the mayor, many of these businessmen adopted a public image of racial moderation that was strongly at odds with their personal racism. Hartsfield's leading patron, Robert Woodruff, played an undeniably important role in advancing desegregation in Atlanta. As late as 1960, however, he privately mocked civil rights laws as guaranteeing "the right of a chimpanzee to vote." Likewise, John Sibley, chairman of the Trust Company of Georgia and a close friend of Woodruff's, championed " 'natural segregation,' a thing that all races with different cultural backgrounds and aspirations always seek." In Sibley's mind, school desegregation would assuredly result in a "mongrel race of lower ideals, lower standards, and lower traditions." In spite of these convictions, however, Sibley would play a pivotal role in bringing about the desegregation of Georgia's schools. For Sibley and Woodruff, and the countless others who took their cues from them, personal racism was ultimately much less important than public prestige. As Atlanta's affluent whites understood, their main concerns—the stability of their city and the success of their businesses—would be damaged by acts of racial extremism. Forced to choose between the social customs of segregation and the economic creed of progress, they readily chose the latter.[37]

At the same time, black leaders approached the political coalition with just as much calculation. They recognized that their partners from the white elite had little genuine concern for civil rights. "Businessmen were pathetically slow in Atlanta when it came to using their refined mechanisms, so good for making money, to achieve some sense of purpose in life beyond dollars and cents," remembered the Reverend Martin Luther King Sr. "On the issue of racial discrimination, there was *no* white leadership at all." At the same time, black leaders understood that, whatever their faults, the white elite represented their best chance for change. Although Hartsfield may not have appreciated it, the black community was, indeed, using the white members of the coalition as much as whites were using them.[38]

In the workings of the coalition, the balance of power between the black community and the business elite was a delicate one. By 1950, for instance, blacks composed well over a third of Atlanta's total population. Continued black migration into the city and white flight from it seemed likely to increase their percentage even further. For coalition leaders, the issue presented a special problem. The alliance relied on black numbers at the polls, of course, and would likely receive a boost there as a result. At the same time, coalition leaders worried that if the black percentage of the population became *too* pronounced, that would work against the coalition. As Hartsfield reminded blacks and whites alike, a black-majority city would be simply unworkable in the South. To Hartsfield and his allies, the solution was simple. Atlanta should annex the surrounding suburbs, thereby increasing its size and, more important, its white population. The mayor had pushed the idea as far back as the early 1940s. In a letter to several hundred "gentlemen" of the upscale Buckhead neighborhood, he presented annexation as a way to bring "decent people"—middle-class whites—into the city. Hartsfield warned of the alternative:

> Our negro population is growing by leaps and bounds. They stay right in the city limits and grow by taking more white territory inside Atlanta. Outmigration is good white, home owning citizens. With the federal government insisting on political recognition of negroes in local affairs, the time is not far distant when they will become a potent force in Atlanta if our white citizens are just going to move out and give it

to them. This is not intended to stir race prejudice because all of us want to deal fairly with them, but do you want to hand them political control of Atlanta, either as a majority or a powerful minority vote?

Still, despite the mayor's repeated pleas, the annexation crusades of the 1940s consistently failed.[39]

In 1950, however, the mayor introduced an ambitious "Plan of Improvement." The plan called for the annexation of eighty-two square miles containing almost 100,000 people. It would triple the city's size and boost its population by a fourth—almost all whites. Ironically, this time around, the "powerful minority vote" inside Atlanta proved to be the key to annexation's success. Although the additional population would dilute their electoral strength, many black leaders supported the Plan of Improvement all the same. Some, like Grace Towns Hamilton of the Urban League, simply took the view that "what was best for the city was best for their community within it." Others, like Clarence Bacote, felt that Hartsfield's record of racial moderation merited their allegiance. The mayor had, by this time, brought street lights to Auburn Avenue and ordered city hall to use the respectful "Mr." and "Mrs." when addressing letters to black residents. "I hope that your administration continues along the progressive lines that it has taken in the past," Bacote wrote the mayor that year, "and, if it does, you can be assured of Negro support as long as you desire to remain a public servant." For still other blacks, the plan seemed to strengthen their political position. The whites annexed by the city were, after all, much like their current partners in the coalition. Politically, they would side with them in future elections; financially, they would contribute to the city's tax base. For all these reasons, the Atlanta Negro Voters League endorsed the Plan of Improvement. As a result, when the plan was put to a popular vote in the spring of 1950, it won inside the city's limits by a huge margin, 23,031 to 2,613. Those on the city's fringes were more skeptical, but the measure passed there as well, 6,560 to 4,816. With the endorsement of the legislature, the Plan of Improvement went into effect on January 1, 1952. As white coalition members had expected, Atlanta's black population dropped from 41 percent of the total population to just 33 percent, literally overnight.[40]

Although black leaders stuck with Hartsfield during the drive for annexation, some complained that the mayor was moving too slowly on their demands. John Wesley Dobbs, for one, had been pressing the mayor to follow up on his reform of the police force by integrating the fire department as well. Hartsfield demurred, noting that because firemen had to live and sleep together, their integration would pose much more of a problem for whites. Dobbs refused to accept that rationale. Shortly before the 1953 primary, he stunned the black community by resigning from the

Atlanta Negro Voters League he had created and throwing his support to Hartsfield's rival, Charlie Brown. As an added blow to the coalition, the *Daily World* announced that it would refrain from endorsing one side or the other. To shore up Hartsfield's black support, Helen Bullard, the mayor's campaign manager and public relations expert, sought the advice of Grace Towns Hamilton, head of the Atlanta Urban League. In a detailed blueprint, Hamilton urged the mayor to call black leaders together for a special meeting. She named fifty-four individuals to be invited, taking care to select an important cross-section of Atlanta's black leadership. She also chose the meeting site—the Butler Street YMCA, a hub of black activity whose selection would underscore the mayor's attempts to meet black leaders on their own terms. Most important, Hamilton urged the mayor to speak frankly. He should stress that his enemies were denouncing him as "the Negro's representative," when he was simply trying to be "mayor of all the people." Hartsfield should list his accomplishments, she advised, but acknowledge "that the Negro did have legitimate gripes. The sore spots should be brought up and discussed—no Negro firemen, more Negro policemen, better schools and parks for the Negroes, appointment of Negroes to planning boards, and the elimination of police brutality. Bringing all these into the open and discussing them fully would rob the disgruntled of their ammunition." Running on Hamilton's advice and Hartsfield's record, his coalition kept the support of black Atlantans. Indeed, in several black precincts, the mayor piled up margins of nearly 90 percent, bringing in enough votes to secure reelection.[41]

Just as black voters supported the larger coalition, so too did the coalition support a black candidate. Dr. Rufus Clement, president of Atlanta University, ran for a spot on the board of education with Hartsfield's hearty endorsement. Aghast, segregationists on the city's Democratic Executive Committee contacted the House Un-American Activities Committee, hoping to find dirt on Clement. But when they sought to spread word of Clement's past membership in left-leaning groups, they found the city's white elite aligned against them. The newspapers denounced the smear campaign as "dirty politics," and no less an establishment figure than Hughes Spalding came to Clement's public defense. With the coalition behind him, Clement beat his white opponent by a margin of roughly 10,000 votes. To the added dismay of segregationists, court rulings forced the Democratic Executive Committee to accept blacks as candidates for its seats. As a result, the largely black Third Ward elected Dr. Miles Amos and Austin Walden as their representatives. In a touch of poetic justice, the men who led the crusade against Clement not only lost that battle but found blacks elected to their own ranks as well. By all accounts, the 1953 elections represented the triumph of coalition politics. Not only had Atlanta returned its moderate mayor to city hall; it had also elected its first black officials since Reconstruction. "You had to experience Atlanta," John Egerton has written of that time, "to get the full flavor of its uniqueness as an urban oasis in the Sahara of segregation."[42]

Indeed, the changes in Atlanta's racial climate forced national observers to take a second look at the city. As late as 1945 the *Saturday Evening Post* still portrayed Atlanta as the backward setting of *Gone with the Wind*. "She's a hot-bread, boiled-greens, fried-chicken-and-cream-gravy town," a reporter noted with a flourish. In his view, the city's worst crisis was "an Old Mammy shortage," which left white women "raising their mammyless children and dreaming for the first time of secondhand washing machines." With the postwar political changes, however, these Old South stereotypes were replaced by New South themes of economic progress and progressive politics. "Here is a city which has been accused of extreme backwardness in racial matters," observed *Christian Century*. Yet the recent "encouraging" political changes meant that Atlantans "have a right to feel proud of themselves." The city had proved it had "more hum than drawl," agreed *Newsweek*. Rejecting racism, Atlanta had become "the nerve center of the New South." Even the *Saturday Evening Post* accepted the image change, running a Ralph McGill piece that praised the "showcase city of the South" for its good political sense and sound race relations. The mayor and his business allies, boosters to the core, had long dreamed of press coverage so positive. Now that the image of Atlanta as a moderate, modern city had finally taken hold, Bill Hartsfield was determined to maintain it. In 1955 the mayor mugged for the National Toastmasters' Club and coined a new nickname for the city. Atlanta, he told the crowd, was "a city too busy to hate." To his delight, the nickname stuck. A few years later, Hartsfield explained what he meant. "We strive to undo the damage the Southern demagogue does to the South. We strive to make an opposite impression from that created by the loud-mouthed clowns. Our aim in life," he concluded, "is to make no business, no industry, no educational or social organization ashamed of the dateline 'Atlanta.' "[43]

Political realities allowed Hartsfield to take a stand against the southern demagogues in his city. "The Mayor," noted an adviser before the 1953 race, "should not let himself be mislead into the belief that he can possibly get any of the really bigoted vote. That's already lost and has been lost since 1946 and no concession should be made to it." Close analysis of voting results made it clear that working-class whites, who sided the most consistently with segregation, were in fact a lost cause. In the 1953 primary, for instance, Hartsfield received 90 percent of all votes cast in a typical black precinct and 60 percent in a typical upper-income white precinct, but just 29 percent in a precinct of lower-income whites. Running for reelection in 1957, the mayor maintained the allegiance of his core constituents but saw his working-class white support plummet to 17 percent. By all appearances, such voters could be safely ignored. Moreover, instead of reaching out to segregationists, Hartsfield learned to hold them at arm's length and thereby hold his constituency together. As he knew, both blacks and businessmen saw working-class, white reactionaries as a common enemy. Outside Atlanta, the forces of rural racism still vilified the city's moderates and blacks alike. If similar forces gained power inside Atlanta, the coalition members understood that years of progress would quickly come to a halt. "If there is anything the coalition fears most," one observer noted, "it is seizure of city government by what are called the 'red neck,' 'wool hat' elements." In this regard, the Hartsfield coalition represented, in the words of another study, a "tacit alliance" of blacks and upper-middle-class whites against the working-class whites of Atlanta.[44]

As this brief overview of Atlanta's political landscape suggests, the idea of "the city too busy to hate" was invented and sustained by a moderate coalition born not out of chance but through careful calculation. For their part, white politicians and corporate leaders were just as segregationist in their thinking as other whites of the city. But they were practical. They discovered to their delight that progressive politics—or the appearance of it, at least—resulted in economic progress and profits. And although the white leadership thought of themselves as "using" their black partners, the African American community used them in return. Like their white partners, black Atlantans forged their own kind of progress, social as well as economic, within the workings of the coalition. Together, both sides stood united through the 1940s and 1950s in pushing an agenda of progress and suppressing the segregationist sentiment of working-class and middle-class whites.

In time, however, these whites would challenge the rule of the Hartsfield coalition. Throughout the 1950s and 1960s, during the peak of the moderate coalition's apparent power and prestige, Atlanta's segregationists slowly gathered steam. As city leaders pressed ahead with the politics of progress, these disaffected working-class and middle-class whites gathered together in a politics of retrenchment. As Hartsfield and his allies bragged about the "city too busy to hate," these whites began to speak a new language of their own, one centered on their beleaguered rights. In the end, their revolt would not only create a separate movement of white resistance in Atlanta but would also irreparably fragment the coalition against which they railed.

CHAPTER TWO

From Radicalism to "Respectability":
Race, Residence, and Segregationist Strategy

IN SEPTEMBER 1946 Holt Gewinner stood in a vacant lot near the Piedmont Mills on Atlanta's West Side and served up a half-hour rant to gathering workers. Something of a semiprofessional fascist, Gewinner stood before the crowd as a featured speaker for the Columbians, the first neo-Nazi organization in Atlanta and, for that matter, the United States. His address covered the usual range of extremist arguments, but he ended with an issue he knew would interest his audience more than anything else. "The reason veterans cannot find housing," Gewinner argued, "is that unscrupulous real estate dealers are selling white property to Negroes, thus forcing all whites in the neighborhood to move." The crowd had been watching with some curiosity until then, but now it cheered "enthusiastically and spontaneously." Gewinner understood the importance of the housing issue to Atlanta's whites and he played it to its fullest. "There are two ways to fight this thing," he roared. "With ballots and with bullets! We are going to try ballots first!" A curious observer roamed through the crowd, "watching their expressions and listening for comments, with a view to finding out whether the talks were going over. I decided that they were." At a folding table near the stage, a brown-shirted man stood by, hoping to recruit new members for the Columbians. The pledge cards he distributed were short and simple. "I want the Columbians to continue the fight for the American white working man," the signers swore. "I want the Columbians to continue the fight to effectively separate the white and black races." Several mill workers inked their names on the spot and urged friends to follow suit. One of them, a bus driver who had arrived late, seemed reluctant. "I don't know anything about it," he protested. One of the newest recruits summed it up for him: "It's to keep the niggers down."[1]

The tensions laid bare at this rally, and countless others like it across Atlanta, demonstrated the ways in which race and residence stood at the forefront of the city's racial politics in the postwar era. For the working-class white Atlantans who cheered the Columbians and their cause, the problem of "transition neighborhoods," where the population shifted from white to black, was their most pressing concern. As these whites knew all too well, their neighborhoods on the city's West Side had become the focal point of residential transition in Atlanta. Just to their east stood

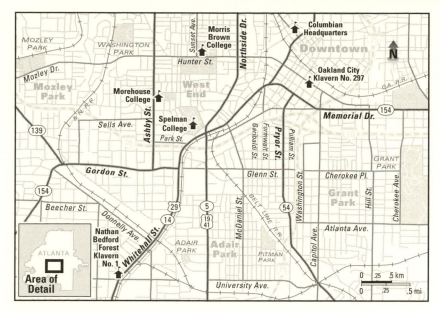

Map 2.1 West End, 1950

the Ashby Street region, which had grown rapidly during the previous decades, emerging as one of Atlanta's most overcrowded black neighborhoods. Indeed, by the 1940s nearly 40 percent of the city's black population lived there, making the enclave's name synonymous with "black Atlanta." (When segregationists sought to paint Helen Mankin as the "Negro candidate" in the 1946 elections, for instance, they simply dubbed her "the Belle of Ashby Street.")[2] But as the region found fame, it also reached a critical mass. The end of World War II brought a severe housing crisis to Atlanta, as thousands of veterans returned home to discover the city had not only failed to build new homes during their absence but actually started to destroy old ones. Black leaders banded together to create new housing on the city's outskirts, but found such projects blocked by local resistance and government red tape. In the end, they had only one option. "Following the pressure of increased population," Atlanta's Metropolitan Planning Commission observed, "their only avenue for expansion has been 'encroachment' into white neighborhoods adjoining their own areas of concentration." Logically, the bulk of the early years of black "encroachment" emerged from the most significant "area of concentration," Ashby Street.[3]

Thus, in the late 1940s Ashby Street became the central place where blacks and whites battled over their relative positions and places in the postwar world. Tapping into working-class white resentment over such residential racial change, three waves of segregationist groups sprang to life there in rapid succession—first the fascist Columbians, then a revived version of the Ku Klux Klan, and finally a homeowners' group known as the West End Cooperative Corporation. In the short term, the Hartsfield coalition held each group in check and allowed the racial transitions around Ashby Street to continue. Although all three organizations were ultimately unsuccessful in preserving white supremacy, their careers still testify to an important evolution of segregationist organization and outreach. Originally, as Gewinner's address made clear, segregationists relied on populist rhetoric and stark racism to harness the discontent of working-class whites. But with each passing year and each new group, segregationists steadily adopted a subtler pitch predicated on appeals to white homeowners with middle-class aspirations of respectability and upward mobility. In time, they would learn to put aside the brown shirts of the Columbians and the white sheets of the Klan and instead present themselves as simple homeowners and concerned citizens. They would tone down their racist rhetoric and stress their own rights instead. And as they did so, the forces of residential resistance found their campaign gaining a wider and wider audience. Although they lost their immediate campaign to "defend" the Ashby Street area from further residential transitions, these segregationists gained much more in the process—a new understanding of how to present their politics in a more appealing package.

The end result of this evolution from radicalism to "respectability" became clear in nearby Mozley Park. In that neighborhood, the Hartsfield coalition seized the initiative from segregationists for the first time. The administration established a structure of negotiated settlements for future crises over race and residence, one that would maintain peace in the city for years to come. But this approach relied heavily on the cooperation of white homeowners' organizations, groups whose means, motives, and membership had directly descended from the blatantly racist organizations of Ashby Street. By empowering these groups to negotiate the course and character of neighborhood racial changes, the Hartsfield coalition thus unwittingly legitimized the very segregationist forces it had just routed. Their voices of resistance, which had only recently seemed so far outside the political mainstream, would now occupy center stage for the remainder of the 1950s and 1960s.

The Evolution of Segregationist Resistance

The Columbians, Inc.

The first segregationist organization to "defend" Ashby Street called itself the Columbians, Inc. The origins of the name remain unclear, but the founders likely drew inspiration from "Hail, Columbia!," a Revolutionary War anthem that often played at their rallies. While the Columbians claimed to be a "patriotic and political group" inspired by an earlier generation of Americans, the organization derived greater inspiration from another, more recent source—Nazi Germany. Indeed, the founders, Emory Burke and Homer Loomis, proudly styled themselves fascists. An Alabama native, Burke had already made his impact on the national stage. According to one source, his name appeared on the letterhead of "nearly every fascist organization in the country prior to World War II." With the defeat of European fascism, Burke hoped to continue the cause in America. "When the American people awaken to the realities of this age," he wrote, "what the Germans have done to the Jews will be a mere tea-party compared with what we are going to do with them!" Burke found a willing partner in Homer Loomis. "His hair was close cropped, Prussian style," an acquaintance recalled, "and his eyes had a Satanical look about them." Loomis had a specific model in mind. "I'm going to be the Hitler of America," he bragged. Friends were asked to greet him with "Heil, Loomis!"[4]

With the war's end, Burke and Loomis launched their crusade. "Atlanta is the logical place to start something," Loomis reasoned. "The South comes by its racial convictions instinctively." Thus, in 1946 they founded the fascist Columbians there. Dressed in khaki army uniforms with a red lightning bolt insignia, its members soon spread across the city, conducting military marches and drilling in the streets. Pointing to the recent rise of black political power, the Columbians asserted "the same right to organize a white block vote in order to maintain political control that is guaranteed the Negro and other minority groups in their attempt to wrest power from us." Although they framed their fight as political, in truth the leadership had more sinister goals. "We're going to show the white Anglo-Saxons how to take control of the Government," they told their associates. "We're trying to show them they have power in their grasp if they'll just organize and assert themselves!" In an ambitious scheme, they hoped to take control of the city in six months, the state in two years, the whole South in four years, and the entire United States within a decade. "There is no end to what we can do through the ballot," Loomis explained. "If we want to bury all niggers in the sand, once we come to power we can pass laws enabling us to bury all niggers in the sand!"[5]

To launch their plan, the Columbians set up headquarters at the edge of Atlanta's warehouse district. Their dirty, three-room office held a library of Nazi histories and a Confederate battle flag. Enlisting was fairly easy. "There are just three requirements," Loomis told prospects. "Number one: Do you hate niggers? Number two: Do you hate Jews? And three: Have you got three dollars?" The result was a collection of social outcasts, but the leaders saw their troops in a different light. "We welcomed all members of the Whiteman's community into our fellowship, but we worked mainly among the underprivileged—those of our brothers and sisters that many of the politicians call 'poor white trash,' " Burke later recalled. Indeed, while the Hartsfield coalition spurned such support, the Columbians consciously targeted the working class. The door to their headquarters pointedly identified them as the "Columbian Workers Movement," and the leadership often professed its common ground with working-class whites as well. "In spite of the smugness of some of our financially well-off White brethren," Burke noted, "there are far fewer betrayers of the Whiteman's Way of Life among the simple and hard-working young textile workers and farmers."[6]

Indeed, the textile mills served as a ripe recruiting ground.[7] In mill neighborhoods across Atlanta—the Exposition Cotton Mills, the Whittier Mills in the northwest section, the Fulton Bag and Cotton Mills on the East Side, and especially the Piedmont Mills off Ashby Street—the Columbians made their pitch directly to working-class whites. Setting up shop in an alleyway or vacant lot, the group worked from a flatbed truck draped with the American flag and the Columbians' lightning bolt banner. Portable speakers blared out renditions of "Dixie," "Atlanta, G-A," and "Hail, Columbia!" so loudly they could be heard several blocks away. Drawn by the music, crowds of curious mill workers and wives drifted in, finding young men in khaki uniforms welcoming them. When two hundred or three hundred had gathered, the music stopped and the speeches began. The speakers varied, but their themes were usually the same. "We're going to them and putting on a show," Loomis explained. "We're telling them stuff they want to hear—that they, the white Anglo-Saxons, are the best people on earth, and that they're entitled to more than they're getting."[8]

All around Ashby Street, in these working-class mill neighborhoods, the Columbians found receptive audiences. "It is in areas as this," the local branch of the Anti-Defamation League warned, "that hate organizations like the Columbians recruit their membership, playing upon the fears, tensions, and insecurities of the people." Another study agreed that "Columbian members were, for the most part, residents of 'transitional' areas in central Atlanta, where housing was rapidly shifting from white to Negro occupancy." Recognizing the housing issue's appeal, the Columbians soon focused entirely on plans for "protecting" white working-class neighborhoods. "White Men and Women" were urged to attend meetings and hear "plans for your neighborhood to keep the Negro out and stop his attack on white people." Burke vowed that his men would bar blacks from the region "if we have to zone them out, walk them out, or throw them out." Signs with the Columbian logo and the words "WHITE COM-MUNITY" were posted in "endangered" areas. The group formed street

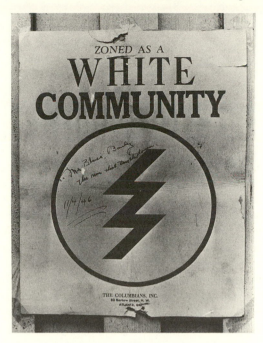

Figure 2.1 Sign posted by the Columbians, Inc., in the "transition neighborhoods" around Ashby Street in the fall of 1946. Although racial zoning was illegal, the Columbians insisted that such areas were, in the words of this sign, "Zoned as a White Community." The symbol at the center is the red lightning-bolt insignia used by the group.

patrols and announced it would "arrest" any black caught in a white section of town. All offenders would be "turned over to the police, beaten with blackjacks, and locked up for being drunk."[9]

The Columbians took this "defense" of white working-class neighborhoods quite literally. On a large map at headquarters, the leaders sketched out the perceived threat. "Here on Ashby Street, the Negroes are driving a wedge toward Bankhead Avenue. And here on Chestnut they're getting another wedge started," Loomis confided to a reporter. "Objective of the enemy here is to cut off this Western Heights section—and make it an 'island' of whites surrounded by Negroes. Then they want to keep moving on in." The former army private continued, jabbing his finger at a dark red line along Garibaldi and Formwalt streets. "We've drawn the color line here," he said, tapping the map, "and that's the line we're going to hold!" All along those streets, his troops patrolled in thirty-minute intervals, armed with .38 caliber pistols and blackjacks. "If you see any niggers so much as walking on the wrong side of the street, stop 'em and whip 'em within an inch of their lives!" Loomis ordered. "After you've whipped them, tell them what you whipped them for. Tell them this is a white neighborhood and they must not pass through it! If one sasses you and you have to kill him, that's what you've got a gun for!"[10]

On the night of October 28, 1946, a young black man named Clifford Hines was walking home along Formwalt Street, where his family had lived for four years. A gang of six Columbians—including one from Garibaldi Street—caught sight of him, whistling and listening to a portable radio. "Ain't this a nigger?" asked seventeen-year-old Ralph Childers. An eighth-grade dropout from Forsyth County, Childers long resented black Atlantans buying homes he could not even afford to rent. In the Columbians, he found a way to vent his anger. By his own account, he had already been involved in the beatings of a dozen or so black men and the bombing of several houses by the time he caught sight of Hines. Chasing him into an alley, Childers and his fellow Columbians proceeded to blackjack the man into screaming hysteria, as Hines's white neighbors stood by, doing nothing. Fortunately for him, police stumbled onto the scene just after the Columbians forced him into the backseat of a waiting car. Unfortunately for Hines, however, the patrolmen arrested him along with Childers, allowing the others to go free. Soon bailed out of jail, Ralph Childers received a hero's welcome and a medal of honor at the Columbians' next meeting. Encouraged, the other troops stepped up their attacks. A black home at the white end of Ashby Street was bombed by the passenger of a passing car on Halloween. Two days later, more Columbians tried to stop another family from moving into a Garibaldi Street home, attracting an angry mob and the police in the process.[11]

Sensing that things were getting out of hand, city and state officials finally decided to crack down. "In those border areas where Negroes and whites live close together," Assistant Attorney General Dan Duke warned, "we have a potential powder keg that could break forth any day in bloodshed." A liberal ally of the Hartsfield coalition, Duke aggressively moved to revoke the Columbians' charter, on the grounds that the group was "peddling hatred and intolerance among our people." The Columbians accepted the challenge. For two days, they drove sound trucks through the tension area, publicizing an upcoming meeting at the nearby Plumbers and Steamfitters Union Hall. Some two hundred residents attended, including many women with children in tow. "A week ago, we were only an organization," Burke announced, "but we have grown because we have helped you with your problem niggers." The Columbians, Burke lied, patrolled the neighborhood armed only with "two fists and an iron will." Without that protection, everything working-class whites cherished would be lost. "Our heroes in Europe didn't die to give a nigger the right to marry a white American girl," he thundered. "That's right!" roared the crowd, which had now become what a reporter could only describe

Figure 2.2 Members of the Columbians at Ralph Childers's trial for the assault of Clifford Hines. The Columbians appear in their official uniform—a khaki dress outfit with red lightning-bolt insignia on the upper arms.

as a "cheering, whistling, Rebel-yelling, foot-stamping throng." Burke shredded the charter and stomped on it. The crowd stomped with him, clapping and screaming "Send the little pieces to the Jews!"[12]

Despite their disdain for the proceedings, Burke and Loomis welcomed the chance for publicity. Responding to the state's allegations, the Columbians claimed they defended Anglo-Saxon civilization from communism, which called for an "ungodly doctrine of one nation and one race." "This doctrine, if not repelled," the Columbians warned, "will bring about a condition where all men will be colored and no man will be white." Although charter revocations are usually a dry matter, this one turned ugly. At one point during the hearings, Assistant Attorney General Duke, a barrel-chested former Marine, responded to an insult by suddenly turning and slugging Loomis across the chin, knocking him out of the witness chair and onto the floor. The Columbian demanded Duke's arrest, but the judge demurred: "I must have looked away for a moment." In the end, an Atlanta jury took only twenty-nine minutes to revoke the charter. As an added blow, the Columbians found themselves added to the House Un-American Activities Committee's list of subversive groups, placed alphabetically alongside the Communist Party they so despised.[13]

By the time of the charter revocation, however, the courts had already caught up with the Columbians on other matters. A number of the rank and file, for instance, were caught hatching an ambitious plan to bomb city hall, police headquarters, the municipal auditorium, and the offices of the *Atlanta Journal* and *Atlanta Constitution*. Others were rounded up on assorted charges stemming from their street patrols. Loomis himself stood trial in early 1947 on charges of inciting a riot, assault, and usurping police powers. In an impassioned two-hour speech to "my fair-skinned brothers" of the jury, his attorney father claimed his son was being "crucified like Christ by the Jews." The jury disagreed, sentencing him to two years on the chain gang and six months in prison. Meanwhile, Emory Burke was sentenced to three years on multiple misdemeanor charges. Neither seemed distraught. "Jail can't hurt me!" Loomis shouted as the bailiffs led him away. "Hitler wrote a book in jail that did all right. I'll call mine *Thunder in the South*!" "They can put me behind forty feet of granite," Burke bellowed, "and I'll still shout white supremacy!"[14]

Although the Columbians had disappeared from the streets of Atlanta, the circumstances that encouraged their growth had not. "The fact that the Columbians were able to rally 200 persons despite all the adverse publicity is an indication of the reality of the issue of interracial housing friction," noted an informant after the Union Hall meeting. "If the Columbians are jailed, it is quite likely that the Klan will mobilize the Columbian followers on the same issue."[15] Indeed, that prediction soon came true.

The Ku Klux Klan

Although the Ku Klux Klan had a long history in Atlanta, the order had been dormant for years. Its postwar rebirth came, appropriately enough, at the hands of an Atlanta obstetrician, Dr. Samuel Green. In late 1945 Green, an unassuming man with wire-rimmed glasses and a toothbrush mustache, anointed himself the Grand Dragon of the Association of Georgia Klans and led his new recruits to Stone Mountain on Atlanta's outskirts. Using a mixture of fuel oil and sand, the men carved out an enormous cross, stretching three hundred feet across the mountainside. Once lit, it was visible some sixty miles away. According to one of the hooded men who constructed it, the blazing crucifix was meant "to let the niggers know the war is over and that the Klan is back on the market." Green returned to the mountain the following May to hold a mass initiation. "America is calling every White Man, who has red blood, into the fight," his invitation intoned. "WHITE SUPREMACY is threatened on every hand. YOU CANNOT FAIL." Sensational newspaper ads attracted nearly a thousand spectators, who watched silently as three hundred men took their oaths and set a ceremonial cross ablaze. At the end of the evening, the Grand Dragon solemnly intoned, "We are revived."[16]

The new recruits came from all walks of life. Cab drivers and truckers, farmers and dairymen, textile workers and factory men, gas station attendants and firefighters were all prominently represented, as were a staggering number of sheriff's deputies and city policemen. An informant snidely reported that the Association of Georgia Klans appealed mainly to working-class whites, who "will not stop to think but will fall in line with 'Dr. Green' as a person of such ranking can easily deceive people who lead an uneventful life."[17] But white collars were just as frequently found under the hoods as blue ones. Tax collectors and assessors were "almost 100% organized," while the clerks and commissioners of other county and state agencies were judged "in good standing." One city councilman's photo was displayed prominently in the East Atlanta post, while two others won door prizes for attracting the most new members at another. Judge Luke Arnold emerged as a popular lecturer at Atlanta Klaverns, and at least three of his fellow jurists were issued special commendations for "conforming with the principles of Klannishness." With such a strong cross-section of working-class and middle-class support, Klaverns quickly cropped up across the city. Weekly meetings took place in rural East Point, along Howell Mill Road to the west, and on Moreland Avenue to the east. Small posts sprang up in the exclusive Northside neighborhood of Buckhead and on the city's suburban outskirts, in Lithonia and Marietta. Despite this sprawl, the two largest and most powerful Klaverns—Nathan Bedford Forrest Post No. 1 and the Oakland City Post No. 297—both stood close to the city's center, not coincidentally near the transitional neighborhoods of Ashby Street.[18]

Because the Klan had so much in common with the Columbians—the same fears, the same enemies, the same base of support in the same neighborhoods, all at the same time—many assumed the two groups were related. "The Columbians are nothing but the juvenile delinquents of the KKK," Dan Duke thundered to the press. "They are one and the same, and ought to be tarred with the same tar!" To be sure, a handful of men wore both the Columbians' brown shirts and the Klan's white sheets. But the organizations themselves were not officially aligned. Publicly, the two groups adopted an attitude of mutual contempt. Each accused the other of peddling hate for profit; each claimed it alone was the true champion of white supremacy. Privately, however, the Klan welcomed the upstart organization. As long as the Columbians remained on the streets, "protecting" white neighborhoods, it did not have to confront the issue. As soon as the Columbians collapsed, however, Klansmen rushed to fill the vacuum.[19]

As it turned out, the hooded order was even better prepared for the task of "neighborhood defense" than the Columbians, given the large numbers of city patrolmen and detectives in its ranks. Sporting nicknames like "Itchy Trigger Finger" and "Shotgun," policemen figured prominently in several of the Klan's more brutal escapades. When one patrolman won a prize for killing his thirteenth black "in the line of duty," he teased the others: "I hope I don't have to kill all the niggers in the South without getting some help from my Brothers!" "Don't worry," they responded. "You'll have plenty of help!" Indeed, in "defending" white neighborhoods, Dr. Green strongly relied on this police presence. At an April 1947 meeting, for instance, a Klansman announced, "I've been told that a family of niggers has moved into an apartment building for whites at 300 Pulliam Street!" At this, the Grand Dragon called out for a particularly ruthless patrolman. "Take three more of your police officers," he ordered, "and go in your police car to that address at once, and report back here!" Four officers tore off their sheets, revealing uniforms beneath, and rushed to investigate.[20]

The weekly meetings at Atlanta Klaverns soon focused on similar stories of black "invasions" in white working-class neighborhoods, especially around Ashby Street. "The West End situation was again brought up," an informant noted after a May meeting, when Grand Dragon Green argued that "the negro is definitely stepping out of his place and that he would have to be put back." But how? The first week of June, a Klansman reported that a black man had moved into a house between two white homes on Sunset Avenue, only one block over from the "black side" of Ashby Street. Neighboring whites had whipped the man and torn the windows out from his house, but he still refused to leave. Now, "it looked like they would have to kill him in order to get rid of him." Likewise, at a July meeting, Klansmen heard about a white man on Ashby who had tried to dynamite a black family from the house next door only to wind up in a gunfight with the man. As they learned of further "outrages" around Ashby Street, the Klansmen called for more extreme measures. One recommended that "whenever they learned of a house being advertised for sale to the negroes that they go out and burn the thing down." Another thought "it would take a riot here to straighten out the negroes."[21]

While the Columbians had engaged in countless acts of reckless behavior, Green tried to stem all talk of Klan violence. Dan Duke, emboldened by his success in revoking the charter of the Columbians, had started similar proceedings against the Klan. Afraid of the consequences, the Grand Dragon did not want to give the prosecutor any more ammunition than he already had. As his men pushed for action, Green merely promised, in the words of one Klansman, that "as soon as the trial comeing up soon is won we would have some demonstrations such as Parades and Kid naping and public gatherings and cross burnings." In the meantime, Green clamped down on all lawlessness, even banning cross burnings for a while, lest they be charged with violating local fire ordinances. Instead, he kept his men busy with improbable public relations stunts. Food was distributed to the needy and twenty pairs of long johns, stamped "K.K.K.," showed up at an old folks' home. In the most memorable act, a Klansman donned a Santa Claus outfit—over his white robe and hood—and presented a 107-year-old black man with a brand new radio.[22]

The Grand Dragon acted so cautiously because he knew informers had infiltrated his Klavern. Any detailed discussions on the protection of white neighborhoods would follow other private plans into the pages of Ralph McGill's *Atlanta Constitution* and onto the weekly radio broadcasts of Drew Pearson and Walter Winchell. The leaks came from Stetson Kennedy, an enterprising writer who had infiltrated the Klan and delighted in airing its dirty laundry. In a particularly inspired move, he contacted the scriptwriters of the *Superman* radio serial and gave them detailed descriptions of Klan ceremonies, right down to the passwords. Atlanta Klansmen soon found their own children imitating the episodes, fighting over who got to be Superman and who had to be the cowardly Klansmen. Humiliated in their own homes, they became obsessed with finding the informer. On one occasion, as Kennedy sat among his fellow Klansmen, Green described plans to "split his tongue, strip him naked and nail his penis to a log, set fire to the log at both ends and give him a straight handle razor and tell him to cut it off or burn up." Despite the considerable thought the Association of Georgia Klans put into catching and condemning Kennedy, it never succeeded. And as long as the informer spied on them, Grand Dragon Green refused to go overboard in the "protection" of white working-class neighborhoods.[23]

In any case, the Klansmen had bigger problems. First, as Green feared, they lost their charter, when the state amassed ample evidence in 1947 that the Klan was neither "non-profit" nor "benevolent." Then, in 1949, they lost their hoods, when moderate forces in Atlanta enacted an anti-mask law. As a final blow that same year, they lost their leader, when Grand Dragon Green unceremoniously slumped over dead in his garden. Green's men tried to carry on without him, but they found the odds stacked against them. "You can't start a new fire in wet ashes," remarked a retired imperial wizard. "Under Dr. Green the Klan might have amounted to something, for he was an old Klansman and the old-timers would follow him. Now it's breaking up into little splinter groups that won't last." The times had changed, he said. "Too many people don't like its methods. Too many laws are now hemming it in. The Klan can't defend the wearing of the mask. And it can't live without the mask. Unmask it everywhere, and in two years it will be dead—no more powerful, politically, than the Red Men or the Maccabees." But the retired wizard was wrong. The Klan did, in fact, learn to live without the mask.[24]

The West End Cooperative Corporation

Compared with the leaders of the Columbians and the Klan, Joe Wallace seemed the embodiment of respectability. Slightly balding, with white hair and round wire-rim glasses, he worked in the scrap business and dabbled as a building contractor on the side. A resident of Park Street, just around the corner from Ashby, Wallace had long been prominent in neighborhood affairs. He was an active joiner, with memberships in the Loyal Order of Moose, the West End Business Men's Association, the Atlanta Tuberculosis Association, the Park Street Methodist Church, and American Legion Post No. 147 on Ashby Street. His most treasured membership, however, was to Klavern No. 297 of the Association of Georgia Klans. There, Wallace made a name for himself as head of their "Housing Kommittee," leading the fight against black "invasions" in the area. As the Klan disintegrated, Wallace branched off from the discredited group and formed his own organization, the West End Cooperative Corporation (WECC). Though technically outside the Klan, the group adopted the hooded order's means and methods, not to mention much of its membership.[25]

Although the WECC built upon the legacy of its white supremacist predecessors in a number of ways, it differed from them considerably in one important aspect—its public image. With their outlandish costumes and crude displays of violence, both the Columbians and the Klan had been ridiculed by Atlanta's moderate establishment as racial extremists who stood outside the circle of respectable life, as rabble-rousers looking for trouble. The WECC members, in contrast, self-consciously presented themselves as honest homeowners confronted with a "social problem" not of their making. In so doing, the organization successfully shifted the terms of debate from one that stressed the defense of white supremacy to one that stressed the defense of home, neighborhood, and community. "You of the middle class," Joe Wallace asked in a typical pitch, "you with that Southern accent, Georgia-born and reared, are you going to stand by and lose your birthright without a struggle?" The mounting wave of "Negro invasions" would ruin the rest of Ashby Street through a drop in property values and the steady spread of decay, he charged. From there, other neighborhoods would follow suit, and then the entire city. "The Negroes will have Atlanta lock, stock, and barrel in less than ten years if we fail to act," he warned. "The Negro race will multiply so rapidly and then we will again even at the edge of town be forced to live with them or move farther out."[26]

Throughout 1947 Joe Wallace reached out to the working-class and lower-middle-class whites of the region with a series of recruitment rallies. Generally, these meetings took place in reputable locations essential to white citizens' sense of their community—the local schoolhouse, a Baptist church, the American Legion post. With small groups of twenty or so, Wallace gave a simple pitch. "We don't hate the nigger," he would tell them. "We love him—in his place!" Unlike earlier groups which had resorted to violence, Wallace promised that the WECC would seek to use capitalism and conversation to solve the problem. If whites would purchase homes from blacks and help them "find homes in the Negro district," he argued, they could effectively "remove all Negroes from the West End." After that, the neighborhood could be permanently protected by a "Great White Wall" of racially restrictive covenants written into the deeds of neighborhood houses. But to create this "paradise," the WECC needed money. It would cost $5 for each covenant and considerably more for repurchasing the homes. Residents of the West End—white residents, at least—could help by purchasing stock in the nonprofit organization. The maximum amount was set at $500 per person, just to keep things democratic.[27]

In addition to fundraising, the West End Cooperative Corporation served, in Wallace's words, as a "sort of a watchdog" for the region. When black buyers were spotted, a careful plan sprang into action. "I put some of our ladies to work making chain telephone calls, and in no time we mobilize quite a crowd around the house where the nigger is trying to move in," he explained to a confidant. "Then I step in and have a little private talk with the nigger. I tell him he has a perfect legal right to move in, and that I will try to protect him. But at the same time I tell him I doubt if I can control more than a small part of the mob, and that if he does move in he'll be endangering his whole family." With the crowd outside, Wallace would move in for the hard sell. "You're too intelligent a Negro to put your family in such a spot," he would say. "Now if you'll just leave everything to me, I'll guarantee to either sell your house for what you paid for it, or our Corporation will buy it, within fifteen days." As Wallace once bragged at a Klan meeting, "Ninety-nine times out of a hundred, that ought to do the trick!"[28]

The scheme of balancing a public image of respectability with private threats of violence worked well for the WECC, especially during its first year. Locals still had a fresh memory of the Columbians' activities around Ashby Street, and thus Wallace's offers of repurchasing black homes found some takers. But with the demand for housing still incredibly high in the black community, the WECC scheme created little more than a temporary truce. In May 1948 the U.S. Supreme Court ruled that racially restrictive covenants were unenforceable, effectively destroying the WECC's only "respectable" tool of defense. With his "Great White Wall" suddenly in ruins, Wallace seemed shaken. Publicly, he still promised a "diplomatic handling" of the housing situation. But without the legal bulwark of racially restrictive covenants, Wallace now only had his hard-sell method to "protect" white neighborhoods in the West End. And by his own admission, that technique required terrorizing his targets.[29]

To that end, Wallace and his allies slipped out of the guise of respectability and stepped up their intimidation campaign. In this regard, the WECC relied on men like H. C. Harris Jr., a pipe fitter in the Southern Railway's repair shop. As the WECC's vice-president, Harris took neighborhood "defense" every bit as seriously as Wallace. For instance, in November 1948, when real-estate agents showed a home at 328 Ashby Street to a prospective black buyer, Harris appeared on the lawn and ominously mentioned that "some property occupied by negroes in the neighborhood had been blown up." Intimidated, the prospect refused to bid on the home. But another black buyer, Bennie Glenn, purchased the house in early 1949. When Glenn's mother Estelle showed up at the home, Joe Wallace was waiting for her. He repeated his usual threats, adding that he would not be responsible "for what harm might happen to them and any negroes in the event they did move in." The Glenns refused to budge. Their old home had been condemned as part of an expressway project; they had nowhere else to go. Refusing to be intimidated, they secured a restraining order against Wallace and Harris, arranged for police protection, and then moved in.[30]

Seeing that threats had failed, the WECC decided to abandon negotiations and resort to violence. Their next chance came in March, when a black beautician, Rose Torrence, purchased a home at 369 Ashby Street, just two doors north of the intersection of Sells and Ashby. Wallace and Harris confronted the new owner immediately. "Mr. Wallace asked me was I the owner of the house," Torrence recalled. "I said yes, then he questioned me about my moving in. He said that it wasn't advisable for me to do so because they were going to bomb it. Then the other white man said that if I moved in I would be running my own funeral." The house exploded that night. With a "deafening blast" heard a mile away, several sticks of dynamite blew out the windows, crumbled the plaster walls, and shot a wooden plank fifty feet down the street and through a neighbor's window. The WECC was apparently no longer content to make empty threats. And yet, with the evidence scattered across Ashby Street and the only testimony coming from a lone witness—and a black woman at that—the Atlanta police were unable or unwilling to charge either Wallace or Harris with the bombing.[31]

In spite of its turn to violence, the WECC still tried to project an air of respectability. It distributed a new neighborhood newspaper, the *West End Eagle*, as a courtesy to "the home owners, residents, and business men of the West End." According to the editors, the paper would simply discuss those issues, such as racial "invasions" in their neighborhoods, which were ignored by the larger Atlanta dailies. "The *Eagle* is definitely NOT a hate sheet," its editors claimed, "but is motivated solely with the idea of promoting better relationships between the white and colored races." However, the advertisement for subscriptions indicated just what sort of relationship the WECC had in mind. "HELP STOP Negro Encroachment into White Areas, Unscrupulous White and Negro Real Estate Agents from Exploiting Negro Home Buyers, Spreading of Communism," the ad implored its readers. "The Eagle will stand for the rights of Southern people." Those rights—to private property, segregation, and self-determination—had been trampled on by petty politicians and minority groups. "Through the columns of this newspaper," the publishers promised, "we will show you how . . . big slogans 'Racial Equality,' 'Civic Improvement,' and other self-righteous, pious, high sounding overworked words have become a tool of exploitation in the mouths of a handful of unscrupulous individuals and organizations, working for their own gain of political, monetary or personal power." At the same time, Wallace played up his personal image as the respectable protector of white working-class and middle-class neighborhoods. "I have been called a rabble rouser and blamed for the delivery of fiery speeches," he claimed. "If a Negro family moved into your block as your neighbor, would you need anybody to rabble-rouse to start you on the warpath? Would you need fiery speeches? No! You would have more need for a pacifier, a diplomat, to cool you down and help you to work out a plan, using the law rather than violence to make a peaceful settlement. That is exactly what I had to do."[32]

Although Wallace tried to portray himself and his organization as respectable, the damage to the image of both had already been done. In its early years, the WECC had succeeded where the Columbians and Klan had failed, largely because it managed to disguise the rabidity of racial violence with the respectability of community politics. Rather than project an air of lawlessness and violence, WECC members presented themselves as hard-working, honest homeowners, concerned about their families, their homes, their neighborhoods and their city. Their motivation was not racism, they insisted, but their rights. But as soon as the organization resorted to outright violence, it ceded all claims to respectability and steadily lost its appeal. Within a few years, Joe Wallace had no credibility and no following. But other segregationist groups in Atlanta looked to the WECC example. They realized that success lay in respectability and a "reasonable" appeal to middle-class values, while violence and open bigotry would only lead to failure.

THE LEGITIMIZATION OF WHITE RESISTANCE:
RACIAL TRANSITION IN MOZLEY PARK

For all the tension and trouble in the Ashby Street neighborhood, its problems were soon overshadowed in the neighborhood immediately to its west, Mozley Park.[33] "Of the postwar tension areas, perhaps the most crucial for Negroes and whites was Mozley Park," reflected Robert Thompson of the Atlanta Urban League in 1960, "not only because it illustrates some of the problems which arise when Negroes move into a 'restricted' area in Atlanta, but because it has had a continuing effect on the thinking and the activities of buyers, sellers, builders, financing agents, and city officials involved in similar situations in other parts of Atlanta." Indeed, as this small and seemingly insignificant area underwent "racial transition" during the late 1940s and early 1950s, the city entered a new era in its struggles over race and residence. Black leaders would shape and reshape their approach to residential desegregation during the neighborhood's transition, forging cautious compromises with city officials and even white homeowners' groups as they went. Those homeowners' groups, meanwhile, would build on the lessons of Ashby Street to create an even stronger and stabler form of white middle-class resistance to racial change. This time around, they staged a more prominent "defense" of their neighborhood in the streets, in the courts, and at City Hall. Though they were ultimately unable to hold back black expansion in Mozley Park, these homeowners' groups would foster the growth of a larger politics of white resistance across Atlanta.[34]

Located three miles west of downtown, along what was then the city limits, Mozley Park stood as a small community of working-class and lower-middle-class white families, living in single-story homes along narrow streets. On the pages of city maps, their neighborhood took the shape of a small triangle, pointing west and extending, along its longest lines, five blocks high and seven blocks wide. Though a small neighborhood, its attractiveness was greatly enhanced by a wide semicircle of parklike public spaces surrounding it. Along the southwest stretched Westview Cemetery, established in the 1880s with nearly six hundred acres of richly landscaped lawns and a strict requirement that all who came there—both visitors and permanent residents—be white. (Fittingly, when Grand

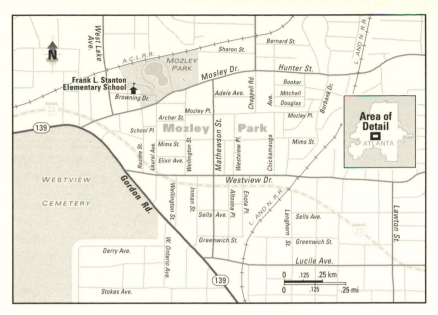

Map 2.2 Mozley Park, 1950

Dragon Green died in 1949, his Klansmen made sure he was laid to rest in one of Westview's whites-only plots.) Then, in the neighborhood's northwest corner stood Mozley Park itself, a thirty-eight acre park that boasted of a large swimming pool, a natatorium, and even a clubhouse, complete with showers and changing rooms downstairs and a hardwood dance floor upstairs. Finally, overlooking the park from the west stood the three-story Frank L. Stanton Elementary School for white children.[35]

Just as these neighborhood spaces—cemetery, park, and elementary school—barred blacks, so too did the residential region enclosed by them. The neighborhood of Mozley Park, however, lay immediately west of the black enclave around Ashby Street. As that area filled to capacity in the 1930s, blacks began edging further west, where the white working-class residents of Mozley Park kept constant watch. When a black physician purchased three lots there in 1937, for instance, he had to abandon his building plans after whites threatened the work crews. The next year, when a black businessman began construction on the neighborhood's out-skirts, a group of hooded whites warned him that black homes would not be allowed in Mozley Park itself.[36]

To "protect" the area from advancing blacks, in 1941 city officials pro-posed the construction of a highway that would seal off the white neigh-borhood from black areas to its east. The West View Parkway, as it would be called, would run south of Mozley Drive down to the Louisville and

Nashville Railroad. Between two parallel lanes of traffic and, more to the point, between the two races, the city would set up a "no man's land" of trees and shrubs, with tall cyclone fences running alongside. Despite a continued push for the program throughout the 1940s, the buffer was never built. Unable to build a new barrier, white residents instead tried to transform an existing street, Westview Drive, into a racial blockade. While the city had thought of using fences and traffic to separate the races, local residents settled for intimidation and threats. Construction crews working for black developer Walter Aiken and others were warned not to build homes within a hundred yards of the thoroughfare. To make the boundary line plain for all parties, the paving of streets leading out from black developments toward Westview Drive abruptly stopped a hundred yards shy of the "white" boundary.[37]

The resistance of these whites to the "encroachment" of blacks resulted not solely from their personal racism but also from the larger manifestations of racism in real-estate practices. By the time these white homeowners confronted racial transition at their neighborhood's borders, the American real-estate industry had completely embraced the idea that such racial transition would, without doubt, lead to a devastating decline in property values. From the 1930s on, leading appraisal manuals linked the worth of property to the status of its occupants, warning that the arrival of "undesirable" racial and ethnic groups would cause home prices to plummet. Shortly thereafter, such ideas became entrenched as federal policy. The Home Owners' Loan Corporation (HOLC), for instance, instituted the practice of "red lining" minority areas—identifying them on color-coded maps as neighborhoods in decline and decay, where property values were in doubt and, therefore, where loans were strongly discouraged as a risky investment. The Federal Housing Administration (FHA) and, after 1944, the Veterans' Administration (VA) adopted HOLC standards in their own massive loan programs to home builders and buyers. To prevent any possible mixture of "inharmonious races and classes" and thereby protect property values, the FHA encouraged the use of racial restrictions, such as restrictive covenants and even physical barriers, to keep blacks from lowering the value of "white" property. As housing expert Charles Abrams observed in the 1950s, the FHA embraced "a racial policy that could well have been culled from the Nuremburg laws."[38]

These new federal policies echoed and amplified the existing racism of the real-estate industry. Until 1950, for example, the code of ethics of the National Association of Real Estate Boards (NAREB) included this canon: "A realtor should never be instrumental in introducing to a neighborhood a character of property or occupancy, members of any race or nationality, or any individual whose presence will clearly be detrimental to property values in the neighborhood." To illustrate the supposed ill effects of black occupancy on the property values of a white block, a NAREB brochure from 1943 warned realtors that

> the prospective buyer might be a bootlegger who would cause consider-
> able annoyance to his neighbors, a madame who had a number of Call
> Girls on her string, a gangster who wants a screen for his activities by
> living in a better neighborhood, a colored man of means who was giving
> his children a college education and thought they were entitled to live
> among whites. . . . No matter what the motive or character of the
> would-be purchaser, if the deal would institute a form of blight, then
> certainly the well-meaning broker must work against its consummation.

Like other local boards nationwide, the Atlanta Real Estate Board took the equation of black ownership and neighborhood decay to heart and stood on guard against such sales. In 1946, for instance, board president A. H. Sturgess confided that his member realtors were "under obligation not to sell to Negroes in predominantly white areas."[39]

Thus, with real-estate officials—public and private, national and local—insisting that the "encroachment" of black buyers on all-white neighborhoods would assuredly depress property values, the white residents of Mozley Park and countless other neighborhoods across Atlanta accepted the idea without question. In truth, most of the Mozley Park properties were already quite modest. For instance, along Mozley Place, one of the streets closest to nearby black neighborhoods, stood simple wooden frame houses, usually just a single story high and situated on small land lots. Much of the housing had been built before the Depression, yet was still of a higher stock than blacks' homes to the east. Unlike most of those shotgun shacks, all the homes on Mozley Place had running water and almost all had private baths.[40] Much like the rest of the neighborhood, the residents there represented a mix of working-class and lower-middle-class whites. Two or three held white-collar positions as clerks or claims agents. Some served as foremen and managers at small businesses, such as a drapery shop or a tire company, while others worked as salesmen on the road or at retail stores like Sears, Roebuck. But the majority worked as skilled and semiskilled craftsmen, including a seamstress, a plumber, a bricklayer, a mechanic, a machine operator, a serviceman, a welder, and a pipe coverer. For the most part, they worked long hours at hard jobs. But most of them—forty out of forty-six—had saved enough money to purchase their own homes. Those homes were by far their largest investment, and their neighborhood a prized possession. All of the authorities in their lives insisted that the presence of blacks would destroy both.[41]

For these working-class whites along Mozley Place, the first sign of "transition trouble" appeared in 1948. William A. Scott Jr., son of the

Atlanta Daily World founder, had returned from overseas service to help his uncle run the paper. For two years, Scott scoured Atlanta for a home but, like many of his fellow veterans, failed to find one in the tight housing market. Therefore, he decided to build one himself, on two lots he had inherited at the corner of Mozley Place and Chappell Road. Although the part of the block along Mozley was completely white, blacks occupied all but two homes on the remainder and owned virtually everything to the east. Nearby whites had apparently accepted this arrangement, though in a less than neighborly manner. When blacks began "taking over" blocks of Hunter Street to the east, for instance, white residents convinced the city to change the name of their part of Hunter to Mozley Drive, so they could avoid the stigma of having a "black" address. The exact dividing line was Chappell Road.[42] Building a home a block below this borderline, at the corner of Chappell and Mozley Place, but still on the "black" side, must have seemed to Scott an uncontroversial extension of earlier expansion.[43]

White residents, however, disagreed. Learning of Scott's plans to make Mozley Place his home, they gathered at Stanton Elementary in hopes of stopping him and preserving property values. First, they tried to have Scott's building permit revoked, but found no support at city hall. Next, they pleaded with him through the minister of a large local church. The pastor repeatedly called the young veteran, begging him to build elsewhere or, at the very least, turn his home around so it would not face Mozley Place. When that approach failed, fifty residents banded together to purchase the lot back from the black owner, in order "to keep them off the street," as one of them later put it. Those negotiations fell through, but yielded an unexpected result. Scott informed them that "Negroes would pay much more for these lots than the whites thought they were worth." Thus, unable to remove Scott, some whites instead decided to remove themselves, placing their homes on the black real-estate market.[44]

The first homes listed were those nearest Scott's site. Ed Turner, a plumber, and his wife Maybelle lived in a small single-story house at 1400 Mozley Place, about a hundred feet across the street. Watching the black veteran lay his home's foundation, Maybelle Turner decided he was there to stay. "I feel like [they] have a right, that this is a free country," she later explained. "I did not object to colored people building there on their property. They owned it." But just as she claimed Scott had a "right" to stay there, Maybelle Turner asserted her own prerogative to sell and leave. "I did not feel like I wanted to be there and be a fence to protect other people," she stated. Soon thereafter, the Turners listed their home with a black real-estate agent, starting a domino effect along Mozley Place. The couple next door at 1406 Mozley, salesman John Ogletree and his wife Ethel, quickly listed their house with a black broker. Margaret Hall of

1416 soon followed suit. "Mrs. Turner and Mrs. Ogletree were selling their houses to colored people," she reasoned, so "I knew no white person would buy mine."[45]

Whites farther down Mozley Place understood what was happening, especially after John Calhoun paid visits to the Turner and Ogletree homes. Calhoun's business cards described him as a "realtist"—the job title used by black real-estate agents who were denied membership in the whites-only NAREB and, as a result, prohibited from using its copyrighted title of "realtor." The occupational semantics spoke volumes about the segregated nature of the real-estate market. But, more important, because black realtists almost exclusively handled property for black buyers, Calhoun's presence in Mozley Park told neighbors that the Turners and Ogletrees were selling their homes to blacks. "He was going back and forward to their houses just like an ant, two or three times a day," recalled one. "We would catch him in there, see him in there, and at night." In response, some whites tried to keep their neighbors from selling. "Well, they had committees come down and suggest that we stay down there and be on the fence and let the colored live there," recalled Maybelle Turner. "They said they didn't blame me, but that they wished that I wouldn't sell, being down there, and stay and protect them." The Turners realized, however, that their neighbors only wanted them to stay on the front lines of defense because they feared blacks would then become *their* next-door neighbors. "I told them that if they objected so much to me selling," Ed Turner scoffed, "they could move on down there to my place, but they didn't want to do that."[46]

While some whites pleaded with their neighbors, others tried intimidation. Chief among these was Ramsey Allen, a bricklayer who had lived at 1433 Mozley Place for fourteen years. Although the white two-story house belonged to his elderly in-laws, Allen was as fiercely protective of the neighborhood as any homeowner. He argued with John Calhoun in August 1948 and William Scott in October, but finally decided to take his case directly to the whites who "betrayed" him by showing their homes to blacks. The brickmason made "a lot of threatening and ugly talk," a neighbor recalled, harassing white sellers and potential black buyers alike. Allen even threatened to import other neighborhood "defenders" from Ashby Street. "Well, he said the Klu-Klux were coming down there," remembered Maybelle Turner, "and he was going to get Joe Wallace to stop us one way or another." Ultimately, however, the threats failed to stop the white owners of 1400, 1406, and 1416 Mozley Place from listing their homes.[47]

All three homes were quickly sold to black buyers. The Turner place was the first to go, bought by the Reverend William Weatherspool, pastor of the Mt. Olive Baptist Church. No sooner had he and his wife arrived at the house, however, than two hundred whites from the neighborhood appeared, with Joe Wallace at the lead. An angry mob of a hundred more stormed the mayor's office, telling him they had "no intention of moving or selling out to Negroes" and demanding a solution. With several city councilmen, the chief of police, and concerned delegations of white and black citizens surrounding him, Mayor Hartsfield met personally with the pastor, begging him to think of the greater good. "That is your property, if you so desire to stay there," he told him, "but in the midst of the tenseness, if you will consider not staying there at night . . . perhaps this will clear up the situation." The minister agreed to remove his family from the property, leaving only his furniture behind. The new owner of 1406 Mozley followed Weatherspool's lead. Meanwhile, Geneva Allen, the third buyer, went a step further and sought to break the sales contract she had signed for 1416 Mozley Place. As seller Margaret Hall recalled, "she said someone came to see her and told her they were going to bomb the house if she moved in it." Hall refused, claiming their contract was binding. The Fulton County Superior Court agreed.[48]

Looking for a way to break the contract, local segregationists tried to nullify the agreement—and get a little revenge in the process—by having the Georgia Real Estate Commission (GREC) revoke John Calhoun's license. Unable to back out of the transaction any other way, Geneva Allen stepped forward to make a charge of "misrepresentation" against the realtist, claiming he had told her the neighborhood was "going colored." The "misrepresentation" charge held a double appeal for segregationists. Internally, it reinforced a fundamental pillar of segregation, the belief that blacks consented to racial separation and would never knowingly purchase a home in a white neighborhood. Externally, the charge let them circumvent recent court rulings. Instead of outlawing residential desegregation, the state would simply make outlaws of those who *enabled* residential desegregation. There was only a slight difference between the two tactics, but the result would be the same. That May, the GREC heard the case and refused Calhoun a license renewal. Not content with putting Calhoun out of business, angry whites sought to put him in prison as well. In Criminal Court, however, a lone juror voted in Calhoun's favor, and prosecutors had to drop the case. The message to others involved in similar "encroachments," however, had still been made.[49]

When the state and county finished their cases against John Calhoun, local whites in Mozley Park tried to correct the "damages" he had wrought in their neighborhood. In April 1949 more than a hundred concerned residents met at the neighborhood's Joel Chandler Harris School to form a new "defensive organization," the Mozley Park Home Owners' Protective Association. In a study of similar groups, historian Thomas Sugrue described the significance of their names. "As protective associations, they fiercely guarded the investments their members had made in their homes," he noted. "They also paternalistically defended neighborhood, home, family, women, and children against the forces of social disorder that they saw arrayed against them in the city." To lead that defense, the new group elected Arnold Kennedy as its president. He had worked with the West End Cooperative Corporation in "defending" Ashby Street and thus seemed a logical choice to "defend" his own neighborhood. Business agent for Local 84 of the International Brotherhood of Electrical Workers, Kennedy surrounded himself with others from the lower-middle-class—a post-office clerk, a drugstore proprietor, a career soldier, a salesman's wife, and a conductor on the Southern Railway. Above all of them, acting as trustee and sponsor for the organization, stood none other than Joe Wallace, who considered this resistance group a branch of his own.[50]

Although most observers neglected to notice, the creation of the Mozley Park Home Owners' Protective Association signaled the legitimization of white resistance to residential transition. Throughout the late 1940s the cause of neighborhood "defense" had passed from one segregationist group to another, with each seemingly more respectable than the last—first, the outlandish fascists of the Columbians; next, their associates in the (comparatively) more reputable Ku Klux Klan; and then the West End Cooperative Corporation, an apparently harmless homeowners' organization that had, in fact, been founded by a Klansman. Now, in Mozley Park, Wallace's WECC helped establish an even more respectable homeowners' group, one that distanced the cause even further from the ugliness of its early days, while still ensuring the same result—the successful "defense" of segregated neighborhoods. While the WECC had never been able to shed its violent image completely, the new Mozley Park group insisted it could solve the "racial problem" solely through nonviolent ways. The key, Kennedy explained, would be raising enough money to buy back the homes and then establishing a "voluntary boundary line for Negro expansion." And so, working in pairs, the homeowners' group visited every house around Mozley Place, quickly raising the needed funds through the sales of bonds. Within a month, 1400 and 1406 Mozley Place were "safely" in the hands of two white veterans. When their fellow veteran William Scott finally finished his home across the street and moved in, he was the only black owner on the block.[51]

This stabilization proved temporary, however. Taking stock of the situation, some whites realized that, by selling to black buyers, their former neighbors had turned a tremendous profit. The Turners, for instance, had originally spent $3,750 for their home but resold it, after years of wear and tear, for $9,050. For some working-class whites, the possibility of tripling their investment simply proved too strong a temptation. In October 1949 eight homeowners along Adele Avenue and Mozely Drive decided to list their homes on the black realty market. To their surprise, many black realtists refused to handle the sales. The largest and most reputable realty firms belonged to the Empire Real Estate Board (EREB), Atlanta's association for black realtists. Their representatives had agreed to the "voluntary boundary line for Negro expansion" that spring, and the members promised to abide by that agreement. There were, however, several unaffiliated black brokers in the city who had no qualms about handling the hot properties. By early spring, all eight of the homes—plus two more—had been sold to black buyers.[52]

The Mozley Park Home Owners' Protective Association tried to fight back the new wave of "invasion" as it had the first. In March 1950 Arnold Kennedy sketched out an ambitious plan, calling for local businessmen to "purchase or resell to Whites" all the recently transferred property—the five homes on Mozley Drive, the three on Adele Avenue, a number of empty lots on various streets, and even the Scott residence on Mozley Place. In addition, he advocated closing virtually every street connecting to Mozley Place and Westview Drive to isolate the neighborhood. White residents welcomed the plan and assumed blacks would once again go along. This time, however, black realtists refused. The original agreement had been easily circumvented by others, they pointed out, and in any case they never enjoyed endorsing a system of segregation that held them in check, both personally and professionally. The entire rationale behind the "defense" of white neighborhoods was preposterous, complained Robert Thompson and Austin Walden. "Negroes have legally purchased property or moved into homes adjacent to or near white sections, and such actions cannot be considered as 'encroachment,'" they asserted. "It is inconceivable to believe that Negroes have gradually or silently infringed upon the rights of the white citizens in the Mozley Park Section of Atlanta, especially when the white residents of the area made overtures first." With all of the black realty firms in agreement, the Empire Real Estate Board decided to stop supporting residential segregation in Mozley Park.[53]

As black realtists collected listings in Mozley Park, each followed his own rules. Some refused to take a house unless every other one on the block was also listed, therefore ensuring "a complete transition from white to Negro occupancy." Others accepted individual parcels, with an expressed agreement that the white seller would remain in his former residence "until conditions permitted the Negro to move in." Furthermore, to avoid alarming whites south of Westview Drive, the realtists decided to concentrate solely on blocks to the north. As an added safeguard, they agreed to contribute a 5 percent commission from each sale to "a separate fund for emergency," such as another lawsuit or licensing trial. The realtists stuck together through the spring and summer of 1951, holding their prized listings until they had secured a majority of the homes along Mozley Place and surrounding streets. At that point, the EREB gave the "go" sign. On the first Sunday of September 1951 black brokers suddenly announced a number of Mozley Park properties in the *Daily World*. Each realtist had his own cache of land: J. R. Wilson displayed a whole block on Mozley Place, Caldwell Realty had eight homes on nearby Browning Street, and the offices of J. L. Wolfe Realty bragged of fourteen more on Mozley Drive. The next week, the pages were nearly filled with listings there. In two-column photo spreads with half-inch banners, the Alexander-Calloway Real Estate Company announced "LET US HELP YOU PURCHASE A BEAUTIFUL HOME IN THE MOZLEY PARK SECTION." Agents encouraged all of black Atlanta to drive through the neighborhood, browse its streets, and attend open houses. "These Home Owners Want to Sell," assured Caldwell Realty. "They Are Friendly People Who Want You to Stop, Look, and Call Us for an Appointment." The whole region was up for grabs, they promised. "If you see a house anywhere in this section you want," read another ad, "call us." An already heavy load of listings grew heavier, as white homeowners further south rushed to put their property up for sale. "Whites panicked and many became anxious to sell to get the top dollar while the getting was good," remembered T. M. Alexander, then president of the Empire Real Estate Board and an active realtist himself. "One Sunday, while driving a Black client around, a White lady stood out motioning to us excitedly to, 'Come look at our house!' " By early October, entire rows of homes on Mims Street and Westview Drive were likewise listed for black buyers.[54]

Selling the homes, however, depended on finding financing. Scarce for black homeowners in general, loans were especially rare for those who wanted homes in "transitional" areas. "In my humble opinion, it is not altogether the Government that is keeping Negroes and other minority groups confined to the central sections of our metropolitan areas," Robert Thompson reported to the National Urban League. "The groups that keep us hemmed in are the officials of banks, building and loan associations, life insurance companies and other approved lending institutions." Around Atlanta, discriminatory lending practices were an open secret. As late as 1959, during testimony to the U.S. Commission on Civil Rights no less, the president of the Atlanta Savings and Loan Association admitted they were a common practice. "We do not want to be a part to creating unrest and dissatisfaction," noted W. O. DuVall. "A loan made in an area of that type"—a transitional neighborhood—"is not so attractive, not so stable. There is a tendency for these houses to be sold, transferred, and it is our general feeling and our experience that it is not so satisfactory."[55]

While most banks refused to make loans in any transitional neighborhood, in the case of Mozley Park they had an added incentive. In an effort to stall racial change in the neighborhood, the Mozley Park Home Owners' Protective Association persuaded at least one white institution against loaning money to blacks in the area. To the astonishment of whites, however, Auburn Avenue quickly filled the void. In late 1951 Citizens Trust Company began working with two black insurance companies to provide mortgage money for black buyers in the area. "Some of these loans," Robert Thompson later noted, "made possible the 'breaking' of the Mozley Park bottleneck." But the bank did more than assist black buyers. It also worked the other end, helping white sellers settle outstanding loans, so they could get their finances in order and get out. By the end of the year, the realtists and bankers had secured the sales of most of the property around Mozley Place. Finally, on January 2, 1952—"Moving Day"—all the black buyers arrived together to take possession of their new homes.[56]

From their home on Altoona Place, a traveling businessman named Donald McLean and his wife Alma saw the "Moving Day" arrivals as the start of a larger "conspiracy." To stop the supposed threat, the McLeans lashed out at the traditional scapegoats, real-estate agents. In May 1952 they filed a suit asking Fulton County Superior Court to enjoin eleven realty firms, both black and white, from "listing or selling to colored persons any additional property" in the neighborhood, on the grounds that such actions were destroying local property values. The neighborhood, as they understood it, included not just the traditional Mozley Park area north of Westview Drive, but a number of still-white blocks to the south, such as theirs. Compared with the section "taken over" on Moving Day, this new area was slightly more middle class. Every single home was owner-occupied and nearly every homeowner held a white-collar job. The McLeans' neighbors on Altoona Place, for instance, included a claims examiner, a supervisor for Atlanta Newspapers, a Hormel salesman, an inspector at the Fort McPherson army base, an accountant for the U.S. Department of Agriculture, an auditor with the army, a career military man, and two business superintendents. (The only exceptions to the middle-class character of the block stood at the very ends—a painter and a foreman for Southeastern Meat and Poultry.) Just as Mozley Park had witnessed a gentrification of the white resistance from Ashby Street, so too did the McLeans' lawsuit represent another small step up the social ladder of respectability.[57]

Indeed, in their lawsuit, the McLeans drew directly on a middle-class self-image, which emphasized the role of the home as a reward for a life of hard work. The residents in their neighborhood, they claimed, had each "established their permanent home in its present location in the belief that they could live out their lives there in peace and contentment." They had done this "at great financial expenditure and personal sacrifice" and now that they had reached middle age, they did not want to abandon "the sentimental and nostalgic memories of their present home where they have spent so many happy years." Unlike earlier crusades for neighborhood "protection," individual homes were no longer the main issue. Instead, the McLeans claimed rights to the entire neighborhood, which they described as "a completely developed and established section of long standing, with white schools, parks, churches, and shopping centers nearby." The neighborhood as a whole belonged to them, the McLeans stated, but real-estate agents sought to steal it. In strikingly militaristic terms, their suit accused brokers of trying to sell blacks "certain strategically located properties" to effect "an encirclement of the city public park for white persons known as Mozely Park, and the city public school for white children known as Frank L. Stanton School." The objective of this "conspiracy," they charged, was "to cause the said public park and the said public school to be turned over to colored persons for their exclusive use, thereby further decreasing the value of petitioners' property and the property of others, and further unlawfully and by means of conspiracy depriving petitioners and others of the use and enjoyment of said public park and school." In other words, if enough homes in Mozley Park "went colored," the school and park would inevitably follow.[58]

The McLeans' charge was not a new one. As early as 1947, when blacks began buying homes north of the neighborhood, white residents spoke knowingly of a similar conspiracy. "The Negroes are slowly but surely surrounding Mozley Park," Joe Wallace warned. "It has been said that the Negro leaders want the Park [and] also the school for the Negro Race." (In a claim that other whites would overlook, Wallace also charged that the "Old Folks Home" of Battle Hill Haven would similarly be "lost" if Mozley Park underwent transition.) As blacks began buying homes closer to these public spaces, whites grew increasingly defensive. Most of them, like the McLeans, considered "their" elementary school and "their" city park the best parts of the neighborhood and refused to abandon them without a fight. Taking stock of the situation years later, a black banker estimated that "95%" of white homeowners in Mozley Park had refused to sell "mainly because of the PARK & the SCHOOL."[59]

In an effort to "steal" their park and school, the McLeans charged, black brokers were deliberately "using the race issue as a weapon and a device to drive down the market value" of white residents' homes. Their lawsuit accused the real-estate agents of spreading rumors that "colored persons will take over at least half the area . . . by January 1, 1953, and force out the remaining white property owners in another year or two." To speed white flight, the unscrupulous brokers were supposedly using a variety of "nefarious schemes" and "conniving practices," including placing ads in newspapers and putting up "For Sale" signs in the neighborhood. Furthermore, through repeated telephone calls, letters, and personal visits, the brokers had asked them directly to sell their homes. As an added insult, their lawsuit charged, the agents "caused persons of the colored race to drive slowly over the area . . . at all hours of the day and night pretending to be searching for houses to purchase which causes apprehension, alarm, and embarrassment to petitioners, their neighbors, and friends."[60]

White real-estate firms claimed the charges were an outrage. Gann Realty, for example, swore that its agents had never violated the sanctity of a white neighborhood in Atlanta. As proof of the firm's sincerity, its attorney informed the court that George Gann was a lifelong southerner, who "verily believes in all the Southern traditions pertaining to the segregation laws and customs of the white race of the South, and especially the State of Georgia." Anyone who said differently was a liar, and "should be indicted and convicted for such false swearing." Naturally, the black firms named in the suit responded differently. The McLeans had no case, they charged, because property sales could not be restricted by race. As for the claim that black neighbors would destroy their peace of mind and property values, that was merely a matter of personal prejudice. In the end, the court reluctantly agreed. "The Supreme Court has already made a ruling in this case, and I can't do anything but follow the rule laid down by the high court," said Judge E. E. Andrews apologetically. "I must administer the law justly and impartially."[61]

Undeterred, the white residents of Mozley Park carried their fight to city hall, asking the mayor to do what the courts could not. In an unusual move for that time and place, Mayor Hartsfield made a personal trip to the black-owned restaurant where the Empire Real Estate Board held its monthly meetings. Before the assembled brokers, the mayor asked them to let "Westview Drive serve as a dividing line of houses for whites and colored in the area." His suggestion struck the realtists as a mixed proposition. On one hand, the proposal would open the rest of Mozley Park for blacks; on the other, the agreement would signal an acceptance of residential segregation. In the end, the brokers decided to strike a delicate balance; they would go along with the mayor's plan, for the time being, but "would not make any boundary line" that might legitimize segregation. In a public letter, they announced their withdrawal from all business south of Westview Drive. All outstanding listings would be turned over to Councilman Milton Farris, who would act as the mayor's representative in contacting white sellers and "asking them to withdraw their property from the market."[62]

The white residents below Westview Drive, however, were unwilling to trust the black real-estate agents. As whites of the West End had done before, they again decided to unite in "defense" of their neighborhoods.

The new group they created, the Southwest Citizens Association, largely resembled its immediate predecessor, the Mozley Park Home Owners' Protective Association. Still devoted to the "protection" of property owners, the new group's name signified a new wrinkle to the ideology of resistance. As "citizens," these middle-class white residents asserted certain rights, such as the right of self-government and the right to private property, but also acknowledged certain duties, such as working with city officials to ensure that their needs and the needs of others were met. In a civic spirit, they sought to help their immediate neighbors, to promote the common good of their region, and to present a unified voice in city politics.[63] Practically speaking, the new organization and its predecessor in Mozley Park were virtually identical. The only real difference was that Southwest Citizens embraced a much larger region of the city and therefore could count on a much larger pool of middle-class membership and financing. Despite its expanded scope, Southwest Citizens remained focused on the problems of Mozley Park. Its president Sid Avery, a transportation engineer with General Electric, lived there on Mathewson Place, one street west of the McLeans, and he well understood the "conspiracy" to take over the neighborhood. Likewise, the group's rank and file, living both inside and outside Mozley Park, believed that the line had to be drawn there to prevent further "encroachments." Naturally, they welcomed the word of the Westview Drive agreement. Whether black brokers were calling it a "boundary" or not, that was exactly what the street was becoming, as the realtists removed themselves and their "For Sale" signs from streets south of Westview.

In order to cement the dividing line, Southwest Citizens worked behind the scenes with Mayor Hartsfield and the ward's councilmen, settling on a foolproof plan. On the evening of October 13, 1952, in the gymnasium of Brown High School, more than fifteen hundred whites gathered to hear the "startling progress" that had been made. On behalf of Southwest Citizens, Richard Florrid gave them the good news, announcing there would finally be a "barrier" between blacks to the north and whites to the south. The mayor, he explained over cheers, had agreed to build a six-lane highway along Westview Drive, running from the far side of Ashby Street all the way to Westview Cemetery. Old calls for a "West View Parkway" had finally been realized, but that was only the beginning. Alongside the highway, Florrid continued, residential lands would be rezoned for light industry and warehouses. Furthermore, the Atlanta Housing Authority promised to build a five-hundred-unit housing project, for whites only, around the Ashby Street and Sells Avenue intersection. Ordinarily, middle-class whites would not have welcomed news that their neighborhood would soon be filled with factories, warehouses and public housing. But the residents of Mozley Park considered these changes a small nuisance when compared with the "threat" of black homeowners. Together, this line of barriers, coupled with the cemetery and park, would provide an unprecedented "buffer zone" between blacks and whites stretching for miles along the West End.[64]

Immediately, black leaders attacked the plan. Though they found the whole scheme reprehensible, critics were particularly incensed by the city's plan to create a housing project merely "as the east anchor of a so-called racial 'buffer.' " Public housing was desperately needed in other "slum areas," the *Atlanta Daily World* editorialized. To waste the Housing Authority's time and money for the purpose of *preventing* citizens from securing homes, instead of its purported goal of *helping* them, seemed a cruel joke. The local chapter of the NAACP agreed, publicly voicing its opposition and even filing complaints with federal authorities over their participation in the scheme. Despite the protests, the Housing Authority pushed ahead with the project, completing it in late 1955 and naming it after Joel Chandler Harris, the Atlanta author of the Uncle Remus tales. Further underscoring the segregating purpose of the Harris Homes, the city constructed high-strength cyclone fences between the whites-only project and the black neighborhood to the north. Although black realtists resented the "buffer plan," they grudgingly went along with it. Practically speaking, they knew, the acquisition of more than seven hundred homes in a fine residential section outweighed the stigma of the "buffer zone." And so, after three years of bitterness, the Mozley Park problem had found a solution.[65]

The transition of Mozley Park, however, remained incomplete. Black residents, having moved into more than seven hundred homes on the neighborhood's streets, now spilled over into blocks to the north. By early 1953 the new residents had, as the McLeans predicted, "encircled" both the park and school. Despite racial changes in the surrounding residences, however, the mayor refused to change the racial designation of these neighborhood spaces. The reason was largely political. Running for reelection, Hartsfield worried about upsetting whites in the region. The "loss" of individual homes had given the mayor headaches enough; he refused to fuel whites' resentment by pushing for the transfer of the prized park and school as well. (Some in his administration thought the mayor might even use the situation to his advantage, by claiming his opponent was "going to put negroes on the Fire Dept. and in the City Hall and in the Sanitation Dept. AND on a population basis give Moseley Park and Stanton School to them.") Hartsfield decided to wait the campaign out, promising to do something after the election.[66]

Only then did the city begin preparation for the transition of the neighborhood's facilities to its new population. The board of education, as expected, announced that Frank L. Stanton Elementary School would be used for black students, beginning that fall. For the new black children in the neighborhood, like Charlayne Hunter at 1306 Mozley Place, the thought of taking over the "white" school atop Mozley Drive was a daunting one. "Of course," she later recalled, "once I had climbed the hill and walked through the doors for the first time, there was nothing white in sight—only the ghost-whites that I conjured up as I climbed the stairs to my classroom and as I sat down in one of 'their' seats for the first time. It was a strange experience, being in one of 'their' schools." Once the school had its racial designation changed, black leaders called for the city to follow suit with the pool and park. The Metropolitan Planning Commission likewise warned in June 1953 that "pressure was very strong in some quarters for the immediate transfer of Mozley Park to the Negroes." But Hartsfield still wanted to wait. Until "a comparable facility for whites" was constructed on the west side as a replacement, Mozley Park would remain all white. In the meantime, Hartsfield shuffled the transfer date back again and again. Ultimately, the park changed hands in April 1954, finally completing the transfer of the Mozley Park neighborhood from white to black after nearly five years of animosity and negotiations.[67]

During that time, the whites of Mozley Park had assumed that the "invading" blacks were of a lower class and cruder background. In truth, blacks in the first wave of residents were very much like their white counterparts, at least in terms of occupation, while the second wave came from a higher class. The stretch of Mozley Place from Ed and Maybelle Turner's home to Mathewson Place on the west was a prime example. When whites fled, their homes were initially inherited by a nearly identical cross-section of blacks. A few were middle-class, such as the principal of an elementary school and an office clerk at Clark College, but the vast majority held working-class jobs, making a living as a painter, a baker, a maid, a day laborer, a laundry machinist, a freight handler, a loader for a trucking firm, and a janitor at Georgia Tech. Once the neighborhood had settled down, however, white-collar professionals moved into the area, including several ministers, faculty members from nearby Atlanta University, and even some of the same real-estate agents who had secured the neighborhood's "transition" in the first place. In a 1957 study, Carson Lee of Atlanta University's sociology department compared the new residents of Mozley Park with the whites they had replaced. In general, he found the new black homeowners generally had higher levels of education, income, property ownership, political activity, and civic involvement. The new population, Lee concluded, was "characteristically stable, mature, upwardly mobile, with a design for respectability."[68]

Like other members of the middle class, these black residents had bought their new homes to escape working-class areas to the east. Two-thirds of the new homeowners, Lee reported, had picked Mozley Park because it had a "better location" or was "less crowded" than older black enclaves. Indeed, in contrast to where they had once been, the neighborhood seemed a paradise. "The house my mother bought was on Mozley Place," remembered one newcomer. "It was twice as big as our [old] house . . . with beautiful grassy lawns in the front and back. The streets were paved, just like the white folks' streets." Not surprisingly, these new occupants wanted to keep those streets in the condition they had inherited them. The main problem with this was, of course, the scorched-earth retreat of the whites who had lived there before them. In keeping with the "buffer plan," two areas of light industry, a center of industrial warehouses and a housing project soon appeared around the neighborhood. With those aspects of the "no man's land" in place, Mayor Hartsfield pressed for the buffer highway as well. "There is a very delicate racial situation along this highway which we are anxious to aid," he wrote his chief of construction in 1954, "and the people out there are going to expect action." The highway project stalled when bonds could not be secured, but later in the decade, the city ensured that a stretch of the new interstate highway took its place. To make way for the project, the state and county condemned much of the black-owned land there in 1959, offering extremely low sums as compensation. Rev. William Holmes Borders, for instance, was offered $992 for a lot he owned, even though homes on that block had been going for nearly ten times that amount. Despite strong protests, the city bulldozed the whole southwestern section of the neighborhood.[69]

Although the freeway presented an obvious instance, public incursions occurred in less obvious ways as well. Typically, once blacks had "taken over" an Atlanta neighborhood, city officials automatically assumed that property values would plummet and the area would become a slum. Accordingly, planners and zoning committees lowered their standards for the region and began approving projects they would have routinely rejected if the residents were still white. After fighting to get into a neighborhood of single-family homes, middle-class black residents now saw cramped apartment complexes and commercial projects springing up nearby. "It's awfully disgusting to pay inflated prices for homes in a residential section and as soon as you begin to get settled, here comes white 'investors' throwing up anything that will get by the inspectors," complained one black Atlantan. "Juke joints and pool rooms will probably be next. Can't we expect any type of protection from our city government?"[70]

Not surprisingly, blacks found this pattern playing out in Mozley Park immediately after their arrival. In December 1952 they discovered that a white landlord on Penelope Road, just two blocks on the other side of the park and school, planned to turn her fifteen acre plot into a two-

hundred-unit apartment complex for whites. Mozley Park residents protested, not merely because the project would present another "buffer" to
the west, but because it would mean more overcrowding. Austin Walden
complained to the Municipal Planning Board, employing a middle-class
rhetoric that resembled that of white residents who protested black "encroachments." "The Atlanta Urban League has worked hard and long to
provide decent housing in desirable locations for Negroes, and we are
naturally opposed to any efforts to destroy the investments of the property
owners," he argued. "To permit the re-zoning . . . is tantamount to admitting that Negroes do not have the same right to protection of their neighborhoods as do citizens of white residential sections." In a coordinated
protest, busloads of homeowners were shuttled to city hall, where they
presented city planners with a petition. "The fifteen acre tract of land is
in the heart of a brand new Negro residential community," they noted.
Construction of such a large project "would tend to lower property values
of the existing home owners" and "would increase the population density,
a major factor in the development of a slum." On this one occasion at
least, their protests succeeded.[71]

While black residents fought to maintain their high standards for the
neighborhood, the city rarely followed suit. This pattern became clear in
the decline of the public park. Prior to the "racial transfer" of Mozley
Park, black Atlantans had only three underfunded recreational sites in the
city, compared with the twenty-two reserved for whites. Even with the
addition of Mozley Park, Atlanta still fell short of meeting the needs of
its black population, due to its segregation policies. "If all park areas were
equally open to all Atlanta citizens, our city would provide one acre of
public recreational land per 200 people," the Atlanta Urban League calculated in 1954. "Under the present arrangements which limit the use of
public recreational space and facilities to separate racial groups, there is
one acre for every 155 white citizens and one for every 1020 Negro citizens." While all black parks suffered from overcrowding, Mozley Park
received the most visitors. Built with white patrons in mind, it was by far
the best-equipped and most attractive spot available to blacks. "Because
there was no other facility like it anywhere in Atlanta," one patron remembered, "it drew crowds of young Black people." Those crowds took
a toll. After the first summer of black use, the *Atlanta Daily World* complained that the lack of other recreational spots created "the necessary
overuse of the Mozley Park" pool and recreation center. "Overcrowding
of Negro parks has long been a sore spot," the reporter noted, adding
that surrounding "residential sections suffer." The city ignored the pleas
of black patrons. Mozley Park stayed underfunded and increasingly over-
used. Just a decade later, the decline was already striking. In 1964 the
Atlanta Inquirer listed a litany of problems that had accumulated across

Mozley Park—windows broken for years, boards on the pool's deck completely rotten, and grounds so untended as to "evoke a feeling of disgust."
"The general run-down conditions," the newspaper noted, "make it hard
for a person to believe that this is the same recreational facility that existed
when it was tabbed 'For White Only.' "[72]

The city's neglect of Mozley Park and its assault on middle-class standards there can perhaps be explained by the fact that white officials, like
white residents, assumed that property values would inevitably decline
once the neighborhood "went colored." In truth, however, the opposite
was true. In spite of all the changes that should have demonstrably lowered property values in the area—introduction of new industrial sites and
warehouses, construction of a housing project and apartment complexes
for the poor, intrusion of an interstate highway, and general neglect by
municipal officials—property values in the black-occupied section of
Mozley Park actually witnessed a boom. A comparison of census block
statistics, taken first in 1950, when the neighborhood was still all-white,
and then a decade later, after the "transition" had long been completed,
shows that property values, measured in constant dollars, rose by an average of 27 percent over the decade. According to the then-dominant theories of real-estate value, a brief surge in prices would be expected, since
"the first black families had to pay a premium to break the color barrier,"
but such a rise would be short-lived and followed by a "drastic decline."
However, in Mozley Park, some of the largest increases were found on
blocks with the longest history of black occupancy. For instance, the four
blocks straddling Mozley Drive, the street where the "transition troubles"
first began, showed price increases of 17, 20, 42, and 50 percent over the
decade. By comparison, on blocks to the south—blocks that underwent
transition later and stood even farther removed from the Ashby Street
enclave—homes of almost identical 1950 appraisal values only showed
increases of 6, 12, and 16 percent over the same period. By all objective
measurements, the transition of property from white to black ownership
did not lower its value but raised it instead. White assumptions that black
ownership would automatically lower home prices reflected not the realities of the free market as a whole, but an artificial market that segregated
not just white and black homes by race, but white and black buyers as
well. Only a slanted perspective, one that interpreted "value" according
to what whites would pay, could see homes in a black neighborhood as
worth less.[73]

Such realities of real estate escaped the notice of white Atlanta. For
them, the visible decline of the Mozley Park neighborhood after the "transition troubles" served as a warning. In truth, the steady decay had been
brought on by city planners who lowered zoning standards, parks officials
who allowed overuse, private companies who slighted the needs of black

residents, and the fundamental economic exhaustion of black buyers, who bought secondhand housing at prices often three times the initial value and therefore had limited funds for repairs or refurnishings. To white eyes, these causes were hidden. In their understanding, the reason was much simpler—blacks had moved in and the neighborhood went down. The decay reinforced their feelings that blacks were lazy, sloppy, and shiftless. As blacks began to move into other "white" neighborhoods around town, the specter of Mozley Park remained in their minds as a warning of what residential transition would bring in its wake.

Although white residents "lost" Mozley Park, and Ashby Street before it, they gained something of tremendous importance. In their effort to defend the region, they had greatly improved the image of white resistance, evolving from fringe groups such as the Columbians and Ku Klux Klan to more "respectable"—and respected—organizations like the Mozley Park Home Owners' Protective Association and, more prominently, the Southwest Citizens Association. In moving their resistance into the mainstream, these whites managed not only to legitimize their cause but to place themselves in positions of influence for the next rounds of resistance. The "defense" of white neighborhoods was no longer the province of racial extremists seeking to sway the opinions of the working class, but instead something woven into the worldview of the upwardly mobile middle class, wholly respectable and admired. Thus, in the course of a few short years and a few short blocks, the cause of neighborhood "defense" had been fundamentally transformed. Mainstream whites no longer saw these residential resistance groups as a threat to the image and ideals of Atlanta; instead, they saw them as legitimate community activists, ones who acted as integral partners in managing the city's peaceful race relations.

CHAPTER THREE

From Community to Individuality:
Race, Residence, and Segregationist Ideology

As RESIDENTIAL racial transitions spread in the postwar era, Atlanta's moderate coalition sought to control its pace. Mayor Hartsfield had been so pleased with the negotiations over Mozley Park that he decided in December 1952 to bring blacks and whites together as a permanent planning committee "to consider the various living, building, and development problems of the west side of our city." To represent black Atlantans, he appointed three prominent leaders: builder Walter Aiken, realtist T. M. Alexander, and attorney Austin Walden. In a move that signified the new strength and status of the white resistance movement, Hartsfield chose the top three officials of the Southwest Citizens Association as representatives of the region's whites: Sid Avery, the General Electric engineer; Richard Florrid, executive secretary of the Atlanta Restaurant Association; and Ernest Sewall, a serviceman for an adding machine company. Together, the six men launched the West Side Mutual Development Committee (WSMDC).[1]

More than any other public or private agency, the WSMDC played the pivotal role in determining the course of residential racial change in postwar Atlanta. Despite its importance, the committee generally reacted to rumors of racial change and conflict as they surfaced. Typically, the WSMDC began by investigating reports of neighborhoods "threatened" by racial transition, gauging the attitudes of local whites with telephone canvasses, written questionnaires, and public meetings. The information collected offers a rare degree of detail and an impressive amount of insight into the processes of residential racial change at the most minute levels. The polls conducted by the committee offer immediate measures of the mood of different neighborhoods, while the house-by-house surveys enable mapping the geography of white resistance with unprecedented precision. Most important, for the WSMDC and its allies in city hall, the reams of information they collected stood as a means to limit the impact of residential desegregation on their city and maintain the peace on its streets.

With such information in hand, the WSMDC would generally call white homeowners' groups and black real-estate agents together to see if some sort of compromise—a boundary line, a program of repurchasing homes already sold to blacks, an alternate site for black homes, and so forth—could be voluntarily worked out. Once such a "gentleman's agreement" had been achieved, the WSMDC used the information "to advise and influence property buyers and sellers, realty and home finance firms, and city departments" about the neighborhood. On the surface, the WSMDC merely made friendly suggestions. But the organization enjoyed public backing from the mayor and aldermen, as well as other planning committees and housing agencies. "The backing of the City government," a WSMDC report noted, "has been a vital force in effecting and maintaining the agreements reached in this [voluntary] way." Furthermore, the committee had the strong support of local newspapers and businessmen, and its members had private connections to major real-estate and financial institutions. As a result, most Atlantans recognized that "unofficial" recommendations of the WSMDC were, in fact, the official word on issues of race and residence.[2]

Throughout the 1950s the West Side Mutual Development Committee used its tremendous influence to negotiate conflicts over Atlanta's neighborhoods "within the framework of the housing market." Practically speaking, this meant working along segregated lines. "There are really two real estate markets—one Negro and one white," the WSMDC conceded in 1958. This resulted not from any public policy of segregation, the committee claimed, but rather from private preferences. According to the WSMDC's technical adviser, Robert Stuart, "the decisions of thousands of individual buyers and sellers of property exercising their constitutional rights [are what] determines whether a particular area is white or Negro." From its own perspective, the WSMDC merely sought to clear up confusion and prevent violence. When committee members spoke of "determining" a neighborhood's racial status, they thought of themselves as trying to discover an objective truth, whether a neighborhood was solidly white or surely becoming black. But more often than not, WSMDC actions "determined" a neighborhood's status in quite another sense. Its pronouncements—this area will stay white, that section is a lost cause—attached an air of certainty to otherwise unpredictable situations. In many cases, WSMDC predictions became self-fulfilling prophecies.[3]

In making those determinations, a single concept of "community integrity" dominated the WSMDC deliberations and, as a result, decided the future of countless neighborhoods. T. M. Alexander explained the idea this way:

A community which has "integrity" as defined by that committee was a complete, homogenous community. It was a community composed of neighbors who were accustomed to living together, and whose children go to the same schools, churches, and parks. It had its own shopping center and a variety of homes in various classes. It had potential growth, and development was already in progress. It was not a "fringe" or "pocket" community nor tied into any other community of similar character.

If a contested area lacked "community integrity," the WSMDC stepped aside and let racial transition continue. But if the WSMDC decided that an area indeed had "integrity," it threw its considerable strength behind private efforts to maintain the racial status quo. When a reporter asked Alexander if the "community integrity" standard wasn't "merely a polite way of masking segregation," the black realtist disagreed. "It has gotten away from the idea of fixed boundary lines, buffer zones, and all the rest," he explained. "I couldn't sell that to Negroes. But we can buy the idea of community integrity." Indeed, Alexander liked the idea so much that he convinced the WSMDC to adopt "We Protected the Integrity of Communities" as its official slogan.[4]

Because the WSMDC relied on community integrity as its "yardstick," white residents consciously tried to measure up to the standard. If they could demonstrate their solid sense of community, past and present, they believed their neighborhood might be "saved" from racial transition. If they could not, they knew their area would be "lost." Therefore, whites in borderline neighborhoods began stressing their common ties, their common rights, and their common goals. They papered over their significant internal differences and tried to present a unified front. To varying degrees, they succeeded. Outside observers largely accepted their claims of "community" without question. But how substantial were such "white communities" in reality? The experiences of several white, working-class neighborhoods in Atlanta demonstrate that "community" was an ideal that was regularly celebrated but rarely experienced. The neighborhood of Adamsville, for instance, seemed to have strong "community integrity" but, in fact, only stayed a white neighborhood through artificial, external measures. Kirkwood, by comparison, seemed to find "community integrity" in neighborhood institutions but ultimately disintegrated under the bitter internal squabbling of white residents. Adair Park, meanwhile, was a small section that tried, and failed, to invent a larger community of whites for its own protection. And as the experiences of Collier Heights, Center Hill, and Grove Park made clear, urban neighborhoods functioned in an interconnected world that made it ultimately impossible for any one "community" to stand alone, regardless of its supposed "integrity."

As these studies demonstrate, the concept of a "white community" was anything but a simple matter in struggles over race and residence. The working-class whites who lived in transition areas assumed that they and their neighbors shared not only the common traits of race and class but also common interests in preserving segregation in their neighborhood and the status quo in local politics. During the course of residential desegregation, however, they discovered that their supposed common ground on these issues and identities was ultimately less important for them and their neighbors than each one's self-interest. As long as individual home-

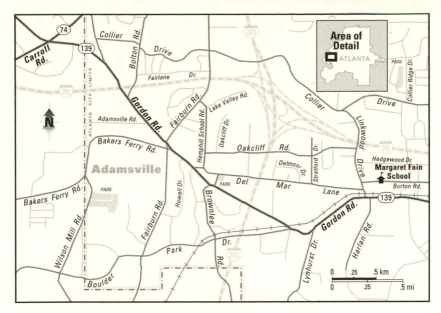

Map 3.1 Adamsville, 1950

owners felt that their individual needs—protecting property values and maintaining a stable home—could be met by working with their neighbors, they did so. Invariably, though, when some whites decided that their needs and the neighborhood's diverged, they resolved to act on their own and in their own self-interest, regardless of the repercussions. The reality of individuality, these whites quickly realized, would always trump the rhetoric of community. And so, during the course of residential desegregation, as more and more working-class white Atlantans made this discovery, they thought of themselves less and less as participants in a larger society, with the attendant rights and responsibilities. For them, connections to other whites, on the same street, in the same neighborhood, or in the city at large, had been proved pointless. Instead of thinking in terms of their supposed community, these working-class whites now started to think of themselves as individuals, set apart from and, indeed, set against the rest of Atlanta.

A COMMUNITY WITH INTEGRITY: ADAMSVILLE

Adamsville had long been an isolated area, only annexed by Atlanta during its postwar sprawl. Even after incorporation, the neighborhood maintained its rural feel. The housing stock was generally poorer than that in the city, with more than a third of its homes dilapidated or without running water. As late as the 1950s the section had no library, no park, no doctor or dentist. It was four miles to the nearest drugstore, and nine to the closest hospital. That sense of isolation, however, quickly faded. "We soon found ourselves in the path of Atlanta's enormous urban growth," the Adamsville Civic Club noted. "Expressways began reaching out to serve our traffic, and people from counties beyond us began using our stores. Open fields became dotted with homes. We were swiftly being transformed into an urban community." And as urban developments spread into Adamsville, so did black residential expansion. By late 1954 black homes were quite literally at its borders.[5]

Alarmed by the approach of black Atlantans, civic groups around Adamsville asked the WSMDC for protection. Tellingly, they all used the language of "community" in their pleas for help. "We are deeply concerned with the continued infiltration of Negroes," wrote the West Manor Civic Club. "This movement is beginning to pose as a threat to some adjoining white communities." Other homeowners' groups agreed. The Adamsville Civic Club, for example, wanted "a new 'Gentleman's Agreement Line' that will respect the integrity of the Adamsville community." Following their lead, neighborhood agencies made a similar appeal. The local parent-teacher association and Women's Thrift Club, for instance, asked the WSMDC to "protect the integrity of the Adamsville community and the interests of its citizens." The Adamsville American Legion Post and its Ladies' Auxiliary stressed the investments residents had made in the area. "[T]his community of Adamsville is almost entirely composed of home owners who established residence here for the purpose of bringing up families and entering their children in white churches and schools," they explained. In a similar vein, the churches themselves begged for help. "In the interest of Christianity and fair play," the pastor and lay leader of Bethel Methodist asked for "a new 'Gentleman's Agreement Line.'" Likewise, the pastor and clerk of the Brownwood Baptist Church wrote to say they were "deeply concerned about our community, our Churches, School, our homes, that the people have worked so hard to have. As you know," they added ominously, "the colored people are moving closer week by week."[6]

By all surface appearances, the people of Adamsville seemed to form a coherent community in contrast to the "colored people" around them. In January 1955 a variety of working-class residents—truck drivers, metalworkers, railroad switchmen, auto mechanics, contractors, plumbers, brickmasons, carpenters, widows—all signed their names to a petition calling for the protection of their neighborhood. "We have invested many years and considerable money in what we feel is one of the best communities in the greater Atlanta area," they asserted. "It is our desire and determination not to sell any of our property which will change the status of our present ADAMSVILLE COMMUNITY." In several cases, this apparent community spirit was amplified when bonds of the neighborhood were reinforced by bonds of a workplace, especially the railroads. Those involved in the early "defense" of Adamsville, for instance, included a switchman, a car repairer, and an engineer for the Southern Railway, as well as a switchman and a clerk for the Nashville, Chattanooga, and St. Louis line. At the top levels of "defense," the ties became even more pronounced. Of the eight residents leading the campaign, for example, two were married to vehiclemen for the Railway Express, while a third's husband was chief clerk there. With these overlapping bonds of home and work, Adamsville seemed a model of "community integrity."[7]

Impressed with this grass-roots response, the WSMDC decided to intervene. Through a series of negotiations with local blacks and whites, Linkwood Road was made the boundary between the "white community" of Adamsville and nearby black neighborhoods. To strengthen the semblance of "community," and thereby cement the "gentleman's agreement," the WSMDC encouraged the Adamsville Civic Club to come up with its own vision of what that community meant to its residents. Its report, *Adamsville: Now . . . and Tomorrow*, began by noting the toll that the city's progress had taken on their once isolated area. "As Atlanta grows larger, small communities like ours begin to lose the personal contacts we once had with our political leaders," the report lamented. "Fewer people vote. Local issues are rarely discussed." But this could change, the civic club promised. In the pages that followed, it sketched out a bold vision of the Adamsville of tomorrow—new streets, schools, parks, and shopping centers, all combined with the traditional values of community that made Adamsville special in the first place. Race was never mentioned. Instead, it existed as an unspoken undercurrent throughout the discussion of creating "a desirable community." For white Atlantans, only an all-white community was desirable.[8]

With Adamsville now defined as a white "community," city planners assumed it would remain so. But it turned out not to be so simple. In 1956 homeowners on Del Mar Lane, immediately inside the Linkwood Road line, discovered that "colored families" not only stood to their east, across the boundary line, but had also occupied homes inside the line to the west, "leaving us completely surrounded by colored citizens." "As you know," they wrote the governor, "the above situation makes our homes unsalable except to colored citizens." Soon, "For Sale" signs appeared along Del Mar. The Adamsville Civic Club sprang into action, cautioning other residents not to panic. At a mass meeting, representatives from the Metropolitan Planning Commission, the West Side Mutual Development Committee, and the Southwest Citizens Association, along with an assortment of mortgage brokers and real-estate interests, all spoke to the residents of Adamsville "for the purpose of stabilizing this area, according to the wishes of the majority." Likewise, the mayor and city council made it known that they, too, would do everything within their power to protect the "community integrity" of Adamsville. The entire city, it seemed, was working together to provide a solution satisfactory to the majority of local homeowners.[9]

The problem with this "majority rule" approach was that whites at the center of the controversy, those living on Del Mar Lane, increasingly felt like a tormented minority. "We have never considered ourselves residents of Adamsville," they insisted, "and we feel that Linkwood Road was arbitrarily set as Adamsville's eastern boundary FOR SELFISH REASONS only." The Adamsville Civic Club had sent letters out asking for their input, but those letters were also sent to people far removed from the crisis area. "Instead of confining the circulation of this letter to *those concerned, residents of Del Mar Lane—from Linkwood to Stratford Drive*," they complained, "it was circulated in a staggered fashion, (*a delaying action, we think*) to residents of Stratford Drive and Oak Cliff Drive, making a total of 70 to 75 letters circulated which places those of us who are REALLY concerned in a great minority group." The entire situation left them feeling persecuted. "Unless the City of Atlanta takes steps immediately to remedy this situation by re-designating the eastern boundary of Adamsville," the Del Mar residents wrote, "we will construe this to mean that not only our civil and legal rights, but even our 'human' rights, have been taken away."[10]

Mayor Hartsfield tried to settle the crisis over what was and was not part of the "white community" of Adamsville, never bothering to question if a "community" even existed. He ordered the WSMDC to do everything in its power to "maintain a white market on Delmar" and thereby return it to the fold of Adamsville. To that end, the committee urged local whites to raise money to repurchase all the black homes inside the boundary line. In just a few days, sixty working-class families pledged a total of $1,100. An additional door-to-door pledge drive and fundraising by the Adamsville Civic Club boosted the total to $13,200. Southwest Citizens contributed its considerable financial muscle, spending over $30,000 more to put four additional pieces of property back in white hands over the winter of 1956–57. Meanwhile, the West Side Mutual Development Committee worked to restore confidence in Del Mar Lane as a "white market." In a mass mailing to mortgage brokers in January 1957, the WSMDC explained the repurchasing program and its conviction that the "integrity" of Adamsville had been restored. "With the previous doubt in regard to race of residents, we understood that the lending institutions were not approving loans for this area, with resulting hardship on the individual families affected," the committee stated. "We believe the area, now, is to be stable for white occupancy, and hope that you will extend full home financing to persons purchasing homes in this area." Additionally, the WSMDC encouraged the development of an all-white realty market on Del Mar throughout the spring of 1957. "The absence of a stable real estate market has been the chief cause of unrest," noted WSMDC planner Charles Allen. "Property owners who, through necessity, have been required to sell their homes have turned to the only available market, which has been the colored real estate market." To secure a "stable market"—in other words, a "white market"—the WSMDC contacted several black realtists and convinced them to withdraw their services and signs from Del Mar.[11]

Despite this massive operation of organizing residents, repurchasing homes, and revitalizing the "white market," the situation remained uneasy. Resting on nothing more than good-faith agreements, the stabilization of Del Mar Lane—and, by extension, all of Adamsville—could be upset by a single black buyer. In June 1957, for example, a black man named M. C. Jackson purchased a home at the intersection of Del Mar Lane and Stratford Road, directly in the crosshairs of earlier conflicts. After repeated requests by the WSMDC and the Atlanta Police Department, Jackson agreed to delay moving into his new home. Meanwhile, Southwest Citizens arranged to repurchase the property at the original price and the WSMDC pulled strings to secure Jackson a spot in public housing. Before the repurchase and removal could be completed, however, arsonists set fire to the home, scorching the roof and gutting the interior. Desperate to remove Jackson, Southwest Citizens decided to buy the home anyway. With his presence erased, the WSMDC renewed its public relations campaign, swearing once more that Adamsville had "integrity" as a white community, recent troubles notwithstanding.[12]

As soon as this eastern boundary of Adamsville had been "secured," however, similar troubles sprang up along the northern border as developers began building homes for blacks there in early 1958. White working-class residents on Fairburn Road, just inside the line, panicked and the whole process of neighborhood transition began again. Once again, the WSMDC sent letters to boost white morale. "The Committee feels that Adamsville has a fine future as a community," it assured residents. But the committee took more aggressive steps, as well. It drew up a petition, on WSMDC stationery, urging local whites to decide "by majority feeling" which real-estate market—black or white, but not both—would function in the neighborhood. After whites followed the WSMDC's lead and voted for a white market, the committee went even further, typing up form letters for homeowners to send real-estate agents. "In view of existing circumstances of Fairburn Road, being a disputed area and all the owners not wishing to sell, and for the best interests of the community," the sheets read, "I wish to notify you that I am withdrawing my property from the market." All homeowners had to do was fill in a few blanks and drop the form in the mail. Afterward, city officials continued to stand guard over Adamsville's boundaries. When a real-estate firm began soliciting business for black buyers on the "wrong" side of the northern line, for instance, the WSMDC strongly discouraged its presence. "You will notice from the map the location of the northern boundary of Adamsville," warned an adviser, adding that the line would remain a racial border until "a clear majority of the property owners" decided differently. To establish the dividing line in more concrete terms, the city planned to make the West Expressway, now Interstate-20, "the boundary between the white and Negro communities." Their intention was no secret, as city construction crews clearly marked the highway's planned route along the way.[13]

In the eyes of city officials at the decade's end, Adamsville was a success story. The neighborhood had weathered countless crises—the dissent of white residents near its eastern boundary, the threat of transition on its northern boundary, the exhausting process of organizing residents, the financial strain of repurchasing homes, and even an occasional outbreak of violence. In spite of all this, the WSMDC noted approvingly that "community integrity" had been maintained. That verdict, however, was somewhat disingenuous. To be sure, Adamsville stood, for the time at least, as an all-white residential area. But that was not the same as a "community." Whites in the region had been unable to hold the neighborhood together on their own and had, in fact, begun to turn against each other when racial residential change loomed large. It was only because of the constant and concerted effort of the city's moderate political, social, and business forces that Adamsville had maintained its segregated status. The neighborhood had staved off racial succession, but it was at heart a hollow victory, one that offered no proof of any "community spirit" at all.

Whereas Adamsville had to be propped up from the outside to maintain any semblance of unity, other neighborhoods in Atlanta possessed their own internal sources of "community integrity," in the form of local institutions. They readily marshaled those sites of local strength in an attempt to do for themselves what Adamsville had relied on outsiders to do. In the end, however, their "community" proved to be just as much of an illusion.

COMMUNITY INSTITUTIONS AND COMMUNITY INTEGRITY: KIRKWOOD

In its private discussions and public pronouncements, the West Side Mutual Development Committee constantly stressed the importance of neighborhood institutions as sources of community strength. "The values of

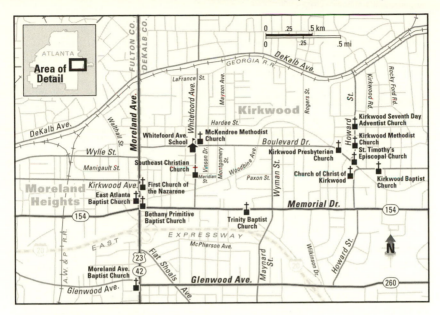

Map 3.2 Kirkwood, 1950

community life built around schools, churches, lodges and other organizations, are built up over a period of years, even generations," an official policy statement noted. "In the sense that the city of Atlanta is made up of a number of parts, the city as a whole suffers a loss when an established community is destroyed." And, in the WSMDC's mind, established white communities were destroyed by residential desegregation. "In my opinion, transition of a large established community from one racial occupancy pattern to the other is wasteful," noted WSMDC adviser Bob Stuart. "Community institutions, churches, schools, lodges, etc., are made up of people. If the people are suddenly changed, these institutions are wiped out." Of all the neighborhoods in Atlanta, the pivotal relationship between "community institutions" and "community integrity" was perhaps clearest in Kirkwood.[14]

Situated in southeast Atlanta, Kirkwood was a white, working-class neighborhood of long standing. Surveys from 1957 showed that more than three-fourths of its residents had lived on the same block for more than five years, although many had been there much longer, some since the 1910s. As in Adamsville, many of the residents not only lived together, but worked together too. Within just a few blocks of each other, for instance, stood the homes of two textile workers, the time-card handler, and a power-room employee at the Fulton Bag Mill. Likewise, three switchmen, a foreman, and the chief clerk of the Atlanta Joint Terminal all lived in close proximity. In rare cases, family ties overlapped with these connections of work and home. Clay Sims, George Sims, and James Sims, for instance, all lived on the same block of Wylie Street and all worked for their family's radiator repair service.[15]

In stark contrast to these close ties of home, work, and even family stood the distinctly separate settlements of blacks to their northwest, around the juncture of the Central of Georgia Railroad and the A. & W. P. Railroad, and to their northeast, between the Central's lines and Boulevard Drive. The whites of Kirkwood watched these black enclaves nervously, waiting for any signs of "encroachment." In 1954, when blacks began looking at homes in the eastern half of Kirkwood, a region known as Moreland Heights, whites sounded the alarm. "An attempt is being made to sell white property to Negroes," warned the Moreland Heights Civic Club. "We believe that those white people attempting to sell to Negroes have failed their responsibility as home owners and neighbors." Whites resented the "infiltration" of black buyers because, in their minds, they threatened their long-standing community. "We have lived in this section for many years and own our homes and we certainly don't want to be surrounded by negroes," a secretary wrote the mayor. But homes were only part of the picture. "We also have our churches near us," she continued, "and don't want them to be taken over by negroes." "If we are force out we will loose our church and school," worried an elevator operator, "and we caint ford to do that." WSMDC planners agreed. "While the problem is difficult, the stakes are very high," Bob Stuart noted. "It is inconceivable that the fine community life and spirit now existing in the Moreland Heights area should be wiped out through a scattering of its present residents."[16]

To determine which community institutions were most important to the integrity of Moreland Heights, the WSMDC surveyed residents in October 1957. "We are asking questions about schools, churches, and so forth which indicate your attitude toward the neighborhood in general," the committee wrote, "because this attitude often has a direct influence on a property owner's decision to sell or stay." Because a majority of Moreland Heights residents were elderly, it was not surprising that relatively few had ties to local schools. A third of those surveyed did have children enrolled and were themselves active in local parent-teacher Associations. One such parent, an auto mechanic, worried that he would have to remove his children from the schools if the neighborhood's racial composition changed. "I have 3 girls," he wrote. "And I would not want them walking to and from school through negros settlers on this street."[17]

Although such ties to schools were limited, the bonds to area churches were quite strong. When asked "Do you attend church in this neighborhood?" more than 70 percent said yes, pointing to one of the many Protestant churches in the area.[18] For congregationally controlled churches like these, neighborhood concerns were church concerns. Not only did the congregations live in contested areas; in almost all cases, their pastors did too.[19] Keeping Moreland Heights white was, therefore, both a pastoral and personal activity for many ministers. For instance, the minister of Southeast Christian, "A Church of Friendly Christians," urged his congregation to discuss "the housing problem" with WSMDC officials. But it was too late. The rush to sell was on, and the neighborhood underwent swift racial succession. By 1960 three-fourths of the homes in Moreland Heights were occupied by blacks. Just as WSMDC planners and local residents had feared, the churches were "wiped out" by the racial transition. The First Church of the Nazarene and Southeast Christian both sold their buildings to black buyers and fled the neighborhood with their congregations. The Whitefoord Baptist Church and an evangelical Christian Fellowship Center closed their doors as well, moving miles to the east, beyond the "transition troubles." And as far as city planners could tell, Bethany Primitive Baptist just disappeared. For many of these congregations, relocation was a financial nightmare. McKendree Methodist Church, for example, claimed an investment of $120,000 in its Moreland Heights property, but hoped to recoup just half that amount after its relocation. Racial transition, by their accounts, proved costly.[20]

As the course of black expansion continued toward the heart of Kirkwood, whites eyed the changes with alarm. "We have enjoyed our modest homes," one white man worried in 1960. "Now a vast flood of Negros are coming East ward & threaten to swamp the area." Like the residents of most borderline areas, these were working-class families. Along Montgomery Street, for instance, stood the homes of a policeman, a firefighter, a cab driver, a baggage handler, a few truck drivers, some railroad men, assorted mechanics and repairmen, and assembly line workers for Ford, General Motors, and General Electric. Much like the working-class whites of Mozley Park and elsewhere, they counted their home as their only investment of note. They too understood racial transition as a threat to property values and reacted accordingly. For instance, when a black family bought the house at 1408 Woodbine Avenue, arsonists set fire to the home before it could even move in. Flammable liquids were poured under the house and ignited, torching the entire back side and burning holes through the roof. Next door to the gutted home stood a sign which simply read: "WHITE AREA." When a black woman and her daughter moved into a home at 1500 Woodbine just weeks later, a similar scene unfolded. As with the rest of the region, huge signs stating "This is a White Area" were scattered up and down the street, including the house next door. Just in case the new occupants missed those warnings, white residents showed up to let them know in person. Only hours after the moving van arrived, knots of people gathered around the small, shingled home. Shortly past sunset, a long caravan of cars wheeled onto the street and swelled the crowd to several hundred strong. Mostly young married couples and teenagers, they shouted insults for hours at the blacks inside. Only after someone shattered the kitchen window with a rock did the police finally order the crowd to disperse.[21]

Although such hostility once remained "hidden violence," incidents such as these have been increasingly brought to light in recent years.[22] But part of this story remains hidden, for white hostility was not simply directed at "Negro invaders." Just as significantly, whites in this apparently united "community" also directed their anger and violence at their fellow whites. This intrawhite hostility stemmed from the fact that whites responded to residential transition in very different ways. When confronted with the fact—not simply the "threat"—of black homeowners in their neighborhoods, whites reacted according to their proximity to racial change. Almost without exception, those nearest the front lines of transition wanted to flee, while those further back wanted to fight. The inherent conflict in those two goals soon surfaced, and a supposedly solid "community" succumbed to bitter infighting. On one side, whites who wanted to sell their homes blamed the others for holding them back. "A few diehards are attempting to interfere with legitimate transactions between home owners and honest real estate salesmen," complained a man from Woodbine Circle. "Many home owners have suffered lost sales because of rabble rousers." Those on the front lines of the transition resented the "interference" of those further back. "From all the discussions I've heard," a plumber wrote, "all of the hell being raised is mostly by people not directly concerned." "They do not want to live next to colored people, but they want us to," fumed another man. "I feel that if they want to control my house, they should buy it themselves. I will be happy to sell it to any of these people who are nailing up the 'WHITE AREA' signs." At the same time, those hoping to stay accused their fleeing neighbors of betraying the "community." Many spoke of Kirkwood as the only neighborhood they had ever known. Several cited hardships of age or infirmity, which made it impossible for them to move, while others feared financial losses. Those who wanted to stay blamed their neighbors for undermining their collective security. "How unfair can things get," a clerk asked, "when you put all you can make and scrap to try and have a home. Then some few who have money and can do better sell you out." Some became so angry they warned neighbors "if they sell to Colored, the house will either be burned or blown up." Tempers quickly reached a boiling point. One resident warned that the transition troubles had "plunged our people to near Riot Stage."[23]

As in other neighborhoods, the white resistance in Kirkwood focused not solely on individual homes but on community institutions. A few worried about what would happen to local schools if blacks moved there. "They have almost surrounded the Whitefoord School," noted a railway worker dejectedly. "The school will go to negroes," another man warned, "with-out white children to fill it up." But, much like Moreland Heights, residents in Kirkwood worried more about the future of local churches. "The churches want to sell if they can get a good price," a homeowner on Boulevard lamented. "They can't keep going much longer without members to keep them up." If the churches caved in, whites rationalized, they would have no choice but to leave as well. "I do not want to live in a community where one church has been Sold to the Colored and the other two are for Sale to them," a Vinson Drive resident worried. "Would you want to live on one white block in what probably will be surrounded by colored by Sept.?"[24]

Hoping to save their churches, Kirkwood residents rallied around Eastern Atlanta, Inc., a corporation formed to repurchase homes and keep "undesirable neighbors" out of the area. Like other homeowners' groups, the organization presented a respectable public face. "We don't have any wild-eyed people in this group," assured Alderman Robert E. Lee Field, a director in the corporation. "We all live here, we own our homes, we're church people. We're just trying to preserve all that." To fund the neighborhood defense, the group reached out to church leaders, asking them to help save the white neighborhood and, thereby, their own churches. The appeal was a natural one, since several in their congregations already had ties to Eastern Atlanta, Inc. The Sunday school teacher at Kirkwood Baptist acted as the corporation's treasurer, for instance, while one of Kirkwood Methodist's stewards served as both a director for Eastern Atlanta and president of the South Kirkwood Civic Club. These overlapping relationships yielded clear results. An October 1960 rally, for instance, featured more than eighty pastors and lay people, representing nine of the fourteen white churches of Kirkwood. B. M. Huggins of the East Atlanta Civic Club reminded the crowd that all the combined church property represented "several millions of dollars in investments," which could only be protected by keeping Kirkwood white.[25]

As the transition "threat" continued to spread, these church leaders assumed ever-greater positions of leadership in their neighborhood's "defense." First, in February 1961, the six main churches of the region— Kirkwood Methodist, Kirkwood Presbyterian, Kirkwood Baptist, Kirkwood Seventh Day Adventist, Trinity Baptist, and St. Timothy's Episcopal—banded together to form the Kirkwood Churches Committee. Each of the six churches lent five members to the cause, usually the pastor and the top lay officials, to create a core of thirty members. Although the group soon changed its named to the Kirkwood Community Committee (KCC), its membership continued to be dominated by the six founding congregations. From the start, the KCC wholeheartedly supported the drive against "undesirable neighbors." At first, it simply "went on record as being willing and anxious to assist the Eastern Atlanta Corporation in the selling of stock subscriptions" to its congregations. It originally allowed others to lead, but soon the KCC decided to spearhead the "defense" itself. For instance, when local aldermen prepared to meet black realtists and work out a new "gentlemen's agreement," the churchmen issued directives from behind the scenes. To underscore the scope of previous white losses and black gains, the aldermen were instructed to note that "the (conceded) Moreland [Heights] area contains 7 churches, the Whitefoord school *and* over 600 houses." The churchmen also wanted the aldermen to stress the current "plight" of their own churches, "with their white congregations moving out of the area" and "the financial losses due to so many religious type buildings going on the market practically at the same time in a relatively small area." Just as the religious leaders directed discussions with the outside world, they also tried to maintain white solidarity within the neighborhood itself. When residents on Paxon Avenue began to list their homes with black realtists, for instance, the churches' organization sent out chiding letters. A "(Negro) Real Estate Company" was soliciting sales in the neighborhood, the religious leaders noted disapprovingly. "We trust the postal cards were returned marked 'NOT INTERESTED.' " Likewise, ministers and lay leaders tried to calm the local whites about their community. "If everyone simply refuses to sell to colored," the pastors assured residents, then everything would be fine. "Please help us 'Keep Kirkwood White' and preserve our Churches and homes."[26]

In spite of the KCC's defensive campaign, the pressures behind black expansion were simply too much. The transition that had overtaken Moreland Heights soon spread through all of Kirkwood. By late 1964 observers commented that the area was already "becoming an all-Negro community." The repurchasing program had delayed the transition but only for a short while. Even with the active participation of local institutions, yet another "white community" rapidly disintegrated. There were multiple reasons for this, of course, but a significant one was recognized by the WSMDC staff long before Kirkwood witnessed its own struggles of race and residence. Community institutions depended on the constant support of individual members for their sustenance. As much as they might try to lead a neighborhood's "defense," the relationship between the institution and the individual was one in which the former was always more dependent on the latter. Once individual whites decided to abandon the "community" or, worse, turned against each other and proved that "community" had been an illusion all along, there was nothing community institutions could do to stop white flight.[27]

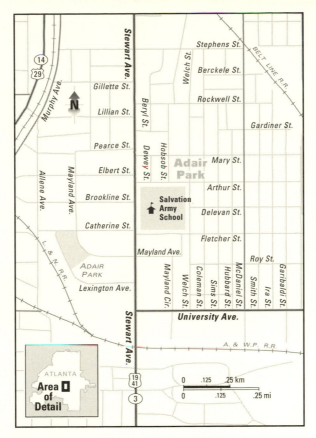

Map 3.3 Adair Park, 1950

Imagining Community: Adair Park

While the residents of Adamsville and Kirkwood made plausible efforts to define and defend their "white communities," Adair Park in south Atlanta lacked any semblance of "community integrity." For one thing, the neighborhood was quite small, only three city blocks wide and six long, with just a handful of short streets. Furthermore, unlike other working-class regions, Adair Park had few illusions of its own upward mobility. With the exception of the Salvation Army School, the streets were only filled with thin land lots and very modest homes. One resident ran a trucking business from home, parking trucks everywhere—on the front lawn, behind the house, and down the street. Another neighbor followed suit, selling used cars. The neighborhood's crude appearance was echoed in the attitude of its residents. "I couldn't sit on my porch for cusing and fighting across the street from me and the police runing over there two or three times a week," complained one woman. For most residents, Adair Park's disrepair was only aggravated by the "encroachment" of blacks. Indeed, by the mid-1950s, blacks surrounded the small white enclave on every side, except for a tenuous western connection to white neighborhoods on the far side of Stewart Avenue. As a result, black Atlantans were a constant presence. "This is a negro neighborhood," one white woman noted dejectedly; "their funerals go by the front of the house all the time and negros are in all of the cars passing by."[28]

In light of the neighborhood's decline, many whites sought to flee. As in other neighborhoods, the transition began with the sale of a single home, on Beryl Street in the fall of 1955. Three homeowners on neighboring Hope Street assumed that complete racial transition was now inevitable and rushed to list their homes with a black realtist. "Some day they will get it & they ought to have it," reasoned one resident. "So why not let them have it." As neighbors saw the "For Sale" signs, reports began circulating that those streets had been "zoned for colored citizens" by the city. To dispel rumors, the WSMDC polled homeowners. According to that survey, eighty property owners were "not desiring to sell" and three were "desiring to sell to whites only." With the exception of the three Hope Street homes already listed, no one else noted they were "willing to sell to Negroes." With this evidence in hand, the Adair Park Civic Club tried to stop the panic. "Negroes are not trying to force you out of the area," the homeowner's group advised. "Do not let your own neighbors force you out with unfounded rumors."[29]

Some residents vowed they would never sell to blacks. As a firefighter from Hobson Street put it, "No body on this St. is trying to sell to nobody." His neighbors agreed. "My home is conveniently located within reach of churches, transportation, school, good neighbors and near shopping area," wrote an area widow, echoing the concepts of community seen in Adamsville and Kirkwood. Selling one's home to a black buyer, many of these working-class whites claimed, would be a betrayal of that community. "We are very interested in our neighbors, and if [our house] was for sale, *we will never sell to a negro*," wrote a paint store salesman. "We are one hundred per cent for our white people to live & stand by each other." Helping blacks move into the area was not merely unconscionable but unpatriotic. "My house is not for Sale," a saleswoman with a home decorating outfit informed the committee. "I am a *red blooded American* and a *true Southerner*." But those nearest the new black residents were not so sure. The whites on Dewey Street, for instance, feared that the racial transition would engulf their street and ruin their property values. One was a widow, living on her own. The rest were working-class families in which, more often than not, both the husband and wife worked. Despite the feelings of the rest of the neighborhood, these whites on Dewey wanted out. They signed a compact the following summer promising to "stick together" by selling their homes on the black real-estate market together and then fleeing the neighborhood en masse. Oddly enough, it was in deserting their "community" that they most acted like one. Soon afterward all of Dewey, along with the remainder of Hope and Beryl, shifted from white to black occupancy.[30]

The streets to the south stayed white for the next two years under an uneasy truce. But in the fall of 1958 familiar rumors spread through Mayland Circle and Mayland Avenue that "the City has zoned these streets for Negro occupancy." Some claimed there was a map in the mayor's office showing as much. The WSMDC tried to dispel the new round of rumors but to no avail. A number of white homeowners panicked and rushed to list their homes with black realtists. Only a year later, the neighborhood had a considerable black presence. "There are now seven Negro families living on Mayland Circle," reported city planner Jim Parham in 1959, with "one home owned, but unoccupied, by Negroes on Mayland Avenue, and some 8 to 10 homes throughout the area with signs indicating for sale to Negroes." As the panic began again, the WSMDC urged the Adair Park Civic Club to do what Adamsville and Kirkwood had done—raise money to repurchase homes already sold to black buyers. Seizing the idea, the homeowners' group established the Southwest Development Company, Inc., for the purpose of buying back the black-owned homes and stabilizing their neighborhood. All interested property owners could fund the company and thereby help save the "white community" of Adair Park. "The certificates are in $10.00 denominations," the Civic Club announced, "and to keep this a community and democratic operation, no one may apply for more than $100.00 for each piece of property owned." The community could save itself, it said. "The plan developed by the ADAIR PARK CIVIC CLUB, INC., is the only way left for us to maintain our Homes, Churches, Schools and Playgrounds," an announcement read. "If you wish to maintain the integrety of your home it now means you and all your neighbors must work together harmoniously to prevent the destruction of our section as a community of white people."[31]

The flaw in this plan of community action was that there was, in truth, little "community" there. Before the racial transitions, Adair Park had been a small area without any strong local institutions akin to the churches of Kirkwood. But by this point, the white area was less than half its former size and shrinking fast. In a bold move, Adair Park tried to enlarge its "community" by simply declaring that it was part of other white neighborhoods to the west and south. It hoped to persuade these whites that the defense of the Mayland Circle area was their fight too. "Don't be mislead by the idea you can stand meekly by and do nothing until a negro buys a house in your block," the Adair Park Civic Club warned. On flyers and letters, it included a map outlining their newly defined "community." "The natural boundaries as shown on the map which have evolved through the years without friction," it argued, "can be taken by all right thinking and fair minded people of both races as a guide so that peace and harmony might be maintained in this section." But as the accompanying map made clear, the boundaries of this imagined community were anything but "natural." First and foremost, the areas to which Adair Park laid claim were nearly fifty times the size of the tiny neighborhood. Second, this sprawling region stood separated from Adair Park by the major thoroughfare of Stewart Avenue on the west and the tracks of the Belt Line Railroad on the south. On the other side of those dividing lines, the contested streets of Adair Park seemed a small and insignificant outcropping that could easily be abandoned. "Adair Park had hoped to get financial support from white communities such as Capitol View and Sylvan Hills, located south beyond the railroad tracks," Parham later recalled. "This support never materialized." Adair Park was on its own.[32]

As bad as this inability to forge a larger community was, the lack of "community integrity" in the original Adair Park area was much worse. White residents there could not agree on a common approach. As in other transition neighborhoods, those living near the new black homes, on Mayland Avenue and Mayland Circle, wanted out. Sara Snead, for instance, had been trying to sell her home on the white real-estate market for three years. "I put my house in the hands of three different agents," she explained, "and they would say, well you know you can't get very much for these houses as they are so close to the negroes." Finally, she gave up and listed the house with a black realtist. Neighboring whites were outraged. They cursed the elderly widow and made angry phone calls at night. "Neighbors have threatened to 'burn the house down,' " a report noted, "and warn her not to leave the house 'or it might nor be there when you get back.' " But Snead was not the only one who had given up hope. Farther down Mayland Avenue lived R. E. Nichols, an employee of the Ruralist Press. When racial transition first "threatened" the neighborhood, he and his wife stood fast. "Our house is not for sale," they insisted in 1955, "and we wish our street and our community to remain for white people only." But four years of uncertainty had changed their minds. They had since moved out of the neighborhood, renting their home to a white tenant and waiting to see what happened. Now they felt it was beyond hope. "There are already too many Negro families living around on Mayland Circle," Nichols wrote in 1959. "I think it will be almost impossible to collect enough money in the area involved to buy back these homes from the Negroes." Although these residents had given up, others still wanted to fight. Homeowners on Hobson Street, for instance, voted to support the repurchasing program of the Adair Park Civic Club, while those along Fletcher Street were even more adamant about holding their ground. "All we want is to get the colord out of Mayland Circle give us our street back white, to the old people of that section," wrote one elderly woman. "Cant there be something done for us white people *Please* Help us to keep our street white." To undermine sales, they tacked up "Disputed Area" signs along Fletcher and elsewhere. In addition, they called banks and mortgage brokers, asking them "not to loan money to colored people who are buying around here." A familiar pattern of white flight surfaced: as some residents tried to flee, their neighbors refused to let them.[33]

With the neighborhood externally abandoned and internally divided, the Adair Park Civic Club became paralyzed. Lacking funds to buy back all the homes, it tried to forge a compromise with black real-estate agents. Properties on Mayland Avenue would be repurchased by the white homeowners' organization, and, in exchange, blacks would be granted a "free hand" along the rest of Mayland Circle. But, as Jim Parham observed, the negotiations were "undermined" by die-hard resisters "who criticize every move to compromise short of 'saving' the entire area." With this minority refusing to make even the slightest concession, the bargain fell through. "Although the leadership tried, it could never shake this millstone," Parham noted a year later, "and the result was its complete inability to negotiate with Negro leadership." A new wave of whites, including some on Hobson and Fletcher streets, put homes up for sale the next spring. The white homeowners even lobbied white banks and mortgage brokers, in an effort to ease the way for prospective black buyers. "Inasmuch as our *only* prospective clients are Negroes," they wrote, "we ask that you grant loans to them so that we may negotiate the sales of our properties." At that, the resistance crumbled.[34]

Without assistance from either the city or other white neighborhoods, Adair Park proved unable to maintain any semblance of "community integrity," even in an artificial way, as Adamsville had. And without any strong internal institutions upon which whites could rely, Adair Park was likewise unable to prolong the campaign of residential resistance. Forced to fend for itself, yet another "white community" disintegrated.

COMMUNITIES AT ODDS: COLLIER HEIGHTS, CENTER HILL, AND GROVE PARK

Unlike the older neighborhoods of Adamsville, Kirkwood, and Adair Park, Collier Heights had a short history. Well into the 1940s, its lands along the northwestern edge of the old city limits remained undeveloped and unclaimed. Soon after World War II, however, a wave of white Atlan-

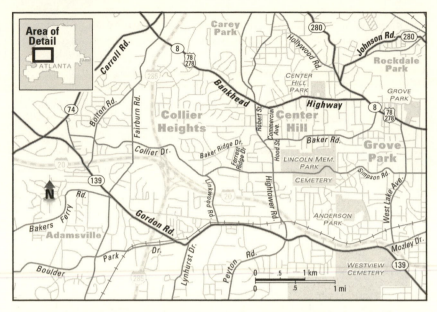

Map 3.4 Collier Heights, Grove Park, and Center Hill, 1950

tans, unable to find housing inside the city, began building a new community there from scratch. Modest homes, priced in the $6,000 to $10,000 range, soon dotted the newly laid out streets. "The thing about Collier Heights that no one in the neighborhood realized at the time," an observer later noted, "was that it lay astride the corridor out which the city's expanding Negro population was moving. Separated from the Negro section by main traffic arteries, no one had given the racial problem a thought."[35]

But the "problem" was, indeed, headed the neighborhood's way. In the fall of 1953 the National Development Company, a black-owned corporation, purchased a thousand acres of undeveloped land west of Collier Heights. In a panic, some whites spread rumors that the whole area would "go colored" soon, rumors they attributed to the Collier Heights Civic Club. When the group's members found out, they became furious and fought back. Indeed, the campaign to dispel the rumors revealed a good deal about the homeowners' organization. Its opponents' means were underhanded, it charged, but their ends were even worse. Selling to blacks meant selling out whites. "It is recommended before you sign," the Civic Club warned, "that each of you take the time to thoroughly think through and consider just what you as an individual stand to lose both *financially* and *morally* by the action of several people in the community selling to colored and leaving you or your neighbor in a predicament created by this selfish few." The powerful Southwest Citizens Association also attacked the "selfish minority" who undermined the community. "We believe that a few persons have deliberately agitated the situation by spreading false rumors," wrote its president, Sid Avery. "We ask you, as a fair-minded individual, to refuse to make a fast dollar at the expense of the majority of the 150 or more home owners in this always white community." Noting that black realtists were not soliciting sales themselves, Avery appealed to the residents' racial pride. "If our Negro real estate people can play fair, certainly our white real estate men can do as much," he chided. "Please refuse to have anything to do with sales of white owned homes in Collier Heights to colored."[36]

In a more concrete way, the homeowners' groups launched an ambitious plan to "save" the neighborhood. Through negotiations with the National Development Company, they secured a new "gentlemen's agreement" that would use a creek as a temporary boundary line between whites to the east and blacks to the west. To cement the line, a highway access road would be constructed along similar lines. In exchange, whites would support the developer in securing sewers, water lines, street curbs, and road paving for the new black community. "The company intends to build *only* in the area to the West of the creek at present and West only of the access road when it is definitely established," the Collier Heights Civic Club informed residents. "All other lots that the company owns outright to the East are for sale to *white people only*." Southwest Citizens echoed these statements, promising that the new black development "will not infringe on Collier Heights."[37]

Although the plan had the endorsements of the mayor, the WSMDC, the Metropolitan Planning Commission, the National Development Company, and the Empire Real Estate Board, it lacked support of one key group—the white residents themselves. Some had sensed this during the negotiations. "I think we can keep the negroes in line," attorney Stephens Mitchell wrote the WSMDC, "but someone else will have to keep the white people in line." Indeed, the ranks of the "selfish minority" who wanted to sell steadily grew. A February 1954 survey showed that 40 percent of white residents planned to sell their homes "as soon as possible." "We sure do want to keep our property for white," a Hightower Road woman lamented, "but there are negros all around us now. Our home is going up for sale." "Since so much has been said about this section going colored," wrote a railroad electrician from Forest Ridge Drive, "then it might as well, because white people will be afraid in it." The Collier Heights Civic Club did not speak for them, they said. "We have had a self appointed committee working to further their own interests," complained a pipe fitter from Baker Ridge Drive. "I will make my own decision when it is necessary to do so." But most had already decided. Virtually all of Baker Road, for instance, noted that they would "sell to colored regardless" of what happened. On another street, a Proctor and Gamble salesman summed up his "personal plans" by snapping he would "Get [the] Hell out!"[38]

Despite this groundswell of dissent, the various organizations pushed ahead with the buffer plans anyway. "We have felt that there existed a sizable group of you who wanted Collier Heights to retain its present white status and have worked to preserve the integrity of your community," the WSMDC wrote in March. In the survey of resident attitudes, 60 percent preferred that Collier Heights "remain white." Likewise, when asked about their personal plans, another slim majority stood against selling; 30 percent swore they would stay put no matter what, while another 25 percent voted to "wait and see what happens." Furthermore, the WSMDC reported that 78 percent agreed to abide by the majority will, whatever it was. Because "a considerable number" in Collier Heights "wish to stay and prefer the community to remain white," the WSMDC assumed the neighborhood would stay that way. It was wrong. The committee failed to appreciate that, for any program of "community defense" to succeed, absolutely everyone—without exception—had to act together. A lone dissent, a single sale to a black buyer, and the rest of the street and, indeed, the whole neighborhood, would follow suit.[39]

Without unanimous support for staying, the alternative of selling gained strength as 1954 wore on. While white homeowners wished to sell their homes to buyers of the same race, they realized that no white buyer would pay full price for homes in a "transition neighborhood" like theirs. Ultimately, financial concerns trumped racial ones. "I will not take a loss on my home," noted a typical resident of Collier Drive. Therefore, much of the neighborhood turned to the black real-estate market, where the homes would sell at much higher prices. In hopes of maximizing profit and minimizing panic, the residents of Collier Heights decided to put all of their properties up for sale at the same time. For three months, they circulated the idea, trying to bring the entire neighborhood on board. "Group captains" were assigned eight houses each, keeping personal contacts with homeowners to assure that everyone stuck to the plan and no one jumped the gun. Finally, when 87 percent of the neighborhood supported the idea of selling, the group decided to list their homes with black brokers. (Absolute unanimity was *not* needed in this instance for the same reason it had been needed for the plan of defense. If a single sale could start a domino effect of white flight, everyone understood, then a vast majority of sales would quickly overwhelm any holdouts.) Indeed, the transition was swift. Within three months, all 135 homes in Collier Heights changed ownership from white to black.[40]

The Collier Heights transition, however, did not take place in a vacuum. Whites in nearby neighborhoods, Center Hill and Grove Park, were stunned to discover that blacks now occupied the entire region to their west. For them, Collier Heights had not been a separate area but an extension of their own community. When racial transition first "threatened" Collier Heights in 1952, for instance, Grove Park and Center Hill took it personally. "The leaders I talked with," noted Philip Hammer of the Metropolitan Planning Commission, "are still strongly of the opinion that the Collier Heights area is definitely tied in with the Grove Park–Center Hill area and should be regarded as an integral part of that community." Other city planners agreed. When the WSMDC set up an advisory panel to try to "save" Collier Heights, for instance, it made sure to include a representative from Grove Park and Center Hill each. And when city planners proposed the access road "buffer plan" to seal off Collier Heights, they also had the neighboring areas in mind. "As you probably know," Mayor Hartsfield wrote his construction chief, "the bi-racial committee is trying to assure residents of Center Hill and Grove Park that the proposed access road will be a boundary which will protect them as Negro citizens move farther out." Both sections felt endangered by the flight of Collier Heights whites; both wanted to stay and fight any similar transition in their neighborhoods. Indeed, the two communities acted in such agreement that observers spoke of a single "Grove Park–Center Hill neighborhood" or even simply the "Grove Park area," which was understood to encompass Center Hill.[41]

Their joint "defense" began soon after the "loss" of Collier Heights. In September 1954 the Grove Park Civic Association pled with the Empire Real Estate Board for a new "gentlemen's agreement." The realtists were reluctant to help support segregation, but they agreed to meet the homeowners' group halfway, setting Hightower Road as the latest boundary line. Blacks would occupy everything west of the road; whites would keep everything east in Center Hill. Whites were thrilled. The Atlanta Baptist Ministers Union, for instance, issued a special commendation praising the Empire Real Estate Board "for refusing to help dispose of the old homes in the old neighborhood of Commercial Avenue to members of the nonwhite population." What these whites failed to understand, however, was that such boundary lines were rarely permanent. "Black involvement in any discussions of this type represented an attempt to avoid the violence that they faced from whites while securing land," historian Ronald Bayor has noted. "Although white leaders saw these boundary lines as final statements on the black land and housing issue, blacks viewed them as temporary and expedient; they expected to eventually cross the boundaries and barriers."[42]

Indeed, the Hightower Road boundary was soon crossed. As in countless other cases, a few whites living along the borderline decided to sell their homes the only place they could—the black real-estate market. "Because of [the] agreement that Hightower Rd would be used as a dividing line between white and black development," a realtist with Alexander-Calloway recalled, "we refused to take listings." But after a black buyer breached the boundary line, apparently without an EREB member's help, white residents on Commercial Avenue, just behind the property, "called incessantly to list their homes." The realty company waited until a strong majority along Commercial—fifteen out of seventeen—wanted to sell before taking the listings, and even then it demanded white homeowners issue "signed statements to the effect that the real estate firm had not solicited the listings, but were accepting them at the insistence of a majority of the residents."[43]

As so many times before, the white community proved to be less than unanimous in its decision to sell. When realtists arrived one Sunday afternoon in November 1955 to show the listed homes to black prospects, they were quickly surrounded by three hundred angry whites at the corner of Commercial and Old Know. Mostly women and teenage children, the crowd carried signs—"Don't Sell to Colored," "Protect Our Neighborhood," "Niggers Must Not Come In." The mob scene only sped the panic, as those on the next block of Commercial Avenue quickly put their homes up for sale. "The problem seems to be getting out of hand," a resident warned. "Seven or eight signs are now posted on Robert's Street, and an additional seven or eight signs are displayed on Baker [Road] below Hood St." Things soon turned ugly. In late February 1956 another mass protest took place, outside an open house off Baker, and this time the crowd numbered nearly seven hundred men, women, and children. A few days later, after a black buyer had actually moved into 2540 Baker Road, his house was bombed. Four days after that, two sticks of dynamite blew up the cellar of another black-owned house at 2431 Baker Road. After the police started round-the-clock patrols, whites turned their rage against them. When a police captain came to inspect the bombings, he returned to find his windshield shattered by a rock. Two patrolmen left their car for a moment and came back to a flattened tire.[44]

As in other borderline neighborhoods, the residents of Grove Park and Center Hill formed a corporation to repurchase those homes sold to blacks. By 1960 it owned nearly thirty homes, making it, in the words of housing expert Jim Parham, "the most successful such organization in the city." Though whites were thrilled with their stabilization efforts, blacks were not. As Robert Thompson noted, "In most, if not all, cases, the repurchase price was less than the price paid by the temporary N[egro] owners." Blacks who refused to go along with the program were given new incentives. A widow and her daughter, for example, had balked at selling her home back to whites. Shortly thereafter, a bomb was thrown at the house. By chance, it bounced off the wall of the front bedroom and rebounded into the street, where it blew a hole in the pavement, shattered windows, and drove nails through a wall. Soon thereafter, the widow decided to sell.[45]

Although the repurchasing program had succeeded, the truce was still a fragile one. In late 1959 whites discovered a new "threat" on Holly Street to the southeast. Blacks had bought two homes there; more problematic, however, a 112-unit apartment complex for blacks was underway, too. Representatives of Grove Park and Center Hill begged the developer to restrict the project to whites only. "Your decision is so crucial to the welfare of our community, that we refrain from contemplating the disastrous effects of an adverse report," the Grove Park Civic League wrote the builder. "The rental of these apartments to colored would cause an immediate break-through and loss of our community with hardship, financial and personal loss of immeasurable proportions." The residents even enlisted the mayor's help but to no avail. The developer sympathized with their plight but refused to budge. "We certainly have no desire to upset the neighborhood," he wrote Hartsfield, "and we would be glad to rent the apartments to white tenants if it could be done successfully. However, due to the proximity of negro dwellings and negro owned property, it is very doubtful." It was a lost cause, he said, because "the Grove Park Civic League has already let the area go colored." Despite years of cooperation between the two white neighborhoods, accompanied by hard work and financial strain, their successful defense meant nothing. Surrounding areas had given up, and that had crippled them.[46]

THE MYTH AND CONSEQUENCES OF "WHITE COMMUNITIES"

As these four studies demonstrate, "community integrity" was a much more complicated concept than city planners first realized. On the surface, the principle appeared to work well. Neighborhoods with a cohesive identity and strong local institutions (such as Adamsville and Kirkwood) were able to hold back residential desegregation, for a few years at least, while a place without such identity and institutions (Adair Park) underwent swift racial transition. By the early 1960s, however, with the advent of the civil rights movement and the continued pressure on the part of blacks seeking homes, all of these "white communities" underwent racial transition, regardless of their "integrity." But even in the 1950s the concept's significant shortcomings were becoming clear. When city planners spoke with pride of "protecting the integrity of communities," they assumed that white neighborhoods could be easily defined and defended by the city. But the threat of racial transition wreaked havoc with any such attempts. The fundamental flaw with the stress on "community" was that city planners sought to impose the boundaries of a community from above, when in reality a community could only be created in the minds of local residents. Whites on the fringes of a defended neighborhood—those living on Del Mar Lane in Adamsville, for instance—often rebelled against their inclusion in a "protected community." The reverse process also happened, when borderline whites attempted to latch onto another community, as in Adair Park's unsuccessful appeal to neighboring whites. In practical terms, a "white community" was impossible to define with precision or permanence.

Even if a "community" were successfully defined, keeping it successfully defended was another matter. A key problem here was the lack of white solidarity. Too often, the threat of "Negro invaders" created cracks in the wall of white solidarity. In places without "integrity," such as Adair Park, these cracks widened rather quickly. But even in areas with supposedly strong institutions and a solid sense of "community," these splits appeared as well. The white residents of Kirkwood, for instance, presented a united front for segregation at first but soon succumbed to bitter internal squabbling. Divided against itself, a "white community" quickly disintegrated. Furthermore, as the example of the Grove Park, Center Hill, and Collier Heights area shows, fissures in white solidarity could appear on a much larger scale, with larger repercussions. The combination of these internal flaws and the constant external pressure for black residential expansion meant that even the strongest defense was eventually overcome. Ultimately, neighborhoods with a demonstrably high level of "community integrity"—Adamsville, Kirkwood, and Grove Park—underwent the same racial transition that consumed more obviously divided areas like Adair Park. The intense planning of and financial strain on whites there did not stop the process but only delayed the inevitable.

For working-class whites in these neighborhoods, and in many more Atlanta neighborhoods like them, the campaign for "community integrity" had accomplished none of its goals. Indeed, if the movement had any lasting legacy, it was the fact that whites in these neighborhoods only came to believe in the importance and, indeed, the existence of their supposed "communities" precisely as those same "communities" crumbled around them. In every one of these white working-class neighborhoods, these Atlantans learned that their fellow whites couldn't be trusted to stand by them, whether it be the whites on the next street or the whites in the next neighborhood. Believing that "community" was meaningless when it mattered most, they moved toward a new ideology that was its antithesis—individuality. As the course of desegregation spread from their neighborhoods to their neighborhood institutions, the trend toward isolation and individualization would only increase.

CHAPTER FOUR

The Abandonment of Public Space:
Desegregation, Privatization, and the Tax Revolt

IN JANUARY 1959 Police Chief Herbert Jenkins found a poem tacked to a bulletin board at his departmental headquarters. Tellingly, the anonymous author had titled it "The Plan of Improvement," in sarcastic tribute to Mayor Hartsfield's 1952 program for the city's expansion and economic progress. The poem looked back over a decade of racial change and spoke volumes about the rising tide of white resentment. It began with a brief review of the origins of residential transition and quickly linked the desegregation of working-class neighborhoods to the desegregation of the public spaces surrounding them:

> Look my children and you shall see,
> The Plan of Improvement by William B.
> On a great civic venture we're about to embark
> And we'll start this one off at old Mozeley Park.
>
> White folks won't mind losing homes they hold dear;
> (If it doesn't take place on an election year)
> Before they have time to get over the shock,
> We'll have that whole section—every square block.
>
> I'll try something different for plan number two
> This time the city's golf courses will do.
> They'll mix in the Club House and then on the green
> I might get a write up in Life Magazine.
>
> And now comes the schools for plan number three
> To mix them in classrooms just fills me with glee;
> For I have a Grandson who someday I pray
> Will thank me for sending this culture his way.
>
> And for my finale, to do it up right,
> The buses, theatres and night spots so bright;
> Pools and restaurants will be mixed up at last
> And my Plan of Improvement will be going full blast.

The sarcasm in the poem is unmistakable, of course, but so are the ways in which the author—either a policeman himself or a friend of one—clearly linked the city's pursuit of "progress" with a litany of white losses.

In the mind of the author, and countless other white Atlantans like him, the politics of progress was a zero-sum game in which every advance for civil rights meant an equal loss for whites.[1]

As the poem suggested, this phenomenon was perhaps clearest in the case of the desegregation of public spaces, which became the focal point of local civil rights activists in the mid-1950s. Emboldened by successes in individual neighborhoods and the growing momentum of the civil rights movement, they pressed for the desegregation of public spaces across the city, especially the bus lines and the municipal golf courses, parks and pools. In each case, a familiar pattern unfolded. First, black leaders would stage a cautious challenge to the racial status quo. City officials would then wait until they were confronted by court orders to desegregate. Then, claiming an inability to do otherwise, they would carefully orchestrate the actual desegregation. Little by little, Atlanta's public spaces were thus desegregated—peacefully, publicly, progressively. And with every successful desegregation, Atlanta's reputation as the "city too busy to hate" grew as well.

Many observers, of the time and since, have accepted the city's claims that it largely obeyed the law and, in doing so, helped close the racial divide. In truth, of course, the story is more complicated. First and foremost, the actual distance between the races remained, even as the legal barriers between them were struck down. Although the two terms are commonly conflated, "desegregation" did not, in practice, mean the same thing as "integration." To be sure, many whites acquiesced to court-ordered desegregation, but that did not mean they were themselves willing to share public spaces with blacks. A majority of white Atlantans recoiled at the thought of social contact between the races, which they more commonly disdained as "interracial intimacy."[2] Accordingly, as public spaces desegregated, whites abandoned them, effectively resegregating those places in the process. In the end, court-ordered desegregation of public spaces brought about not actual racial integration, but instead a new division in which the public world was increasingly abandoned to blacks and a new private one was created for whites.

The second complication of Atlanta's seeming success story is related to the first. Court-ordered desegregation, instead of closing the old divide between blacks and whites, actually aggravated a new one between classes of whites. In the eyes of working-class whites, the desegregation of public spaces was nothing short of a disaster. The thought of sharing public spaces with blacks was anathema to them, as it was to most whites of this time and place. But unlike the upper class, Atlanta's working-class whites long held a close connection to neighborhood parks and pools, municipal golf courses, and modes of public transportation. They used those facilities regularly and had, under the auspices of legalized segregation, come to think of these municipal services as "their" buses, "their" golf courses, "their" parks, and "their" pools. Upper-class whites had no similar attachment because, unlike the poor, they had plenty of private alternatives. They belonged to private country clubs, had access to private pools, and drove private cars. Accordingly, they knew the desegregation of public spaces would not affect them in any meaningful way. To the shock of working-class whites, who had long assumed that all white southerners stood united in support of segregation, these upper-class whites not only went along with court-ordered desegregation but then had the gall to brag about it.

In reaction, working-class whites were furious. Throughout the late 1950s they held bitter protests to prevent the "loss" of their buses, golf courses, parks, and pools. In the end, however, the combined power of the courts, the city's upper-class whites and the civil rights community overwhelmed their "defensive" efforts. Within a few years, all of the city's public spaces were thoroughly desegregated. Ultimately, the failed fight over these spaces showed working-class whites that there was a growing chasm between their own commitment to segregation and the commitment of wealthier whites. In the immediate sense, the class divide sparked by desegregation was felt in local politics, as working-class whites rebelled against the drive for civic improvements which they assumed would solely benefit blacks. In a broader sense, however, their anger over the desegregation of public spaces dovetailed with their anger over the desegregation of their neighborhoods to prompt their flight from the city. Their withdrawal was physical, of course, as working-class whites abandoned the city for the still-segregated suburbs. But their retreat also took place in a larger sense, as working-class whites withdrew their support—financial, social, and political—from a society that they felt had abandoned them. Just as the desegregation of their neighborhoods had led them to reject the concept of "community," the desegregation of the public spaces around those neighborhoods led them to rise up against Atlanta's plans for progress, too.

The Desegregation of City Buses

As a rule, public space in the South was strictly segregated, parceled out in distinctly separate and decidedly unequal ways. This pattern was perhaps clearest in the physical nature of public space, in that municipal authorities generally granted each race distinct spaces to call its own. Public transportation proved to be the exception to this rule, because transit companies found it impractical to provide completely separate vehicles for each race and decided to separate the races within a single vehicle instead.

Thus, trolleys, streetcars, and buses stood as the public space in which whites and blacks came into the earliest and closest contact.[3]

Although blacks were allowed on streetcars, their interior movement was strictly controlled. If the two races came into "intimate contact" there, whites believed violence would be inevitable. An Atlanta judge, for instance, admitted that contact between the races could enrage even a patrician such as himself. "If a big black man got into the streetcar and pressed up against my wife," he confessed, "I would brain him." To prevent such contact, Georgia had passed segregation statutes for streetcars in 1890, the first such laws in the South. Under the legislation, conductors of private transit companies had almost unlimited police powers. They could order paying customers to move anywhere they chose, eject them from the trolley, and, if they deemed it necessary, resort to physical force. The pattern of segregation that conductors enforced, however, was ill-defined. To be sure, signs indicated that the streetcars ran segregated. "White People Will Seat from Front of Car toward the Back," passengers were reminded, "and Colored People from Rear toward Front." But the precise dividing line remained fluid, to be moved forward and back at the driver's discretion.[4]

For many white Atlantans, such arrangements were not enough. No matter how rigidly or ruthlessly the segregation statutes were enforced, the simple act of sharing public space with blacks was too much for them. In 1920, for instance, an angry Atlantan wrote the president of Georgia Power, the company that ran the streetcar lines, to voice his neighbors' objections to the line running through their "very desirable residential section" off Ponce de Leon Avenue. "Especially during the rush hours of 7:00 to 8:30 A.M. and 5:00 to 7:00 P.M., this car is continually crowded with negroes, and it is very displeasing to have to ride in a car filled with this 'aroma,' " he noted. Rather than put up with the presence of black passengers, he and his neighbors wanted the entire line discontinued. Other whites rejected the sharing of streetcar space as well. In 1926, for example, white residents of the Fifth Ward complained about the single-car trolleys used in their neighborhood, charging that "the manner of separation of White and Colored passengers on such cars is improper, and that the continued operation of these cars will ultimately result in personal injuries to passengers, and serious racial friction." Upset at having to share public space with blacks, however strictly segregated, they petitioned city commissioners to ban all such streetcars "on any line serving Fifth Ward."[5]

Although many whites boycotted the streetcars, large numbers continued to ride, taking comfort in the knowledge that the racial code would be strictly enforced by the conductors. Under their watch, any black who challenged the rules of behavior was dealt with swiftly and harshly. In-

deed, the violent behavior of Georgia Power's drivers became so pronounced that company officials worried it would hurt business. "We just
can't have men who are not able to control themselves and handle the
negro passengers," lamented the president. Often, white drivers could
control neither. A black Atlantan, for instance, recalled a wartime incident
between a white driver and a black rider. "At one of the stops a working
man got on the car, which was extremely crowded," he remembered. "He
was in overalls, . . . covered with the dirt of his trade." When the car
started, he failed to move back. The motorman slammed on the brakes
and ordered him to the rear. But the worker quietly replied that he was
too dirty to "move through all those people." Furious, the driver
wrenched loose an iron tool and struck the man on the head. The passenger, however, wrestled the tool away from him. As the rest of the car
looked on in horror, he beat the driver nearly to death and then fled the
scene. Shortly afterward, all Atlanta motormen were deputized and
armed with revolvers.[6]

But arming the drivers only made matters worse, as they became prone
to use deadly force against even verbal infractions of the racial code. For
instance, in March 1946, three young blacks asked a driver on the West
Fair–Magnolia line for a free ride into town. After he refused and they
cursed him, the driver shot one in the stomach. Two weeks later, more
blood was spilled on an Irwin Street car. Madison Harris, a black veteran,
exchanged "remarks" with the driver, T. H. Purl, but left the trolley. As
Harris walked away, Purl pulled out his gun and flung open the doors.
"When the victim saw the motorman's gun," a witness told reporters,
"he put his empty hands in the air. And as he did so, the motorman shot
him." On a downtown line, another exchange of words between a white
driver and a black veteran led to similar bloodshed. Again, the passenger
walked away from the argument, only to be followed out of the car by
the driver, W. D. Lee, who pulled his pistol and dared the man to "repeat
those remarks." As the unarmed man stood there with his hands at his
side, Lee killed him. Still not satisfied, the driver moved closer to fire more
shots at the corpse, stopping only when his pistol jammed. Several white
men from neighboring businesses rushed onto the street with their own
guns drawn. Too late to aid the motorman, they followed his victim's
friends down the street and forced them to bring the dead man's body
back to the scene.[7]

In all of these shootings, the city sided with the drivers. The police
classified Purl's murder of Madison Harris, for instance, as merely "disorderly conduct—shooting another." The courts were even more lenient,
dismissing the case without trial. "To me," Judge A. W. Callaway ruled,
"this is nothing but a case of justifiable homicide." Likewise, when W. D.
Lee appeared in Callaway's court, his incident was also dismissed, despite

Lee's own admission that he stopped shooting only because his gun jammed. The driver, who laughed during several witnesses' descriptions of the shooting, was set free and sent back to work. Officials at Georgia Power also sided with their drivers. A letter of protest from a black veteran, for instance, merely received a polite note that the company looked upon such shootings "with a great deal of disfavor." "We do not intend to excuse the issue," the manager continued, "when we say that a few of our passengers, either through ignorance or a premeditated desire to rob, make it necessary for the operators on some of our lines to protect themselves, and I believe you will agree that in a few instances this has been justified." In all, the motormen felt vindicated. "Now," Purl gloated, "I guess they'll see where we stand."[8]

This was Atlanta of the mid-1940s—before the rise of Bill Hartsfield's biracial coalition and before the city started to worry about the impact that racial conflicts had on its image. The Klan and the Columbians were still roaming the streets of Atlanta and, in some instances, operating the very streetcars where these shootings took place. In their eyes, such shootings were not only necessary but praiseworthy. For instance, Vester Ownby, a member of both the Klan and the Columbians, wrote the *Atlanta Constitution* to praise the streetcar operators for their "defense" of whites' public space. They were good men, he wrote, heroes forced to do battle with "serpents in human form, bipeds, drunk or doped, bearing death-dealing weapons, dangerous to all humankind." White Atlantans, he insisted, owed them their thanks. But black Atlantans, then beginning their campaign for political inclusion, refused to back down. The Atlanta Baptist Ministers Union wrote to Georgia Power, protesting the "outrageous shooting and killing" of black trolley patrons. Representing more than two hundred black ministers, the group expressed its "fear that if this situation is allowed to continue [it] will lead to more serious crises." Others tried to rally the community in protest. "Two Negroes within 3 weeks have been shot by Street Car operators," an announcement warned. "Your boy, brother, or husband may be next."[9]

As the Hartsfield coalition took shape, brutal acts of violence gave way to subtler suppression. At the most basic level, drivers seemed to delight in the power they had to order black riders to move back or stand at the driver's whim. In 1948, for instance, a white passenger complained of how a driver on the Marietta Street trolley had treated a black passenger in "a most humiliating and ungentlemanly manner." Even though he was already sitting behind the color line, the passenger was ordered to move farther back. Likewise, on several lines, drivers moved the color line back during rush hours, but refused to readjust it when whites left. While most of the seats before them remained empty, blacks had to huddle in the aisle. "It breaks my heart to see white people act so rude," one woman wrote. "I am white and not what is known as a 'nigger lover' but I do like common decency." Others agreed. "I have found trolley drivers consistently rude, inconsiderate, and in many cases just plain mean," another complained. "They seem to despise all their customers and take a delight in passing them whenever possible—especially their Negro customers." Other insults faced by blacks were actually part of the transit company's policy. While all passengers paid and entered by the front door, for instance, blacks alone were required to exit at the rear.[10]

While segregation turned individual streetcars into contested terrain, it had an equally important impact on the city at large. Service patterns of the private transit companies often reinforced residential segregation, helping to isolate black communities further. The Southern Regional Council, for instance, reported in 1945 that "no outlying Negro sections are served by trackless trolleys and buses, nor are there any of these sections served by feeder bus lines. These services are made available to many, although not all, outlying white sections of the city." Specifically, Georgia Power had "refused service to the colored people in the new Dixie Hills and Pine Acres section," the report continued. "The company said the Negro population of this area did not warrant its extension of services." As demonstrated in Mozley Park, neighborhoods that underwent racial transition were often denied bus service for years. And once transit companies finally did provide service to these areas, black riders had to pay high prices. "Many steady, hard-working colored couples have long wanted to buy lit-new clean houses instead of living at a rental of over fifty dollars monthly in half of a dilapidated house discarded by white people," one black Atlantan wrote the mayor. But now that their dreams had been realized, many were finding it impossible to pay the high fares needed to get to work. What were they to do? "A high official in another group answered my query with: 'Let the negroes either give up the new houses they have bought or give up their present jobs and get others near [the downtown district of] Five Points.' " As an added problem, the few buses that did make it out to their neighborhood were woefully overcrowded and getting worse. "I am afraid that when many more negroes move into the completed houses," he continued, "there will be racial trouble on the little Gray Line bus, negroes filling the seats."[11]

Black leaders in Atlanta tried to address these problems through the city's traditional approach of private negotiations. At first, their efforts focused on the small indignities. In 1949, for instance, the local NAACP chapter met with officials of Georgia Power to discuss "relieving congestion in busses serving Negro areas and restrictions to exit from rear doors only." Thereafter, the NAACP maintained polite and open communication with Georgia Power and, after the company changed hands in 1950, the Atlanta Transit System. President Robert Sommerville spoke proudly of his "harmonious meeting with local negro leaders." Ultimately, how-ever, communication did little to solve the problems. Transportation seg-regation, company officials repeatedly pointed out, had been legislated by the state assembly and upheld by the courts. As a private business, they were obligated to live by these laws.[12]

Unable to negotiate a change, black leaders decided on another course of action, inspired by Atlanta's own Martin Luther King Jr. A pastor's son from Ebenezer Baptist Church and a graduate of Morehouse College, King had since moved to Montgomery, Alabama, where he famously led protests against that city's segregated bus lines in 1955–56. Six months into the Montgomery boycott, Atlanta ministers made tentative steps of their own. On the first week of June 1956, a group of black activists, led by Rev. John Porter, spread out in the front seats of an Irwin Street bus. At the next stop, several whites boarded, paid their fares, and stopped dead in the aisle, stunned by what they saw. The operator whirled around and shouted at Rev. Porter, "Boy! Get up, move to the back, and let those folks sit down." The minister refused to move. "Boy! I am talking to you!" the driver yelled again. Rev. Porter said he heard him, but stayed in his seat. For several minutes, the two sides remained motionless, as the driver "glared in mounting anger and fury." Ultimately, the protestors backed down and left the bus without further incident. A few weeks later, Rev. Porter tested another of the segregation statutes—the rule that blacks had to leave by the back door. When the bus he was riding reached the corner of Walton and Broad, Rev. Porter got up and walked to the front exit. The driver told him to leave by the back, but the minister proceeded out the front. Outraged, the driver suddenly closed the mechanical doors as Rev. Porter was halfway through them, pinning the preacher. Only through his own efforts was he able to free himself.[13]

These initial challenges gained strength and support when the Supreme Court settled the Montgomery boycott in November 1956 by striking down segregation on its buses and other modes of public transportation. Emboldened by the ruling, Rev. William Holmes Borders and other minis-ters launched the Love, Law, and Liberation Movement to apply the deci-sion in Atlanta and thus end segregated transportation there as well. In keeping with the Atlanta approach to race relations, the ministers met with Mayor Hartsfield to discuss their plans in advance. All they wanted to do, they told him, was secure grounds for challenging the state's segre-gation statutes in court. Always mindful of his city's public image, Harts-field asked if there was any way it could be done without arresting the ministers. "Impossible," they replied. Without arrests, they would lose face in the black community.[14]

Confronted with the inevitability of their challenge and convinced of the likelihood of its success, Mayor Hartsfield carefully orchestrated the desegregation of his city's buses. The first step involved a peaceful test. Together, the Love, Law and Liberation Movement and the Atlanta Transit System carefully arranged the challenge beforehand. "We are going to ride until these buses are desegregated," Rev. Borders announced to a crowd of twelve hundred at his Wheat Street Baptist Church. "If they take the bus to the barn, we'll ride it to the barn and then get another. We'll take every bus in Atlanta to the barn if necessary." Despite these bold words, the challenge was meant to be as conservative as possible. Ministers alone would ride the buses, they announced. Public support was not sought and, indeed, directly discouraged. In addition, while they would be breaking the rules of segregation, the ministers promised not to violate taboos of racial intimacy. "We will not sit by a white person," Rev. Borders cautioned. "Under no circumstances will any of us sit by a white woman."

The next morning, January 9, 1957, twenty ministers boarded a bus, paid their fares, and, as the driver remembered, "took seats in my trolley coach wherever they pleased to sit." The incident did not take him by surprise, however. "I was aware," he attested, "that there had been talk of an attempt by certain colored persons to board a vehicle of my employer and ride such a vehicle on a 'desegregated' basis." The young driver said nothing to the ministers but refused to move the bus. "It's not going anywhere," someone shouted from outside, and all the white passengers filed off the bus, except one. An Atlanta Transit System manager soon arrived, telling the driver to switch the sign to "Special" and drive the bus straight to the barn—just as Rev. Borders had predicted. As the driver carried the singing and praying ministers away, one reporter remembered, a "cavalcade of press and television cars" stretched out behind the bus, saving every moment for public scrutiny. Once at the barn, the ministers exited—by the front door—and left the scene without any ugliness. In fact, the only clash occurred when a white passenger tried to take a camera away from a white reporter who had just taken his photo.[15]

After the challenge, the ministers' arrest was just as carefully scripted. At Hartsfield's direction, Police Chief Herbert Jenkins went through the formality of obtaining warrants for their arrest, even though no one—not the mayor, the police chief, the county solicitor, not even the judge himself—thought the ministers should be punished. "He said that he did not believe the warrants would be worth the paper they were written on," Jenkins said of the judge, "but if I believed it would help defuse a potentially explosive situation, he would issue them." Jenkins hoped the ministers could quietly come to the police station on their own; Hartsfield even offered to send city limousines. But Rev. Borders insisted on the spectacle of being carried away in the paddy wagon. Obligingly, the police chief asked him for a convenient time and place for the arrest and arranged for two of his most level-headed men, Captain J. L. Moseley, white, and

Detective Howard Baugh, black, to lead the detail. The arrest was an even bigger event than the ministers' ride the day before. Huge crowds came out to Wheat Street to watch. "The people knew why we were there, why the police were there," Rev. Borders recalled. "People quit work. They stopped cooking meals. They left beauty shops. They came out of stores. They thronged the streets." So many turned out, however, that the paddy wagon was unable to leave until Rev. Borders climbed out and asked the crowd to part. Moseley and Baugh chatted amiably with the ministers all the way to the station, and a representative from Time-Life rode along with them, chronicling his trip in the South's first integrated paddy wagon. At the station, the ministers were booked, bonded, and released within two hours. Their brief visit included time in a detention cell, but the door was never even closed.[16]

By the end of the day, everyone involved was satisfied. The ministers had secured grounds for a test case against state segregation laws and were satisfied to fight it out in the courts. "We've accomplished our objective," Rev. Borders told his supporters. "The fight will be in the courts and we won't attempt to ride the buses integrated again until it's settled." At the same time, the mayor safeguarded the positive public image of his city. "Atlanta has an excellent record before the nation for its good race relations," Hartsfield crowed. "We in Atlanta have felt that this was a desirable thing, not only for the sake of decency but from the standpoint of business as well." After the ugliness of the Montgomery boycott, the nation marveled at how smoothly, almost effortlessly, Atlanta had desegregated its buses.[17]

Unlike other spots in the South, where whites responded to bus desegregation with violent attacks, Atlanta witnessed little in the way of violence. To be sure, Rev. Borders soon grew accustomed to answering phone calls for "that damn bus preacher" and heard that whites would dynamite his Wheat Street church in retaliation. But nothing happened. Instead of attacking the activists behind bus desegregation, Atlanta's segregationists struck back by boycotting the buses themselves. Many whites had long promised that desegregation would drive white patrons away and bring the end of public transportation altogether. "In our opinion," the *Metropolitan Herald* noted after the initial challenges, "the eventual sufferers will be those who will be left with no means of public transportation to get to and from their jobs, as transit systems are forced to go out of business." Once the court case had been won, segregationists again urged whites to abandon the buses. Georgia's attorney general Eugene Cook, for instance, praised the white passengers for leaving the bus when Rev. Borders and the other ministers first arrived. Likewise, the director of the segregationist States' Rights Council of Georgia encouraged white flight. "White people should refuse absolutely to be integrated on the city

Figure 4.1 Rev. William Holmes Borders. As a leader of the Love, Law, and Liberation group, Rev. Borders orchestrated the desegregation of Atlanta's city buses.
Working closely with city officials, the organization secured a test case in January
1957 for challenging the segregation statutes. His jail cell, which he is here seen
leaving, was never locked during his brief stay at the police station.

busses of Atlanta," he urged. "In no event should white people remain
seated when these NAACP agitators become disorderly and unruly in
sitting by them." These leaders' revulsion resonated deeply with their
fellow whites. "There is nothing more intimate and integrated," one Atlantan wrote disgustedly in 1959, "than a black nigger sitting beside a
white girl on the trolley." A northern man warned Chief Jenkins about
what would happen to Atlanta's desegregated buses as whites fled in fear.
"As of today, Detroit, Chicago, Cleveland public transportation systems
are mere shells of their former place in public utility," he noted. "They
are almost abandoned to the private car—bumper to bumper, one man
to a vehicle—definitely to avoid Integration." Whites and blacks simply
could not coexist, the writer insisted. "Too many toes were stepped on
with no apologies, for it is noted that negroes do not apologize for a

social error," he sneered. "Too many women were molested; too many men were knifed, too many bus drivers were attacked in trying to maintain order on public vehicles."[18]

Indeed, white patronage on Atlanta's buses *did* plummet after the January 1957 challenge to desegregation. The Atlanta Transit System compared its usage from the previous year and found significant and steady declines across the board. By that May, passenger fares had dropped off 7 percent; by November, they were down 13 percent. "It was felt," the board recorded, "that this decline was definitely influenced by publicity on desegregation and by the recent court suit filed by the NAACP in respect to segregation on Atlanta buses." The drop-off in white usage, however, was not due to the *actual* desegregation of the buses but their *threatened* desegregation. The ministers' lawsuit took two years to work its way through the court; meanwhile, they urged blacks to abide by segregated seating patterns. Apparently, they did. An Atlanta University sociology student rode the buses in April and May 1957, for instance, and found that the old patterns of segregation persisted. "Of the total number of white passengers riding the buses, the largest number preferred to sit from 'front to center,' " he noted on a rush hour bus. "Whites did not change their seats for Negroes. Most of the white passengers boarded by the front entrance and departed by the front exit." That might have been expected, but the observer found that blacks also abided by the old codes. "Negro passengers elected in the majority of the cases viewed to sit from 'center to rear,' " he observed on a residential line. "Most of the Negroes boarded by the front entrance and departed by the center exit." In the three weeks he rode the buses, he witnessed only a single conflict between blacks and whites, a verbal one at that.[19]

Even after the Supreme Court ruled in favor of the ministers and forced the official desegregation of Atlanta's buses in January 1959, blacks rarely challenged the old concepts of race and place. "You are free to ride anywhere you choose," Rev. Borders told a rally of twenty-five hundred after the decision. But he cautioned restraint. "We don't want one single incident, and that is what we are working for," he announced. Blacks should be neat, be orderly, and never sit next to white women. In all, Borders and his fellow ministers did little to encourage the exercise of that newly found freedom. "There will be no concentrated mass effort to ride desegregated," noted Rev. B. J. Johnson. Therefore, months after the decision, city buses remained effectively segregated. "So far, here in Atlanta, I have not seen a single negro on the street cars sitting by a white person," a white man wrote in March 1959. "I don't think they, in the mass, are anxious to mix with us anywhere." White riders, however, were even less anxious to "mix" with blacks. Census reports from 1960 demonstrate that, as some had predicted, whites had indeed fled the system and taken to private cars in large numbers. In several neighborhoods, working-class whites now used private cars to get to their jobs instead of public transportation, by a 2-to-1 margin. Meanwhile, blacks in neighboring tracts—sections that were likely to share bus routes with these white areas—trended in precisely the opposite direction, choosing public transportation over private cars by a 2-to-1 margin. A private survey of bus usage from 1960 echoed the fact that blacks were becoming a predominant presence on the lines as working-class whites fled. Although African Americans represented only a third of the city's population, the report noted, they made up "59 percent of the bus patronage during the rush period." And over the next decade, as desegregation picked up speed, so too did white flight from the lines.[20]

THE DESEGREGATION OF GOLF COURSES, PARKS, AND POOLS

The anger of working-class whites over the "loss" of bus lines was nothing compared with their outrage over the desegregation of Atlanta's municipal parks. Unlike the buses, which had always been contested terrain, these public spaces had been reserved for whites since the days of Reconstruction. Indeed, it was only after the First World War that the city established any "colored" park space at all. And even then, the small lands conceded for black use were woefully underfunded and underdeveloped. A 1954 report from the Atlanta Urban League noted that, though blacks represented more than a third of the city's population, they could use just 3 of 132 park areas operated by the Atlanta Parks Department. The distribution of recreational facilities, the report pointed out, was just as bad. There were ninety-six tennis courts in the city, for instance, but blacks could only play on eight, none of which was lighted. The city ran eight community centers, but blacks could use just one; likewise, only one of the city's seven gyms admitted blacks.[21]

The most glaring discrepancy in the distribution of these services, however, stood in the municipal golf courses. While blacks had at least some access to other sites, they were barred completely from the city's five golf courses. Nearly a quarter million white golfers visited these courses a year. But if Atlanta's blacks wanted to play a round, they had to haul their equipment beyond the city limits, to the privately owned Lincoln Country Club. Realizing that the unequal distribution of Atlanta's public spaces was most evident in this area, those seeking the desegregation of city services thus targeted the golf courses first. On July 19, 1951, a foursome arrived at the Bobby Jones Municipal Golf Course: Dr. Hamilton Holmes, an elderly physician; his sons Alfred, a former Southern Amateur champion, and Oliver Wendell, a seminary student; and Charles T. Bell, a friend

and real-estate agent. They were a respectable, middle-class group. However, as the golf pro pointed out, they were also black. Because of that
detail, he refused to let them play, citing a city ordinance barring blacks
from "public areas designated for whites." Although the golf pro had the
law on his side, Atlanta's leaders understood the foursome's challenge
presented a serious problem. Nervous officials in the Parks Department
announced that plans were "in the blueprint stage for a Negro golf
course." Years passed, however, with no steps made toward creating a
course for blacks. Meanwhile, two new ones were built for whites.[22]

Accordingly, Hamilton Holmes filed a federal suit in June 1953, seeking
$15,000 in damages and demanding that all of Atlanta's courses be
opened to blacks. A year later, Judge Boyd Sloan of the U.S. District Court
ruled that there was "no legal obligation" for the city to set up public
courses. But if it did, it had to allow everyone access. Although Judge
Sloan found in favor of the black plaintiffs, he left room for continued
separation of the races. "Segregation," the *Atlanta Journal* assured its
readers, "can be maintained." Black leaders, however, were not satisfied.
Several of the NAACP's leading legal minds, including Thurgood Marshall
and Robert Carter, were brought on board to handle the appeal. Emboldened by *Brown*, they pressed the case to the Supreme Court, in hopes that
the justices would strike down any semblance of segregation. On November 8, 1955, the Court did just that. In a ruling of just fifty-eight words,
the justices decided unanimously that lower courts had been wrong to
apply the "separate but equal" doctrine to public facilities. Blacks had to
be admitted to Atlanta's golf courses on a completely equal basis.[23]

Segregationists were outraged. Blacks did not want equality, they
charged; they wanted social intimacy. "They do not want to play on golf
courses where only Negroes are playing," spat an angry Herman Talmadge. "They want to play with White men and women and they are
determined to force themselves on the White players." Blacks should have
respected whites' wishes for separate facilities. "Instead," the former governor and future senator complained, "they yell for the Supreme Court
like spoiled brats." Governor Marvin Griffin, Talmadge's successor, likewise charged that the lawsuit had been brought by "a handful of disgruntled Negroes, manipulated by the NAACP." He predicted the ruling would
be "a definite disservice to their own people."[24]

In what would emerge as a recurring theme of segregationist resistance,
these political leaders offered a drastic solution. Unwilling to let municipal
spaces be integrated, they instead urged the city to abandon its public lands
altogether. Talmadge, for instance, suggested the city sell its parks and
playgrounds to private interests who could keep them white. The Supreme
Court's ruling, he predicted dourly, would "probably mean the end of
most public golf courses, playgrounds, and things of that type." Governor

Griffin agreed. "I can make the clear declaration that the state will get out of the park business before allowing a breakdown in segregation in the intimacy of the playground," he announced. If he had been in charge of the courses when the ruling came down, the governor said, he would have "plowed them up next morning and planted alfalfa and corn."[25]

But Mayor Hartsfield was in charge, not Governor Griffin, and he took a quite different approach. "Atlanta has a good reputation before the nation, and we hope to preserve it," the mayor announced. "I have no doubt that Atlanta, as usual, will do the right thing." Publicly, he refused to say what "the right thing" would be. Privately, however, he carefully prepared for peaceful compliance with the court's orders. Hartsfield first convinced Judge Sloan to delay the delivery of the desegregation order until the Christmas holidays, to give the city time to comply. In the meantime, Hartsfield again worked to engineer peaceful desegregation. First, he met with leading members of the black community to secure their cooperation. "The Negro leadership was agreeable to any plan that would desegregate the golf courses without incident," Police Chief Jenkins recalled, "and agreed to make no move to integrate the courses until the city had an opportunity to work things out." Next, the mayor met with the nearly one hundred employees of the golf courses. There were just two choices, he told them—comply or close. Reminded that closing the courses would mean losing their jobs, the employees voted unanimously for compliance. As a final touch, Hartsfield shut down the locker rooms and shower facilities, hoping that might lessen whites' fears of "interracial intimacy." To the press, he claimed with a straight face that the lawsuit had nothing to do with it: "We decided that since most people travel to and from the courses today, the showers just weren't needed any more." By the time Judge Sloan finally handed down the decree to desegregate on December 23, 1955, Hartsfield had thus carefully laid the groundwork for calm compliance.[26]

Now faced with the order, Hartsfield said Atlanta would "accept [it] without question." Still, he tried to downplay the importance of the ruling. "Golf, by its very nature, is a segregated game," he rationalized. Even if a black foursome appeared on a course, white players would have little personal contact with them, if any. Hartsfield listed similar southern cities that had already desegregated courses without trouble and reminded whites that other public facilities, such as playgrounds and swimming pools, would still be segregated. Following Hartsfield's recommendations, the same group that had first sought to play golf on the Bobby Jones course four years earlier announced they would finally play the next day. "It was Christmas Eve," the mayor later explained, "and we counted on everybody being full of the Christmas spirit, not to mention tired from all that shopping and going to parties." Not everyone was in the holiday mood, however. During the night, a number of angry whites snuck onto several courses and scrawled obscenities in yellow paint across the pavilions and benches. But Hartsfield was prepared. He had work crews out before dawn, painting over every word. When reporters arrived at the Bobby Jones course, there was no trace of the vandals' work. However, there was also no trace of the Holmes family. Fearing an outbreak of violence, the mayor convinced them to play on another course. "They had promised the television people they would appear," Hartsfield recalled. "I said, 'Those TV boys aren't interested in watching you hit the ball. They want to get pictures of you getting beat up!' " In the end, his careful preparations paid off. When the foursome arrived at the North Fulton course to play, there was no ugliness.[27]

Although the desegregation seemed to go smoothly, whites in neighborhoods near the courses were outraged. The conflicts over race and residence, which had already consumed Ashby Street and Mozley Park and were even then raging in Adamsville, Collier Heights, Center Hill, and Grove Park, had not affected these neighborhoods to the north. Thus, the desegregation of "their" golf courses stood as their introduction to the battles over race and place. Originally, they thought it would never happen. When the desegregation order came down from the Supreme Court, the local *Northside News* sarcastically addressed the likelihood of black golfers coming to "their" courses. "Oh, we'll be able to tell when the invader's really coming, in person," the editors scoffed. "He'll have a big crowd, coming north on North Side Drive from down there by the West By-Pass! This'll be a live show. The road's all paved. They'll be yelling 'Fo', white boy! Don't you heah me yellin' fo' at you? The saints is marchin' in.' " Ultimately, these whites believed they could stop the "invasion" of the golf courses just as their fellow whites seemed to be stopping "invasions" of the neighborhoods to the south. Indeed, they drew explicit comparisons between the two forms of resistance. "We held them back last Sunday in Center Hill when they started crowding in there with their open house stunt," the editors noted with pride. "We'll hold 'em off at the golf course, too. Shucks, they won't even cast their eyes toward Malon Court's tennis court over there on the edge of the golf course and run complaining to Jedge Warren that we don't want nobody for tennis, either."[28]

But when desegregation really did arrive, the *Northside News* interpreted it as a personal attack. "There are seven public golf courses in Atlanta," they pointed out. "Only two are in the North Side, the other five being much more convenient to the Holmes boys and their friends who live in southwest Atlanta." Blacks had targeted the Bobby Jones and North Fulton courses not because they were the city's finest, the paper charged, but because the "NAACP wants nothing short of all-out war." The Northside courses had been chosen because they stood in neighborhoods that were still all white. "Under the NAACP strategy," the editors warned, "the Negro invading forces strike first at the Pearl Harbors and not at the nearby Asiatic islands. The first attack must humble the self-satisfied whites who believe that the Negro problem will never strike close to their homes. That, itself, is an incident Northsiders need to note."[29]

Tellingly, the paper charged that the city's moderate coalition would, in time, dismantle segregation in all public spaces. "With a smugness that would be laughable were it not so alarming," they wrote bitterly, "the *Atlanta Journal* declares that the admission of Negroes to white golf courses does not mean that Negroes will be permitted to use the swimming pools with white people. That is like saying the infant who learns to crawl will not learn to walk." No, the golf courses were just the first step. In less than a year, they warned, the mayor would announce that "he and the merchants welcome the integration of whites and blacks in swimming pools, in all restaurants, on all buses—and maybe, in the public schools." The *Northside News* reminded whites that many of them had been recently annexed by the city because Hartsfield wanted to suppress the rising percentage of blacks in the population. " 'The Negroes,' he said, 'are taking over the City of Atlanta as it is today. The whites have got to put those Negroes in their place and see that Atlanta continues under a white mayor,' " they remembered angrily. "The North Side came to his help. Now the North Side finds Mayor Hartsfield surrendering, without even a mild protest, the North Side's playgrounds to the South Side's Negroes he once wanted to keep in their place." They were disgusted: "That is really the lowest one could expect from an elected caucasean in the betrayal of public trust."[30]

Because of white outrage, the golf courses remained contested terrain for years after their official desegregation. In the summer of 1959, for instance, working-class whites in the city's southwest learned that black golfers were planning to hold a "National Negro Golf Tournament" on the eighteen-hole course at Adams Park. They were furious. A "large contingent of aroused residents" marched to the mayor's office, demanding he stop the tournament. "The whites were by no means the rough element that bothers trouble," judged the *Atlanta Journal-Constitution*; "they were people of middle income, living in a nice section." But the mayor dismissed them. "City officials (which in Atlanta means the mayor) refused to take a stand, pleading impotence," one resident remembered with disgust. So whites "defended" the course themselves. "With dogged determination," he noted with pride, "the white people publicized plans to clutter the course from daybreak until dusk, for the duration of the tournament, and the Negroes backed down. The National Negro Golf Tournament was called off."[31]

White resentment over the desegregation of golf courses, though poten-tially explosive, never reached a state of true crisis. Whites could, of course, simply refuse to play desegregated courses. But if they did play, they would rarely encounter any black players. As the mayor liked to point out, golf was by nature a "segregated game" in which there was little or no contact between groups. With no contact, there could be little conflict. In other spaces of public recreation, however, such as park facili-ties and swimming pools, the degree of personal contact would be much more pronounced. And, accordingly, so would the resistance of segrega-tionist whites.

After the golf courses had desegregated, little else changed in the distri-bution of park space for black Atlanta. To be sure, as the 1950s wore on, there were small improvements, especially when black homeowners took over white communities and inherited the neighborhood parks. The trans-fer of Mozley Park, for instance, added thirty-two acres of land, two unlit tennis courts, a swimming pool, and much-needed playground equipment to the park space open to blacks. But such gains were haphazard and, in any case, did little to erase the real disparities in provisions made by the city for its black and white citizens. A study from 1960 showed that mu-nicipal facilities were still offered on a decidedly unequal basis: 20 football fields for whites, none for blacks; 22 baseball diamonds for whites, 3 for blacks; 16 recreation centers for whites, 3 for blacks; 119 tennis courts for whites, 8 for blacks; and 12 swimming pools for whites, 3 for blacks. The major municipal parks were still predominantly white spaces, with 42 reserved for whites, but just 3 for blacks. Accordingly, in 1961, civil rights activists launched a legal campaign to desegregate the city's parks.[32]

As with the golf courses, the city tried to evade the issue. Its attorneys stalled for time, challenging everything from the class-action nature of the lawsuit to the fact that the plaintiffs were representing themselves. Once the case received serious attention from district court judge Boyd Sloan, the jurist who had desegregated the city's golf courses in 1955, the city's attorneys suddenly claimed the issue was moot. The parks were already desegregated, they said. Park officials and police officers denied enforcing the segregation statutes and insisted that it was merely "by custom and practice" that the races in Atlanta tended to "segregate themselves in the use of the public facilities and otherwise." Despite the official claims of innocence, Atlanta's parks and recreational facilities were still very much segregated, if in subtler ways. At the Bitsy Grant Tennis Center, for in-stance, blacks were turned away in May 1961 on the grounds that they had failed to sign up for courts in advance. When another group appeared there in August, they found the courts full of white players, including Georgia Tech's famed football coach Bobby Dodd. They walked down-stairs to register, but in the short time it took to get there, the manager

cleared the courts and announced they were now "closed for repairs."
The district court saw through the city's subterfuges, however, and ordered Atlanta's parks, pools, recreation centers, and tennis courts to desegregate, fully and officially, in 1962 and 1963.[33]

Again, large numbers of working-class whites fiercely opposed the desegregation of public parks. More than anything, they were outraged that
the city's public pools would be desegregated in June 1963. "That summer people talked about the integration of the swimming pools and little
else," Police Chief Herbert Jenkins remembered. "Frankly, the police
hoped for a rainy summer, for there were more eyeballers and agitators
driving around trying to see how many Negroes were using the pools than
there were people swimming." Indeed, on the first desegregated day at
Piedmont Park, between 40 and 60 people swam in the pools, while a
crowd of 250 whites stood outside the fences and watched. Hoping to
cut down on the number of clashes between white and black teenagers,
the city employed high school coaches to manage the pools that summer
and kept uniformed police and plainclothes detectives on hand as well.
Aside from a few fistfights, the early weeks of pool desegregation went by
calmly.[34]

In truth, pool desegregation went smoothly not because whites accepted the decision, but because they had decided, once again, to flee from
these desegregated spaces. For many whites, integrated pools represented
a level of "interracial intimacy" they simply could not stomach. Indeed,
the image of black and white children swimming together was so repug-
nant for them that some segregationist groups sent photographers to Atlanta's pools to get pictures for future propaganda. Such a reaction from
hard-core segregationists was to be expected, but even those who embraced integration in other areas refused to support shared use of pools.
Even biracial religious groups, for instance, drew the line at integrated
swimming. "They had quite a few negroes at Lake Junaluska last year
and they took part in all the activities," one man noted of a retreat held
by the Methodist Church. "However, when four or five of the negroes
decided to go in the pool one afternoon, they immediately drained the
pool." Many whites—segregationists or not—believed that blacks carried
diseases that might be spread in shared waters. "For the protection of all
swimmers," one woman proposed, "would it not be possible for the City
to require health cards for admission?" Likewise, a segregationist outside
the Piedmont Park pool handed out leaflets to everyone entering. "The
negro race is a reservoir of venereal infection," they read. "Will you expose yourself and your children to the deadly threat? Keep your children,
especially, out of the public pools." The rumors of health hazards became
so prevalent that the *Atlanta Journal* had to remind its readers that syphilis and gonorrhea "are not spread by water, food, or air."[35] In all likeli-

hood, however, such warnings only reinforced whites' assumptions that a great number of blacks really did carry such diseases. Not surprisingly, white attendance at the pools plummeted that year. Even Chief Jenkins, who had prayed for a rainy summer, was alarmed at the "noticeable drop" in attendance. On opening day the year before, for instance, the popular pools at South Bend and Oakland City took in 400 visitors each; on the first day of desegregated use, attendance was down to 155 and 259 respectively.[36]

As whites abandoned the pools, they asked the city to follow suit. And in many ways, Atlanta did. The next summer, for instance, hours of operation were cut back at most public pools. The change had been made, Mayor Ivan Allen Jr. noted, "so as to lessen racial tension wherever possible." But the city did more than simply reduce the operating hours of its pools; it also reduced their size and scope. Instead of the old system, in which large pools served broad sections of the city, Atlanta launched a new "neighborhood pool policy," which relied on smaller "walk-to" pools enclosed in individual neighborhoods. Given the segregated nature of those neighborhoods, such a move could easily be seen as a way around the order to desegregate. For some whites, however, these changes in policy were still not enough. They demanded an end to public pools altogether. In Candler Park, for instance, 850 whites signed a petition calling for the closing of their neighborhood pool, which they claimed had been "a menace to the peace and tranquillity of the community" ever since it had been desegregated. "This community is mad as hell," noted the head of the local civic club. When pools such as the one at Candler Park were closed, segregationists delighted in it. In 1966, for example, a tour bus driver entertained visitors with a joke about the changes at Grant Park. "There used to be a swimming pool here," he announced, "but when the integrationists made us let Nigras in we fixed them by filling it in and now it's a bear pit." His riders laughed appreciatively.[37]

Unwilling to share public spaces with blacks, white Atlantans once again looked for a private alternative. In the case of the public parks, some whites hoped to move municipal lands into private hands. Citing "social changes . . . largely due to the racial situation," the head of the Atlanta Council of Civic Clubs called for the privatization of the entire park system. Community civic clubs, neighborhood churches, and "patriotic and historical organizations" could take ownership of the parks, he suggested, and thereby maintain the racial patterns in them. Ultimately, privatization of large city parks was simply not feasible. But private pools were a realistic alternative and many whites rushed to start construction in their own backyards. Indeed, the demand for private pools was so sudden and severe that a number of fly-by-night construction crews cropped up in the city, fleecing desperate customers. Eventually, Atlanta's legitimate builders had to form a new organization, the Greater Atlanta Swimming Pool Association, just to clean up the industry's reputation.[38]

Working-class whites, of course, could not afford their own pools. For them, the only alternative to swimming at an integrated pool was not swimming at all. And thus, while almost all whites complained about the self-imposed "sacrifices" they were making in their flight from desegregated public spaces, once again only the working class had no real alternative. They angrily attacked the white members of the moderate coalition as hypocrites who pushed a social policy on the poor but escaped its ramifications themselves. "Don't forget to report on how many of the Atlanta Mayor's official family did or did not attend the opening of the city swimming pools for a nice integrated swim," complained one man to the *Atlanta Constitution*. As he and many others realized, neither the mayor nor his allies in the white business elite would be affected by the desegregation of public parks, pools, or golf courses, because they held memberships in exclusive, still-segregated private clubs. (Indeed, the most exclusive of these, the Peachtree Golf Club and Piedmont Driving Club, did not accept black members until well into the 1990s.) "Integration for everyone but the *Rich* high & fancy," is how one angry white put it. "When the black horde (masses) start banging on the doors of your fine homes & segregated districts & segregated clubs & pools you will sing a different tune. Oh yes & how you will. Integration is just fine as long as it doesn't touch (*in your* opinion) God's chosen few and their Ivory Castles."[39]

Thus, as Atlanta desegregated its parks and pools, working-class whites once again reacted in a now familiar pattern. First and foremost, they believed that these public spaces, which they considered their own, had been "stolen" from them and "given" to another race. As before, working-class whites once again understood the process of court-ordered desegregation not as one that brought down barriers to black citizens but, rather, as one that erected new barriers for themselves. Second, in their anger, they blamed not just black Atlantans but the upper-class whites who had aided and abetted the entire process of desegregation. That anger quickly took the form of a full-fledged tax revolt inside Atlanta and, in time, greater white flight from it.

RACE AND THE TAX REVOLT

White flight from these public spaces was made all the more bitter because whites felt that these public spaces were "theirs" and theirs alone. This resulted partly from the history of segregation. For most whites in Atlanta, these spaces "belonged" to them as a racial birthright. But whites' sense of ownership of these public spaces went much deeper than that. As they saw it, whites paid the vast majority—or, in some interpretations, all—of the taxes in the city. Whites alone had paid for these public spaces, they argued, so whites alone should be allowed to use them. When the city opened these public spaces to blacks, whites felt that their belongings and their birthright had quite literally been "stolen" from them.

The perception that whites paid more taxes than blacks was quite common in Atlanta during the late 1950s and early 1960s. To be sure, because of discriminatory policies of public and private lending institutions and real-estate agencies, comparatively few black Atlantans owned their own homes. In direct terms, therefore, only a small portion of Atlanta's black population paid property taxes. But indirectly, through often exorbitant rental payments on their homes and businesses, blacks did contribute their full share to the city's tax base. Still, white Atlantans assumed that they alone shouldered the vast majority of the tax burden. In some cases, this assumption was expressed in a benign, though paternalistic, way. "The white people have paid lots more taxes for schools, highways, and the other necessities of life than the colored people have paid," one Atlantan claimed, "but we have no regret about that because we have tried to be a help to them." Many of his fellow Atlantans, however, expressed plenty of regret. "Where would the Negroes be if it were not for the taxes of the white people?" one woman wanted to know. "Very few of them pay any taxes." "Do you know that Atlanta's population is one-third niggers?" read a typical segregationist pamphlet. "They are paying five per cent of the taxes and receive a strong margin of seventy-five per cent of the tax for their race."[40]

This supposed disparity between the tax burdens of whites and blacks took on a strongly racist tone, as whites charged that they unfairly bore the financial burden for a welfare system that catered to blacks. "I believe in them having good things but in their own *negro sections* and I believe in them working by the sweat of their brow as 'God' states in the Bible instead of hand-outs from White organizations," one man complained. "Welfare office, etc. give them about $50 of white peoples tax money for every illegitimate 'youngster' they have & do they breed fast?" "A majority of negro women have no morals and breed like swine," another agreed, "and the white people of the city are taxed to keep them and their illegitimate offspring up." Segregationists used this popular sentiment to disparage blacks' calls for desegregation and other civil rights measures. A mock application for membership in the NAACP, for instance, appeared in Atlanta in 1957. "I believe in equality that niggers is better than white folks is," the pledge read, "and that the White folks should pay more taxes and us Niggers should have more and more welfare." In a similar vein, this segregationist poem made the rounds in the city:

Po' white folks must labor, 'tween sun and sun,
To pay welfare taxes whilst we has de fun,
We doan pay no taxes, we doan make no goods,
We just raise little niggers, way back in the woods.

Dey pay us to vote and rewards us to sin,
While dem sweet demmycrates keeps de checks cumming in,
We waits every month for the slips and de figgers,
An dats all we do—we is damn lucky niggers.

For angry whites, the implication was clear. "SHALL YOU CONTINUE TO PAY FOR THEIR PLEASURE?" one segregationist sheet asked. "While they sit in the shade and spoon in the moon light, multiplying like rats, we continue to bleed ourselves with heavy taxes to carry the socialistic burden of feeding and clothing them. They do not remain as slaves and therefore are certainly not your wards."[41]

When white neighborhoods were "threatened" by the approach of black buyers, resistance groups often tapped into the resentment over taxes to rally angry whites. Many, for instance, called themselves "taxpayers' organizations," "taxpayer leagues," or "property owners' associations." Even those which went by other names still stressed the rights of white taxpayers in their propaganda. "We are faced with the problem of encroachment upon our community, by the Negro race," warned one group in 1958. "If our community is lost, then who will be the loser, except you the property owners and taxpayers. You can not as a property owner, taxpayer, man, woman, or child, sit by and let this situation go as it appears. You must have the intestinal fortitude to stand up and fight these battles wherever and whenever you can." Now, with the desegregation of public facilities, these whites invoked their beleaguered role as taxpayers even more. "Common use of recreational and sanitary facilities supported by taxation—of which the Negroes pay about one-thirtieth—together with all forms of public transportation, seems inescapable," one Atlantan lamented in 1958. "But the die-hard segregationist can still claim and retain his prerogative of strap-hanging in the crowded trolley, wisely holding his temper and tongue. Similarly, he can exercise, for himself and his progeny, the option of staying away from contaminated swimming-pools and bathing at home." Because of their refusal to share these public spaces with blacks, whites essentially made their old complaint come true. Their taxes *were* being used to fund services enjoyed largely by blacks. Whites refused to acknowledge that this was a result of their own racism, however, and instead blamed the city for "surrendering" these public spaces to blacks.[42]

White anger over desegregation and the tax revolt soon made itself felt in Atlanta politics. The Hartsfield administration and its admirers in the

national press often cited Atlanta's successful desegregation of neighborhoods and public spaces as proof of the city's progress. Increasingly, local
segregationists equated the two as well. In the eyes of working-class whites,
the "progress" that the mayor and his allies often bragged about had come
at their expense—in the "losses" of their neighborhoods and their public
spaces, as well as in the price they paid in taxes. One Atlantan, for instance,
told Hartsfield that he and his neighbors were sickened by what the mayor
called "progress." They saw it another way: "Many of the progress viewers
now live in the county [outside] of the city. You see, their neighborhoods
were taken over by the negro race. Their neighborhoods became slums."
Another angry woman shared this assessment. "I will certainly give the
mayor credit for giving one of the largest swimming pools in West End to
the Negroes," she complained, referring to Mozley Park, "and replacing it
with a pool about the size of a pocket handkerchief." For such Atlantans,
the city's growth meant nothing alongside their own perceived losses. Municipal services offered by the city meant nothing either. In 1953 one of
Hartsfield's supporters described a conversation he had with a neighbor, in
which he tried to stress the civic improvements Hartsfield had championed.
"I asked my next door neighbor how often her Garbage was taken up
under the old plan," he reasoned, "and if she had ever seen a street sweeper
before." But there was only one thing on her mind: "Her cry is 'nigger,
nigger, nigger.' " In the end, the woman became so enraged that she and
the Hartsfield supporter had to be pulled apart.[43]

As such stories made clear, many white working-class Atlantans believed that their losses had actually been *caused* by the city's pursuit of
"progress." Increasingly distrustful of the city's moderate leadership and
increasingly resentful of the course of racial change, they soured on the
talk of "progress" that was central to both. In the early 1960s, as Atlanta's leadership proposed a new slate of civic improvements, these whites
decided to draw the line. The new spaces would be desegregated as well,
they reasoned, and they would therefore stay away. So why should they
fund them? The growing white backlash on issues of race and public space
became clear in the battles over two bond initiatives in 1962 and 1963.
The first bond issue called for $80 million for a number of improvements
on schools, streets, sewers, and other public works, as well as proposals
for a new civic auditorium and a new cultural center at Piedmont Park.
Whites, angry over the "loss" of their old public spaces, refused to pay
for two more spaces that would be used by blacks. Although Mayor Ivan
Allen Jr. touted the auditorium as a way for the city to attract national
conventions and hold large events, working-class whites saw it as another
space exclusively for blacks. A crude cartoon circulated by the Klan, for
instance, depicted a black speaker, labeled "Martin Luther Coon," addressing an integrated audience. "I's been advised by de mayor dat de

white folks is going to raise dere bond taxes and build us a new auditorium for future NAACP meetings," the caption read. "We is making progress." The proposal for a cultural center caused even greater controversy. Located in the heart of the city, Piedmont Park was perhaps the most prized public space in Atlanta, one originally landscaped by the famed Olmsted Brothers. Hoping to add to its value with a new cultural center, Mayor Allen soon found that the politics of race and space were more complicated than he had imagined. Prior to the bond vote, the Woodruff Foundation, a charitable group founded by Coca-Cola magnate Robert Woodruff, donated $4 million to the project, but with the provision that the foundation's name be kept out of it. "The redneck elements started screaming that the Piedmont Park plan was really an effort to integrate the park," Mayor Allen later recalled, "and that the $4 million anonymous gift was 'nigger money.' " Meanwhile, real-estate agents warned surrounding neighborhoods that the cultural center would spark a mass migration of blacks to the area, rumors that only increased white anger. "Piedmont Park suddenly blew up in my face," Allen remembered, "and became a raging racial issue."[44]

The bond went down to a stunning defeat. As the *Atlanta Journal* noted, nearly 58,000 turned out at the polls, "a record number as far as bond referendums go." Basic improvements in schools and street works lost narrowly, but plans for the auditorium and cultural center died in a "smothering defeat." The latter proposal, for instance, was rejected by a margin of almost two-to-one, with the vast majority of opposition coming from working-class and even middle-class whites. In their minds, the reason was clear. The tax burden for the projects, one man complained, would rest on "90 per cent of the white people" while blacks would get most of the benefits. Others agreed. "I think that this is another step," one man reasoned, "where the taxpayers are tired of paying hard-earned money for things that they will not be able to enjoy because of the prospect of forced integration, which means that the facilities would be used almost entirely by the Negroes." After the recent changes in the political and social scene in Atlanta, he continued, "the white people who pay all the bills have decided to stick a little closer and vote accordingly." Mayor Allen tried again the next year, introducing a second bond referendum pared down to the "bare essentials." Although most of the controversial aspects from the year before had been excluded, whites still fought the proposals. A letter from Allen to the local NAACP, for instance, was doctored to make it seem as though the mayor took orders from civil rights groups. Copies appeared across the city, with a warning at the bottom. "Don't give the 'CAPTIVE MAYOR' of the Minority Bloc a blank check to use against the OTHER voters and tax-payers of Atlanta," the sheet warned. "VOTE AGAINST BONDS!" Allen responded by pouring $25,000 into a public relations campaign for the measure and marshaling the votes of upper-class whites and the black community. Only then did the bond pass, and still, there was sizable protest. "The negative vote came from sections of the city and county where white segregationist sentiment traditionally is strongest," the *Atlanta Journal* noted. "And the vote went heaviest against projects where integration or benefits for Negroes might have appeared to be involved—urban renewal, parks, libraries, the auditorium." Indeed, as the bond vote demonstrated, for many whites, public works and "benefits for Negroes" now meant the same thing.[45]

The white revolt over the "loss" of their neighborhoods, their golf courses, their buses, their parks, and their pools represented only the beginning of the white backlash. Notably, the desegregation of these spaces had largely affected only working-class whites. They were the ones living in neighborhoods like Mozley Park, Adamsville, Kirkwood, and Adair Park, where the "transition troubles" had been unfolding for well over a decade. They were the ones who relied on public transportation to get from those neighborhoods to work; they were the ones who needed public golf courses, parks, and pools to relax outside of work; and thus they were once again the ones most impacted by the desegregation of those public spaces. The next stage in Atlanta's desegregation, however, centered on another public institution, the public school, which was just as close to the hearts of middle-class whites as it was to working-class ones, if not more so. As the city's struggles over segregation entered the realm of education, white middle-class Atlantans found themselves flirting with resistance for the first time.

CHAPTER FIVE

The "Second Battle of Atlanta":
Massive Resistance and the Divided Middle Class

WHEN THE SUPREME COURT delivered its landmark decision against segregated schools, Herman Talmadge stood in the small town of LaFayette, Georgia. As the governor started his speech—on the state's successes with separate-but-equal education, no less—he learned the *Atlanta Journal* had been frantically trying to reach him. "I immediately knew what had happened," he recalled. "Within minutes, I had borrowed a DC-4, and in less than an hour I was back in Atlanta." Soon thereafter, Talmadge was on the lawn of the governor's mansion staring into rows of newsreel, television, and newspaper cameras. He denounced the decision in no uncertain terms. "The court has thrown down the gauntlet," Talmadge thundered. "Georgians accept the challenge and will not tolerate the mixing of the races in the public schools or any of its tax-supported public institutions." His statement delivered, the governor strode back into the mansion, settled into an overstuffed armchair, and started taking calls from across the nation. He chatted with reporters for a while, defending segregation strongly but with as much southern charm as he could muster. Soon tired of it all, he told his wife to inform future callers that the governor was busy outside, reviewing the Confederate troops.[1]

As Talmadge and his political machine set Georgia on a course of "massive resistance," they combined their defiance with an equally apparent confidence in the structures of white supremacy and their own abilities to defend it. Lieutenant Governor Marvin Griffin, already anointed as Talmadge's successor, promised the races would never be "mixed" in the state, "come hell or high water!" Likewise, Attorney General Eugene Cook boldly claimed the *Brown* ruling did not apply to Georgia and insisted the state's schools would remain segregated "until we are forced to abandon it by legal action applied to every school in the state." Georgia's leaders, of course, were not alone in their resistance. Similar statements of defiance came from statehouses and governors' mansions across the South, with each echoed and amplified by hundreds more like it. When the cries of resistance made their way to Washington, they found expression in the "Declaration of Constitutional Principles" of March 1956. Better known as the "Southern Manifesto," the declaration was a joint statement from 101 of the region's 128 representatives in the Senate and

House, including the entire Georgia delegation. Condemning the "unwarranted decision of the Supreme Court" and announcing support for southern resistance, the manifesto was, in the words of one legal scholar, nothing less than "a calculated decision of political war." Taken together, these pronouncements assured that segregationists projected a united front of opposition to desegregation. Even the name they chose for their cause, *massive* resistance, suggested that southern whites would be both unified and uniform in their response to court-ordered desegregation.[2]

Despite that confident image, in private conversations segregationists admitted that massive resistance was neither as immobile nor as monolithic as they led others to believe. First, although Georgia's segregationists insisted that massive resistance would preserve the racial status quo precisely as it stood, their programs embodied fundamental changes from the very start. At the heart of their plan to defend school segregation, for instance, stood a revolutionary scheme called the "private-school plan." In 1953, a full year before *Brown*, Governor Talmadge advanced a constitutional amendment giving the General Assembly the power to privatize the state's entire system of public education. In the event of court-ordered desegregation, school buildings would be closed, and students would instead receive grants to attend private, segregated schools. "We can maintain separate schools regardless of the U.S. Supreme Court," Talmadge promised, "by reverting to a private system, subsidizing the child rather than the political subdivision." The General Assembly and the voters agreed, ratifying the amendment in the next elections. From then on, Governor Talmadge and his successors, Marvin Griffin and Ernest Vandiver, relied heavily on the scheme as the centerpiece of the state's resistance to school desegregation. During the 1956 legislative session, for instance, the General Assembly strengthened the plan with several new laws. Legislators laid out a plan to transfer all public-school property and functions to private hands. No detail was left untouched. Procedures for fire marshal examinations of private schools, for instance, were reworded and made to conform to the standards for public ones. Likewise, the legislature amended the state retirement program to ensure that all public-school teachers would maintain their coverage at private institutions. If the courts ordered their schools to desegregate, the governor could thus switch everything to a nominally "private" system without missing a beat.[3]

As the private-school plan made clear, massive resistance had the potential to reshape the political and social landscape of the South. Although its proponents framed their resistance as a way to stop the clock on racial change and preserve the customs of the past, in truth the movement represented the first significant step toward a new conservative politics more attuned to the future. For it was in their challenge to integration that white southerners in Atlanta, and across the region, first considered major changes that they otherwise might never have contemplated—including complete abandonment of public education, establishment of an ersatz private system in its stead, and introduction of a system of tax breaks and tuition grants to fund the scheme. Massive resistance may have been presented to the people of the region and nation as an uncompromising preservation of the status quo but, as the experiences of Georgia demonstrate, from the very beginning, the politics of massive resistance represented fundamental and far-reaching changes.

In much the same way, segregationists' insistence that massive resistance encompassed all white southerners was also a calculated overstatement.[4] In their more candid moments, the leaders of massive resistance admitted that the region was by no means of one mind. On their own, liberals, moderate businessmen, and urban political machines each presented problems for the massive resisters' plan to maintain white supremacy through white solidarity. In Atlanta, of course, these forces came together in a combination that segregationists feared would prove lethal to their cause. This reality was recognized by none other than Roy Harris, a four-time speaker of Georgia's General Assembly and leader of massive resistance in both the state and the South. Harris was an undisputed political power. (Decades later, an *Atlanta Constitution* columnist noted that, in the 1940s and 1950s, a candidate only needed two things to become governor—"$50,000 and Roy Harris.") And when it came to the state's program of massive resistance, Harris readily understood its weak spot. "Atlanta," he warned, "could be the Achilles' heel in the fight to keep segregation in Georgia."[5]

Despite such fears, the image that state-level segregationists had of Atlanta's moderates was just as misleading as the one segregationists presented for themselves. While Atlanta's leaders claimed to welcome racial change as demonstrations of their commitment to the rule of law and their pursuit of progress in all things, in truth they always followed the path of least resistance. Throughout the struggles over segregated education, white moderates allowed for only the minimum amount of change needed to preserve the city's progressive public image. They fought the NAACP's lawsuit for a decade in the courts and, once defeated there, instituted a program of minimal compliance with the court's ruling. Although Atlanta would make a great show of its initial day of desegregation and reap tremendous rewards in the realm of public relations, the reality was that the city had enacted a minimalist program of tokenism that amounted to the smallest commitment to desegregation imaginable.

And, again, much as segregationists masked the significant degree of dissent inside their state, Atlanta's moderates tried to cover up the considerable amount of segregationist resistance in their own ranks. Working with their allies in the press, the churches, and the business community, the moderate coalition largely succeeded in projecting an image of Atlanta that omitted much of the segregationist sentiment there. When such feelings became undeniable—with a sudden explosion of violence or a public demonstration of protest—the Hartsfield administration dismissed the sentiment as coming from "outside agitators" or lower-class "rednecks," and thus unrepresentative of the "real" Atlanta. The moderates who stood up to protect public education from the consequences of massive resistance self-consciously portrayed themselves as the embodiment of middle-class values. In truth, however, they were not the only ones with a claim to that identity. As Atlanta's struggles over school segregation make clear, there was a considerable body of homegrown, middle-class segregationists who insisted that the loss of public education would be a smaller price to pay than the loss of what they saw as their rights as parents, citizens, and taxpayers.

These middle-class segregationists stood at the center of the struggle over separate-but-equal education. From their vantage point, the state segregationists and the local moderates each seemed to be living in delusion. Georgia's whites, they knew from experience, were not as united in defiance of the Supreme Court as the forces of massive resistance made them out to be. But Atlanta's "respectable" whites, they also understood, were not as committed to the cause of desegregation either. Caught between the segregationists in the state capitol and the moderates in city hall, these Atlantans recognized that the struggle over segregated education would reveal, on both sides, internal conflicts and discrepancies between public image and practical reality. These middle-class segregationists understood the deep divisions on all sides and appreciated the magnitude of what would come next. The struggle over segregated schools, they predicted, would be "the Second Battle of Atlanta." The first had destroyed the city; the second would remake it.

FROM MASSIVE RESISTANCE TO LOCAL OPTION

Despite its growing reputation as the "City Too Busy to Hate," in the 1950s Atlanta seemed too busy to desegregate its schools. For forty years, the local NAACP had been pressing for equalization of Atlanta's educational expenditures but with little success. Thus, in 1950 the organization broadened its attack, filing a federal lawsuit demanding complete desegregation. For four more years, the city stonewalled, insisting that its reluctant efforts to equalize school funding made the suit moot. The *Brown* ruling did nothing to change that approach. The original decision alarmed whites, but once the Court slowed the pace of desegregation to "all deliberate speed" with the second *Brown* ruling, whites became convinced that

Figure 5.1 Segregationists protesting rumors of public-school desegregation in Atlanta. Demonstrations such as these were a common sight in 1950s Atlanta. Note the connection between communism and civil rights in their signs, as well as the invocation of their supposed rights as whites.

school segregation would never end. "The idea of integrated schools scared people to death," Police Chief Herbert Jenkins remembered. "They would rush up to me and swear that it could never happen—people just thought it never could happen." Indeed, in spite of *Brown*, the city's leaders acted as if nothing had changed or ever would. "The City of Atlanta is now engaged in defense of segregation in the public schools of Atlanta," announced Mayor Hartsfield, "and we expect to continue to defend that suit." Realizing that only a direct court order could desegregate the city's schools, ten parents filed a class-action suit against the superintendent of schools and the Atlanta board of education in January 1958.[6]

As the case, *Calhoun v. Latimer*, made its way to trial, a serious rift grew among Georgia's whites. Segregationists at the state level immediately dug in their heels. Governor Marvin Griffin blamed Hartsfield for the suit, claiming that his "middle-of-the-road" stance on the golf courses and buses had encouraged "race-mixers" to target the schools. Lieutenant Governor Ernest Vandiver ominously predicted that the suit would "mean the end of the public schools" in Atlanta. In all, the state's segregationists were perfectly willing to follow the "private-school plan," abandoning Atlanta's public schools to preserve segregated education in the rest of

Georgia. Atlanta's leaders, however, refused to see their city sacrificed. In December 1958 Mayor Hartsfield advanced an alternative, the "local option" plan. The people of Atlanta and other localities, he said, should decide the fate of their own schools, not the state legislature. Essentially, Hartsfield took the rationale of massive resistance—segregationists' insistence that states could handle racial affairs better than the federal government—and used it against them, making state politicians the "outsiders" interfering with local affairs. Atlanta's delegation to the General Assembly quickly seized the "local option" idea. Fulton County representative Muggsy Smith, for instance, called for the repeal of all school closing laws and urged a statewide vote on a simple proposition: "We want public schools—or—we do not want public schools." Segregationists reacted predictably. "Some people in Atlanta are hollering before they're hit," Governor Griffin complained. "The mayor of Atlanta cannot throw in the towel for me or any other Georgian." George Whitman Jr., chairman of the state board of education, agreed. All talk of a "local option" approach to the school problem was "so much hogwash," he sniffed. The people of Georgia could maintain segregated education as long as they were willing to stick with the private-school plan. "The only thing we have to fear," he solemnly intoned, "is fear itself."[7]

Developments elsewhere, however, showed that the private-school plan might not be the ideal defense its creators claimed. In Arkansas, Governor Orval Faubus sought to evade court-ordered desegregation by closing Little Rock's high schools in September 1958. White children, he assured voters, could still be educated in private schools that could rely heavily on the buildings, property, and finances of the abandoned public school system. The local district court, however, ruled that neither public property nor public funds could be transferred to supposedly "private" hands to avoid integration. Likewise, Virginia tried to dodge desegregation by shutting down only the school district named in its lawsuit, encouraging local whites to arrange for their own private schooling while it maintained public schools elsewhere. But it too ran afoul of federal courts in January 1959. The state had no obligation to operate local schools, ruled the three judges of the U.S. District Court, but if it provided public education anywhere in the state, it had to provide it everywhere. Such decisions meant that Georgia's plan to shut down only the schools specifically targeted for desegregation and then finance private replacements for them with public funds was, in the words of one Atlantan, "dead at birth."[8]

When the U.S. District Court in Atlanta finally convened to hear *Calhoun v. Latimer* in June 1959, all sides recognized that the legal landscape of massive resistance had been radically altered. The case was heard by Judge Frank A. Hooper, a native Georgian, onetime member of the General Assembly, and longtime associate of segregationist Senator Richard

Russell. Despite his background, Hooper believed massive resistance was doomed. "Even the most ardent segregationists in the land," he remarked, "now recognize that racially segregated public schools are not permitted by law." In light of recent federal court decisions, he held, Atlanta's segregated school system was clearly unconstitutional. "To make any other ruling," Hooper noted, "would only add to the confusion which already exists in the minds of so many of our good citizens, and to build up in the breasts of our citizens hopes of escape which would soon be torn to shreds." Still, Hooper recognized the problem posed by the private-school plan. If he ordered Atlanta's schools to desegregate immediately, the state would shut them down. To avoid this doomsday reaction, the judge delayed implementation of his ruling and granted Atlanta—and the state—time to clear away the traps of massive resistance.[9]

Immediately, Atlanta's leaders pressed the "local option" idea again. This time, the campaign for a local approach had a base broader than just the city's politicians. Religious leaders, for instance, had been slowly moving toward such a stance. During Little Rock's school troubles, eighty Atlanta clergymen made a cautious but clear break with the segregationist status quo through a public statement of conscience. "The public school system must not be destroyed," they urged. "To sacrifice that system in order to avoid obedience to the decree of the Supreme Court would be to inflict tremendous loss upon multitudes of children, whose whole lives would be impoverished as a result." The "Ministers' Manifesto," as it was known, sparked public debate on the issue of desegregation, but it was short-lived. As Little Rock's crisis passed, so too did the chance for dialogue in Atlanta. Just a year later, however, the cause gained greater momentum when white supremacists dynamited the Temple, Atlanta's oldest synagogue. Rabbi Jacob Rothschild had refrained from signing the original "Ministers' Manifesto," but only because it had been strongly couched in Christian rhetoric. He praised those who did sign and urged compliance with the Court's decisions. Rothschild realized his outspoken position might make him a target for extremists. "To date, no churches have been bombed," he wrote a friend in March 1958. "Although, between us, I confidently look forward to such incidents if the present blatant disregard of law and decency is allowed to continue." When the Temple was dynamited that fall, it literally shook the city. The blast woke hundreds of Atlantans from their sleep, including Marvin Griffin at the governor's mansion and an elderly woman who mistook the clamor for Union cannons. In a larger sense, the attack roused the rest of Atlanta's religious community. Nearly four hundred clergymen quickly issued a second "Ministers' Manifesto," more forceful than the first. Calling for open discussion of the school crisis, it urged the governor to appoint a citizens' commission to hold hearings across the state.[10]

That same fall, the "local option" campaign gained even greater strength with the formation of Help Our Public Education, Inc. (HOPE). The organization began simply, after a conversation between two housewives sparked a series of morning coffees for mothers concerned about the "school situation." By December 1958 those small meetings had evolved into mass rallies and, eventually, official incorporation as a nonprofit group. Although chapters sprang up across the state, HOPE never had a formal structure of organization, not even a membership list. "That way, if anyone ever wanted to crack down on us and asked for our membership lists," activist Frances Pauley confided, "they're impossible to get because truthfully we don't have any." On the whole, however, HOPE members were typically upper-middle-class, college-educated, white mothers, many with children then in the public schools. In a number of ways, they had natural ties to the Hartsfield coalition. Many lived in elite Northside neighborhoods, and several were married to local politicians or rising stars in the business community. Likewise, in terms of tactics, HOPE followed the "local option" approach favored by these same forces. "Hope Inc. will not enter into the controversy of segregation vs. integration," Pauley promised. "It will say that we want schools, public schools, operating legally. When this means desegregation in some places, then Hope will say that this will be accepted." Indeed, the dissociation from "the desegregation question" was so complete that the organization itself remained segregated. As one organizer put it, HOPE had to be "administered by white citizens who actively seek the support of other white citizens." An integrated organization, in her mind, would surely fail. Not surprisingly, the mayor threw his support behind the group, and his allies in the press and the Atlanta Chamber of Commerce followed suit. Although HOPE presented itself as simply an organization of "concerned mothers," it had become, in many ways, the unofficial voice of official Atlanta on the topic of open schools.[11]

The Hartsfield coalition and its allies in the press portrayed HOPE as the voice of the respectable middle class and dismissed segregationists as uncultured "rabble-rousers," but in truth Atlanta's middle-class whites were sharply divided on school segregation. In the 1954 elections, for instance, slightly more than half of Atlanta's middle-income whites voted for the private-school amendment. If public schools were "forced" to desegregate, they wanted them shut down and a system of private education erected in their stead. Four years later, many still felt this way. "Yes, I would like to cooperate with you to keep our Public Schools open, but never at any cost," an Atlanta attorney replied to a HOPE mailing. "Private schools or home study would, to me, be far preferable to Public integrated Schools and I hope that you feel the same way. I cannot understand how any native Georgian could take any other position." Other middle-class whites reacted with similar disbelief. "In a state where 40% of our population is Negro," the president of an art supply company asserted, "we can certainly look forward to amalgamation of the races if they are mixed in our schools. How anyone with intelligence can want this in the state of Georgia or the city of Atlanta is beyond my comprehension."[12]

Although middle-class whites remained divided on the matter, both sides sought to claim their class's respectable identity for themselves and characterize their opponents as representatives of other classes. The Hartsfield coalition painted segregationists as "rednecks" who stood in the way of progress. Meanwhile, segregationists responded by charging that only those in the "silk-stocking crowd" were pushing policies of integration, which, if they came to pass, would never affect them. Indeed, throughout the late 1950s, working-class and middle-class whites who lived on the city's still-shifting racial fronts repeatedly stressed that if school desegregation came, it would certainly come in their neighborhoods. The richer whites who supported HOPE and Hartsfield would be shielded from desegregation, because blacks lived nowhere near them. "Millions cannot understand why mothers of white children—and I suppose you are a mother—can support a political inspired issue such as the school mixing mess under the guise of loosing your public schools," a suspicious Atlantan wrote to HOPE's Frances Pauley. "Are you a wealthy parent where mixing will not touch you and yours?" Often, this class division was reduced to simple geography. The rich whites of the Northside, segregationists groused, were sacrificing middle-class whites of the Southside. "I have been so busy during the past few days," fumed one segregationist in late 1958, "that I am unable to quote the latest bounty offered for the scalp of North Siders, who strive so earnestly, to thrust the negro in our South Side schools, while they are free from the threat." However, he warned, when the "Day of Agony" finally came, "the value of a fine pelt from an especially active North Sider will increase greatly."[13]

Infuriated by HOPE's "brainwashing," these Atlantans formed the Metropolitan Association for Segregated Education (MASE). In keeping with the shift away from the uglier, race-based segregationism of the Old South and toward a more respectable, rights-based conservatism for a New South, MASE refused to cede the middle-class middle ground to HOPE and its allies. (Indeed, the group's original name, the Northside Association to Continue Segregated Education, demonstrated that much of its initial membership came from HOPE's own backyard.) At the helm of the organization stood Thomas J. Wesley Jr., a lifelong Atlantan whose family ran a real-estate agency. The *Atlanta Journal* judged him to be "perhaps the most literate and articulate local exponent of the separate but equal point of view." Indeed, Wesley wore the mantle of mild-mannered respectability well. He spoke softly, with reserve and intelligence,

Figure 5.2 Thomas J. Wesley Jr., leader of the Metropolitan Association for Segregated Education (MASE). A prominent spokesman for middle-class segregationists in Atlanta, Wesley challenged the claims of the moderate coalition that their opponents were simply uncultured "rednecks" from the working class. In his opposition to desegregation, Wesley employed a language that avoided crude racism and instead stressed the supposed rights of the white middle class, especially the right to "freedom of association."

and in a language that accentuated middle-class ideals of family, individual rights, equal opportunity, and upward mobility through hard work. "Some people are saying 'Save our schools,' " Wesley stated in one speech. "We say 'Save our children first.' We want the Negroes to have full opportunity for self-advancement, but see no reason why this necessarily entails their forced inclusion into places where they are not suited."[14]

Taking charge of what they called the "Second Battle of Atlanta," MASE staged massive rallies throughout early 1960. To welcome the new legislative session, for instance, MASE brought to town one of the South's leading segregationists, Robert Patterson, executive secretary of the Citizens' Councils of Mississippi. Organizers reserved the Lenox Square Auditorium, assuming that only a few hundred would show up. Nearly a thousand did, tripling the hall's capacity. Two weeks later, five hundred more parents met at the suburban Marietta High School. Another fifteen hundred well-dressed, middle-class Atlantans packed the Tower Theater in early February, and twelve hundred more at a second rally shortly thereafter. In such settings, MASE rallied middle-class segregationists against

Hartsfield and his "elitist" allies in HOPE. "They're the biggest bunch of hypocrites I ever saw," Roy Harris said. "They don't care if there is murder and rape and beatings in every schoolroom in Atlanta, and they don't care what their daughters' relations with the Negro boys are. And you know why?" he asked. "Because they live on the Northside, that's why." State Democratic chairman James Gray agreed. "Some of the best known integrationists in our state," he said, "already have their children safely tucked away in private schools." Presenting themselves simply as parents concerned with their children's education, MASE members insisted that they alone spoke for the middle class.[15]

By the spring of 1960 the "Second Battle of Atlanta" had settled into siege warfare, with opposing politicians and constituencies sharply divided. On one side, Mayor Hartsfield and HOPE insisted that segregated education could never last and promised the "local option" approach could keep integration to token levels. On the other, segregationists in MASE and the state capitol stood by the private school plan, which they hoped would preserve segregation and education alike. The segregationists had their opponents outnumbered—in terms of popular support, political strength, and legislative power. But their shrewder leaders realized that Judge Hooper's rulings in *Calhoun* signaled a crucial change in the balance of power. Schools in Atlanta would be forced to integrate or close, they understood, and the rest of the state would invariably face the same choice soon thereafter. Realizing they had backed into a corner, Governor Vandiver and his aides searched for a way out. It wouldn't be easy. "If we had had a vote on closing the schools, by a popular vote," aide Griffin Bell recalled, "they would have been closed." Instead, they established an advisory body in February 1960, the General Assembly Committee on Schools, to hold hearings across the state and poll the public on school segregation.[16]

The schools committee was more commonly known as the Sibley Commission, after its head, John Sibley. A grandfatherly figure from Atlanta, Sibley had been an attorney, a judge, and now a successful banker. Although personally a segregationist, he understood that massive resistance was doomed to fail. "John Sibley was nobody's liberal," a HOPE activist recalled, but he wanted to keep the schools open. "In traveling throughout the state and going to every Congressional district and hearing people speak, he was just embarrassed at the racists. He didn't want to be a part of that." Officially, the Sibley Commission had been established to gauge public opinion. But in fact, Bell confided, the real purpose was "to let people sort of blow off steam." In this regard, the commission had the ideal chairman. Sibley had "the patience of Job," a reporter marveled. Unfortunately, he had the problems to match. Day after day, Sibley suffered through speeches from segregationists great and small, enduring the

Figure 5.3 The Sibley Commission Hearings in Atlanta. Of all the sessions held by the General Assembly Committee on Schools, the meetings in the gymnasium of Henry Grady High School were, without doubt, the most hotly contested of all. Although the session attracted the "open schools" forces of HOPE, Inc., and the segregationist members of MASE in equal numbers, the crowd bears a uniformly middle-class appearance.

repetition and posturing as best as he could. "The most excruciating pain in the world," he reasoned, "is the pain of an undelivered speech." In truth, however, the commission did more than simply solicit opinion. In a fundamental way, it helped reshape Georgians' thinking on the subject of segregated schools itself. When witnesses were brought forth to testify, Sibley allowed them to vote for either the continuation of public schools, with a small degree of desegregation, or the abandonment of public education altogether. Thus, the desegregation "dilemma" was pared down to a simple decision: "public schools or no schools." To the moderates' delight, this sounded just like the "local option" approach.[17]

While its hearings had seen heated exchanges in rural sections of the state, the Sibley Commission found Atlanta the most contested site by far. HOPE dedicated itself to ensuring that the hearings would "be flooded with sentiment for uninterrupted public education." MASE, of course, urged its supporters to pack the meeting as well. "Unless we do so," Thomas Wesley told the press, "we will find ourselves being represented by integrationists such as Mr. Hartsfield who arrogate unto themselves a monopoly on wisdom and virtue and the prerogative of being spokesmen for all the people." The two sides kept up their attacks when the hearings began in the gymnasium of Henry Grady High. For their part, supporters of the "local option" plan presented an impressive array of endorsements. Representatives of HOPE and black organizations spoke out for "open schools," of course, but so did a dozen PTAs, the Atlanta Chamber of Commerce, the Junior Chamber, the Atlanta Council of Churches, B'nai B'rith, Active Voters, and the League of Women Voters organizations of Georgia, Atlanta, and DeKalb County. Atlanta's school board also supported the "local option" approach and, in that vein, offered a new plan for compliance with Judge Hooper's rulings. There would be only token desegregation, Chairman Pete Latimer noted, with a handful of black students "integrated" under a complex pupil placement scheme. Most students, he assumed, would stay put under a policy of "voluntary segregation." Although there could be no official racial discrimination in student placement, school administrators noted that other forms of discrimination, especially residential segregation, would keep city schools largely segregated. "We think and believe," Latimer assured the crowd, "that geography is probably the one single factor that will deter any mass mixing of the races in Atlanta." Even black leaders supported this rationale. "Less than 100 Negro students would be involved in Atlanta," Rev. William Holmes Borders agreed. "Where they live will determine where they attend school."[18]

Despite such assurances, most whites still supported segregation. Some did little to conceal their anger. A representative of United Auto Workers Local No. 34, for instance, strode to the microphone to deliver the results of his union's vote on the matter. "We want segregated schools at any cost," he stated, "and when I say any cost, I mean any cost—the cost of lives if necessary." "We are for segregation at any cost," echoed a minister from the Evangelical Christian Council. "Last night, an overflowing crowd—they authorized me to speak to this Assembly here and to this group and that they were 100% behind segregation and they would stand for segregation at any cost and all cost to the bitter end." In their eyes, those who called for compliance with the Supreme Court should have been ashamed. "These white people who throw up their hands and holler, Oh, Lord, we are whipped, don't shoot—I think that you ought to go crawl in a hole and quit," spat a plumber. At this, the crowd thundered its approval, so loudly and for so long that Sibley threatened to stop the proceedings. "We can't have this hooping and hollering," he remonstrated, "we can't have a meeting with this sort of thing."[19]

The strongest case for the segregationists, however, came from MASE president Thomas Wesley. In a statement that reflected his organization's middle-class sensibility, Wesley avoided racist sentiments and instead stressed the rights that whites felt were being taken from them. "To swap forced separation for forced integration is to exchange a lesser evil for a greater one," he reasoned. "If the right to associate transcends the right not to associate, then nobody's privacy is safe. We feel that everyone should be permitted to associate with those he chooses—if the desire for association is mutual." In his mind, the private-school plan protected those threatened rights. "The state should peacefully and legally resist to the last, any tyrannical usurpations of power by the Federal government," Wesley read. "When we can no longer operate as we wish and elect our public schools—which we erected with our money and operate with our money—then we should close them, dispose of the buildings, and educate our children by other means." The crowd erupted in a strong and sustained applause, cheering and clapping until Sibley managed to restore order once more.[20]

The unscientific tabulations of the Sibley Commission showed that the day's testimony supported the segregationists, who had come out in force.[21] In fact, public interest was so strong in Atlanta that the commission decided to return for a second day. This time, the "open schools" forces showed up in greater numbers, offsetting the initially strong showing by segregationists. In the end, when the *Atlanta Constitution* scored the two-day political prizefight, it found that more than two-thirds of the speakers at the Atlanta hearings had favored "open schools." Statewide, however, the scorecard read differently: closing schools won by a margin of 831 to 731. The Sibley Commission's final report proved to be just as divided. The majority report, signed by eleven members, including Sibley, endorsed the "local option" approach. Individual school districts could decide if they wanted to continue public education. If a district decided to keep its public schools, strict pupil placement laws would prevent wholesale integration, and white parents would be able to move their children to segregated schools wherever possible. Alternately, parents could accept a tuition grant from the state to cover the price of private schooling. The Sibley report proposed, quite simply, the most grudging degree of desegregation imaginable. The recommendations were limited and did not themselves change any of Georgia's segregation statutes, but Judge Hooper took them as a sign of the legislature's good faith. Soon after the report was released, he again postponed implementation of the *Calhoun* decision until May 1961. In public pleas, Hooper urged the legislature to let Atlanta deal with its school desegregation problem without the hindrances of the state's massive resistance program. The alternative, he warned his old colleagues in the General Assembly, was "to risk the dam breaking and the whole state being flooded."[22]

In January 1961, as the General Assembly convened in Atlanta to resolve the city's desegregation dilemma, the "dam" suddenly burst elsewhere in the state. In a series of quick rulings, federal judges ordered the University of Georgia at Athens to admit two black applicants, Charlayne

Hunter and Hamilton Holmes. The pair had applied for admission in 1959, but university officials turned them down, citing a lack of space in the freshman class. School officials refused to acknowledge that the two students had been rejected for racial reasons and insisted that the University of Georgia did not follow a policy of segregation. It was simply a coincidence that no blacks had attended the school in its 175-year history. The NAACP's legal staff disagreed and filed suit. In a swift series of orders in early January 1961, Judge William Bootle of the U.S. District Court in Macon and then Chief Judge Elbert Tuttle of the Court of Appeals ordered the two applicants to be admitted immediately.[23]

Notably, both students hailed from Atlanta, where they had each experienced the city's struggles with desegregation firsthand. Charlayne Hunter's family had participated in the racial transition of Mozley Park, moving into a formerly white home on Mozley Place in 1951 and sending Charlayne to Stanton Elementary when it was first transferred to black use. Hamilton Holmes, meanwhile, had ties to a different chapter of Atlanta's desegregation struggles. His grandfather, father, and uncle had been in the first black foursome to challenge segregation on Atlanta's municipal golf courses and the first to play there.[24] As it turned out, both would have reason to draw on their Atlanta experiences in Athens. The night of the initial court order, two hundred angry students gathered around the campus's historic entrance. From the wrought-iron gate, adorned with the state's motto of "Wisdom, Justice, Moderation," white students hung a black-faced effigy and serenaded it with choruses of "Dixie" and chants of "Two, four, six, eight, we don't want to integrate!" That was only the start. After Holmes and Hunter attended their first classes, a violent riot erupted outside Hunter's dorm. A "howling, cursing mob" of nearly two thousand surrounded the building, holding a message for the new occupant: "Nigger Go Home." The mob raged for an hour, leaving chaos in its wake. "The area around Center Myers looked like a deserted battlefield," recalled an eyewitness, "with bricks and broken glass on the lawn, small brush fires in the woods below the dormitories, and the bite of tear gas still in the air." Despite the resistance, the district court refused to budge. "The lawful orders of this court," Judge Bootle announced, could not "be frustrated by violence and disorder."[25]

With the University of Georgia integrated, the stakes for segregationists had suddenly become much higher. Many legislators would have willingly, even gleefully, closed schools in Atlanta, but this was another matter. "The University of Georgia is just part of the fabric of Georgia," Governor Vandiver remembered. "Every family in Georgia has somebody that went." Because shutting it down was unthinkable, the governor searched for a way to stop the machinery of massive resistance. Vandiver had little to lose, since he was already taking blame for the admission of

Holmes and Hunter. (Segregationist wits around the state capitol invoked his campaign pledge that no black student—"no, not one!"—would attend a white school while he was governor. He had kept his word, they joked: "No, not one—two!") Calling the state's segregation legislation an "albatross" around their necks, Vandiver urged the General Assembly to abandon much of it. Legislators quickly repealed old statutes and passed new measures that allowed a "local option" approach, clarified the "pupil placement" process, and established tuition grants for private schools. Individual school systems, such as Atlanta's, could now survive court orders to integrate without being shut down or shut off from state funding. The "Second Battle of Atlanta" had become a strictly local skirmish.[26]

ATLANTA'S PUBLIC SCHOOL DESEGREGATION IN IMAGE AND REALITY

As moderates prepared for the desegregation of public schools in Atlanta, they closely examined the experiences of other southern cities. First and foremost on everyone's mind were the lessons of Little Rock. Much like Atlanta, it had a reputation for moderation in race relations, one founded on its successful desegregation of public parks, buses, and hospitals. As the 1957 school year approached, Little Rock planned to admit nine black students to Central High School. But, as in Atlanta, the city's moderates found themselves attacked by the state's segregationists, especially Governor Orval Faubus, who called out the National Guard to prevent desegregation and thereby sparked a constitutional showdown between the state and federal governments. In the short term, Faubus lost, as the Supreme Court rejected the state's rationale for massive resistance in the landmark case of *Cooper v. Aaron*. Thereafter, federal troops kept the schools open and desegregated for the remainder of the school year. Faubus refused to back down, however, and ordered all of Little Rock's high schools closed for the 1958–59 school year. The courts forced the schools to reopen in 1959, but a great deal of damage had already been done. Lawlessness fell on Little Rock during these years, as segregationists bombed the offices of the mayor and school superintendent, fired gunshots into the home of an NAACP leader, and made countless threats against black students. In the end, the pressure proved too much for the man charged with keeping the peace. Shortly after the schools reopened, Little Rock's police chief sat down at his kitchen table, fired three bullets into his wife and then turned the gun on himself.[27]

Atlanta's leaders also watched with apprehension as New Orleans struggled with desegregation in the fall of 1960. Again, moderates in another southern metropolis found their campaign for "open schools" thwarted by state-level segregationists. As in Georgia, Louisiana's leaders had promised to defend white supremacy at any cost, even if it meant abandoning public education altogether. While Little Rock's reputation had been badly damaged by its segregationist outburst, whites in New Orleans took violence to new levels. The degree of desegregation in the city was barely noticeable, with just four first-grade girls entering two elementary schools. Still, thousands of whites rioted in New Orleans' streets, throwing rotten eggs and tomatoes at the first transfer student, a six-year-old girl. Crowds of angry mothers, known as "the cheerleaders," vented their raw hatred at other whites, too, spitting and screaming at the dwindling number of white parents with children still in the schools. Their ugliness stunned most observers. Searching for words to describe the scene, John Steinbeck called their shrieks "bestial and filthy and degenerate." But the protests succeeded in speeding white flight from the two schools. By the third day of desegregation, just nineteen white students remained in one school, and only two at the other. The mobs gained strength throughout the year, using an intimidating combination of violence, vandalism, and economic reprisals against anyone, black or white, who dared oppose them. As the mayor and business leaders refused to take charge, New Orleans spiraled dangerously out of control.[28]

For moderates in Atlanta, Little Rock and New Orleans provided stark lessons about how segregationist resistance could ruin their city. "I do not think it is any exaggeration to say that had Atlanta—strongly assisted by the state government—chosen to be the center of resistance rather than compliance, it would have torn the city apart," Police Chief Jenkins reflected. "Atlanta would have become another Belfast." Luckily, the city still had Mayor Hartsfield at the helm. As his campaign manager Helen Bullard recalled, "we could have out-Little-Rocked Little Rock easily if it hadn't been for that old man Hartsfield." Just as he had handled the desegregation of the golf courses, buses, and various neighborhoods, Hartsfield guided Atlanta through its latest and greatest desegregation crisis. Again, he stressed the politics of progress. "We're a city too busy to hate," he bragged in an interview with *Look Magazine*. "Atlanta does not cling to the past. People who swear on the old Southern traditions don't know what the hell they are. I think of boll weevils and hook worms." Under Hartsfield's watch, Atlanta would desegregate its schools just as it had other spaces—with a great deal of image control and token degree of desegregation.[29]

Drawing on the lessons of Little Rock and New Orleans, Hartsfield hoped to convince local businessmen that it was in their own interest to guarantee the peaceful desegregation of city schools. "It will do little good to bring about more brick, stone, and concrete," he told them, "while a shocked and amazed world looks at a hundred thousand innocent children roaming the streets." To prove his point, the mayor reminded them that Little Rock had resisted desegregation and lost millions in business as a result, ranging from a $10 million shopping center to other assorted enterprises. Hartsfield commissioned a study of that city's economic losses and made sure Atlanta's top businessmen all received copies. Members of the Little Rock Chamber of Commerce were even brought to Atlanta to counsel their counterparts. They displayed a letter from an industrial leader who refused to build a factory in Arkansas after Little Rock: "We have no desire to be involved in the segregation problems current in that state." Other leaflets spoke of the "Cost of Little Rock," warning that resistance meant ruin. "Don't be misled into believing that business in Little Rock is 'as usual,' " wrote an Arkansas resident in a HOPE newsletter. "The downswing has just begun." "Little new Industry since 'Little Rock,' " another reported grimly. The "2 most profitable businesses now are Moving Van companies."[30]

While Atlantans looked elsewhere to understand the economic costs of massive resistance, they realized that the violence then raging in New Orleans could just as easily erupt in their city. Segregationist tempers remained raw in the wake of bus desegregation, and after that Atlanta's civil rights movement only picked up speed. Student sit-ins swept the city in early 1960, bringing protests and counterprotests on scales never before seen. Publicly, Mayor Hartsfield took the arrival of the civil rights revolution in stride; privately, he worried that rising tensions would explode in the public schools. A month before schools opened, Hartsfield frankly confided to Burke Marshall, assistant U.S. attorney general for civil rights, that he was "concerned about the continual belligerent attitude of our Negro agitators. They are moving against us on all fronts, making all sorts of accusations just at a time when a little restraint and cooperation would be in order." Thus, as the racial climate of the city, and indeed the country, became ever more charged, many Atlantans worried that school desegregation would cause the city to explode.[31]

As if to prove this point, before dawn on December 12, 1960, a bomb blasted the English Avenue School. The school had switched from white to black use when the region underwent racial transition, and local whites quickly linked the bombing to lingering racial resentment. When "the community's beloved school equipment was given to Negroes," a former principal reflected, local whites had suffered. "It meant loss and hardship and leaving familiar home surroundings for many of my longtime friends," she told reporters. "I remember a community meeting to protest the loss of the school to white children. There were more than 1,000 people present. But not one city official, not one member of the school board, was on hand to talk to the families, to explain what was happening, or to try to clarify the situation. Perhaps if residents of the section had been dealt with more sympathetically," she admonished, "this sad and ugly incident would not have taken place." Local and state leaders denounced the bombing, but no one was more outraged than Mayor Hartsfield. Glossing over the considerable middle-class support for segregation, the mayor blamed the usual suspects. "Such senseless destruction of property is the work of the lowest element," he spat, "an ignorant rabble, inflamed by political demagogues and encouraged by the silence of our most substantial civic leaders." He begged the city's elite to speak out for open schools. "It is time for the substantial citizens of Atlanta—the people who own its great stores, office buildings, plants, and factories—to assert themselves," the mayor pleaded. "Otherwise, a few little, loud-mouthed racial demagogues will be mistaken for the voice of Atlanta."[32]

Fearing that the experiences of Little Rock and New Orleans would be echoed in their own city, Atlanta's businessmen finally took a stand. For most, this meant putting aside their personal prejudices first. "I am just as much in disagreement with the Supreme Court decision as anyone," noted banker Mills Lane. "Yet you cannot look at the experience of our other Southern neighbors in any but a practical way." The Atlanta Chamber of Commerce, under the leadership of future mayor Ivan Allen Jr., realized that its own self-interest was at stake. "They weren't a bunch of do-gooders," the chamber's Opie Shelton said of his fellow members. "They were hard-headed businessmen who realized that you can't sell peanuts at a funeral." Hoping to create a climate of peaceful acceptance, the chamber convinced television and radio stations to donate prime time for countless announcements by political, business, and religious leaders. In the week before schools opened, the television stations alone carried 150 spots. Meanwhile, the chamber ran full-page advertisements in both the *Atlanta Constitution* and *Atlanta Journal* with a challenging question: "How Great Is Atlanta?" Riots and disturbances, the ad implied, would damage the city's standing. "Everything we did, we overdid," Shelton remembered. "Zealous is the word to describe it. We wanted to feel like that, if we couldn't get by without trouble, then there was no way a city could prepare itself."[33]

But the Atlanta Chamber of Commerce was not alone in its public relations campaign. In the spring of 1961 "open schools" activists created a new umbrella coalition—Organizations Assisting Schools in September (OASIS)—to "help accomplish desegregation in a peaceful and orderly manner." As an "organization of organizations," OASIS represented fifty-three different religious, civic, and service agencies and thereby encompassed hundreds of thousands of Atlantans. Throughout 1961, in an endless stream of speeches and public programs, OASIS stressed the need for civility and compliance with school desegregation while avoiding any discussion of the merits or morality of such changes. In stressing "open schools," OASIS followed HOPE's approach. While this helped attract a broader base of support, it also highlighted key divisions within the moderate coalition. Liberal activist Eliza Paschall, for instance, related a telling conversation she had with a more moderate OASIS leader. "When I said there should be more Negro participation, that we cannot prepare for something by avoiding it, she said, 'But you see, our objectives are not the same. The Negroes are working for a desegregated community. We are working for peaceful situation in the schools.' " It was, Paschall noted, a "bit of a blow to have it said in so many words."[34]

The combined campaigns of OASIS and the Chamber of Commerce stunned local segregationists. "Our city is making history," complained Separate Schools, Inc., an offshoot of MASE, "in that this is the first time a brainwashing campaign has been announced in advance by authorities." Reflecting the pervasiveness of the public relations blitz for "open schools," this segregationist group warned of forced conformity in the days ahead: "Stubborn PTA units which are not 'prepared' to accept the Africans will be given special treatment. Teachers will be threatened with the loss of their jobs if they do not do the 'right' thing. Parents will be told that success of the children and their subsequent promotion will depend upon their ability to 'adjust to the new conditions in a changing world.' " But the "most important part of the brainwash campaign, however, has been reserved for the students who will be exposed directly to the Congolese infiltration," the group warned. "Pupils will be submitted to every conceivable hardship and embarrassment if they appear to be reluctant in accepting socially their new dark 'brothers.' " To counteract the "brainwashing" campaign, Separate Schools sent out mass mailings, urging white parents to boycott desegregated schools and keep their children at home on opening day. Instead of submitting to desegregation, the group urged whites to use tuition grants and send their children to still-segregated private schools.[35]

Although segregationists predicted that "hordes" of black students would sweep into formerly white schools, such a scenario was never likely. To keep integration to a bare minimum, Atlanta's school board adopted a "pupil placement" plan. In the late 1950s such schemes emerged as segregationists' surest way to slow desegregation down to a trickle. No mention of race was made in such legislation, but segregated schooling would be maintained all the same, through the application of highly restrictive standards to black students seeking transfers to formerly white schools. In 1958 the Supreme Court allowed Alabama's pupil placement program to stand and, from then on, segregationists relied on the complicated plans whenever they could. Atlanta's board of education, for instance, effectively preserved segregated education in the city with a wide variety of pupil placement statutes, ranging from the availability of transportation or classroom space, to the applicant's "scholastic aptitude" or "relative intelligence," to a catchall consideration of the "possible friction or disorder" that the transfer might cause. Despite the many obstacles, Atlanta school superintendent John Letson insisted that no limit would be placed on the number of black students transferred. But in more candid moments, school officials acknowledged that the scheme would guarantee minimal desegregation. Fulton County school superintendent Paul West, for one, noted that other states had used such programs to "hold school integration to a minimum." North Carolina, he noted, "has had desegregation for six years," but there were still just "eight Negroes in the white public schools." Surely, he implied, Atlanta could do the same.[36]

Atlanta ensured token levels of desegregation in other ways, as well. While other cities, such as Dallas, Nashville, and New Orleans, had begun desegregation in their elementary schools, Atlanta focused on high schools instead. Only seniors and juniors would be eligible to transfer in the first year; the plan would expand by one grade a year after that, working backward through the ranks. Thus, it would take until 1971 before desegregation reached Atlanta's first graders. Many educators pointed out that such a top-down plan made no sense, since younger children would be less indoctrinated in their racial outlooks, less set in their social circles, and generally less committed to the status quo. In the minds of segregationists, of course, that was precisely the problem. Beginning with the top grades, they felt, would keep the number of transfers to a minimum. Some school officials later admitted as much. As Superintendent Letson confided, "I firmly believe that it was done on the assumption that there would be fewer black students who would want to leave their schools."[37]

In truth, the demand for transfers was strong, but the pupil placement system rebuffed most of them. Nearly 300 black students made the trip to city hall to pick up transfer applications in May 1961. The window for returning them was tight, just two weeks, and less than half completed the complicated forms by the deadline. From that pool of 133, only 16 made the final round of interviews and just 10 had their requests approved. Of those, only 9 would actually make the move. Meanwhile, nearly 50,000 black students remained in still-segregated schools. The black community was, of course, frustrated by the obstacles presented in the pupil placement system. "We've got a saying around here," an NAACP officer noted, "that it's easier to go to Yale than to transfer from one public school to another in Atlanta." Besides limiting the number of black students integrated, the pupil placement plan limited the number of schools involved, too. As segregationists had predicted, two of the schools were in transitional neighborhoods: Murphy High School, just southeast of Kirkwood, and Brown High School, in the West End. The other two, however, were not: Northside High, near the affluent Buckhead area, and Henry Grady High, site of the Sibley Commission hearings.[38]

As the opening day of school approached, the Atlanta Police Department did everything it could to ensure that those four schools witnessed none of the violence seen in other cities. Chief Jenkins understood that the task would be theirs and theirs alone. Governor Vandiver had announced that "not one National Guardsman nor state patrolman will ever be used to integrate a school." U.S. attorney general Robert Kennedy offered to send federal marshals, but Jenkins turned him down. "I told him that if the Atlanta Police Department could not handle the peaceful desegregation of the Atlanta schools, then I would need more than federal marshals," he remembered. "I would need the U.S. Third Army." In truth, Atlanta's policemen had been preparing for school desegregation for years. "We've had men from our force in Little Rock and New Orleans studying what they did wrong," the mayor told reporters. "When racists come in *this* town, they know they're going to get their heads knocked together." In case extremists still failed to get the message, Chief Jenkins established a special unit to monitor "crackpots" with round-the-clock surveillance. His informants infiltrated so many white supremacist groups that at least one decided to leave Atlanta "in search of freedom."[39]

The Atlanta police planned for the first day of school with what Superintendent Letson called "a care for detail that characterized the D-Day landing." Chief Jenkins knew the students and their parents were worried. Some had been threatened repeatedly over the phone. Other parents, especially ones living in transitional neighborhoods, worried that their homes would be bombed. When the police intercepted a Klan flyer listing the transfer students' names and addresses, they placed their homes under protection. The journey from home to school was likewise covered. Undercover cars carried the students to and from school during the first days, with a black detective driving and the route detailed, street by street, minute by minute. And the schools themselves were guarded with equal care. Days before the desegregation began, Jenkins placed all four schools under twenty-four-hour guard. To scare off bombers, canine units patrolled the grounds from 8 p.m. to 6 a.m. A half-dozen uniformed and plainclothes policemen stood ready outside each school, with a policewoman and more officers stationed inside. A special mobile squad, paddy wagons, a helicopter, and the evening motorcycle squad would all be on call as well. Jenkins was so concerned that the desegregation go well that he had his force hold a "dress rehearsal" a few days before. There could be no mistakes. "It is most important that this operation be completed quietly, lawfully, and without confusion," he told his "school squad" leaders. "We also have a great public relations job to do because there will be so many members of the press present and the eyes of the world will be focused on you and your school during this period."[40]

Figure 5.4 A police officer standing guard outside Murphy High School on the first day of desegregated schools, Wednesday, August 30, 1961. By all outward appearances, the desegregation of four of Atlanta's high schools went by without a flaw.

Indeed, the city had gone to great lengths to ensure a positive public image. OASIS assembled an informational handbook for reporters called *Background: Atlanta*. It detailed facts about the transfer students and offered statements from city leaders. Eager to present a positive image, Hartsfield created an elaborate media center at city hall. Private lines to the principals' offices were set up and run into the city council chamber, and police radio kept the press constantly updated. Hartsfield, Jenkins, and school officials were all present to answer questions. The Coca-Cola Company catered the entire affair, and city hall scheduled a bus tour of the city, a cocktail party, and a dinner for the press. Reporters were stunned. As *Newsweek* noted, "Old hands who had been harassed and badgered by city officials on the integration beat from Little Rock to

New Orleans were awed by Atlanta's anxious effort to cater to the working press."[41]

On the first day of classes, Wednesday, August 30, 1961, reporters began gathering outside the schools as early as seven o'clock. The police stood ringed around the buildings. At Henry Grady High, the site of the Sibley Commission hearings a year before, patrolmen quickly ushered white students inside. After the starting bell rang, a police captain alerted reporters that the two transfer students would be there in five minutes. On cue, a green Oldsmobile pulled up to the curb. Out filed Madelyn Nix, 15, and Lawrence Jefferson, 17. As the pair walked the concrete path to the schoolhouse door, everything was silent. Police had stopped traffic along Charles Allen Drive to let photographers get a good shot, and the only sound anyone could hear was the subdued commentary of CBS correspondent Robert Pierpont. "You have just seen something," he said as the pair disappeared inside, "that many people predicted would never happen in their lifetime." Traffic started moving again. As reporters stood around, assessing the anticlimactic result of a decade-long struggle, a black Ford pulled up beside them. "Signal Adam—OK!" shouted Mayor Hartsfield. Content that things had run smoothly at Grady, he drove on to the next school, leaving the photographers in his wake.[42]

Surprisingly, few protests marred the day. What one journalist called the city's "jail-now, ask-questions-later" approach had scared off most troublemakers. "A man would be a fool to go down there knowing that he's going to get locked up," one staunch segregationist told a reporter. Still, scattered dissent did surface. A man in a panel truck drove slowly by Grady early in the morning, shouting racist curses at no one in particular, and police discovered "Boycott Mixed Schools" signs on the lawn of Murphy High. Later in the day, the police were quick to move any passersby away from the schools. At Northside High, for instance, patrolmen rushed down to the corner when they spotted two suspicious-looking men. They turned out to be FBI agents. In the end, only five arrests were made. Four were just teenagers out looking for trouble; the fifth was Bill Cody of the American Nazi Party, who showed up at Grady shortly after the mayor, demanding his right to protest. His trial for disorderly conduct, held that very day, only lasted a few minutes but remained memorable. Halfway through the proceedings, Cody tore off his khaki shirt to reveal a white undershirt with large red letters: "WHITES HAVE RIGHTS TOO." Unmoved, Judge Luke Arnold sentenced Cody to thirty days in the stockade. The young Nazi then clicked his heels, gave a stiff-armed salute, and shouted "Sieg Heil!" before being led away by bailiffs. The judge's identity was noteworthy. In the late 1940s Luke Arnold had been held in "high esteem" by local Klansmen; but now, with the eyes of the nation upon him, he readily supported the city's public relations effort. He even allowed photographers into his courtroom, "to put the world on notice that Atlanta runs a fair and impartial court, but at all times protects its citizens, especially its school children."[43]

Aside from such isolated incidents, there was no trouble. Separate Schools had predicted a mass student boycott, but attendance seemed normal. Speaking to reporters over the loudspeakers at city hall, principals proudly reported that there had been no incidents. "It's even more normal than usual," said one. City leaders were ecstatic. "I don't believe we could have written a script and made it any better than the way it turned out," beamed Opie Shelton. "Luckily, we saw Atlanta rise to its full measure of greatness." "We are very proud of Atlanta," Mayor Hartsfield announced with relief. "We hope the whole world will witness how a proud Southern city is obeying the law of the land." Even some who opposed desegregation were pleased with how the day turned out. "I use taxis all the time," Helen Bullard recalled, "and the drivers that I knew were segregationists. I mean, just red-necks from the beginning. They were so proud. 'Well . . . I guess they didn't get much of a story when they came down here, did they?' "[44]

But the lack of a story *was* the story. Atlanta's uneventful compliance with court-ordered desegregation was, in Shelton's words, "a silence heard around the world." As Hartsfield hoped, the city's courtship of the press brought forth an abundance of praise. *Newsweek* toasted "a proud city" and the *New York Times* praised Atlanta for providing a "new and shining example of what can be accomplished" by "people of good will and intelligence." *U.S. News and World Report* heralded a "New Mood in the South," while the *Reporter* proclaimed there was now "hope for us all." Likewise, *Look* anointed Atlanta "the leader of the New South." *Life* singled out the police department for congratulations, while *Good Housekeeping* told the tale of "How Women Won the Quiet Battle of Atlanta." The ultimate praise, however, came from President John F. Kennedy, who opened his evening news conference with congratulations "for the responsible law-abiding manner" with which Atlanta desegregated its schools. "I strongly urge all communities which face this difficult transition to look closely at what Atlanta has done."[45]

To the delight of the Hartsfield coalition, "The City Too Busy to Hate" had pulled off its greatest public relations coup. In spite of the incredible odds against it—the state's "massive resistance" machinery, the dedicated opposition of segregationists, the internal divisions of its own white community, and the ever-present threat of violence—Atlanta had shone before the nation. For those at city hall and the chamber of commerce, it was Atlanta's brightest moment. The national press had come to inspect the city and the South, but Atlanta had passed muster. Images of black students walking into four formerly white schools, without incident, were replayed on newscasts and reproduced in newspapers across the country. From then on, most observers assumed that the city's "school problem" had been settled.

The black students shown in those pictures, however, understood that their ordeal had only just begun. Away from the cameras, they lived a much different day than the one portrayed by the national press corps. The experiences of Martha Ann Holmes and Rosalyn Walton were illustrative. On the way to Murphy High that morning, the two girls traveled through Kirkwood, a neighborhood that was still embroiled in its bitter struggles over race and residence. The Waltons had moved into the heart of Kirkwood a short time before, while the Holmes family lived in the earlier transition section of Moreland Heights. Just the summer before, the same streets they now traveled—Boulevard Drive, Whitefoord Avenue, Memorial Drive—had been covered with signs warning: "This is a White Area." A number of homes along the route had been surrounded by angry white mobs; a few had been torched or even dynamited. Martha Holmes feared her family's home on Wylie Street would be next. "She expects trouble because she lives in what she believes to be a troubled area," a detective reported. "Student also feels that her house may be bombed."[46]

Inside Murphy High, the girls received a cold welcome. During the first week of classes, as detectives kept watch, white students remained "standoffish." In the lunchroom, for instance, the two girls ate alone at a table for twelve. "Those few Murphy students who wanted to be friendly," a reporter noted, "hesitated for fear of exposing themselves to the heckling meted out to a 'nigger-lover.' " When the police disappeared, things got even worse. Students crayoned "Nigger" on the girls' lockers and slipped crude notes inside: "Go back to Africa, Jungle Bunny." As the girls walked to and from classes, students would sneak up behind them and utter vulgar curses. "I tried not even to look back at them in the halls," Martha told a reporter, "so they wouldn't think we were paying attention." But things were no better in the classrooms. In Martha's physics class, for instance, the boy who acted as a teacher's aide would mark her examination booklets with a swastika or the words "NAACP Approved." Once, he took the liberty of lowering her grade himself. In English class, meanwhile, the boy who distributed test papers refused to hand Martha hers. He simply threw them at her. As students saw teachers ignoring such slights, they grew bolder. One afternoon, a boy at the blackboard hurled a piece of chalk at Martha, striking her directly between the eyes. After that act went unpunished, students tormented Martha with a wide arsenal of everyday items, such as pennies and berries. "One day," she remembered, "I was just picking nails out of my hair."[47]

Figure 5.5 Rosalyn Walton, inside Murphy High School. Inside the supposedly desegregated schools, black students found themselves isolated and ostracized. Here, one of the first two black transfer students to Murphy High, Rosalyn Walton, sits alone with her teacher in a typing classroom. Throughout the school year, she and fellow transfer student Martha Ann Holmes were singled out for verbal and physical attacks by their white classmates.

The trials of Martha Ann Holmes and Rosalyn Walton were perhaps the worst experienced by Atlanta's transfer students, but they were by no means unrepresentative. At all the desegregated schools, white students made their hatred of their new black classmates clear. Even after the first year of token integration, white students still resented the "invaders." As the first black students entered O'Keefe High in the fall of 1962, for instance, white students reacted as they had at Murphy the year before. "The niggers are here!" one shouted in alarm. Stunned that "their" school had actually desegregated, white students stared at the new arrivals. One girl pulled a friend aside in disbelief: "Did you see those Niggers in my home-room?" Shock gradually gave way to anger and violence. Black students were pushed, tripped, spit upon, cut, and cursed on a daily basis. Their classmates knocked books out of their hands, left angry notes in their lockers, and threw almost every object imaginable at them. To one degree or another, white students singled out and ostracized the new arrivals. School officials, still concerned with appearances, tried to put a positive face on the hostility. In the words of the deputy superintendent of schools Rual Stephens, the attitude was simply one of "chilly correctness."[48]

Other observers, however, had more to say. Dr. Robert Coles, a child psychiatrist who studied student reactions during the desegregation of

Atlanta's schools, reported that almost all white students reacted with hostility to blacks in "their" schools. "By far the largest number are quiz-zical, annoyed, or would just say that they don't want them," Coles reported. This "quietly disapproving or careless majority," as he called them, simply stood by while a "small but articulate" group of whites attacked the black students. In interviews with these white students, Coles carefully recorded "chief themes which come up again and again." Echoing the racism of their parents and neighbors, white teenagers argued "that Negroes will lower standards"; "that they are dirty and diseased"; "that they are like animals"; and "that they are not like white people, inferior, less intelligent, born and made to serve." Again, just as their parents reacted to the integration of public spaces and neighborhoods, these students interpreted the integration of public schools as a personal loss. "Themes of betrayal, of being cheated and hurt come to their minds and words," Coles noted.[49]

Through their silence or support, teachers only fueled the hostility of white students. A handful tried to make the transfer students feel welcome, but most reacted to desegregation just as their students had. "I just didn't believe it would work," one teacher later admitted. "I've known nigras all my life, and I didn't think they would adjust to our schools. I have nothing against them. I just thought their minds weren't like ours." To be sure, some teachers went to great lengths to ensure that black students could never "adjust." One, for instance, made all the black students sit in one corner of her class. She addressed only the white children while lecturing, and sometimes gave the two races different homework assignments. Another instructor delighted in telling racist stories and jokes before black students. In many classrooms, teachers even encouraged attacks on black students. For instance, when one girl complained that a white boy kept throwing papers at her, the teacher reprimanded the girl for not facing the front of the class. At another school, a white boy asked permission to say a prayer "to get rid of the Negroes in our class." The teacher simply smiled. In a study of other desegregated schools, sociologist Mark Chesler found that the collusion between Atlanta's teachers and white students was sadly typical. "Some of the teachers will try to be funny," one black student reported. "When they get to a word like Negro, they call it Nigger or else try to make fun." Other times, the involvement of teachers in attacks on black students ran much deeper. "When we got in there they started throwing rocks and crayons at us," another black child recalled. "I told the teacher and she went back there, and they all started laughing, and she was laughing with them. And then they went outside and they brought more rocks and they started throwing them."[50]

In Atlanta's desegregated schools, official and unofficial policies only reinforced the pattern of ostracism. At Murphy High, for instance, Princi-

pal George McCord noted pointedly that he did not favor "personal relationships" between white and black students. He reasoned that Martha
Holmes and Rosalyn Walton should expect to be spurned by their white
classmates. When reports of the attacks reached his office, he refused to
intervene. "He'd try to tell me things happened because I was just another
student," Martha remembered, "not because I was colored." Making
matters worse, school officials discouraged the two from taking part in
any extracurricular activities, even from attending pep rallies for the football team. At other schools, principals went even further, assigning black
students to specific tables in the cafeteria and telling them which
restrooms they could use. And, in a variety of ways, black students were
discouraged from attending social events. For instance, several schools
required female students to have escorts from the school for all dances.
Because very few transfer students were male, most black girls could not
find escorts and were conveniently barred from the dances. Even at gradu-
ation, students were segregated. At one ceremony, white seniors marched
according to height, while the school's two black students were paired
together, even though one was just 5' 3"? and the other 5' 11"?.[51]

In off-campus outings, the ostracism of black students was even more
blatant. Atlanta's white high schools, for instance, traditionally held their
senior picnics at the privately owned Callaway Gardens. After the start
of school desegregation, Atlanta's high schools continued to hold class
picnics there, even though the Gardens barred blacks completely. (Noting
the white flight from public parks, the management insisted that black
guests would cripple their business. "Callaway Gardens is a private venture," they reminded a civil rights group. Unaware of the irony, they
added, "in order to make it serve the largest number of people, we have
not opened it to interracial groups.") At the close of the 1961–62 school
year, as the annual trip approached, one principal called the black seniors
into his office. "You can go if you want to," he told them, "but this is a
private place and they wouldn't let you in, so I'll save you the embarrassment of going and being turned away." The school board supported
this approach, claiming that such discrimination was ultimately in the
best interest of the black students. "To intercede and cause the outing to
be called off would result in unfavorable reaction of the class, the student
body, and the community towards the student involved," a board member
reasoned. Thus, for years, white seniors in Atlanta's "integrated" schools
continued to take their class trips without their black classmates. Likewise, black seniors were barred from baccalaureate services, traditionally
held at neighborhood churches. "The principal said the minister said it
would be alright with *him* for me to come but of course he couldn't say
what some of the people there might do," one black student reported.
"He said if my parents came, some people might move when they sat

down next to them." The student shrugged this off. Her parents had already been shunned at PTA meetings; this would be nothing new. However, as the principal predicted, ugly incidents did occur at some services. For instance, at the 1962 service for Henry Grady High, black parents received a harsh reception at the First Baptist Church. A woman who had been warmly greeting other parents simply snapped at them: "You know you are not welcome here."[52]

Thus, in practice, token integration was often just a new form of segregation. Black students sat by themselves in classes and the cafeteria. Students attacked them in the halls, teachers ignored or insulted them in the classrooms, and school officials excluded them from school activities, both on and off campus. For white liberals, the treatment of the transfer students dashed their faith in Atlanta's progress. "When you hear 9 children say nobody spoke to them at school & nobody sat with them at lunch," one activist reflected, "it doesn't make you feel very happy." But most white Atlantans believed that the white students' "chilly correctness" was understandable under the circumstances, perhaps even appropriate. A number of white Atlantans, however, wanted to remove themselves and their children even further from black students. Keeping their distance inside a desegregated school was simply not enough. They wanted out.[53]

CHAPTER SIX

The Fight for "Freedom of Association":
School Desegregation and White Withdrawal

As ATLANTA SCHOOL officials read through the transfer requests in May 1961, they found an application quite unlike the others. Sandra Melkild, a seventeen-year-old, middle-class white girl, sought a transfer from Northside High, which would desegregate that fall, to Dykes High, which would remain all-white. The reason for Sandra's request, her application stated simply, was her desire "to maintain freedom of association." "The rights to equal education are inseparably connected with rights to freedom of association," insisted her father William, an engineer with AT&T. "This freedom is the right to associate with whom one pleases and the right not to associate with whom one pleases." Sandra Melkild, he argued, had a right not to be "forced" to attend school with blacks against her will.[1]

As such complaints made clear, William Melkild and similar segregationists saw their children as the victims of the civil rights movement. "Disallowing the transfer of Sandra Melkild, who is seeking freedom of association, while [permitting] the transfer of 10 Negroes seeking forcible association," he charged, would "set the most disturbing precedent in this city and state since Reconstruction days." School officials, however, worried about setting other precedents. First, they feared that giving whites the freedom to change schools would allow blacks to change as well. That precedent would destroy the pupil placement program and thus, the attorney general warned, "lead to massive wholesale integration of the worst sort." Second, the Atlanta school board worried that other whites would make transfer requests, too. Only the Melkilds had thought to make the request during the two-week window for applications, but many more expressed interest after the window closed. For these reasons, the school board believed that letting Sandra Melkild change schools would destroy the city's entire program of token integration. Accordingly, it rejected the request.[2]

Convinced of his rights, William Melkild secured a hearing before the state board of education in August. As in earlier appeals, he claimed his daughter had been denied a fundamental freedom, "the right to associate with whom one pleases and the right not to associate with whom one pleases." Unlike those earlier appeals, however, this plea found a receptive audience. Much of the state board had been appointed by Governor Ernest Vandiver, who had frequently spoken of "freedom of association" and "freedom of choice" in his speeches on school desegregation. As Georgia's massive-resistance legislation crumbled, he even tried to push through a constitutional amendment declaring that "freedom from compulsory association at all levels of public education shall be preserved inviolate." While the governor's amendment never passed, his political appointees loyally followed his lead. Reviewing the Melkild matter, Paul Stone of the state board of education claimed the Atlanta school board had "grossly abused its discretion" in the matter by "forcing a child to go into a situation that is very distasteful" to her. When the attorney for the Atlanta board argued that "freedom of association" had no legal foundation, Stone retorted that it had the backing of "human law." In any case, he announced, "I would not force any white child to go to an integrated school." By a 7-2 vote, the state board swiftly reversed the earlier decision.[3]

Suddenly, just weeks before the desegregation of Atlanta's schools, the city's plan for controlled, token integration had been thrown into chaos over "freedom of association." For once, the conflict between state and local authorities was not rooted in a difference of goals. Both boards wanted to "defend" segregated education. The state board took a near-sighted view of the problem, focusing on the "plight" of a single white student without appreciating the wider impact of such a decision. The Atlanta board, meanwhile, worried that accepting the Melkild request, with its obvious racial inspiration, would bring down the wrath of Judge Frank Hooper, who had barred the board from using race as a grounds for student transfers. Accordingly, it petitioned the district court for a "clarification of its rights and duties." Hooper, who had maintained jurisdiction over Atlanta's desegregation suit, issued a restraining order against the state board. As many predicted, Hooper claimed that the Melkild transfer request was motivated by racial factors and therefore invalid. "She didn't show any reason for a transfer except for the fact that some Negroes had been admitted to a school that she was attending," he later recalled. Ultimately, the judge ruled against the Melkilds not because of any enlightened racial sensibility but rather because he, like the Atlanta school board, feared wide-scale white flight. "If the Atlanta Board of Education was compelled (as sought to be compelled by the State Board of Education) to allow a transfer from Northside High School of all the white students," he ruled, "the practical effect would be to vacate the school as to all white students desiring to transfer." The remainder of the "desegregated" school system would invariably follow suit, he predicted, since "whenever any Negro students transferred into an all white school," that school would "be abandoned by all who desired to do so." Hooper refused to sanction such an exodus. The request of the Melkilds was once again denied; the state was summarily enjoined from interfering.[4]

Regardless of the court ruling, many whites still considered freedom of association a fundamental right. They had embraced the concept long before the Melkild dispute, and a judge's opinion would do little to change that. "Is it not every father's and mother's inalienable right and duty to choose, for their children, associates and companions for life?" asked one father in 1956. "If you do away with segregation in schools, churches, and public places, for our children and young people, you tie the hands of our fathers and mothers to make the kind of homes they would like to have for their off-spring, and which is the very foundation of our schools and churches and the very spirit of the Constitution." Others agreed. "We can't choose who we send our Children to School with, and it won't be long before we will have to ask who we can visit and who can visit us," complained another man in 1957. "How far are we from a Russian form of Government?" As "freedom of association" became a common theme at the grass roots, segregationist leaders learned to follow suit. MASE president Thomas Wesley, for one, repeatedly hammered the theme. "My views on the 'school crisis,' the 'sit-ins,' 'kneel-ins,' etc., remain summarized in the phrase 'freedom of association,' " Wesley wrote in a 1960 column for the *Atlanta Journal*. "It is perfectly alright if people who want integration have all the integration they want, provided those who feel otherwise (including me, of course) are granted the same 'freedom of choice' " to do otherwise.[5]

As such sentiments made clear, "freedom of association" stood as a deep-seated and far-reaching concept in segregationist ideology. The idea found its full expression during the debate over school desegregation, but it had stood as an implicit rationale for white resistance and white flight during earlier stages of segregationist defiance, as in the struggle over transitional neighborhoods. Notably, the whites who invoked "freedom of association" did not define the concept *positively*, in terms of what outside groups they could join, but *negatively*, in terms of what groups of outsiders they could shun. Blacks were entitled to their rights, these parents reasoned, but not at the expense of whites' rights to choose their own associates. "I want the negro to enjoy his freedom but I dont want any part of them," said another. "I dont want any one to tell me Ive got to sit with them have my children go to school with them invite them into my home. . . . which shall it be? give us liberty or give us death?" In their struggle to preserve segregated education, these white parents insisted they had a right to choose what kind of schools their children attended and, more important, what kind of children attended school alongside their own. Although this seemed a narrow concern, "freedom of association" would serve as a unifying principle for the different strands of segregationist resistance, linking the homeowners' organizations of the past, who insisted they had a right to choose their neighbors, with the future campaigns of businessmen, who insisted they had a right to select their customers. Taken together, these movements in defense of whites' "freedom of association" accelerated the earlier movement away from community and consideration of common interests and instead toward individuality, privatization, and the concern for self-interest above all else.[6]

In the end, the resolution of the Melkild case did not shake the faith segregationists had in freedom of association, but it did radically transform the ways they could put the concept into action. Once Judge Hooper ruled against racially motivated transfers within the public school system, it became painfully clear to whites that if they wanted their children to attend public school in Atlanta, they had to attend the school in their neighborhood. While the "defense" of schools and "defense" of neighborhoods had always been closely aligned, suddenly the stakes in both were much higher than ever before. And for segregationist whites who lost the struggle over their neighborhoods and neighborhood schools, the only remaining option was another phase of withdrawal, to the last bastion of segregated education inside the city—private schools.

NEIGHBORHOOD SCHOOLS: THE INTERSECTION OF RACE, RESIDENCE, AND EDUCATION

Throughout the "transition troubles" of the 1950s and 1960s, segregationists warned that racial change in a neighborhood would inevitably lead to racial change in that neighborhood's schools. During the desegregation of Atlanta's high schools, their predictions came true in many ways. At Murphy High, both Martha Ann Holmes and Rosalyn Walton came from sections of Kirkwood settled by new black homeowners just a few years before. And so, to a great degree, did the black students who followed them to Murphy High in the later years of desegregation. In 1962, for instance, all twelve transfer students again came from these transition areas in Kirkwood. One student's house had been targeted by segregationists in 1960; another lived down the street from a home bombed in 1956. In 1963 another thirty-five students, almost all from those same contested streets, also transferred to Murphy. In such ways, the desegregation of neighborhoods and neighborhood high schools generally involved the same families, the same students, the same struggles against segregationist resistance. But the connections between the two forms of desegregation went well beyond the placement of select transfer students in targeted high schools. In regions where residential transitions were sweeping, school officials reluctantly recognized that they would have to do more than simply transfer a few black students to white high schools. They would, instead, have to transfer entire schools to black students. Importantly, this policy applied not just to high schools, the only ones then desegregated under the grade-a-year plan, but to elementary and middle schools as well.[7]

For their part, school officials appreciated the impact residential changes had on the city's school system. "It is very evident that many white residents are moving to the suburbs," Superintendent John Letson announced in 1960, "and many white areas in the city are becoming Negro residential communities." As a result, he noted, the ratio of black students to white was rapidly expanding. During the 1959–60 academic year, for instance, the school system lost 1,627 white students and gained 2,668 black students. The next year, Atlanta's public schools lost another 1,072 white students and gained 3,064 more blacks. Instead of realloting resources to address the expanding black student body, officials tried to make do with already overtaxed and overcrowded facilities. As white classrooms remained half-filled or stood empty, black students were forced into cramped classes and taught in half-day "double sessions." As the situation approached a crisis state, school officials reluctantly reached the obvious conclusion. "At some point," Letson announced in July 1961, "we must convert a white school to a Negro school."[8]

Such an approach was nothing new. The school system had regularly, if reluctantly, changed the "racial designation" of public schools as white neighborhoods shifted to black. In fact, during the early 1960s such transfers took place in all of Atlanta's key transitional neighborhoods. The population shifts in Collier Heights and Grove Park, for instance, led the school board to transfer James L. Mayson Elementary to black students in February 1961, despite loud protests by hundreds of angry whites. Likewise, as Kirkwood changed hands, so did the neighborhood's Whitefoord Avenue Elementary, in June 1961. And transition "troubles" in Adamsville led the school system to consider transferring Margaret Fain Elementary to black students that same summer. Notably, all three schools had seen their enrollments plummet from white flight. Whitefoord, for instance, had enrolled 610 students in 1959, 567 in 1960, and then just 242 in 1961, when the board finally decided that it would be impossible to keep the school "white." Likewise, Fain dropped from 444 students in 1959 to a projected enrollment of half that number for 1962. Although bitter protests by white parents kept the school board from changing its racial designation that year, the school was soon transferred to black use. All across Atlanta, as neighborhoods switched from white to black, so too did the neighborhood schools. Indeed, between

Map 6.1 Public and private schools in Atlanta, 1961

1961 and 1971, school officials changed the racial designation of twenty-seven formerly white elementary schools, roughly a third of all the elementary schools that were "white" at the decade's start. (Because the high schools faced actual desegregation from the start of that period, the school board officially reclassified only eight of them.)[9]

Although changing a school's racial classification became more commonplace after the city began to desegregate high schools, it was still politically explosive. In July 1962, for instance, school officials decided to redesignate the James L. Key School to relieve chronic overcrowding at three nearby black elementary schools. Whites in neighboring Grant Park were outraged. More than three hundred residents turned out to protest, forming what one city hall reporter judged "the largest board audience in years." On their behalf, James Allgood, a local upholsterer and president of the Grant Park Civic Association, made a panicked plea for keeping Key white and, by extension, Grant Park as well. Local aldermen joined in, pleading for the "preservation and protection" of "a great white community." Whites were already fleeing the area, they warned. Just the news that Superintendent Letson *might* recommend the school's transfer had caused seventeen homeowners on Atlanta Avenue to put their homes up for sale. "In turning this school over to Negroes," Alderman James Jackson thundered, "you are not just changing a school—you are changing a community." School officials voiced their sympathy but still decided to designate the Key School for black use. The white crowd was furious. Some promised to "blow up" the school rather than see it "lost" to blacks, an ominous threat after the English Avenue School bombing. Others, meanwhile, directed their anger at the board members themselves, shouting "We'll beat your heads off!" For half an hour, they huddled in the aldermanic chamber, afraid for their lives, as the angry mob milled about outside. Only with a police escort could they escape the building.[10]

In the weeks after the "loss" of the Key School, the surrounding community rapidly moved toward racial transition. Real-estate agents, the Grant Park Civic Association charged, began barraging homeowners with solicitations for sales. "The Grant Park Area is zoned for Negroes," they reportedly said. "We are going to take over the Grant Park Area and you had better sell now." Enraged, the homeowners' organization staged a resistance campaign during the summer of 1962. "ATTENTION BLOCK BUSTERS," read ads from the group's Home-Protection Committee, "YOU HAVE FAILED TO TAKE OUR HOMES AWAY FROM US! You have failed to scatter and panic us and our neighbors! Your treacherous tactics have turned our neighborhood into a battleground!" The ad tried to convince whites elsewhere that this was their fight, too. "Today the problem is ours—tomorrow it may be yours! Don't sleep while the blockbuster prepares to take your homes from you." Finally, the ad ended by paralleling the pleas of Sandra Melkild: "Help us in our struggle to remain free from forced ASSOCIATIONS with any group." Despite the impassioned "defense," the panic that began with the school transfer ultimately swept the entire neighborhood into the hands of black buyers. All across Atlanta, a similar pattern prevailed: wherever white schools desegregated, white neighborhoods self-destructed. "Hundreds upon hundreds of white homes in these areas [with desegregated schools] have been placed on the market," noted the *Metropolitan Herald*. " 'For Sale' signs have sprung up overnight. White parents are literally running away just as quickly as they can sell."[11]

Not surprisingly, as school desegregation picked up speed, white flight kept pace. In early 1964 the Atlanta Board of Education responded to pressure from federal courts and greatly accelerated its plans for integration in the upcoming school year. No longer would white facilities remain unused, while black schools became dangerously overcrowded. "We're going to fill every empty seat in high school classrooms this fall," board member Sara Mitchell announced in April. Transfers, which had heretofore been tightly limited, were suddenly granted in great numbers. While only 85 requests had been approved in 1963, the school board granted more than 700 in 1964. Segregationists were horrified. "It will mean only one thing," the *Herald* promised. "White residents of these areas will sell their homes and leave the city limits just as quickly as they can." "Call it prejudice, ignorance, or whatever you like," the editors stated, but "white families are not going to live long in a school area where massive integration of the schools is in effect. They are not going to expose their children to such an explosive condition for long."[12]

The impact of mass transfers was perhaps best seen at West Fulton High School. As early as 1957, city officials warned that residential racial changes would soon affect the school. "There seems to be an impending change—already in progress—partly brought about due to the Negro population moving closer," a report noted. "This socio-economic situation is a grave problem." As long as the school system limited the number of black students transferred, changes in the surrounding neighborhood had little impact. In 1962, for instance, just 2 black students attended West Fulton; in 1963 only 9. In a school whose total enrollment approached 1,200, this meant that the degree of actual integration was negligible. The acceleration of Atlanta's desegregation plan ended that. In 1964, more than half of the transfer requests granted by the city were to West Fulton. When the school opened that fall, blacks outnumbered whites by a slight margin. Stunned by the sudden changes, whites withdrew their children with astonishing speed. After just one week, white enrollment had plummeted from 607 to 143. School officials tried to stop the white flight from West Fulton, but had little success. Superintendent John Letson, for instance, met with hundreds of students to convince them that, in the wake of the Melkild decision, there would be no "mass transfers" to other, "less-heavily integrated" schools. The students, however, swore they would never return and devoted their time to overwrought eulogies to the "old West Fulton." One girl became so choked with emotion she was unable to finish her prepared remarks; another fainted and had to be revived by a school nurse. Their parents proved to be just as stubborn, as more than 200 angry mothers and fathers stormed the school board meeting the following week. The school board caved, granting transfers for 150 white students who wanted to leave. As the school went, so went the surrounding neighborhood. Just a month later, the changes were striking. "It's virtually a Negro community now," observed a short-order cook across the street from the school. "I sure hoped I wouldn't be around to see it."[13]

A similar pattern developed that year at Kirkwood Elementary. Although Atlanta's elementary schools had yet to be desegregated, a group of black parents showed up at the still-white school in August 1964, hoping to register their children there. All the nearby black schools, they noted, were horribly overcrowded. Whitefoord Avenue Elementary, for instance, had been converted to black use just a few years before, but it was already dangerously full. Students there, like some 5,400 other black elementary students in the city, were taught in half-day "double sessions."

Classes convened in hallways, the teacher's lounge, a clinic room, and even the janitor's washroom. As enrollment at the black school surged to nearly 650 students over capacity, still-white Kirkwood remained 750 under capacity. When the black parents were turned away, they staged pickets at the white school and launched a boycott of the black ones. Under pressure, the school board announced in December 1964 that black children would be allowed to attend Kirkwood Elementary after the holidays. White students, however, would again be offered a way out. "Pupils enrolled at Kirkwood may remain," Superintendent Letson wrote parents, "or may request transfers to other schools. Transfer applications will be honored up to the capacity of the school requested." As an added insult, white teachers were allowed to flee as well. The results were dramatic. On the Friday before the black children were to arrive, there were still 470 white boys and girls enrolled at Kirkwood Elementary, plus a full slate of white teachers and staff. When the black students showed up the following Monday, they found only 7 white children in the building, with just the white principal. By the start of the next school year, Kirkwood Elementary had become exactly what black parents hoped to avoid—yet another overcrowded, all-black school.[14]

Thus, desegregation unfolded in public schools much as it had in other public spaces. Once city officials were confronted with court orders, they carefully orchestrated desegregation, minimizing the number of blacks involved and maximizing the amount of public relations hype. And though the actual scope of desegregation was limited in every way possible—in the number of students and schools involved, in the grades and neighborhoods affected—the vast majority of white Atlantans found it to be too much. As they fled from the schools in record numbers and at record speed, yet another desegregated public space passed from segregation to resegregation, with barely any time spent on true "integration" at all. From there, whites completed the familiar pattern as they had so often before, recoiling from desegregated public spaces and retreating to still-segregated private spaces instead.

PRIVATE SCHOOLS: SEGREGATION ACADEMIES AND RELIGIOUS SCHOOLS

As whites abandoned public schools, private schools surfaced as an attractive alternative. In truth, white Atlantans' movement toward private education had been underway for a decade, ever since the creation of Talmadge's "private-school plan." But at the end of the 1950s, when it seemed increasingly likely that conflict between the state's massive-resistance legislation and federal court orders would force all of Atlanta's public schools to close, this interest in private schools surged. In the fall of

1959 private academies in Atlanta reported record numbers of requests for admission. One school tripled its enrollment that year, while another enrolled a thousand students and turned away nearly twice as many more. The rush for private schools was so great, in fact, that a number of new schools were hastily thrown together to satisfy the demand. A wide variety of Atlantans, from neighborhood church leaders to the commander of a local air force base, created contingency plans for their own private schools in case public ones closed. These plans, however, were merely preparations for a worst-case scenario that never came. As the school closing crisis passed, so too did they.[15]

More ominous were the "segregation academies" established as a permanent escape from the public schools, whether they were closed or kept open on a desegregated basis. The Ku Klux Klan, for one, announced in January 1960 that it would start a school in Atlanta. All the city's white children would be welcome, Grand Dragon Lee Davidson announced, not simply the sons and daughters of the hooded order. Not to be outdone, segregationist suburbanites presented their own plans. Twenty businessmen in Marietta, for instance, obtained a corporate charter for a segregated school in January 1959 and mailed out a thousand applications to prospective parents. Another group, the Cobb County White Citizens for Segregation, claimed it would construct two additional academies for white children the following year.[16]

The success of these segregation academies, however, rested on their affordability. Many whites wanted segregated education for their children, but few could pay for it on their own. Therefore, supporters of segregation academies tried to tap into state funds to help parents of all classes send their children there. Initially, they hoped to use new legislation that allowed Georgians to give money to private schools instead of paying their state income tax. Similar tax credits had been installed by segregationists in Virginia, as a way of channeling public tax money to private segregated schools, and Georgia hoped to follow their example. In April 1959 Atlanta attorney Moreton Rolleston and several white parents chartered a new organization for segregated education, which they not-so-subtly called the Patrick Henry Schools, Inc. Immediately, they applied for tax-exempt status. However, the state commissioner of revenue worried that approval would set a dangerous precedent and bankrupt the state. Using authority granted to him by the law, he refused the request. With no private schools able to qualify for tax-exempt donations, the whole plan proved pointless.[17]

Supporters of segregation academies then turned to the state's Tuition Grant Law, part of the original "private-school plan." Simply put, the law guaranteed every child in Georgia money for a private education. Although it made no mention of race, the legislation noted that students seeking to escape certain "intolerable conditions" in public schools could avail themselves of the grants and thus maintain their "freedom of association." As with the tax-exemption route, state and local officials hesitated to dole out public funds for the scheme and forced a legal showdown. Once again, Moreton Rolleston appeared in an Atlanta court to defend whites' "right" to publicly financed but privately controlled education. His client this time was Carla Aikens, an eleven-year-old enrolled at the Arlington School, and her parents, who wanted the money promised them. The case was heard before Judge Durwood T. Pye, an outspoken champion of segregation who predictably ruled that the "right to the grant is clear and absolute," as long as the applicant was a school-aged resident of the system and the private school was "non-sectarian" in nature.[18]

With the courts supporting the scheme, tuition grants seemed to be the solution for segregationist parents. By the fall of 1962 more than one thousand tuition grants had been approved for a total exceeding $186,000. Closer inspection, however, showed that the grants were not a way for all whites to place their children in segregated private schools, but merely a handout to upper-class whites who already had their children there. A study by the *Atlanta Constitution* reported that 83 percent of the recipients had been enrolled in private schools well before the desegregation struggle. (One beneficiary of the grant program was a local black educator, who had long been sending his children to a northern prep school and was now happy to have segregationists help pay their way.) Furthermore, hundreds of the recipients lived in areas outside Atlanta, where no desegregation existed and, thus, where there was no "need" to flee the public schools. Such stories convinced many Georgians that the tuition grants were not a universal solution to desegregation, but rather one only for the rich. Indeed, since the average grant covered far less than half of the tuition at most private schools, the program only helped wealthy parents who could afford the remainder. As such disparities came to light, many legislators soured on the plan. Even State Senator Garland Byrd, who had personally championed the Tuition Grant Law while lieutenant governor, now denounced the plan as a "subterfuge," which only helped "a privileged few." Instead of enabling all Georgians to attend segregated schools, the tuition grant program was "simply . . . making the public school system poorer and the rich richer." The legislature tightened the administration of the law and, by the time the 1963 school year began, not a single tuition grant had been sought throughout the state.[19]

As tuition grants dried up, so too did the "segregation academies" around Atlanta. It was no coincidence that the two had risen together, and no coincidence that they now fell together, too. From the plan's inception, tuition grants had been restricted to "non-sectarian private schools." Georgia's legislators had included this requirement to ensure that the legislation would not run afoul of Supreme Court rulings forbidding the use of public funding for religious schooling. (Challenging *Brown*, it seems, was more than enough for them.)[20] However, this restriction meant that Georgians could not use the tuition grants at most established private academies in the state, because they almost always had a religious affiliation of one kind or another. Thus, as white parents sought to use tuition grants in the early 1960s, "segregation academies" sprang up to answer the new demand for segregated but nonsectarian education. And, likewise, as the tax exemption and tuition grant schemes dried up, the demand for these schools also disappeared. Accordingly, the few true "segregation academies" scattered around Atlanta collapsed, nearly as quickly as they had risen.[21]

For many observers, of the time and since, the short, strange career of the city's segregation academies seemed evidence that Atlanta's school desegregation was a story played out solely in the realm of public schools.[22] To be sure, "segregation academies" as they were commonly defined—private schools established by leading segregationists, in direct response to court rulings against public school segregation, and for the explicit purpose of evading those rulings—did not play a major role in the resistance of Atlanta's whites. But other private schools, established by major religious denominations, long before rulings against segregated education, did, in truth, provide shelter for segregation. Most scholars have neglected to address their role in white resistance, but in many ways, they deserve as much attention as the more obvious segregation academies, if not more. Segregation academies were, in a perverse way, proof of segregationists' sincerity, a sign of the lengths to which they would go to maintain white supremacy. But as segregation persisted in older, more "respectable" private schools, it contradicted these schools' outspoken support of desegregation elsewhere. It was proof of what could charitably be called a double standard of class, but what was at the time denounced as simple hypocrisy.

By the early 1960s, with the token integration of Atlanta's public schools and the total collapse of Atlanta's segregation academies, the city's established private schools found themselves in the uncomfortable position of being the last bastion of segregated education in "the city too busy to hate." Nowhere was this unease more keenly felt than in private religious schools. During the late 1950s religious leaders and educators stood at the forefront of Atlanta's moderate coalition in counseling the calm acceptance of court-ordered desegregation. Through the "Ministers' Manifestos," a series of columns published in the *Atlanta Constitution*, and countless sermons to their congregations, these religious leaders had taken a principled public stand for the acceptance of desegregated schools. But by the early 1960s these same religious leaders found themselves confronted with the same situation in their own still-segregated institutions. Wrestling with this problem publicly and painfully, many found it hard to practice what they had literally been preaching.[23]

Some quickly moved to correct the problem. Roman Catholic schools, for instance, made it clear they wanted no part in segregation. Soon after his appointment to the Atlanta archdiocese in 1962, Archbishop Paul Hallinan aggressively pressed for the desegregation of all eighteen elementary and high schools under his jurisdiction. Because the city had desegregated its schools, he announced, the church could do no less. "We decided to move at this time to desegregated archdiocesan schools," he stated, "first, because it's right, and second, because an excellent climate of opinion and action already exists here." That fall, parochial schools in Atlanta—as well as ones in Marietta and Athens, where public schools remained segregated—all integrated without incident. While some observers pointed to this as yet another sign of Atlanta's progress, Archbishop Hallinan dismissed the praise. "To call this action courageous," he noted pointedly, "is a reflection on this community." Other religious schools in the region, he knew, were still strictly segregated.[24]

Shortly thereafter, the Greater Atlanta Council on Human Relations took stock of those schools. The largest and most popular private academies, they found, generally hedged the issue. For instance, the main Presbyterian schools, Westminster and Trinity, noted that they had technically accepted applications from blacks, just not black students themselves. Trinity corrected that oversight in April 1963, enrolling the daughters of Andrew Young, a civil rights activist and future mayor of Atlanta. Westminster, meanwhile, took a different approach. Blacks remained barred from attending the academy and, on the rare occasions they were allowed on campus, were required to obey the customs of segregation. Still, officials at Westminster tried to distance the school from the subject. Its headmaster, Dr. William L. Pressly, claimed that the school had never capitalized on racial controversies by taking in "refugees" from the public schools. "Westminster started before the Supreme Court decision [on school segregation] and was full before the decision, were full at the time of the decision, and are still full," the headmaster lectured a reporter in the early 1960s. "The only difference it has made is that we had more applications," he admitted. "Two years ago, when Atlanta was first worried about the schools closing, we had 1,900 applications and took 100." After that, only announcements about the limited class size could stem the tide of application requests. From then on, requests from white children posed no problem. Those from black children were another matter. "The policy of the school up until either June 1962 or Dec. 1962," noted Eliza Paschall of the Greater Atlanta Council on Human Relations, "was to accept *for testing* any student, but there had never been any clear policy by the trustees as to what they would do about a qualified Negro student who applied for Westminster." In 1963 the school faced precisely such a scenario when a black professor of anthropology at Atlanta University tried to enroll his daughter. Despite her academic qualifications, the head-master was not optimistic about her chances. "He said it was very disturbing," Paschall reported, but "that unfortunately a lot of people who have money are opposed to it." As expected, her application was denied.[25]

A similar but more sensational situation unfolded that same year at Westminster's Episcopal counterpart, the Lovett School. Founded in 1926 as a small tutoring institution, Lovett grew rapidly through the late 1950s, boosting its student enrollment from one hundred to one thousand in only four years. Headmaster Vernon Kellett, an elderly Englishman, readily admitted the impact of public school integration on the academy's growth. "In all candor, the segregation-desegregation struggle gives impetus to the development of private schools," Kellett confided to a reporter. When the NAACP lawsuit for the desegregation of the public schools had been delayed a year, he noted, "we had forty cancellations in one week." Still, the headmaster argued that race was "a factor, but not a prime factor." "There is a cry for places in the independent schools regardless of the color question," he insisted. "Lovett School is going along not because of integration, but because people are interested in the best education, and in those things that go along with it."[26]

Indeed, on the surface, Lovett seemed to have no racial restrictions. The school had no formal policy on segregation, one way or the other. But the Episcopal Diocese repeatedly stated that "segregation, on the sole basis of race, is inconsistent with the principles of the Christian Religion." Bishop Randolph Claiborne had taken a forthright stand against all forms of discrimination. For instance, in 1955, when the state board of education adopted a resolution to revoke "forever" the license of any teacher presiding over a racially mixed class, Bishop Claiborne delivered a strong public rebuke. The measure, he warned, was "an effort to bring about state control of thought, opinion, and expression that line us up with Nazi Germany or Communist Russia." Likewise, both the bishop and several prominent pastors signed the "Ministers' Manifestos," with positive results. Dean Alfred Hardman of the Cathedral of St. Philip's, the largest Episcopal church in town, said that "not one person" of his congregation of 3,000 had "come up to say they didn't like what I did." Thus, Bishop Claiborne noted in 1963, the diocese's stand against segregation had been demonstrated "over and over and over." "Any demands for a new resolution of what has already been stated," the bishop told reporters, "seems to me to encourage doubt as to our sincerity in both principle and practice, which have been clearly demonstrated." That same year, however, it became clear that the diocese did not, in fact, put those principles into practice.[27]

The "Lovett Crisis," as it would forever be known, began simply enough on a flight between Albany, Georgia, and Atlanta. Rev. John Morris, a liberal Episcopal priest, found himself in conversation with an African American woman, Coretta Scott King, wife of Martin Luther King Jr., about school segregation back in Atlanta.[28] "She asked about Lovett, whether it was segregated, etc.," Morris later recalled. "I knew of no policy, but promised to advise her about it later." Finding no policy at the school, the priest took his bishop's public statements and press releases at face value. He informed the Kings that Lovett would welcome children of all races; accordingly, they submitted an application for their son. Confronted with the challenge of desegregation in their own institution, the Lovett trustees tried to reconcile their public rhetoric with their private realities. "Personally I have been in complete sympathy with the negro in his quest for decent treatment," noted Dean Hardman, who served as chairman of the Lovett board. "I am still willing to stand up and be counted as being in accord with his seeking the right to vote; to public transportation; to hotel accommodations; to worship in any church, etc." But Lovett was another matter. "I feel strongly," the dean confided, "that both the negro and the white man has some individual rights. Among these I would include the right to pay for and operate a school accepting only those he chooses and to reject any applicant he doesn't want for any reason he deems good." Relying on such a "freedom of association" rationale, Headmaster James McDowell sent a curt letter in February 1963, informing the parents of Martin Luther King III that his application had been denied.[29]

The school's rejection was disheartening, but the diocese's reaction was worse. Bishop Claiborne swiftly distanced the church from the school. "The Diocese of Atlanta has no official connection with Lovett School," he told a national Episcopal weekly. Though technically true, the unofficial connections between Lovett and the diocese were many. Since 1958 the academy had gone by the name of the "Lovett Episcopal School," and its charter stated that the "Episcopal faith" was to be taught there as "contained in the Book of Common Prayer." More important, since 1954 the school had been under the ownership and direction of the diocese's most prominent church, the Cathedral of St. Philip. An ordained Episcopal priest served as the school's headmaster, while two-thirds of its trustees were required to be Episcopalians, with half of that number drawn from the cathedral's congregation. The dean of St. Philip's held a permanent seat on that board; at the time of the request, he served as its chairman.[30]

As such "unofficial" connections came to light, Bishop Claiborne announced in June 1963 that Lovett's "church-related" status would be withdrawn if it "remains in effect a segregated school." When the school's trustees unanimously reaffirmed that segregated status, the bishop revoked all "implied or official" Episcopal support for the school and announced the resignation of the Episcopal priest who served as the school's headmaster. Immediately, however, it became apparent that Lovett was still very much an Episcopal institution. The day after Bishop Claiborne's announcement, for instance, the trustees sent letters to Lovett parents announcing that the school would still have "religious teaching" and "Episcopal services in chapel" in spite of the bishop's statement. A month later, the acting headmaster, a trustee of the Cathedral of St. Philip, again assured parents that the school's religious ties would remain in effect. "The rumour is rife that there will be no more daily chapel, no Wednesday morning communion services, no teaching of religion and an abandonment of all religious emphasis," J. A. Rabbe wrote. "Nothing could be further from the truth. All of these will be continued just as in the past and have the approval of the Bishop."[31]

For some in the Episcopal Church, these revelations over Lovett demonstrated a good deal of religious hypocrisy. "It seems that this amounts to a prostitution of the Prayer Book and an insult," Rev. Morris noted after the trustees' decision. "Having been spanked, they indicate that business will be as usual." Although his response might have been expected, others not involved in the dispute were just as incensed. Ralph McGill, perhaps the most prominent lay member of the cathedral congregation, stunned them by leaving in protest. "I must confess a bitter disappointment in the Cathedral leadership in regard to the Lovett School opportunity," he wrote Dean Hardman. "The Cathedral means much to me, but, Dean, I honestly don't believe I can sit there and listen to sermons about Christian responsibility . . . without a feeling of being very, very uncomfortable knowing these principles have been meaningless in the one test that has come." Too often, he noted in a second letter, the cathedral spoke one way and acted in another. "I know that there is the window-dressing of admitting any colored persons who appear at the sanctuary," he offered as an example, "but I also noted that the last two times I was present, a colored person or so was at a distance, and the invitation to the coffee hour carefully was omitted from the announcements." Convinced the cathedral had been engaged in "a lot of cheap hypocrisy," McGill refused to return.[32]

As the summer wore on, the situation only became more combative. The Episcopal Society for Cultural and Racial Unity (ESCRU), a liberal religious organization founded by Rev. Morris, formally entered the fray in July 1963. Protesting "the enormity of the Trustees' action," several ministers and lay members from ESCRU began a long campaign of protests and pickets around Lovett that September. Although the sight of

priests picketing their own church's institutions presented a public relations nightmare, the Episcopal Diocese's problems were only beginning.
In late September, the church's monthly magazine, *Diocese*, conducted an
interview with Ralph McGill. In the course of their conversation, Rev.
Alfred Hatch asked McGill if he thought Lovett were still "Episcopally
affiliated." "Oh, it certainly is—inescapably so," he replied. "I think the
Cathedral leadership has acted with hypocrisy, and I think that this is too
bad." When Canon Milton Wood, editor of *Diocese*, learned of McGill's
comments, he rushed to the diocesan print shop. Finding that press run
finished, Wood ordered all thirteen thousand copies of the magazine immediately destroyed. Instead, he printed new versions with McGill's comments deleted. The professional press still picked up on the story and,
within weeks, news of Canon Wood's censorship appeared in the *New
York Times* and *Time*. (Other local news outlets followed the story, but
refused to report it. As a *Newsweek* stringer put it, "I dare not, in effect,
call the Bishop a liar until I have really checked and re-checked. Hell, he's
my Bishop.") Ironically, in trying to keep McGill's criticism from reaching
thirteen thousand local readers, the diocese inadvertently spread it to millions more worldwide.[33]

Despite the intense pressure on the diocese, Lovett's trustees refused to
desegregate. As they knew, many of the leading members of the church
not only supported their stand but insisted upon it. "We commend the
trustees of Lovett School for frustrating the effort of agitator Martin Luther King to niggerize our very excellent institution," ranted a segregationist member of St. Philip's congregation. "When a trustee would risk
destroying the school to carry out his perverted ideas on race," he urged,
"his resignation should be accepted promptly." But church leaders had to
contend with more than just crude political posturing; they also understood the considerable financial pressure that was brought to bear on
them. For instance, Philip Alston, a wealthy lawyer and a senior warden
at St. Luke's parish, had raised more than $350,000 for Lovett's building
campaign—including one gift of $100,000 which had been made on the
explicit condition that the school remain closed to black children.[34]

With such incentives to stay segregated, Lovett did so for several years.
And with equal determination, ESCRU maintained its protests against
Lovett. Each year, they picketed the baccalaureate services held at the
Cathedral of St. Philip. Instead of slowly fading away, their protests became more intense over time. In 1966 two clergymen fasted on the cathedral's lawns for a week before the ceremony. Their protest attracted a
good deal of national attention and, fittingly, a personal appearance by
Rev. Martin Luther King Jr., whose son's application had sparked the
controversy years before. "It is quite interesting, I think, to mention that
the public schools have had some form of integration for the last four

years in Atlanta, and yet we find a church-related school still holding out and refusing to integrate," Dr. King noted. "This is another example of the fact that the Church can be, if it is not careful, the tail-light instead of the headlight in our society; and it would be tragic, indeed, if the Church turns out to be the last bulwark of segregated power."[35]

Indeed, throughout Atlanta and much of the segregated South, religious schools did serve as the one of the last refuges for racism. Despite their past support of public desegregation, many religious leaders and educators argued that their church-affiliated schools were private organizations, with a right to accept or exclude individuals, or entire races, as they saw fit. This continued resistance made them, of course, no better or worse than the private "segregation academies" that sprang up elsewhere or the public school systems, which only desegregated under court orders. All offered resistance, on separate—if parallel—tracks. The public schools and segregation academies worked together in disguising public resistance with a "private" face. But older private schools, such as Lovett, were genuinely "private" all along. In this regard, the churches and their schools simply represented one aspect of a larger trend, the privatization of segregation. The retreat to and defense of private schools and private churches was, in essence, another aspect of the larger retreat of elite whites into private communities, private clubs, and private businesses.

In truth, white southerners of all classes hoped for a privatized, racially selective world. But only upper-class whites had the financial wherewithal to exercise those "rights." Originally, they supported public desegregation and then retreated into their private world, secure in the knowledge that desegregation would never touch them. Meanwhile, once again, working-class and now middle-class whites were left behind, just as unwilling as elite whites to take part in an increasingly integrated public society, but unable to create their own private segregated society. In the end, they too retreated, although not as comfortably or callously as the upper classes had before them.

To the surprise of the white elite, however, desegregation ultimately did spread from the public sphere into their private realm. Throughout the 1960s, as the civil rights movement began to target private restaurants and businesses, upper-class moderates who had hoped to hide in their isolated world were forced to confront the contradiction between their long support of public integration and their defense of private segregation. All of these arenas were private spaces that whites assumed could be defined, and defended, as precisely that—private. Leaders of the civil rights movement, however, understood this private world as a simple extension of the public one and challenged segregation there just as strongly as they did it in the other. As the civil rights movement turned its attention from segregated schools to segregated lunch counters, restaurants, hotels, and department stores, this fundamental difference of opinion—over the dividing line between what was "private" and what was "public"—would widen considerably. And as black activists and white businessmen found themselves on opposite sides of the racial debate for the first time in over a decade, the coalition that held Atlanta together would be placed in dire jeopardy.

CHAPTER SEVEN

Collapse of the Coalition:
Sit-Ins and the Business Rebellion

ATLANTANS OPENED their morning papers on March 9, 1960, to find an advertisement that would change the tone of the city's race relations and set the agenda for a decade of civil rights protests. "An Appeal for Human Rights," a full-page ad signed by student leaders from all six colleges of the Atlanta University Center, sounded a stirring manifesto for a new generation of black activists. "We do not intend to wait placidly for those rights which are already legally and morally ours to be meted out to us one at a time," the students announced. "We want to state clearly and unequivocally that we cannot tolerate, in a nation professing democracy and among people professing Christianity, the discriminatory conditions under which the Negro is living today in Atlanta, Georgia—supposedly one of the most progressive cities in the South." The call-to-arms continued, listing with exact detail the inequalities faced by blacks in education, employment, housing, voting, hospitals, restaurants, movies, and law enforcement. "We must say in all candor," the students concluded, "that we plan to use every legal and non-violent means at our disposal to secure full citizenship rights as members of this great Democracy of ours."[1]

The publication of the "Appeal" represented a watershed in the course of race relations in Atlanta and, indeed, the nation. Just a month earlier, another group of black college students staged what they called a "sitdown protest" at segregated lunch counters in Greensboro, North Carolina. Although similar protests had been tried before, the Greensboro campaign caught fire in a way that nothing else had. Within days, the protests—now known as "sit-ins"—spread throughout the state and then across the South. That the sit-ins arrived in Atlanta surprised few; that they were announced with such insistence and intelligence certainly did. "It caused a firestorm," activist Julian Bond later recalled. "You can't imagine. Because these people here were not used to young people, students, saying these kind of things—and, particularly, not saying them well—and saying them with data, facts, figures." The students quickly followed their words with deeds. Within days, they held their first protests. Within a week, they formed a new organization, the Committee on Appeal for Human Rights (COAHR), to press their demands. And within another month, they joined forces with other sit-in leaders to form the

Student Non-Violent Coordinating Committee (SNCC), the organization that would stand at the vanguard of civil rights activism in the 1960s and house its headquarters in Atlanta.[2]

The city was stunned by the "Appeal" and the civil rights revolution it heralded. Atlanta was then still adjusting to the widespread desegregation of neighborhoods and public places of the late 1950s, and deeply embroiled in the debate over desegregation of public schools. Tensions in the city only increased with the news that Martin Luther King Jr. would soon return to Atlanta, his hometown, and base the Southern Christian Leadership Conference (SCLC) there as well. Even moderates reacted with trepidation. "I must say," remarked Ralph McGill, "I feel like a citizen of a medieval walled city who has just gotten word that the plague is coming." In this climate, the "Appeal" struck a nerve with the city's segregationists. From the capitol, for instance, Governor Vandiver dismissed it as a "left-wing statement . . . calculated to breed dissatisfaction, discontent, discord and evil." It carried "the same overtones," he noted suspiciously, "which are usually found in anti-American propaganda pieces."[3]

While the segregationist reaction was expected, the true impact of the "Appeal" was felt within the moderate coalition. In a telling sign of things to come, Atlanta's moderates found the pace of race relations, which they had controlled for a decade, suddenly slipping from their control. When the *Constitution* first received the ad copy, for instance, Ralph McGill's staff was stunned. A nervous advertising executive called editor Eugene Patterson to examine the text. "Gene, you better come in here," he said. "I'm in something way over my head." Patterson, too, was shocked by the militant tone. "I thought this was communism," he later recalled. Still, he felt obligated to print the piece, to show that Atlanta had an open mind. Likewise, Mayor Hartsfield found himself balancing his private concerns with a public image of calm. The declaration performed a "constructive service," he announced. "It must be admitted that some of the things expressed are, after all, the legitimate aspirations of young people throughout the nation and the entire world." Privately, however, the mayor had serious reservations. "I went out and tried to talk them out of it," he later admitted. "I was afraid that any demonstrations would incite counter demonstrations, would bring out the Ku Klux and that sort of thing."[4]

Hartsfield and his allies reacted with such unease because they feared the sit-ins would upset not simply the public order but the political order, too. As they understood, the sit-ins could easily destroy the moderate coalition of blacks and businessmen that had kept them in power for so long. The merchants that the students would target were, after all, the mayor's strongest political allies. Therefore, Hartsfield and members of his coalition, such as black college presidents and white ministers, tried to dissuade the students from initiating sit-ins. Citing the business community's long record of involvement in negotiated racial settlements and good-faith agreements toward token desegregation, the mayor asked the students to meet the merchants and talk things out. The COAHR leaders agreed, hoping the businessmen might welcome the chance to change. They didn't. After listening in stony silence to the students' presentation, the businessmen attacked them angrily. Their demands "smacked of communism," one man charged. Another spoke for his colleagues by stating flatly that they were "not even thinking about thinking about doing away with segregation!"[5]

Thus, in fundamental ways, the sit-ins threatened to tear the moderate coalition apart. Together, blacks and businessmen had maintained peace and progress in Atlanta since the end of World War II, but suddenly the two groups found themselves directly at odds. On one side of the sit-ins stood a new generation of black activists. The students pressed an aggressive civil rights agenda that alienated not just white moderates but the elder generation of black leaders as well. For decades, the old guard had worked with white leaders at a slow but steady pace, which guaranteed a gradual course of desegregation, as well as positions of prominence for themselves. In contrast, the student activists proved to be much more militant than their elders in every way. Instead of negotiations, they issued ultimatums; instead of compromise, they sought confrontation. Most important, instead of helping to promote Atlanta's positive image, the students shrewdly sought to use that image—and its contrast with reality—to achieve their ends. Faced with these fundamental differences of tone and tempo, the old guard came to feel that the students threatened not only their past accomplishments but their present positions as leaders of the black community. Not surprisingly, a significant gap grew between the generations. And as the sit-ins expanded, it soon became clear that Atlanta's black community—long understood by all sides as a monolithic "Negro bloc"—was, in truth, several communities with contrasting experiences and expectations.

On the other side of the sit-ins stood the city's leading businessmen. Before the protests struck Atlanta, these men had, to one degree or another, gone along with a cautious and limited course of desegregation. Their political allies in the Hartsfield coalition had convinced them that such changes were in the city's interest and, therefore, their own. But the sit-ins undercut such arguments, as merchants who once accepted the idea that racial progressivism and economic progress went hand-in-hand instead came to believe that the civil rights movement might cost them on several fronts. For one, the sit-ins threatened their public prestige. Under the auspices of the moderate coalition, these businessmen had adopted a paternalistic attitude that simultaneously stressed their own contributions to the "betterment" of black Atlanta and sharply contrasted their own stance with that of strident segregationists. To their shock, the student activists challenged both claims, arguing that the business community's past accomplishments were insignificant and that their current discriminatory policies made them no better than the more rabid racists. While such arguments made merchants uncomfortable, the practical costs of the protests alarmed them even more. The sit-ins distracted their employees, scared away their customers, created bad publicity, and, in general, choked off their profits. On a more fundamental level, these businessmen took offense at the ways in which the sit-ins challenged key assumptions of their world—the supremacy of the free enterprise system, the right to private property, and the identity and autonomy that they, as businessmen, had under both. In the eyes of the business elite, the sit-ins threatened not only their stature but their very way of life.

As the moderates' coalition weakened from within, its enemies chipped away at it from outside. In earlier phases of the civil rights struggle, segregationists had made strong appeals to middle-class whites who felt threatened by the course of desegregation, only to find their arguments thwarted by similar appeals from the other side. During the struggles over residential segregation, for instance, homeowners' organizations had sought to rally whites in defense of their "community" to keep black buyers out. But civil rights activists countered by asserting that an even more fundamental middle-class value, the right to private property, trumped those concerns. And as the courts agreed that the power over one's surroundings was less important than the power over one's belongings—in this instance, the ability to sell a home to whomever one wanted—residential desegregation gained considerable traction. With the sit-ins, however, this earlier logic was upended. Now, businessmen were told that they could no longer do as they pleased with the establishments they owned and operated. The power over one's belongings—here, the power to do business with whomever one wanted—now had to yield to the expectations of their surroundings. Segregationists had always presented whites as the "victims" of the civil rights movement, but with the advent of the sit-ins, they could make their strongest case yet.

Over the course of the 1960s, as student activists became ever more strident and white businessmen responded in kind, the political coalition that had once held them together seemed dangerously close to falling apart. Black Atlanta became embroiled in a generational conflict that threatened to push the two sides ever farther apart. Meanwhile, the white business elite found itself increasingly at odds with its longtime political allies, and increasingly tempted to join forces with the segregationists it had helped suppress for the better part of two decades. The sit-ins thus represented more than a simple escalation of the civil rights movement.

They represented a political crossroads, a chance for the dissolution of old alliances and the creation of new ones, an opportunity to reassess past politics and consider new paths for the future.

THE SPLINTERING OF THE MODERATES

As the student leaders planned to stage sit-ins in the spring of 1960, they searched for the perfect venue. At first, the activists singled out the eating establishments at public places, such as city hall, the state capitol, and the Fulton County courthouse. "We decided, because of the question of the legality of sit-ins, that we would put ourselves on absolutely safe ground," Julian Bond remembered, "and only go to public places, government-owned places." Then, the activists targeted the A&P Groceries, to dramatize the economic plight of black Atlantans who, while allowed to shop at such stores, were only hired for the lowest-paying positions. Neither target resonated with the students, however, since public buildings seemed too timid a target and the equal employment issue too complicated a cause. So they decided to focus on the city's downtown department stores, where protests would be highly visible and the problem easily understood by all sides. Once the students made their decision, they quickly came to focus their energies on a single, and singularly important, company— Rich's Department Store. The largest chain in the South, Rich's was locally owned as well. As such, it occupied a leading position in the power structure of the city and, therefore, the students' planning. "I decided that we ought to employ a kind of domestic domino theory," student leader Lonnie King later recalled. "We would take on Rich's department store as being the kingpin, and if we can topple Rich's, all we have to do is just kind of whisper to the others." "Rich's was the gem," Julian Bond agreed. "Rich's was the pinnacle." If it desegregated, the other retail stores in town—Davison's, Woolworth's, McCrory's, Kresge's, Kress's, W. T. Grant, Sears-Roebuck—would invariably follow suit.[6]

As the students prepared to target Rich's, they understood they would be on their own. After decades of successful negotiations and "gentlemen's agreements" with their white counterparts, much of the black establishment balked at the thought of sit-ins and street protests. Even Martin Luther King Jr. understood that his father's generation would discourage such tactics in "their" town. ("They didn't have to say it to him," Andrew Young remembered. "He knew it.") But they did say it to the college students. The old guard saw them as outsiders to the community—too young to understand how things had "worked" in the past, too transient to have a stake in how things would stand in the future. When the sit-ins began, the black establishment did all it could to slow them down. For instance, C. A. Scott, the *Atlanta Daily World* publisher who represented the public voice of the old guard, refused to aid the students in any way. When they approached him with their "Appeal," he grudgingly agreed to print it, but demanded they pay the full advertising rate. From then on, Scott issued a steady stream of editorials that discouraged further protests and urged the students to let the older generation handle things. When they returned with a second advertisement, Scott refused to run it.[7]

While the older generation balked at protests in general, it particularly opposed any such protest against Rich's. The store had "deep roots in the community," the old guard lectured the students in an April meeting. It had been the first to offer credit to black customers and the first to make salespeople use the titles "Mr." and "Mrs." when addressing black buyers. Although the students refused to heed the adults' advice, they understood Rich's popularity. "We knew that a Rich's charge plate in the black community was like running water," Lonnie King recalled. "There was one in everybody's house, and people didn't want to get rid of it." Hoping to convince black Atlantans to do exactly that, the students launched a massive campaign for a fall boycott. They printed up a publication, "The Student Movement and You," and distributed thousands of copies in churches every Sunday. "You know, we just showed 'em all parallels," King later remembered. "We asked, 'How is it you have to drink "colored" water if you going to spend that kind of money?' " They called upon blacks to "close out your charge account with segregation" and "open up your account with freedom" instead.[8]

Although black Atlantans had long patronized Rich's, they were certainly aware of the store's strict policy of segregation. Black customers were not allowed to try on clothing prior to purchase; the store held that whites would never buy items worn by blacks, however briefly. More galling were the restaurant and restroom facilities set aside for blacks' use in the subbasement. Notoriously filthy, they were avoided at all costs. "Quite frankly, unless an emergency arises, we do not use the rest room or eating facilities," read a typical complaint, "because we feel that for reasons of comfort, sanitation, and self-respect, the token facilities which you provide for us do not reflect the spirit of 'welcome' accorded us in other areas." Having received "a number of complaints" in the late 1950s, owner Dick Rich admitted that "our rest room facilities for Negroes are not up to the standard we would like." His store soon began construction of new restrooms for blacks on another floor. He refused, however, to move or improve the restaurant.[9]

If any one man embodied the plight of Atlanta's moderate business leaders in the sit-in struggle, it was certainly Dick Rich. As the sit-ins first appeared in Atlanta, Rich remained convinced that such protests would never surface at his store, given his own track record in amicable race relations. "The Negro problem has not been a difficult one here at Rich's," he confided to a white customer in April 1960. "We cater primarily to the better class of Negro customer, and we have not run into any problems whatsoever in servicing them in the past and do not anticipate any in the future." But as rumors spread that his store would become a main target of the sit-ins, Rich found himself caught in a controversy he desperately wanted to avoid. A practical businessman at heart, he wanted nothing to do with social change or political matters. As his friend Morris Abram remembered, "He just wanted to sell shoes, furniture, and perfume." Rich tried to maintain his distance, arguing that segregation was a public policy and, as such, should be first addressed in the public sphere, through school desegregation. Private business, he fumed, should not be made the "bellwether of change." Moreover, Dick Rich resented the students' decision to focus on his store. "He felt that they weren't doing anything that other people weren't doing," another contemporary recalled, "and 'why put the finger on us!' "[10]

In spite of his best effort to remain above the fray, Dick Rich soon found his company embroiled in a controversy of national stature, with no easy way out. As bad as a boycott would be for business, the alternative seemed no better. "He was in terror that his company would be charged with caving in to black pressure, a public relations gaffe that could cost him millions of dollars," Abram recalled. "Moreover, what would happen if black crusaders should then target en masse on Rich's to really integrate its segregated dining and rest room facilities, while his competitors had a free ride?" In spite of the pressure, Rich and his associates decided to hold their ground. "I was on the board of directors at Rich's then," Ivan Allen Jr. recalled years later. "We began discussing the students' demands, going so far as to determine the exact volume of Negro business, which wasn't much in dollar value, and giving consideration to making Rich's an all-white store." Confident that they had a "good relationship" with blacks, the store's leaders were sure that any protest would be minimal and ineffective. They decided to risk a boycott.[11]

To the astonishment of both these businessmen and the old guard of black leaders, the student boycott worked. "Nobody could believe that you could get the Negroes who were trading and had accounts at Rich's— Nobody hardly believed you could stop them," recalled Atlanta University president Benjamin Mays. But the fall campaign against Rich's caught fire. Soon the older generation was backing the protests it had first fought. In a telling sign of the changing climate, John Wesley Dobbs, the embodiment of the black establishment, returned his charge plates to Rich's with an angry explanation. "I find that my Conscience and Self-Respect will no longer allow me to support a business that shows so much unfairness to its Colored Patrons," Dobbs wrote in September 1960. "Your policy of 'JIM-CROW' treatment to your Colored Patrons is positively WRONG, and UNFAIR. You are caught on the wrong side of a MORAL ISSUE." Recognizing the significance of Dobbs's challenge, Rich's general manager, Frank Neely, penned a personal reply, trying to distance the store's segregated facilities from the stigma of racism. "While it has not been the custom through the years of your married life for white and colored to dine together, accepting such social differences, we long ago provided a restaurant and rest rooms for our colored patrons equipped as those of the white customers, and food cooked in the same kitchens," Neely argued. "So far as we are aware, we have tolerated no so-called 'Jim Crow' or unfair practices to race and color." Not surprisingly, such arguments fell flat in the black community. Indeed, as Mays remembered, so many black leaders followed Dobbs's example and closed their accounts that "Negroes were scared to be seen in Rich's."[12]

As the boycott gained strength, members of the moderate coalition again tried to slow the students down. In keeping with the coalition's penchant for informal talks, Chief Jenkins asked student leaders to stop by the police department, where they found Dick Rich waiting for them. Rich tried to strike a common bond with the students, explaining that, as a fellow minority, as a Jew, he sympathized with their plight. Still, he warned that sit-ins would be dangerous. If the students would wait until schools desegregated the following year, Rich promised, he would then get downtown merchants to desegregate their stores. The students refused to wait. They dismissed his proposal as "a lot of Uncle Tom business" and promised to continue their campaign. Rich refused to back down either. As Lonnie King remembered, "Dick Rich said to me that 'We didn't arrest you today, but if you come back down to my department store again, I'm going to put you in jail.' And I said, 'Well, Mr. Rich, we are coming back, so you may as well put us in jail right now.' " Unable to dissuade the students, Dick Rich snapped that he could get along without black customers. He would never yield to intimidation. After that, whenever longtime friends prodded him to negotiate with the students, Rich would only give a curt reply: "We don't do anything under pressure."[13]

As Lonnie King promised, roughly seventy-five students protested at segregated lunch counters on October 19, 1960. Though sit-ins took place at eight downtown department stores, Rich's remained the main target. At exactly eleven o'clock, protesters tried to gain access to all of its white eating establishments. In the subbasement, three protesters tried to get seats in the Barbecue Room. A white woman pushed one black girl aside roughly; another patron flashed a Ku Klux Klan card. All three students were arrested. Meanwhile, one floor up, two more protesters fared no better at the Cockerel Grill. "I feel that if you invite me in to use my Charga-plate elsewhere in the store," one protester insisted, "you ought to invite me to use my Charga-plate in here." The employee held his ground, as bystanders offered suggestions. "I know what to do with uppity niggers," spat one. After a half-hour standoff, the two students were led away by police. The real showdown, however, unfolded upstairs. Ten protesters, including Lonnie King and the Reverend Martin Luther King Jr., appeared at a lunch counter on the covered bridge between the two halves of the Rich's complex. Taking sandwiches and drinks in hand, they asked either to be served "or be arrested." Waitresses simply cleared the tables and vanished. Undaunted, the activists moved on to another target, the posh Magnolia Room on the sixth floor. Minutes after taking their places in line, they found themselves surrounded by the store's plainclothes detectives and Frank Neely. Holding a list of "Atlanta Mixing Organizations," the Rich's executive demanded to know if they belonged to any of them. To his outrage, the students refused to give direct answers. "I am here representing myself," said one. When policemen asked if Neely wanted the protesters arrested, he gave his approval. Six were taken away, down the elevator, out the front doors, through a picket line, and into waiting police cruisers. In the Magnolia Room, Dick Rich sat down and wept. To his dismay and the students' delight, the sit-ins had finally secured a dramatic demonstration of blacks' plight—the arrest of Martin Luther King Jr.[14]

King's arrest intensified the pressure on Dick Rich and increased the national interest in the Atlanta sit-ins. "I don't feel that I did anything wrong in going to Rich's and seeking to be served," King explained at his arraignment. "We went peacefully, non-violently, and in a deep spirit of love." Like many of the students, he refused to post bail and promised instead to "sit in jail ten years if necessary." Meanwhile, the students kept protesting, submitting to arrest or at least causing panicky managers to lock up their restaurants. Each day, the sit-ins spread. On the first day, eight stores had been targeted; on the second, eleven; on the third, sixteen. From the Fulton County Jail, Lonnie King announced that students would demonstrate "all day, every day" if needed. Meanwhile, segregationists started their own counterprotests. At Woolworth's, a white man marched along the counters with a crude sign pinned to his lapel: "LONG LIVE Jim Crow." Later, another young man swaggered up and down the aisle, spraying black students with room deodorant. Most ominously, the Ku Klux Klan called on white organizations to fight back and urged the governor to mobilize the National Guard to protect whites against the "advancing Negro race."[15]

With protests and counterprotests threatening to spin out of control, Mayor Hartsfield stepped forward to negotiate a truce, in the Atlanta tradition. On October 22, he convened a meeting of sixty leaders from all walks of the black community—students, college presidents, ministers, businessmen, and political leaders. After hours of intense negotiations, Hartsfield agreed to pardon those in the city jail and lobby for the release of those in the county's custody, such as Lonnie King and Martin Luther King Jr. In addition, the mayor promised to pressure the downtown merchants to desegregate their lunch counters. For his efforts to be successful, Hartsfield said, the demonstrations would have to stop. "I can't negotiate at gunpoint," he told the students. Reluctantly, they agreed to halt protests for thirty days. Elder blacks were elated by the meeting's end. Rev. William Holmes Borders, for one, called the Saturday summit "the best meeting we've ever held in the City of Atlanta."[16]

Unknown to those present that day, however, larger political forces were also at work. During a break from his meeting with black leaders, Mayor Hartsfield heard that Harris Wofford, an aide on Senator John F. Kennedy's presidential campaign, had inquired about the negotiations. Suddenly, Hartsfield had an idea. He would announce that Kennedy himself had asked him to engineer the release of Martin Luther King Jr. and the others. With Kennedy's name behind it, the negotiated settlement could overcome the objections of both black militants and white businessmen, and thereby heal the rift in his coalition. Hartsfield tried to push the plan, but he was unable to overcome the strong objections of Wofford, who feared the scheme might kill Senator Kennedy's chances in the South. He was also unable to contact the candidate, then on a whirlwind tour of Kansas. Ever the maverick, Hartsfield decided to make the announcement anyway. "Now, I know I ran with the ball farther than you expected, Harris, my boy," he told an enraged Wofford, "but I needed a peg to swing on and you gave it to me, and I've swung it."

Hartsfield's maneuverings stunned the Kennedy campaign, but his feint had the desired effect in Atlanta. With the apparent support of a popular presidential candidate, the mayor arranged for the release of protesters in both the city and county jails. There was one problem, however. Martin Luther King Jr. remained in custody. From neighboring DeKalb County, Judge Oscar Mitchell had issued a warrant denying King's release on the grounds that his role in the Rich's sit-in violated the conditions of an earlier suspended sentence. In one day, King found himself transferred to the DeKalb County Jail, brought before Judge Mitchell, stripped of his probation, sentenced to four months' hard labor, and transferred once again to the maximum-security prison in Reidsville. The events sparked a political firestorm, ending only with Kennedy's courtesy call to Coretta King and her husband's subsequent release on bond. By the time the tumult subsided, Kennedy had won the presidency, due in part to a sudden surge of black support nationwide. In Atlanta, a number of locals, ranging from Bill Hartsfield to Martin Luther King Sr. to the students, all took credit for freeing King and electing Kennedy. In fact, so many claimed responsibility that Thurgood Marshall teased King's attorney: "They tell me everybody got King out of jail but the lawyers."[17]

As exciting as the King and Kennedy controversy had been, Hartsfield realized there was still real work to be done in the sit-ins. With time running out on the truce period, Hartsfield spent November trying to bring businessmen to the bargaining table. While he had success in convincing smaller merchants of the need to negotiate, the mayor was unable to get a Rich's representative to a single meeting. As a member of its management later reflected, "We just weren't prepared to involve our store in politics." Rich's refusal to take part scuttled Hartsfield's hopes for a quick conclusion to the sit-ins. "I am having a hard time getting the merchants together on the subject of lunch counter service," he confided. "Of course, the key to the situation is Rich's. The other merchants are determined not to be used ahead of them." Meanwhile, the mayor noted, "the Negro group is becoming more restive and more impatient as I fail to give them any indication of settlement." As white businessmen and black students pulled in opposite directions, Hartsfield feared they would tear his coalition apart.[18]

Indeed, with Rich's refusing to participate, negotiations proved worthless. By the end of November 1960, with the thirty-day truce over, students resumed where they had left off, returning to old targets and starting protests at new sites as well. As the sit-ins stretched into a second week, owners and operators of the targeted stores prepared for what the *Atlanta Journal* grimly predicted would be a "long sit-in siege." Several variety chains made plans to keep their lunch counters closed indefinitely. As the manager at Newberry's put it, "it doesn't look like a break is in sight." Larger department stores were digging in their heels as well. Rich's management entered a state of denial, refusing to address the sit-ins raging around their store and hoping the problem would simply go away. When a black leader proposed a citizens' committee on the sit-ins, Dick Rich dismissed all such meetings as "fruitless." When a white activist offered to mediate new discussions between the store and the students, Rich scrawled across the letter: "I think we should ignore this." Throughout his store, workmen boarded up the lunch counters and installed vending machines instead. Restaurant workers were let go, with no assurances of being rehired. Even the Magnolia Room closed. Yet again, white Atlantans made it clear that, when faced with the "threat" of desegregation, they would abandon a public space, no matter how prized, rather than see it integrated.[19]

As civil rights groups pressured Rich's to drop its racial restrictions, white groups likewise lobbied the store to stand by segregation. "WE MUST SUPPORT merchants who continue to operate their food facilities and rest room facilities on a segregated basis," exhorted one group of segregationists. "Encourage your merchant for his persistence to the lawless 'sit-ins.' " In this regard, Rich's was singled out for praise. "I want to congratulate Frank Neely and Dick Rich," declared Roy Harris. "If it hadn't been for those two gentlemen, your lunch counters would now be integrated. I hope you'll at least go down and buy a pair of socks or a tie for somebody for Christmas and let them know you appreciate it." Meanwhile, segregationists pressured whites to stay away from businesses that "surrendered" to student protesters. Petitions made the rounds in Atlanta, with signers promising, "We do not intend to trade with any store which maintains integrated eating facilities or integrated rest rooms." Within two weeks, the campaign had secured more than eight thousand signatures. "We are continuing to receive many requests for petitions in addition to the several hundred already circulating greater Atlanta," the petitions organizer told Rich's treasurer, "with the number of supporters increasing daily."[20]

Trapped between black boycotts and white counterboycotts, Rich's management must have thought things couldn't possibly get any worse. To their dismay, the Ku Klux Klan proved them wrong. When the sit-ins started, the hooded order—now known as "the U.S. Klans"—rushed to Rich's aid. In late October 1960, just prior to the truce, Klansmen established their own picket line around the embattled store. "We Will Not Accept Race-Mixing in Georgia," one sign warned. When the sit-ins resumed, Klansmen grew bolder. They returned to Rich's in late November, this time walking a double-file line in full regalia—the rank and file in white, their leaders in crimson satin. For several days they marched around the department store, holding sway over the sidewalks. "The men members of the Klan paraded the streets of Atlanta so that women folks and children would know they could walk safely on the streets if, and when, Hartsfield's and King's army decide to take over Atlanta," a Klan newspaper thundered. "THERE WILL BE PROTECTION IN ATLANTA should a crisis arise!" On a few tense afternoons, Klan pickets and student protestors mingled on the same sidewalks. Hoping to lighten an increasingly tense mood, Mayor Hartsfield joked that it was simply another sign of Atlanta's progress. "With the help of the Ku Klux Klan, it can be the first to claim integrated picketing," he noted playfully. "At least we are handling our problems in a progressive way."[21]

With pressure now coming from both sides of the civil rights struggle, Rich's management and its allies in the business community began to buckle. Too many customers, they complained, had been scared away by the countless boycotts and counterboycotts. The Christmas shopping season had been a bust, and students were now talking of a wider campaign for Easter. In February 1961 Ivan Allen Jr., then head of the Chamber of Commerce, and Robert Troutman Sr., legal counsel for Rich's, offered to meet with black leaders on behalf of the merchants. "The joint opinion of these businessmen was clear: they were in a hell of a pickle," Allen later recalled. "They were being criticized from all directions, and they didn't care to go on much longer like that." Without dissent, they authorized him to work out a solution to the sit-ins, even if it meant the end of segregation. And so, for nearly a month, representatives of the business community and black leaders sat in the plush fourteenth-floor boardroom of the downtown Commerce Club, bargaining back and forth. The businessmen first tried to limit the degree of desegregation but soon wore down. "Open the goddamned stores and give it to them, if you need to," Dick Rich told Allen. "But for God's sake do something! I'm so damned tired of this thing. Get me off the hook."[22]

By March, Allen had hammered out a compromise. The merchants agreed to open up their lunch counters, restrooms, restaurants, and changing rooms, but only after the public schools desegregated that fall. The student leaders balked at this catch. "It was clear that if there was trouble with the school desegregation," Lonnie King recalled, "this would fall apart, too." When he asked for permission to bring the proposal before the broader student body, King found himself attacked—not by the businessmen but by the older blacks. "Boy, I'm tired of you!" shouted Martin Luther King Sr. Shaking an angry finger at the stunned student, the minister lectured, "This is the best agreement we can get out of this." Others in the old guard agreed, though in calmer terms. "I've been segregated all of my life," John Calhoun noted. "I don't see where another six months is going to make a difference." Against their better judgment, the students caved in. The stores would remain segregated, but with a commitment to desegregate along with the schools in the fall. Until then, the sit-ins would cease.[23]

Although the growing generational divide in the black community had been apparent at the Commerce Club meetings, it surfaced even more strongly when the agreement was made public. In the eyes of many students, the settlement seemed a significant tactical blunder. (Even Lonnie King recognized it as such. Immediately after signing the truce, he offered to resign as leader of the student movement.) To address the students' growing disgruntlement, the adults convened a mass rally, with more than a thousand students, at Warren Memorial United Methodist Church. There, the generational tensions again boiled over. When Austin Walden took the stage to say that desegregation of the lunch counters was certain, several mocked him from the pews. "You'll have to take my word for it," he added defensively, but that only spread laughter through the crowd. Daddy King then addressed the skeptics. Reminding them of his credentials, he noted that he had been fighting for change in Atlanta for thirty years. At this, a woman shouted, "And that's what's wrong!" The crowd erupted in cheers. Over the next few hours, others from the old guard, such as Rev. William Holmes Borders and Rev. Sam Williams of the NAACP, were likewise dismissed by the students. As the hours wore on, it seemed quite likely that the sit-in agreement would be abandoned. At the end, however, Martin Luther King Jr. took the stage. Stung by the attacks on his father, he denounced the growing "cancer of disunity" in the room. Where the elder King's generation failed, the younger King succeeded, convincing the students to abide by the agreement. "If this contract is broken, it will be a disgrace," he said. "If anyone breaks this contract, let it be the white man."[24]

That fall, Atlanta's lunch counters were desegregated, much as other spaces in the city had been—through a carefully constructed and well-orchestrated plan of token desegregation. According to the settlement, limited numbers of blacks would make the first appearances at specific spots and during selected times. The mayor asked the papers to limit their coverage, in order to keep things quiet, and store managers met with the students ahead of time, to discuss how the day would unfold. (One merchant proposed that only light-skinned blacks be used in the first days, since they would supposedly be less threatening to his white clientele. While the activists generally tried to accommodate the businessmen, they balked at this suggestion.) With these "control programs" planned down to the last detail, the actual desegregation of Atlanta's lunch counters went smoothly. At Rich's, for instance, the agreement called for eight blacks to dine at the Magnolia Room on six consecutive days, but never during the busy luncheon hours. And so, shortly after 2 p.m. on September 28, 1961, four young black women, well-dressed and well-mannered, arrived at the Magnolia Room. They were promptly seated and quietly served. White patrons, a reporter noted, paid little attention, as did whites at other integrated establishments.[25]

Although the races could now dine together in Rich's, and in other department stores in downtown Atlanta, a significant distance remained between the store owners and the student protestors. Indeed, their stand-off reflected a growing gap between the larger communities of black Atlantans and white businessmen. For over a decade, these two groups had worked together to maintain a spirit of progress and progressivism in Atlanta and also keep the white working class at bay. Now, these former allies found their interests diverging and themselves increasingly at odds. As the gap between them grew, the city's segregationists saw an opportunity, at long last, to drive a wedge between them and bring the city's influential businessmen to their side.

The Revolt of the Small Businessmen

Before the advent of the sit-ins, Atlanta's leading businessmen had, to one degree or another, gone along with limited desegregation. Their allies in the moderate coalition had sold them convincingly on the theory that such changes were "good for business." For the most part, the experiences of their southern neighbors and the reactions of national observers seemed to have proved that theory right. But the sit-ins upended that line of thinking, making it clear to the merchants that the civil rights movement could actually hurt their profits and, even worse, limit the power and prerogatives they had long enjoyed as individual businessmen. Major merchants, such as Dick Rich, only realized this dilemma when they faced protests themselves. Smaller businessmen, however, had foreseen the clash for years. Unlike the larger businesses and local corporate branches, they had little connection to the outside world and, thus, little concern with what it thought about race relations in Atlanta. Focused instead on the more immediate concerns of their community and their customers, these businessmen had long warned about the rising "threat" that the civil rights movement presented to many of the ideals they held dear—the right to private property, the system of free enterprise, and the now familiar defense of "freedom of association."

If small businessmen had a champion, it was certainly Lester Maddox. Growing up around the steel mills of central Atlanta, Maddox started scraping for work at a young age. At ten, he regularly walked downtown to buy raw peanuts, hauled them home to roast, and then walked back the next day to sell them on the streets. At twelve, he peddled newspapers. At sixteen, he renovated an old pigeon house to sell soft drinks and penny candy on McMillan Street. His entire life, Maddox wanted to operate his own business. "I had seen men standing in the doorways of their stores and shops, and I had seen the contentment and pride and accomplishment reflected in their faces," he later recalled. "That was what I wanted, to stand in my own doorway, to plant my feet firmly on just one small piece of God's great earth and to know in my heart that this was mine to do with as I saw fit." Maddox realized this dream by starting the Pickrick Restaurant, a cheap cafeteria-style establishment that specialized in skillet-fried chicken and folksy charm. ("Pick," customers learned, meant "to select, to fastidiously eat," while "rick" meant "to pile up or to heap, to amass." "You PICK it out," the slogan promised, "we'll RICK it up.") A self-made man in the truest sense, Maddox built the business himself. "I was my own prime contractor, architect, [and] engineer," he remembered, "and I did a lot of the sawing, nailing and bricklaying as well." With his hard work ethic, Maddox and his restaurant fit their working-class environment well. Students from nearby Georgia Tech and workers at the surrounding steel mills, rail yards, and trucking lines flocked to the Pickrick for its cheap, filling meals.[26]

Although he seemed ill-prepared for the role, Lester Maddox quickly emerged as the most outspoken and effective critic of Atlanta's moderate coalition. His rise to prominence began in 1950, when he began placing ads for the Pickrick in the Saturday newspapers. Full of quaint and funny commentary, the pieces became increasingly political and increasingly popular as the decade wore on. "Most people would get the Saturday paper," remembered one Atlantan, "then go straight to the 'Pickrick Says' ad to see who Lester was lambasting in his column." More often than not, Maddox's attacks centered on the dangers of desegregation, in all its manifestations. Maddox emerged as a strong voice for the status quo, someone who always shifted the desegregation debate to stress the potential "losses" that civil rights changes would bring to whites. He framed the issue of school desegregation, for instance, to stress the inconveniences and injuries white students would suffer. "Shall we keep our schools segregated, our races pure, peace and harmony in our schools and state," he asked in 1958, "or will we give it all up, throw our children to the wolves (politicians) and let those who are most dear to us come face to face with the diseases, crimes and wickedness that has come to all large integrated cities?" Maddox addressed residential change in the same light. "Mixed neighborhoods," he charged in 1960, were "destroying white churches, homes, businesses and white communities. Thousands have been trapped and forced to sacrifice their homes and thousands more are trapped and unable to get anything for their homes."[27]

As hundreds of such examples made clear, Maddox's defense of segregation was always deeply enmeshed in a broader defense of what he regarded as inherent, individual rights. Much like the white middle-class parents who opposed "forced" school desegregation partly because of racism and partly because it threatened their understanding of "freedom of association," Maddox opposed "forced" desegregation in other realms because he was convinced, to his dying day, that such interference from the federal government weakened what he took to be the pillars of American life—the right to private property, the system of free enterprise, and, again, the freedom to associate with whomever one wanted in the private sphere. "If you can't have private property rights and the free enterprise system," he reflected in a 1965 interview, "then none of these other things can be ours that we've enjoyed and appreciated so much in America."[28]

For Maddox, the sit-ins represented the ultimate threat to both segregation and private property. In his mind, the lunch counter protests were more than just the latest assault of "integrationists" on segregated society.

In an important change, he noted, these latest protests targeted private policies, not public ones. Maddox believed, as most white businessmen did, that private property rights gave him the freedom to run his establishment however he saw fit. Regarding racial policies, his own preference was clear. "I am a segregationist," he noted simply, "and I chose to operate my restaurant on a segregated basis." Thus, in the months and years after the students first presented their "Appeal for Human Rights" in the local newspapers, Maddox used those same pages to claim that their movement threatened his own human rights. "Rights of property owners are completely ignored by lousy politicians who care more for votes and power than for their souls and their fellow men," he charged in a typical ad. "Why are 'Civil Rights' more important than human rights, human decency and human respect?"[29]

To defend the right to private property against the "assault" of the sit-ins, Maddox sprang into action and organized Georgians Unwilling to Surrender (GUTS). The name and its initials were an obvious call to arms. Notably, in much of their coverage of the group, the *Atlanta Journal* and *Atlanta Constitution* often referred to it not as "GUTS" but instead by the more innocuous-sounding acronym "GUS." Given the antagonistic relationship between Maddox and the moderates the papers supported, it is likely this stemmed not from a journalistic commitment to grammar but a desire to needle the Pickrick proprietor. For Maddox, however, the new organization's name symbolized everything he believed was threatened by the sit-ins. GUTS members, he recalled decades later, were "unwilling to surrender your right to private property" and "unwilling to surrender your constitutional right to safety and security." Individual rights were jeopardized by "forced integration," Maddox believed. And he refused to give them up without a fight. Throughout the winter of 1960, thousands of white Atlantans joined him in that fight, attending GUTS rallies and funding the cause.[30]

In waging war against the sit-in movement, the segregationists of GUTS urged local businessmen not simply to stay segregated, but to join the fight themselves. In a December 1960 ad, for instance, Maddox directly challenged the city's merchants. "Atlanta businessmen who believe in our system of free enterprise and freedom of choice," he wrote, "should speak up and be heard, before Atlanta is falsely recognized as being controlled by 'so-called' liberals." Just as Bill Hartsfield had once implored the city's businessmen to stand up for the greater interest of the city, Lester Maddox now urged them to stand up for their own self-interest. "What about it, Mr. Businessman? Will you speak out or continue to excuse yourself by saying: 'Being in business, I can't afford to speak out?' Are you a man or a mouse? Will you wait to lose control of, or lose altogether, your business before you have the GUTS to speak out?"[31]

When Rich's and the other downtown department stores "surrendered" to student demands, GUTS and its allies felt bitterly betrayed. "I guess they must prefer a white boycott to a black boycott," Maddox mused. In a similar vein, flyers titled "RACE-MIXERS, INC." spread across the city in April 1961. Listed among the "five-star generals" of the mock organization were not simply Mayor Hartsfield and Ivan Allen Jr. but the reluctant Dick Rich. "If you want complete Racial Integration in Georgia, please do all you can for the listed public officials and merchants," the sheet said with sarcasm. "They are leaders in the integration effort and we should encourage them by giving them all the business we can." Another group, the Committee on Human Rights for White People, urged whites to "FIGHT BLIGHT—BUY RIGHT!" The stores that signed the settlement had made a "shameful capitulation to the black mobs" and should be shunned accordingly. "These firms have shown that they care more for their colored customers than they care for white patronage." A white boycott was the solution. "Hundreds of whites are protesting by closing their accounts NOW and by trading with stores that have not surrendered to the blacks," noted the segregationists. Indeed, the white boycott soon took its toll. In the last week of May 1961 delighted segregationists announced that, according to Federal Reserve figures, downtown revenues had fallen a stunning 14 percent. "Atlanta merchants who had capitulated to a mild boycott of black intruders and had surrendered their last white dining and rest room facilities," they later crowed, "began to realize that they were facing a white boycott that would make the slowdown of the blacks look like child's play."[32]

Empowered by the strong segregationist reaction to the sit-ins, Maddox decided the time was right to run for the mayor's office. He had tried once before, in 1957. In that race, Maddox had entered late and with little experience, leading most observers to assume he would only provide comic relief. "They laughed," he recalled, "said I wouldn't get 2,500 votes." Just to be safe, Hartsfield's aides conducted a poll. To their amazement, they learned that Maddox led the mayor in six of the city's eight wards. "That," Maddox remembered, "was the day they stopped laughing." To counteract his surprising support, the moderate coalition sprang into action. Atlanta's leading businessmen raised an unprecedented $50,000 in just two nights and then Hartsfield went to work. A consummate campaigner, the mayor stressed his proven record of prosperity and peaceful race relations. "You must choose between progress and discord," he told the city on the eve of the election. "Do you want another Little Rock, another Montgomery and Birmingham in Atlanta?" The appeal worked. The old coalition of blacks and upper-class whites once again rallied behind the mayor, giving him a solid 41,300-to-23,987 victory. Despite their success, the moderates saw something alarming in the election returns. No one was surprised that Maddox had run strongly in white working-class precincts, taking in about two-thirds of their votes. But as closer analysis showed, Maddox demonstrated significant support in middle-class and even upper-class areas as well. According to the calculations of historian Numan Bartley, he took in two-thirds of the vote from "middle-income whites," over half of the vote from "semi-affluent whites," and, most surprisingly, a full quarter of the "affluent white" vote that represented the core of the Hartsfield coalition. "I wish I were wrong," a friend informed the mayor, "but I am afraid I am not. Pickrick got a majority of the white vote."[33]

In 1961 Maddox hoped to build on his earlier strong showing and win the office outright. In many ways, his chances looked good. In his first try, Maddox had run on a short timetable and little experience, but this time he would be able to run a stronger, sustained campaign. More important, as he discovered on the day he announced his candidacy, he would not have to face his biggest obstacle. "MAYOR BOWS OUT," blared the *Constitution* in bold block letters. "Hartsfield Calls It Quits after 23 Fateful Years." Throughout that period, the mayor's moderate coalition had dominated Atlanta's political scene. But now, its charismatic head was retiring, just as the component parts of the coalition, white businessmen and black activists, found themselves at odds. In this climate, Maddox suddenly had a realistic chance to win the office. With the popular incumbent out of the way, others saw their chance and rushed to join the campaign, too: Ivan Allen Jr., the head of the Chamber of Commerce and the clear favorite of the white business elite; Charlie Brown, a state senator defeated by Hartsfield in the 1949 and 1953 races; Muggsy Smith, a coalition ally in the statehouse; and Jim Aldredge, a county commissioner. Despite the crowded field, Allen and Maddox focused largely on each other in their campaign appearances and advertisements. As a result, the race effectively became one between them alone.[34]

Because neither Allen nor Maddox had any real political experience, they both drew on their more extensive backgrounds in the business world instead. While both stressed their past in the private sector, their stories could not have been more different. Maddox represented, in the words of one liberal columnist, the "boy who came up [the] hard way," someone of absolutely no means who literally built his business from the ground up and ran its daily operations with considerable pride. "As a businessman," Maddox bragged in one ad, "I started with a capital investment of $4.00 and that investment, as of today, has increased by more than one hundred thousand times." In contrast, Ivan Allen Jr. was a privileged son who had been born into one of Atlanta's wealthiest families and married into another. During the Depression, he attended Georgia Tech, blocks from the future site of the Pickrick, and then took a prominent position in his

Figure 7.1 Ivan Allen Jr. (*left*) and Lester Maddox (*right*). Despite their smiles in the newsroom of the *Atlanta Journal-Constitution* on election night, 1961, these two rivals in the race to replace Bill Hartsfield as mayor were bitter enemies. Maddox took in an overwhelming majority of the white vote, but Allen relied on the old coalition of upper-class whites and the black community to secure victory.

father's firm, the Ivan Allen Company, a leader in the office-supply business. As he rose to become president of both the company and the Chamber of Commerce, Allen found his longtime friends rising to similar positions in the city's power structure. As he later recalled, "We were the presidents of the five major banks, the heads of the Atlanta-headquartered industries like Coca-Cola, the presidents of the three big utilities, the heads of the three or four top retail establishments, the managers of the leading national-firm branches for the Southeast, the man in charge of the city transit system, the heads of local businesses, like the Ivan Allen Company and the Haverty Furniture Company, and the leading realtors." Thus, although the two main candidates were both businessmen, they represented vastly different parts of that world—one the well-connected, corporate executive, the other the small-time, independent operator.[35]

As the embodiment of the business elite, Ivan Allen campaigned on Hartsfield's proven themes of progress and progressivism. "It seemed pretty obvious that I should run on a promise of continued prosperity, emphasizing my background as a business leader and as former president of the Chamber of Commerce," he noted later. "None of [the other candidates] had the personal associations in the higher echelons of the city that I had. None of them had the experience of doing big business, of dealing in terms of millions of dollars." Again, like Hartsfield, Allen linked economic progress to racial progressivism, warning that segregationist resistance could only bring Atlanta the same financial ruin that had struck other cities. In this regard, he could have had no better opponent than an outspoken segregationist like Lester Maddox. "You represent a group which would bring another Little Rock to Atlanta," Allen shouted at their first debate. "You spread hatred and lawlessness, but we will settle it this summer with God's help." At another rally, Allen waved a report on Little Rock's losses, noting that the city had lost a quarter of its population and much of its industry since its upsurge of segregationist resistance. "Little Rock," he pointed out, "hasn't had the job expansion, the opportunity, or the admiration of the rest of America that Atlanta has had."[36]

While Allen argued that integration would help the city's economy as a whole, Maddox instead stressed the losses it would bring to individuals. Because Atlanta's whites had been complaining about the "costs" of desegregation since the start of residential transitions in the late 1940s, this theme resonated well. Integration, Maddox warned in one ad, would damage "religious, residential, educational and business investments" throughout the city. "If you have lost your home, business, church or other investment because of this problem, you know what I mean," he wrote in another campaign ad. "If you haven't been involved, can you afford a $5,000, $10,000, $20,000 or greater loss to your investment?" For a decade, the Hartsfield coalition had been arguing that racial moderation meant financial success, but Maddox attacked such reasoning directly. When Allen repeated the moderate mantra that Little Rock had demonstrated the dangers of segregationist resistance, for instance, Maddox refused to accept his arguments. "Was the Little Rock emigration motivated by the violence, which had already been quelled before anyone moved out," he asked, "or was it the fear of the consequences of compliance with the newly discovered 'law of the land'?" It was *acceptance* of "forced integration" that crippled a city, he charged, not resistance.[37]

As such language suggested, Maddox insisted that businessmen had lost not simply money in their struggles with desegregation but some of their fundamental rights. He followed the lead of the middle-class parents who insisted their right to "freedom of association" had been trampled upon by school integration and argued that the sit-in movement had likewise violated the same rights of businessmen. The "big issue" in the election, Maddox insisted in a campaign ad, "is whether we will return to sensible and constitutional government BY and FOR you, the people, or if we will continue to compromise, surrender, and place ourselves under the control of those who would harm our families, destroy our property values, take our jobs, direct our businesses, tell us where to work, who to hire, where to live and what to think." The real threat, Maddox said, was not integration in and of itself, but "forced integration" imposed by an out-of-control federal government. If "forced segregation" had been proved wrong by the courts, then "forced integration" should have been discredited as well. "If there is a right to integrate, there is a right to segregate," Maddox argued. Individuals had a right, grounded in their "freedom of association," to select their friends, neighbors, and customers. "The freedom of choice of association is a fraud," Maddox insisted in a campaign ad, "unless there is a freedom of choice to NOT associate."[38]

As many expected, Allen and Maddox led the field in the primary election, taking in 38,820 and 20,914 votes respectively, out of more than 100,000 ballots cast. Since neither secured a majority, the two businessmen were forced to face each other in a runoff election. In launching the second phase of his campaign, Maddox exploited the tensions created during the previous year's sit-ins. He reminded his fellow businessmen of Allen's role in the desegregation of department stores, which was still weeks away from becoming a reality. "Mr. Allen made a deal to integrate lunch counters downtown when the schools were desegregated," Maddox announced, "but he and his Negro friends have postponed doing so until after this election." Furthermore, Maddox insisted, Allen next wanted to desegregate "all businesses licensed by the city government." Portraying Allen as an enemy of small businessmen, Maddox's advertisements tore into the supposedly identical "DEMANDS OF THE NAACP and IVAN ALLEN, JR. with respect to integration of the races in restaurants, hotels, and private businesses." Insisting that Allen was now "obligated to surrender all that you have," Maddox claimed the voters' choice was clear. "If you want integration of housing, swimming pools, businesses, public and private facilities . . . and if you want to lose all your investment in Atlanta," his ads suggested, then "vote for Ivan Allen." In contrast, he countered, "LESTER MADDOX BELIEVES that every person who is engaged in private business has a right to choose the customers of his business. The law gives him this right," he insisted. "When I am your Mayor, the police department of the city of Atlanta will protect this right. I will NOT ALLOW sit-in demonstrations to deprive them of this right, whether they are participated in by whites or Negroes."[39]

As Maddox portrayed himself as the defender of whites' individual rights, his campaign reinforced Allen's image as an integrationist. A carload of white and black teens made the rounds of upscale Buckhead, for instance, waving Ivan Allen cards and giving the impression that a vote for Allen was a vote for "race mixing." Anonymous callers peppered real-estate agencies with pointed questions. "Do you rent to Negroes?" they would ask, knowing the answer would be "no." "Well," the callers said, "you just wait until after Friday, if Ivan Allen is elected." Finally, on election eve, the Maddox camp published a photograph showing white and black volunteers socializing at Allen's headquarters after the primary. "This is what Atlanta can expect if IVAN ALLEN, JR. is elected! Are you ready for this in your BUSINESS, SOCIAL, RELIGIOUS, EDUCATIONAL, AND POLITICAL LIFE?" asked the ad. "If you love your FAMILY, CHURCH, HOME, SCHOOL, AND YOUR CITY, VOTE FOR LESTER MADDOX! His stand is the same as yours." In response, Allen stood firm. Instead of dodging the innuendo of Maddox's attack ads, Allen faced them directly. After Maddox published photos of Allen's integrated primary night party, for instance, Allen made a television appearance with his own movies of the celebration. It was true, he said. All Atlantans—black and white—were joining together to support his candidacy and build a better Atlanta. That, Allen insisted, was the real issue of the election. "Let's get on with the business of building a city," he urged. Borrowing the boosterish slogan of Bill Hartsfield, the candidate implored: "We are a city too busy to hate."[40]

For the Allen camp, the talk of progress remained the key theme to sustain the old coalition of blacks and white businessmen. "Mr. Allen will keep us in the mainstream of progress," the *Atlanta Journal* noted in an endorsement. "Mr. Maddox's policies mean stagnation in the brackish backwaters. It is onward and upward with one, backward with the other." For Maddox and his supporters, however, "moving backward" was not necessarily a bad thing. Indeed, Maddox embraced the label, claiming he stood for a return to traditional values of segregation, free enterprise, and law and order. "Will we move BACKWARD TO HONOR, DECENCY, AND GOVERNMENT BY THE PEOPLE in ATLANTA," he asked in a newspaper ad, "or will we move FORWARD to forced racial integration and amalgamation of the races?" Many whites, he knew, equated "progress" with the "losses" brought on by desegregation. Their neighborhoods, golf courses, parks, and buses had already been "taken" from them; public schools and downtown stores were starting to "go colored" as well; and the swimming pools were supposedly next. For many of these whites, the 1961 campaign was a last stand. At one rally, a young man stumping for Allen found himself shouted down by an angry crowd of three hundred Maddox backers. "The white people of Atlanta have their last chance in this election," a Maddox man yelled. "If we don't win, we might as well leave town!"[41]

To the dismay of Maddox's supporters, Allen won the runoff easily. Following Hartsfield's blueprint, Allen polled strongly in upper-class white neighborhoods and in the black community and thus took in 64 percent of the total vote. Bitter in defeat, Maddox blamed the "Negro bloc vote" for his second loss at the polls. The charge held some truth. In ten largely black precincts, for instance, Allen trounced his opponent 17,683 to 95. Though Maddox captured just a third of the total votes, he once again took a commanding majority of white votes. Among working-class whites, he once again polled extremely well, winning roughly two-thirds of their ballots. While this segment of the white population supported him much as it had in 1957, Maddox's totals in middle-class regions rose significantly. As historian Numan Bartley's analysis has demonstrated, Maddox now took in 72 percent of "middle-income white" votes and 63 percent of "semi-affluent white" votes as well. Likewise, to the shock to the moderate coalition, more than a quarter of the white elite—Ivan Allen's friends and neighbors—went for Maddox instead.[42]

Together, the 1960 sit-ins and the 1961 election made it clear that the moderate coalition had cracked into three distinct parts, perhaps irrevocably. For a decade and a half, the moderates had worked together to keep Atlanta on the path to economic progress and racial progressivism, but now each faction eyed the others suspiciously. Student leaders dismissed the old guard as "Uncle Toms" who helped maintain the racial status quo in exchange for a place at the table, and they attacked the white businessmen as hypocrites who gave lip service to their city's greatness but actually did nothing in their own companies to exact racial justice. The elder black leaders, meanwhile, found themselves in the awkward position of trying to sustain the old system of negotiated settlements in the new civil rights climate of confrontation. As a result, they were attacked by the students for dragging their feet and criticized by the business elite for going too fast. And those businessmen, finally, felt deeply betrayed by the combined pressure of two generations of black activists who seemed willing to dismiss decades of "good race relations" and pick fights instead.

In this climate, white businessmen found themselves increasingly attracted to the logic of segregationists. Throughout the reign of the moderate coalition, these forces had steadily expanded their defense of segregation to move from a negative argument founded in starkly racist fears to a more measured rationale predicated on the middle-class entitlements and individual rights that "forced integration" supposedly threatened. In the earlier rounds of the struggle over segregation, such arguments had found ready audiences among working-class and middle-class whites. But in the wake of the sit-ins, they held a much broader appeal, and earlier class divisions within the white community seemed ready to be wiped away. The white elite who usually dismissed segregationists as "rednecks" complaining about nothing now found that they too worried about the personal costs of civil rights change. While the privileges of class had let them escape the course of residential desegregation and school desegregation, such differences did nothing to shield them from the sit-ins. Their fellow whites had reconsidered their politics in the wake of their personal confrontations with the civil rights movement, when residential desegregation struck working-class neighborhoods and when school integration alarmed middle-class parents. Now, as the civil rights movement struck home for them, too, the white elite found itself forced to do the same.

CHAPTER EIGHT

"The Law of the Land": Federal Intervention and the Civil Rights Act

ON JULY 26, 1963, Mayor Ivan Allen Jr. walked into the hearing room of the Senate Commerce Committee, dressed in a dark suit and more than a little nervous. Here, the crowd recognized, was a political curiosity, if not a complete contradiction in terms—a white southern politician coming to urge the federal government to enact the strongest and most significant piece of civil rights legislation in the country's history, what would become the Civil Rights Act of 1964. As Allen began his testimony, one of the spectators, Alistair Cooke, noted that he spoke in "a soft, almost apologetic Southern tone . . . without bombast and without much self-esteem, either." "Atlanta has achieved some success in eliminating discrimination in areas where some cities have failed, but we do not boast of our success," Allen began. "We say with humility that we have achieved our measure of success only because we have looked facts in the face and accepted the Supreme Court's decisions as inevitable and as the law of the land." There had been successes in the struggle over segregation, but it wasn't over. What Atlanta and the rest of the nation needed now, he insisted, was "a clear definition from Congress" on how to uproot racial discrimination. "I have heard dozens of businessmen say that if there had been a court order or definition by Congress, it would have been easier to desegregate," the mayor testified. Congress's failure to act, he said, "would amount to an endorsement of private business setting up an entirely new status of discrimination throughout the Nation. Cities like Atlanta," he warned, "might slip backward."[1]

Predictably, the committee reacted along sectional lines. Senator John Pastore of Rhode Island, the acting chairman and an advocate of civil rights legislation, praised Allen for his "courage." From the other end of the spectrum, Senator Strom Thurmond of South Carolina, a die-hard segregationist, tried to trap the mayor. "I observe from what you say," he noted, "that the progress that has been made in your city, though, in almost all cases, has been by voluntary action." "Yes sir," Allen replied. "Don't you feel," Thurmond continued, "that less tension results when there is voluntary action?" Allen saw the trap. Thurmond was trying to use Atlanta's past successes in civil rights as a reason for *not* passing the legislation. Allen held his ground, insisting that businessmen wanted some direction. Thurmond continued to press the attack, until Pastore stepped in, charging that his colleague was merely seeking to bring "embarrassment to the witness." As Thurmond responded with an angry rebuttal, the chairman used his gavel to drown out the South Carolinian as the galleries cheered. "I can tell you who is in here," Thurmond fumed to the crowd. "It is a bunch of leftwingers who favor this bill, and who are taking your position, and you know it." Years later, Allen reflected on his duel with the Dixiecrat. "We got under his skin pretty bad," he recalled. "I had the audience 100 percent."[2]

The confrontation between Ivan Allen and Strom Thurmond represented a larger struggle between the moderates of the New South and the die-hard segregationists of the Old. A central premise of massive resistance had been the South's insistence that its racial problems could only be settled at the local level and that "federal interference" would only make matters worse. Perhaps more than any other city in the South, Atlanta had real reasons to claim it could solve racial problems locally. From the first stirrings of residential transition through the desegregation of schools and public places, the city had relied on a loose confederation of biracial committees, negotiated settlements, and "gentlemen's agreements" to maintain a measured pace of racial change satisfactory to all sides. To be sure, much of the city's progress had been prompted by outside developments, such as court rulings and civil rights protests. But the tone and tempo of Atlanta's race relations had always been determined by Atlantans themselves. With the advent of the sit-ins, all that changed. The moderate coalition found itself internally divided and externally challenged by the resurgent resistance of segregationists on one front and the increasingly militant demands of civil rights activists on another.

Ultimately, Atlanta's moderates realized the local deadlock could only be resolved at the national level, where the civil rights movement and the federal government were converging to address the central racial problems of the decade. Thus, Atlanta's leaders, long seen by the nation as perfect examples of how localities could solve racial problems on their own, now urged the federal government to take charge. Atlantans consulted with two administrations in the White House, testified before the U.S. Senate, and addressed crowds spread across the National Mall. The end result of their work in Washington, the Civil Rights Act of 1964, would be a crucial breakthrough not simply for Atlanta but the country as a whole. This landmark legislation proved, without question, that active intervention by the federal government was essential for the success of the civil rights movement. Indeed, without its involvement, the racial impasse in Atlanta and countless other communities might never have been solved.

This same federal intervention, however, provoked an equally powerful and equally important reaction in the opposite direction. To no one's surprise, the Civil Rights Act outraged segregationists. But in fundamental ways, countless other whites—in the South and elsewhere—found themselves disturbed not by the act's goals but by the means used to reach them. Whatever these whites may have felt about the significant changes the act enabled in race relations, they were much more troubled by the revolutionary ways in which the new legislation expanded the power of the federal government and constricted the prerogatives of private businessmen. Indeed, in the eyes of many Cold War–era conservatives, the Civil Rights Act seemed to be nothing less than communism, because it undermined capitalism, limited individual decision making, accelerated the growth of the centralized state, and further entrenched the federal bureaucracy. And so, just as liberal and moderate Atlantans had traveled to Washington to support and celebrate the passage of the Civil Rights Act, conservative Atlantans also journeyed there to challenge the legislation before the Supreme Court. In the end, their challenge failed, but the conservative counterrevolution continued to grow.

The Limits of Local Action

In the wake of Atlanta's successes with the desegregation of schools and lunch counters, the National Association for the Advancement of Colored People (NAACP) announced it would hold its annual convention there in July 1962. With nearly two thousand black activists coming to the city, the NAACP hoped to pressure local hotels into desegregating. "If the facilities of the hotels are not made available, we will hold the convention anyway," warned Regional Director Ruby Hurley. "But such action certainly would give Atlanta a black eye." With this in mind, the Atlanta Hotel Association surveyed its members on the prospects for desegregation. "They're all against the idea," a spokesman told reporters in March. "But you know—we're all trying to make Atlanta look good. Most everybody has sort of gone along with the idea that if it was an all-around deal they'd probably go along with whatever is decided." An early straw poll, however, showed members evenly split over the proposal. Problematically, the city's most prominent hotels—the Dinkler Plaza, Henry Grady, Biltmore, and Piedmont—refused to provide any leadership in the matter. As a result, the drive for consensus soon fell apart. "We're in a dilemma over this thing," one hotel operator confided. "It looks like the more we work on it, the further away from a settlement we get."[3]

To be sure, some small signs of progress had already been made in the realm of hotel desegregation. In April 1961 a visit by Secretary of State

Dean Rusk to the Atlanta Bar Association's meeting at the Biltmore Hotel sparked a minor controversy. Shortly before Rusk's visit, several black physicians had been arrested for trying to dine at the hotel restaurant during a medical conference; as a result, civil rights leaders urged the statesman to avoid the hotel. With public pressure rising, the management of the Biltmore and other leading hotels agreed in April 1961 to a compromise. Blacks could attend convention events, they resolved, but with restrictions. "No Negro can have anything to drink but water," the managers agreed; "no Negro can go above the second floor." After this meager beginning, a few smaller hotels relaxed their policies of segregation. The Peachtree Manor, for instance, announced in May 1962 that it would welcome interracial baseball teams from the International League. Likewise, the Atlanta Cabana accepted an occasional black guest. The segregationist backlash was swift. Klansmen distributed a crudely racist cartoon depicting a figure labeled "Martin Luther Coon" addressing a crowd of caricatured blacks. "I's one of de selected nigers to stay at de Atlanta Cobana Motel," stated one. "My brother is staying at de P-Tree Manor Motel," echoed a second. Another hate sheet mocked the motels with a fake contest. "The United Klans of America, Inc., KKKK are seeking the poorest and largest Negro family in Georgia for an expense paid weekend vacation in Atlanta. They will stay in the Atlanta Cabana Motel," the flyer promised. "Do not be afraid! Mayor Allen and the Atlanta Police Department will protect you night and day. He welcomes you, the Motel Manager welcomes you."[4]

Afraid to face an even wider backlash, the Atlanta Hotel Association dropped all talk of desegregation. In late June, just days before the NAACP convention, the group announced that its twenty-eight member hotels were free to integrate or segregate as they pleased. "The Atlanta Hotel Association has taken no action in the matter," noted its president. "It can only be determined by each individual member, each for himself, to take whatever action he feels is in his own best interest and to the interest of the citizens of Atlanta and the State of Georgia." Most hotels continued to follow policies of segregation quietly, but a few went out of their way to make their stance known. Moreton Rolleston Jr., the attorney who had led the legal drive in defense of "freedom of association" in education, now sent letters to past patrons of his Heart of Atlanta Motel. "We want to advise you that we have never accepted a Negro guest at this Motel, that we have not agreed with anyone to accept Negro guests now or in the future, and that it is our considered and firm policy that we will not accept Negro guests at this Motel at any time," Rolleston wrote. "We believe that a high percentage of our guests will welcome this policy."[5]

When NAACP delegates arrived in July, they discovered how rigidly segregated the city's hotels were. The airport Hilton, for instance, refused to honor the reservations of an interracial group of twelve. The Atlanta Cabana Motel, under fire from segregationists, reversed course and now rejected reservations for two black delegates. Accordingly, the first night of the convention, the NAACP delegates voted unanimously to picket the city's segregated hotels and restaurants. For several days, hundreds of blacks picketed outside sixteen hotels but with little impact. Atlanta had already seen its share of mass demonstrations; this scattering of sign-boards raised few eyebrows. Still, some tried to give the protests a positive spin. "The time is not far off when Negroes will be accepted in Atlanta hotels without discrimination," predicted United Nations undersecretary Ralph Bunche. However, he realized that time was not at hand. The Nobel Prize winner had been refused a room himself at the Dinkler Plaza Friday morning, even though he had a reservation. "I do not miss the hotel," he said to the convention. "But I resent the rejection as an affront to my group, just as I experience deep insult whenever I see the hateful sign 'colored' and 'white.' "[6]

With the picket lines unsuccessful, the NAACP tried to address the problem with a lawsuit. Dr. Eugene Reed, a dentist and president of New York's state branch, was one of those whose reservations had been withdrawn by the Atlanta Cabana Motel. He promptly sued for damages, claiming he had "suffered great distress as a result." Instead of simply styling the suit as a civil rights matter, the NAACP legal team also filed it as a breach-of-contract complaint. Georgia still had an antiquated "innkeeper's statute" that obligated proprietors to accept guests of "good character." Reed's attorneys argued that hotels were thus agents of the state and, therefore, their discrimination was discrimination by the state itself, a violation of Reed's rights under the Fourteenth Amendment. In settling the dispute, *Reed v. Sarno*, Judge Lewis Morgan of the U.S. District Court ruled that policies of a private business could not be construed as "state action." If a businessman wanted to discriminate in his choice of customers, he had that right. Reed's attorneys appealed the decision, but to no avail. Under existing laws, they noted, there seemed little chance of securing a judgment against segregation in private places. "My hopes are high," wrote one of his lawyers a year later, "that the problem of hotel desegregation can be solved outside the courts."[7]

With their protests stalled in both the streets and the courts, the NAACP tried a third tactic, political pressure. In April 1963 the local branch called for a municipal public accommodations law that would compel hotels and restaurants to open their doors to all customers, regardless of race. Playing on the city's deep investment in public relations, NAACP leaders praised the "positive steps" taken in the desegregation of buses, schools, parks, and lunch counters, but prodded city officials to do more. "While this is good and right," they wrote, "we feel this is not enough. There are many places, licensed to do business with the public, that refuse to accept the patronage of the Negro solely because he is a Negro." The NAACP realized, however, that white moderates were not receptive to the idea of public accommodations legislation. John Sibley, who had guided Georgia through its school desegregation crisis, shuddered at the thought of businessmen compelled to serve black customers against their will. In the editorial offices of the *Atlanta Constitution*, publisher Ralph McGill complained privately that such measures trampled on free enterprise; his editor Eugene Patterson agreed. In retrospect, Mayor Allen admitted that public accommodations were simply too much for the moderate coalition. "Atlanta *had* made strides during the first three years of the sixties, but the battle line had been drawn quite clearly at the restaurants and hotels," he remembered. "Everything I had tried in those areas had failed. There had been endless meetings with the hotel and restaurant people over the past three or four years, and no matter what agreement was reached everyone involved would be split in every direction." Although Atlanta had solved countless other racial problems with negotiated settlements and political compromises, it seemed that such arrangements would fail in the field of public accommodations.[8]

By early 1963 the local campaign to desegregate hotels and restaurants had stalled on every single front. After three years of demonstrations and the full pressure of the NAACP, protests had only desegregated the department stores and a scattering of other facilities. And, as the *Reed* case made clear, lawsuits worked no better. Finally, as far as the traditional Atlanta solution of negotiated settlements was concerned, the issue of business desegregation was beyond the pale. Moderate leaders had seen how close the sit-ins had come to destroying their political order, and the businessmen who backed them wanted no part in such discussions. In local terms, the prospects for progress in public accommodations looked bleak.

On the national scene, however, the climate for a civil rights breakthrough was rapidly improving. Along with the rest of the country, Atlantans watched as the most significant events unfolded in nearby Alabama. In May 1963 networks and newspapers across the country brought home the brutality of segregation as civil rights protests in Birmingham came to their climax. Images of local lawmen battering black children with high-pressure hoses and attacking them with German shepherds shook the national conscience and raised serious doubts about the wisdom of leaving racial issues in the hands of local forces. Then, little more than a month later, Governor George Wallace staged his famous "stand in the schoolhouse door" at the University of Alabama. Wallace had come to Tuscaloosa to block the admission of two black students to the all-white school, but the intervention of the Justice Department forced him to back down, with a crowd of photographers and cameramen recording the confrontation. Once again, the nation was treated to an ugly image of segregationists—sneering, defiant, and somewhat ridiculous. This time, however, Americans could see their government fighting back.[9]

Among those closely watching events in Alabama was President John F. Kennedy. To that point, the president had done relatively little to support the civil rights movement, afraid that any action might alienate southern Democrats. Alabama changed that. The brutalities of Birmingham made him "sick," he admitted. The school showdown in Tuscaloosa, meanwhile, led him to believe that racial conflict would only grow worse in the South if the federal government remained uninvolved. What was needed, he decided, was strong civil rights legislation. On June 11, as the first black students registered at the University of Alabama, the president impulsively decided to announce his plans while the nation's attention lingered on civil rights. At eight o'clock that evening, Kennedy addressed the nation in strong tones. "We are confronted primarily with a moral issue," he declared. "It is as old as the Scriptures and is as clear as the American Constitution." Kennedy described the routine injustices faced by blacks for an imagined white audience. "If an American, because his skin is dark, cannot eat lunch in a restaurant open to the public; if he cannot send his children to the best public school available; if he cannot vote for the public officials who represent him; if, in short, he cannot enjoy the full and free life which all of us want," the president asked directly, "then who among us would be content to have the color of his skin changed and stand in his place? Who among us would then be content with the counsel of patience and delay?" The time had come for action, he insisted. "I think we owe them," Kennedy said, "and we owe ourselves, a better country." He then listed the proposals he would put before Congress. The first and most specific recommendation, he said, would be "legislation giving all Americans the right to be served in facilities which are open to the public—hotels, restaurants, theaters, retail stores and similar establishments."[10]

For those on the front lines of the civil rights struggle, the president's address was a godsend. From his home in Atlanta, Martin Luther King Jr. drafted an immediate response. "I have just listened to your speech to the nation," he wrote with haste. "It was one of the most eloquent profound and unequiv[oc]al pleas for Justice and the Freedom of all men ever made by any President." Meanwhile, in Jackson, Mississippi, the family of the NAACP's state field secretary, Medgar Evers, waited up late to see what he thought of the speech. Around midnight, the children heard his Oldsmobile pull into the driveway. Evers got out, picked up a stack of sweatshirts stenciled "Jim Crow Must Go," and turned to enter his home. Across the street, hidden among the honeysuckle vines, a white fertilizer salesman named Byron de la Beckwith squinted through the scope of his

30.06 Winchester rifle, squeezed the trigger, and ripped a bullet through the man's back. At the crack of the gun, the children inside threw themselves to the ground, precisely as their father, a veteran of the Normandy invasion, had trained them. When no more shots came, they hurried outside to find their father, face down and bloody. An hour later, Evers was pronounced dead.[11]

In Georgia, segregationists were less brutal in their reaction but just as bitter. As usual, many vented their anger at Ralph McGill. Although the editor had privately spoken out against the public accommodations measures, he kept his misgivings out of his weekly column. Segregationists assumed he favored the plan and attacked him anyway. "You and your kind are a disgrace to this country," wrote one. "You, the Martin Luther Kennedy's and all other White Trash should be deported to Africa." "The damn niggers & lousy damn Kennedys have wrecked this country and half-breed [BAST]ARDS like you are doing all they can to help," sneered another. "You should be with Evers!" Not surprisingly, the city's segregationists swore they would never support the civil rights bill. Doing so, argued one man, would mean "surrendering" their private property and "turning it over to the Negroes." "I pay all the insurance and all the taxes on my property and I am going to be the boss and operate my property so long as there is life in my body," wrote another. "And if a bunch of these Punks come into my Place to sit all over the floor or any place to infringe and obstruct my business, they are going out. And to hell with what you or either of the Kennedy say."[12]

Mayor Allen was well aware of segregationists' resistance to the civil rights bill. He considered Kennedy a political hero, but believed that the president's bill—the public accommodations provision in particular— was more than the nation and his city were ready to accept. In early July 1963 he met with Morris Abram, then an adviser to the administration, about the bill's prospects. "I don't know a single important official in the South who's come out for it," the mayor told his guest. "Ivan," Abram replied, "the President wants you to support the bill. He wants you to go to Washington to testify." Kennedy needed southern support for the bill, Abram explained, and Atlanta, with its recent successes in desegregation, was the ideal source. Allen had yet to cement his stand on the bill, but he was sure that supporting it publicly would end his political career. Only a personal call from the president convinced him. After shoring up support from his business backers and the black establishment, Allen headed off to Washington.[13]

In his Senate testimony, Mayor Allen warned that, without any clear direction on desegregation, cities like Atlanta "might slip backward" and resegregate. Indeed, the very day he spoke in Washington, back in Atlanta the Southern Regional Council announced that forty-five restaurants which had supposedly desegregated were once again barring blacks. "The situation is changing from day to day," warned Eliza Paschall, "and more often for the worse than the better." A month later, in August 1963, the Greater Atlanta Council on Human Relations polled local restaurants and hotels about their current policies on segregation. Most restaurants bristled at the call, but many hinted that they were, as Allen suggested, looking for a way out. "We'll integrate if [a] law is passed," said the Ship Ahoy Restaurant, "and not before." Others admitted that they, too, would serve blacks, but "only under pressure." When asked why, most cited a fear of alienating their white clientele. "I agree and am in sympathy," said a voice at the Camellia Gardens, "but we are in business to make money." Likewise, the manager at White Shutters was pleasant on the phone. Could the caller bring a black client to lunch, then? "Goodness, no!" the man answered. "They would all walk out." The hotels, meanwhile, were much more direct. Would the Briarcliff Hotel welcome black guests? "Nigger, no!" spat the clerk. "I have been prepared for this," said the voice at the Peachtree-on-Peachtree Motel: "No!"[14]

Under this "voluntary" approach to integration, no one could be sure which hotels and restaurants accepted black guests. Civil rights activists tried to maintain up-to-date lists of "integrated establishments," but the situation was constantly changing and incredibly confusing. A few hotels accepted black visitors, but usually with the provision that they were part of a larger convention and, as a group, composed no more than 3 percent of the total conventioneers. For restaurants, "integration" was even more convoluted. A reporter for *Newsweek* explained the problem to his home office: "Some said they were integrated, but would accept no more than two Negroes at a time; some said they wouldn't accept mixed parties; some said they were integrated only between one and two p.m.; some would agree on the telephone they were integrated, but would close the door in the face of negro patrons; some did vice versa." It was, the journalist noted, an exasperating pattern of "confuse-and-divide."[15]

This confusing state of restaurant "integration" meant that seeking service could be a baffling ordeal for blacks. In September 1963, for instance, a black Spelman College graduate and her white co-worker spent a Sunday afternoon looking for a place that would serve them. A friend had seen Mammy's Shanty on a list of integrated restaurants and suggested they try it. But the hostess there halted them at the door and asked the black woman for identification. Since her Massachusetts driver's license did not include a listing for race, the hostess asked the woman "what nationality" she was. "American," she answered. The two were told to leave. Next, they went to the new Holiday Inn on Piedmont, only to be rejected there as well. The ladies then tried the Davis Brothers Cafeteria on Peachtree. The day before, they had dined there without any problem.

This time, however, the cafeteria staff—including the same man who served them then—refused to admit them. Yesterday, he said, had been a mistake.[16]

As such experiences became commonplace, civil rights leaders recognized that "voluntary integration" had failed. In October 1963, therefore, nine groups—including the Committee on Appeal for Human Rights and local chapters of the NAACP, the SCLC, and SNCC—joined together to form the Atlanta Summit Leadership Conference, an umbrella organization that would orchestrate their policies and protests. In November the summit coalition released "Action for Democracy," their plan for the "total desegregation" of Atlanta. The document recommended a variety of improvements in the city's racial climate, including complete school desegregation, the installation of fair employment practices, an open-occupancy housing law, relaxed voter registration requirements, and the appointment of more blacks to city positions. As its first priority, however, the statement called for the swift passage of a public accommodations measure. "Limited desegregation of hotels, motels, and restaurants," the document warned, "is completely unacceptable." These goals, the Summit Leadership Conference hoped, would be reached "through cooperative action, rather than through conflict." But if that failed, the coalition would once again resort to protests and picket lines.[17]

Segregationists, of course, reacted to the summit recommendations with horror. "WAR HAS BEEN DECLARED UPON WHITE ATLANTA," proclaimed Lester Maddox. "Every man, woman, and child is included in the immediate threat being made by the Communist-inspired racial agitators. Your family, home, church, job, business, profession, labor union, school, civic club, and your city are under this immediate, direct, and publicly announced threat of invasion and ruin." The public accommodations proposal, in particular, was "inhuman, unconstitutional, and un-American." Even if the measure became law, Maddox said, he would never obey it. "We have a divine right to discriminate," he claimed. To protect that "right," in June 1963 Maddox formed another segregationist organization, the People's Association for Selective Shopping (PASS). "Let all who read this understand that if there is a general breakthrough of integration in the hotels, motels, restaurants and other business concerns in Atlanta," warned a press release, " 'PASS' will immediately activate a massive and never ending campaign to keep all 'PASS' members and supporters from doing any shopping, whatsoever, in downtown Atlanta." Borrowing a page from civil rights activists, Maddox distributed lists of integrated places to supporters. "STAY AWAY FROM THESE PLACES," urged one such sheet. "DO NOT SLEEP OR EAT INTEGRATED." Under Maddox's leadership, the city's segregationists were kept on full alert through the summer and fall of 1963. Thus, when the Summit Leadership Conference recommended its November reforms, PASS reacted as if the anticipated "war" had finally arrived. "All that is ours is being swapped for votes at Atlanta City Hall," the group warned in panic. "Every white citizen is under attack—your family, home, and job."[18]

At the same time, civil rights activists were likewise moving closer to renewed protests of their own. As negotiations proved fruitless, the generational gap in the black community once again broke open in late November. "There was a secret meeting of the Negro leadership . . . in which tempers flared," a reporter informed his editors, "and, it is whispered, the old-line leadership called the youngsters rabble rousers and said they were more [like] a mob." It was becoming clear, he noted, that the pace of civil rights change was slipping out of the older generation's control "and there is the strong smell of a take-over by the young militants." The Summit Leadership Conference tried to keep the generations together, with a mass rally in Hurt Park on December 15. While organizers had predicted tens of thousands would turn out for the "Pilgrimage for Progress," it actually attracted only a fraction of that support. Two weeks later, the summit's steering committee decided that negotiations had failed. Direct action, it seemed, was the only solution.[19]

Thus, in January 1964, the students launched a new wave of sit-ins, protests that would stand as the most confrontational and controversial in Atlanta's history. Their first protests, against the Krystal and Morrison chains, quickly turned ugly. On January 10, for instance, a crowd of college and high school students entered a Krystal shop, only to find whites inside pushing back. One waitress jumped on the counter and struck students with a broom, while another grabbed a female student and threw her against an iron post. As the students sang "We Shall Overcome," policemen arrived and begged them to leave. They refused, however, and were arrested. Segregationists responded to the protests with picket lines of their own. On January 18, for instance, ten Klansmen marched into a student-targeted Krystal and sat down. As the hours wore on, the number of demonstrators outside grew and the confidence of the Klansmen inside dwindled. "The day has come," shouted SNCC Director James Forman, "when the Ku Klux Klan is afraid to come out!" When a student outside was arrested, others rushed to protest, throwing themselves in front of the paddy wagon. "Under the wheels!" Forman called. "Under the wheels!" At this, the normally calm Atlanta policemen snapped and started arresting more students, showing fits of frustration. SNCC Chairman John Lewis, for one, found himself smashed against the side of the paddy wagon by five officers. Ultimately, the police took away seventy-five students and cleared the entire block. At that, the Klansmen took off their robes, folded them under their arms, and sheepishly left the restaurant. Later that night, fifty more students marched to the city jail to protest the "brutal handling" of their friends. After a second confrontation with police, they too were arrested.[20]

Atlanta's moderate leaders tried to keep a lid on the protests and counter-protests, but events rapidly spun out of their control. On January 24, a twelve-member United Nations Subcommission on Discrimination and Minorities arrived for a weekend visit in Atlanta. The purpose of the trip, ironically enough, was to study the city's "successes" in race relations. What the visitors saw was something altogether different. At the airport, they found students with signs reading, "Welcome to a Segregated City." The next day, as the UN delegation lunched at Atlanta University, three hundred more students gathered outside. "What are they singing?" a Soviet interpreter asked. "Freedom songs," came the answer. "Ahhh, freedom," the Russian replied softly. The delegation's chairman, Hernan Santa Cruz of Chile, stopped for a moment to join in a few bars of "We Shall Overcome." As the music died away, James Bevel of the Southern Christian Leadership Conference collected students for a two-mile hike downtown. Getting word of the march, the Krystal chain closed every one of its restaurants.[21]

The students, however, were headed not to Krystal's but to Leb's Restaurant. In recent years, owner Charlie Lebedin had emerged as one of the most stubborn opponents of integration. The students responded by making his restaurants, especially Leb's at the corner of Forsyth and Luckie Streets, frequent sites of their sit-ins. On January 25, the confrontations at Leb's reached a peak. Forty students swept into the restaurant, with SNCC leader John Lewis, in the words of a reporter, "letting people in like a headwaiter." When the police refused to intervene, Lebedin decided to lock up the restaurant with everyone inside. Barring the restroom doors and switching off the water and lights, he locked the front doors at four o'clock and left. As the hours passed, the students abandoned their nonviolent ways. They smashed drinking glasses to the floor, overturned coffee urns, and flipped a few brown-and-yellow leather booths upside down. With the restroom doors still locked, some demonstrators relieved themselves on the floor. Lebedin was outraged. "I never was a segregationist," he said. "But I am today." Just as dismayed were civil rights leaders, who called for students to leave Leb's before vandalism escalated into serious violence. But the damage was already done.[22]

Indeed, the Leb's incident severely undermined the civil rights movement in Atlanta, causing a number of moderate whites to rethink their support of desegregation. The mainstream newspapers had taken moderate-to-liberal stands on the civil rights movement until then, but after Leb's they soured on the student protests. The *Constitution* charged that SNCC had "fouled the nest of equal rights." The protestors were "wrong-headed zealots," the *Journal* agreed, no better than the Klan. The impact

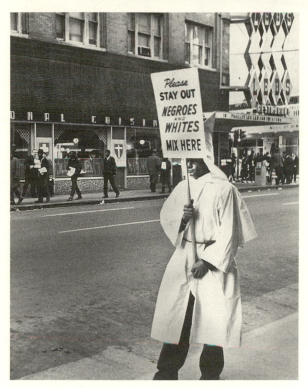

Figure 8.1 Klansman protesting an integrated restaurant at the corner of Luckie and Forsyth Streets in downtown Atlanta, 1964. Across the street stands Leb's Restaurant, which was a frequent target of sit-in protests during 1964.

of Leb's on moderate whites was perhaps best seen in the mind of their most prominent spokesman, former Mayor Bill Hartsfield. Watching from retirement, Hartsfield was thoroughly disgusted. In an address titled "Is Urination Non-Violent?" he charged that the demonstrators had undermined their own cause. From then on, Hartsfield grew increasingly suspicious of black activists. Only a year later, he wrote Congress to complain about "certain communists who were identified with the famous Leb Restaurant incident in Atlanta."[23]

As protests continued at Leb's and other segregated sites, chances for a local solution to the public accommodations impasse seemed slim. For their part, the student activists insisted on immediate change. Seventy-five gathered outside City Hall on January 26, carrying a large sign: "We Want a Public Accommodations Law." SNCC leader Prathia Hall, who had helped write John Lewis's speech for the March on Washington a few months before, directly challenged Atlanta's carefully crafted public appearance. "Despite its 'liberal' image, Atlanta is still a segregated city," she announced. "We wish we could rely on the good business sense and moral righteousness of Atlanta officials and businessmen. They have proven to us that we cannot." Two days later, Mayor Allen responded by convening a televised meeting with the city's top business and civic leaders. In a remarkable address, the mayor frankly discussed the different meanings blacks and whites gave to "racial harmony." "The white community as a whole tends to define racial harmony as the absence of disturbance," the mayor noted. "The Negro community—to a man—defines it as the establishment of their full rights as American citizens. I am determined to use all of the authority I have to see that, in Atlanta, both definitions are fulfilled." Hoping to convince both sides of the other's goodwill, he urged the students to cease their demonstrations and the city to consider the summit recommendations, even the controversial public accommodations measure.[24]

The passage of such a law, however, seemed unlikely, as Atlanta's businessmen dug in their heels. On January 27, the Atlanta Restaurant Association ran a full-page ad in the *Atlanta Journal*. "We feel that as individual operators of our establishments," the restaurant owners wrote, "we still have the freedom of choice to operate our businesses as we see fit—in the best interest of our customers, our employees and our families." Recent talk of public accommodations legislation, in their view, was part of the "ever-increasing trend toward centralized control and regulation," which "must stop before socialism is an accomplished fact." In the end, they tapped whites' growing sense that the civil rights movement was endangering their own rights. "This matter has transcended the consideration of civil rights alone," the restaurateurs stated. "It now involves the basic right of an individual, any individual of whatever race, creed, or color, to engage in business." That, they held, was sacrosanct. The next day, the association proposed that all restaurants shut down for a day, in essence, to protest the protests. "Our quarrel," restaurateur John Evans said, "is with extremist groups and government at any level which seeks to strike down the individual rights of businessmen." At the mayor's Wednesday meeting, other merchants rallied around the restaurateurs. Rawson Haverty, Allen's successor as Chamber of Commerce president, said he would "heartily endorse" all the mayor's proposals, except the public accommodations measure. That, he said, was completely unacceptable. Even those who had desegregated their own stores balked at the plan. Ed Negri, owner of Herren's Restaurant, explained his own experiences with integration. "I'm happy in my decision," he said, "and I will not back down." But the decision to desegregate had been his own. "If you're going to force a man to integrate," Negri warned, "you'd better think of some way to support him. I'm over the hump, but some of my friends are struggling." He surprised many with his next words. "Mr. Maddox—and he's a friend of mine—would be out of business if this law is passed," Negri told the crowd. "He should be able to operate the way he wants to." In the wake of the businessmen's stand, the board of aldermen quietly tabled the mayor's proposals at its next meeting and ignored the topic thereafter.[25]

After four years of fighting for desegregation of the city's hotels, restaurants, and other public accommodations, civil rights activists realized that local actions—whether protests in the streets, lawsuits in the courts, or negotiations in city hall—would never secure the victory they sought. Atlanta had weathered countless racial crises, from thousands of unheralded residential transitions to the much-touted desegregation of public schools, but it seemed clear that this was a legacy of segregation that was too deeply entrenched for even the "city too busy to hate" to overcome on its own. Increasingly, civil rights leaders and white moderates in Atlanta and other cities looked to Washington for a way out.

THE COURSE OF FEDERAL INTERVENTION

As the push for public accommodations legislation stalled in Atlanta, the campaign in Washington gathered speed. In the wake of John F. Kennedy's assassination, Lyndon Johnson had connected the nation's mourning with the cause of civil rights. "No memorial oration or eulogy could more eloquently honor President Kennedy's memory than the earliest possible passage of the civil rights bill for which he fought so long," President Johnson told the nation in his first formal address. "We have talked long enough in this country about equal rights. We have talked for one hundred years or more. It is now time to write the next chapter, and to write it in the books of law." At the time, the civil rights bill was bottled up in the House Rules Committee by Representative Howard Smith, an eighty-year-old Virginian and ardent segregationist. With Johnson's speech lifting public support over 60 percent, Smith was unable to keep the bill back. On January 31, 1964, just days after the Atlanta drive stalled, the Rules Committee released the bill for consideration by the full House. The core of Kennedy's proposal, the public accommodations measures, remained intact. In fact, at Johnson's insistence, they had been considerably expanded. After a perfunctory debate and some slight tinkering, the House passed the bill by a strong margin of 290–130, on February 10, 1964. It was, in the words of the *Congressional Quarterly*, "the most sweeping civil rights measure to clear either house of Congress in the 20th Century."[26]

In the Senate, the Civil Rights Bill faced longer odds. Georgia's Senator Richard Russell, powerful head of the southern bloc and Johnson's former mentor, tore into what he called "one of the most dangerous" measures in the nation's history. In particular, Russell singled out the public accommodations section, which, in his words, violated the "inalienable rights" of Americans "to choose or select their associates." The law would establish a dangerous constitutional precedent, which could be used "to sustain the validity of legislation that will compel admittance into the living room or bedroom of any citizen." As the House bill moved to the Senate, Russell decided to strangle the legislation with a filibuster. He hoped the administration would come to the bargaining table, but Johnson refused to bend. "They can filibuster until hell freezes over," he said privately. "I'm not going to put anything on that floor until this is done." Instead of compromising with his former mentor, Johnson reached across the aisle to moderate Republicans, then headed by Senate Minority Leader Everett Dirksen. Russell was just as stubborn as his former student, however, and subjected the Senate to three months of debate on the matter anyway. Finally, the bill's supporters secured cloture and the issue headed to a final vote. On June 19, 1964, exactly one year after Kennedy had submitted the matter to Congress, the Senate adopted the bill, 73–27. On July 2, the House accepted the revised version as well. That same day, President Johnson signed the landmark bill into law.[27]

Within the hour, the first challenge to the Civil Rights Act was launched in Atlanta. Moreton Rolleston, owner of the Heart of Atlanta Motel and a shrewd constitutional lawyer, took advantage of an often-overlooked rule that required federal court clerks to remain on duty at all times. As the bill signing ceremony drew to a close, Rolleston drove to the clerk's home in Decatur, knocked on the front door, and formally filed his suit against the United States of America. As the motel owner challenged the Civil Rights Act, Atlanta's restaurant owners took different routes. Charlie Lebedin reluctantly resigned himself to defeat. He posted signs of compliance in his restaurant's windows, dramatically draped with black crepe paper. "I intend to obey the laws of the United States and Georgia," read one sign, "as I have done for the past 15 years." Lester Maddox, meanwhile, resolved to fight. "They're coming out to polish up on Lester's chicken bones," he predicted darkly, "but when they get here we're ready for 'em." He soon had the chance to prove his point. On July 3, 1964, the afternoon after the bill became law, three black ministers wheeled into the Pickrick parking lot in a black Chevrolet. Standing guard at the front door, Maddox rushed out to intercept. As Rev. George Willis opened his door, Maddox slammed it shut. When Rev. Albert Dunn made it out the passenger side, Maddox and his son confronted him. The father held a pistol, while the son brandished an ax handle like a baseball bat. With the crowd swelling behind them, they drove Dunn back into the car. Maddox had made his response clear. He would "defend" his restaurant at all costs.[28]

Maddox immediately became a folk hero for segregationists. The next day, at a Fourth of July rally he organized in Atlanta's Lakewood Park, over 11,000 whites showed up to hear him and a slate of segregationist all-stars. With ninety-five degree heat and thick humidity, the afternoon soon grew ugly. Halfway through an address by former Governor Ross Barnett of Mississippi, three black men began booing. In the crowd, two white factory workers looked at each other and, without a word, picked up steel folding chairs and began beating the hecklers on the head and shoulders. As the crowd screamed "Kill 'em!" and "Get those niggers!" others joined the attack, throwing bottles and rocks and then pounding them with fists, feet, and folding chairs as well. The black men broke for cover, but the crowd was everywhere. Two were trapped at the corner of a chain-link fence. One of them fell to the ground, blood spurting from his ear; when he tried to get up, he was knocked down by another chair. The third, separated and surrounded by the crowd, stumbled toward what he mistook for an exit and wound up trapped as well. As flying chairs struck him, he fell to his knees. The police rushed in to hold the crowd back, allowing the man to climb a fence and escape. The officers, however, were themselves attacked by the crowd, as was a white woman linked to the men. "She was smirking when she came in here," an eyewitness noted. "They beat her up, but I wish they'd killed her."[29]

As police rushed the injured to Grady Hospital, Alabama Governor George Wallace took the stage. His shirt already drenched with sweat, he attacked the Civil Rights Act with ferocity. It was a "cruel irony," he said, that right before Independence Day, "the President of the United States has just signed into law the most monstrous piece of legislation ever enacted." True patriots would resist such tyranny. "We must destroy the power to dictate, to forbid, to require, to demand, to distribute, to edict," he shouted. "We must revitalize a government founded in this nation on faith in God!" The crowd ate it up. Grand Dragon Calvin Craig, on stage at Maddox's invitation, called it "the finest speech I've ever heard." The crowd agreed. Long after Wallace had ended his talk, he strode the stage, arms stretched overhead in a V-for-victory salute. Wallace was always a hard act to follow, but Maddox matched him that afternoon. He simply strode to the microphone and said deliberatively: "Never! Never! Never!" By one reporter's account, that received the loudest applause of the day.[30]

Throughout the rally and, indeed, in all their resistance to the Civil Rights Act, segregationists repeatedly insisted that the legislation was communist in its origins. Maddox promoted the rally as a "no-holds barred dissection of the Communistic blueprint for the Sovietization of American society," while Wallace insisted the act was taken straight out of the *Communist Manifesto*. While many observers have dismissed such charges as mere grandstanding, these segregationists sincerely believed them. In their eyes, the Civil Rights Act embodied both the means and the ends of communism. Practically speaking, the new law restricted the power and prerogatives of individual businessmen and, therefore, threatened capitalism itself. At the same time, the legislation greatly expanded the power of the central government over local authorities and, therefore, infringed on individual rights and grass-roots democracy. Finally, as segregationists repeatedly liked to point out, the goal of the act, racial integration, was a cause long embraced by both domestic and foreign communists and, thus, fundamentally suspect. All told, the Civil Rights Act seemed to segregationists the embodiment of communism. As Grand Dragon Calvin Craig charged, "It is just as much COMMUNIST as if the RUSSIAN Government passed it."[31]

The supposed connection between the Civil Rights Act and communism was clearly and repeatedly made by Lester Maddox, especially during a press conference he convened in the Dixie Ballroom of the Henry Grady Hotel. For a half hour, the Pickrick owner poured out his heart in an overwrought statement, which he recorded and later sold as an album, "If I Go to Jail."[32] The Civil Rights Act had stolen the Pickrick from his family, he said. "Our business and our property does not belong to the government, the communists, the mayor of Atlanta, the President of the United States, the news media, the National Council of Churches, Martin Luther King or other civil rights leaders that cheat their people and cheat a great America," Maddox insisted. "It belongs to me, my wife, and children—free Americans—and we are sole owners. So help me God, we shall continue in that position." Should he be forced to close his restaurant, Maddox said, he would know who to blame. At the top of the list, he said, were "the communists," closely followed by "the President of the United States and members of the United States Congress who have violated their oath to uphold the United States Constitution." After them, blame rested with "the news media that continues to follow the socialist-communist plan to destroy our great nation and even today will not allow much of my statements to reach the people." The "weak and cowardly business leaders who care more for dollars than they do for the soul of America" were just as guilty, he charged. With these forces aligned against him, Maddox sighed, he would surely go to jail. But he wouldn't go alone. "Behind those dark doors will go states' rights, constitutional government, individual freedom, and the American free enterprise system, racial pride, racial integrity, independence, the right to employ or be employed, freedom of speech, the right to buy, own, or rent property, and, yes," he added with a flourish, "the right to live in a free country."[33]

As if to prove Maddox's paranoia about the powers aligned against him, the U.S. Department of Justice soon began legal proceedings against the Pickrick. Acting on the complaint of the ministers Maddox had chased away, Attorney General Robert F. Kennedy swiftly secured a three-judge trial for July 17, 1964. There, the government would be represented by none other than the head of the Civil Rights Division, Assistant Attorney General Burke Marshall, and a battalion of federal lawyers. Furthermore, from the NAACP Legal Defense Fund, director Jack Greenberg, his chief assistant Constance Baker Motley, and local attorney William Alexander weighed in as well. Maddox felt overwhelmed by the forces arrayed against him. "If the United States had about three of these cases at the same time," he joked, "they'd have to pull out of Vietnam." For his defense, Maddox was simply represented by William G. McRae and Sidney Schell. Although able lawyers, neither man was regarded as much of a constitutional heavyweight.[34]

The government's lawsuit against Lester Maddox was paired with Moreton Rolleston's lawsuit against the government. Combined, the two cases, *Heart of Atlanta Motel v. U. S.* and *Willis v. Pickrick,* formed the first challenge to the Civil Rights Act. The presiding judges—Chief Judge Elbert Tuttle of the Fifth Circuit Court of Appeals and Judges Frank Hooper and Lewis Morgan of the U.S. District Court for the Northern District of Georgia—understood the intense interest in the cases and decided to impose tight security when the hearings began. On July 17, the entire third floor of the Old Post Office Building was sealed off by federal marshals and, hours before the 9:30 trial time, a line of hopeful spectators stretched down the hall. Because no one would be allowed to stand inside, seats became a prized commodity. Anyone who left the courtroom, for water or a smoke, returned to find his seat taken and a new spot waiting for him at the end of the line. There were no exceptions. At least three men flashed sheriff's badges at the door, but marshals refused to let them by. Press credentials fared no better; one reporter waited in the hall all day without seeing the courtroom.[35]

The first arguments heard were for *Heart of Atlanta Motel*. Dressed in a blue wash-and-wear suit, Moreton Rolleston explained that his lawsuit was not about segregation. "We could get along with Negro guests," he said. "They would hurt our business, as we've alleged, and it's true. [But] we could get along with them." Instead, Rolleston said, his lawsuit was about the unconstitutional and unchecked expansion of federal power. "I took the position," Rolleston recalled, "that if the federal government could tell me who to have as my customer, they could tell me to do anything." The Constitution, he told the court, expressly forbade such an expansion of government power—not once, but twice. "The Fifth Amendment says you can't take a man's liberty or property without due process; and you can't take it, his property, without compensation," the attorney argued. "Have they taken our liberty at the Heart of Atlanta Motel? We used to could say who could come there and who could not come there and we would turn [people] away for whatever reason we wanted. We don't have that liberty under the prohibitions of this act if the act is good." Furthermore, Rolleston continued, "the Thirteenth Amendment provided there be no slavery and no involuntary servitude. In our case," he asked, "how can we say that we are subject to involuntary servitude? We say that we had the right to run the motel like we wanted to before the act was passed. We now have the right to run the motel like the Government says." For a case that questioned fundamental aspects of federal rule, the *Heart of Atlanta Motel* hearing was stunningly brief. Moreton Rolleston called no witnesses; Burke Marshall brought only two for the government. Since both sides accepted the facts of the case, the only disagreement rested on the issue of the Civil Rights Act's constitutionality. In all, the presentations took less than two hours.[36]

The *Pickrick* proceedings, however, lasted much longer. First of all, Maddox seemed determined to hold the spotlight. Arriving in a black Pontiac Grand Prix, with an American flag flying from the antenna, he spent the lunch recess chatting up spectators and shaking hands like the celebrity he had become. And unlike Rolleston, Maddox's attorneys refused to concede a single point of fact. Early in the trial, for instance, an NAACP attorney offhandedly asked that it be noted, for the record, that a departing witness "was a member of the white race." "I think we would require some testimony on that," interrupted Sidney Schell for the defense. Judge Tuttle was dumbfounded: "Are you serious? You want some testimony on that?" "Very serious," the attorney answered. "Well," Tuttle shrugged, "call the witness back in."[37] Likewise, Maddox's attorneys refused to admit that the Pickrick was engaged in interstate commerce, an important point, since Congress had grounded the Civil Rights Act in its own authority to oversee such trade. To prove that the Pickrick had, in fact, served out-of-state customers, FBI agents were forced to track down visitors from Virginia, Tennessee, and Alabama. To prove that the Pickrick had, in fact, bought food from outside the state, the plaintiffs interviewed wholesalers and had a customer recall the bottles on her table—ketchup from California, tabasco sauce from Louisiana, and worcestershire from New Jersey. Still, Maddox's attorneys denied that purchasing out-of-state goods involved the Pickrick in interstate commerce. Maddox had bought them from a local warehouse, they argued, and that meant the commerce was purely local. Plus, William McRae added, the consumption of those goods was a local event as well. "When they get to Lester Maddox's restaurant and they are served to a person that sits down and eats at his table, are they still in commerce? The fellow who eats 'em will evacuate 'em and they'll go into the Chattahoochee River as waste," said McRae, with an unfortunately vivid sweep of his arm. "There's no more commerce there."[38]

Although Maddox's defense dwelled on minutiae, McRae and Schell remained mindful of the larger ramifications of their case. Much like Moreton Rolleston, they argued that upholding the Civil Rights Act would set the stage for future federal interference in private affairs. "The whole question here, may it please Your Honors, is whether or not we are going to destroy the historic foundation of our dual system of government," McRae argued, "whether or not we are going to commit to the Federal Government the power to absolutely control and dominate every phase of our activity and to prevent us from making any discrimination at all." And discrimination, McRae continued, was not bad. In fact, it was a fundamental American right. "The Constitution of the United States was designed to preserve the freedom of man to discriminate," he claimed. "When you talk about rights and freedom, what is a greater freedom than the right to select your own associates; the right not to serve anyone that you don't wish to serve? That's real freedom," McRae concluded, "and that's what we are battling to preserve in this country."[39]

On July 22, 1964, two days after the hearings concluded, the judges called the parties together to hear their verdicts. Outside the clerk's office, both sides waited nervously. "Even if they take everything," Maddox joked, "I'm not going to worry. Didn't Lyndon Johnson say he was going to eradicate poverty?" Within a few minutes, the clerk delivered the ruling. In a unanimous decision, the judges upheld the constitutionality of the Civil Rights Act and enjoined the Pickrick and the Heart of Atlanta Motel from barring customers on racial grounds. Both businessmen remained defiant. Rolleston filed an appeal just minutes after the announcement, while Maddox vowed he would continue his struggle as well. He soft-pedaled his earlier promise to "go to jail," however, stating now that he would close the Pickrick "if the Supreme Court rules against the rights of free enterprise." When the Supreme Court refused to grant a stay on the injunctions, he grew bitter. Maddox took a fully dressed mannequin outside the Pickrick, placed it face-down on a park bench, hammered a knife into its back, and poured red food coloring around it for effect. In case anyone missed the symbolism, he tacked up a sign: "This manikin represents what has happened to the American free enterprise system. It has been stabbed in the back."[40]

Despite the injunctions, Maddox continued to bar blacks for several days. Soon, the threat of contempt charges convinced him to close the restaurant. Rather than back down, Maddox transformed the Pickrick building into a monument to free enterprise and conservative politics. Over the loud speakers, dining music was replaced by fife-and-drum renditions of "Yankee Doodle Dandy" and other marches. On long tables outside, Maddox offered customers recordings of his "If I Go to Jail" speech and copies of right-wing booklets. Car owners could buy a license tag with the Confederate battle flag or a "Goldwater '64" bumper sticker. Cans of "Gold Water" soft drinks were available as well, twenty cents warm, twenty-five cents cold. Maddox's best-selling items, however, were ax handles, which he had made a defiant symbol of segregation. Sales were so strong that Maddox cleaned out two local suppliers and five other factories as well. "I probably supplied him 10,000 in all," mused a friend in the hardware business, "and he got some others on his own." When asked just what people would do with the ax handles, Maddox flashed a mischievous grin. "Aw, just souvenirs," he said. "People are picking them out to match their woodwork—crossing them over their doors and fireplaces." To boost sales, Maddox built a three-story, white-frame tower in the Pickrick's parking lot. On a chilly Sunday afternoon in September 1964, he dedicated his new "shrine to the death of the free enterprise system." A crowd of five hundred bought tickets—thirty-five cents for adults, twenty-five for children—to listen to Maddox and other segregationists deliver speeches from the back of a flatbed truck. Afterward, ticket holders were allowed to walk inside the "shrine." There, they found just a black casket, containing a copy of the Constitution and quotations from Maddox, Daniel Webster, and Lyndon Johnson from his more conservative days.[41]

Gimmicks and grandstanding could only carry Lester Maddox so far. A few days after the monument's dedication, he admitted he was in "horrible financial condition." The fire insurance had been canceled, and the second mortgage-holder was demanding coverage. "I've got to do something to survive," he said, and that meant reopening his restaurant. But it would not be the Pickrick anymore. That was a corporation which had ceased to operate and would remain "out of the food business unless and until the U. S. Supreme Court kills the Civil Rights Act of 1964 as it applies to public accommodations." (To illustrate his point, the old Pickrick sign was covered in a black tarp with the words "Light Turned Out by L.B.J.") This would be a "new" restaurant, Maddox insisted. As proof, he obtained a new license and new tax numbers for the Lester Maddox Cafeteria, which would be run not by the Pickrick corporation but by Maddox himself. To most observers, the changes were superficial. It was, after all, the same owner, the same building, the same employees, and the same food as before. But there was, actually, an important change in the cafeteria's customer relations. Hoping to exempt this "new" restaurant from the Civil Rights Act, Maddox announced he would not bar people because they were "red, yellow, black or white" but because they were "integrationists." That, he claimed, was a form of political, not racial, discrimination and, as such, was not covered by the act. For two days, the Lester Maddox Cafeteria attracted huge crowds. Lines of white customers often stretched out the door for a block. On the third day, four black customers appeared at the door. Maddox knew them well. Three were the same ministers involved in the July 3 showdown: George Willis, Albert Dunn, and Woodrow Lewis. Barring their way, Maddox shoved the men back. "Get off my property!" he yelled. "I can run it the way I want to!" On the ministers' complaints, Judge Frank Hooper held that the Lester Maddox Cafeteria, despite the cosmetic changes, was subject to the same injunction against the Pickrick. A show-cause order for civil contempt was issued within hours of the confrontation, but the trial date was repeatedly delayed until February. Meanwhile, the Lester Maddox Cafeteria continued to prosper.[42]

In early October, as court proceedings stalled in Atlanta, the U.S. Supreme Court convened to hear arguments in the fall term's first case, *Heart of Atlanta Motel v. the United States*. Moreton Rolleston made the first presentation of the day. Unlike Maddox, who forced federal officials to prove his involvement in interstate commerce, Rolleston now admitted that his motel was engaged in such business. In spite of these concessions, Rolleston still had serious objections to the Civil Rights Act. "The fundamental question," he charged, "is whether or not Congress has the power to take away the liberty of an individual to run his business as he sees fit in the selection and choice of his customers. This is the real important issue." The question of "alleged civil rights" was "purely incidental" to the case, Rolleston reasoned, "because if Congress can exercise these controls over the right of individuals, it is plausible that there is no limit to Congress's power to appropriate private property and liberty." At the close of the day's proceedings, Rolleston added a novel twist to his argument. As he had prepared his case, he told the justices, he perceived "that in the writings of members of this Court there is still a great facet of personal liberty that this Court stands for. This Court, under the Constitution, is the last bulwark of personal liberty. Where else can a man go to defend personal liberty?" Supporters of the Civil Rights Act had naturally argued that the measure expanded individual rights. Rolleston argued that the opposite was true. The Civil Rights Act, he charged, threatened the rights of the individual—to choose his associates, his customers, and his livelihood. Seizing on Congress's reliance on the commerce clause, Rolleston made the landmark legislation seem no loftier than a bit of tariff law. "Congress has the right to remove burdens from interstate commerce if it pertains to commerce," he said dismissively. "But I believe that the rights of individuals, the rights of people, the personal liberty of a person to do what he wants to, to run his business, is more important and more paramount than the commerce of the United States."[43]

Ultimately, Rolleston's appeal failed. On December 14, 1964, the Supreme Court unanimously upheld the Civil Rights Act's constitutionality. After reading the ruling, Rolleston issued a grim statement. "This decision opens the frightful door to unlimited power of a centralized government in Washington, in which the individual citizen and his personal liberty are of no importance," he announced. "It makes possible a socialistic state and eventual dictatorship. . . . This is a sad day for the cause of individual freedom." Despite his misgivings, Rolleston would abide by the Court's decision. He wouldn't be alone. In swift announcements, the representatives of Atlanta's major hotels, motels, and restaurants readily accepted the Court's ruling. "The hotels will obey the law," assured the president of the Atlanta Hotel Association. His counterpart at the Atlanta Restaurant Association agreed. The Civil Rights Act was "now the law of the land," he said; "I urge that all our members comply." Where voluntary negotiations and civil rights protests at the local level had failed, the clear and concrete intervention of the federal government succeeded, just as Ivan Allen had insisted. After nearly five years of unrest and upheaval, Atlanta's places of public accommodation had finally accepted desegregation.[44]

To no one's surprise, Lester Maddox proved to be the lone exception. "I'm not ever going to integrate," he vowed. "I'd be committing an act of treason against my country, a sin against God and a crime against man if I did." Despite his statements, Maddox's defiance was fast drawing to a close. On February 1, 1965, his trial for civil contempt began before Judge Frank Hooper. Maddox still maintained that his "new" restaurant, the Lester Maddox Cafeteria, should not be bound by the injunction against his "old" restaurant, the Pickrick. Furthermore, his attorneys insisted, the Lester Maddox Cafeteria restricted its clientele according to political—not racial—classifications. "Color doesn't have anything to do with rejection of customers from my place of business," Maddox testified. "I will never serve integrationists regardless of race, color, creed, or national origin." For the defense, Sidney Schell prodded the prosecution's witnesses, asking each if he were an "integrationist," which he defined as "one who holds the political belief that the federal government has or should have the power to require an individual to render personal service to another against his will." That was too much for Judge Hooper. "I do not approve of this line of questioning," he interrupted. Lawyers for the plaintiffs, however, pressed the issue themselves, to show how ridiculous it was. William Alexander asked Maddox directly: "How do you know an integrationist when you see one?" "Well, the white ones," Maddox replied evasively, "they just look like integrationists." In his ruling just days later, Judge Hooper rejected the segregationist's sleight-of-hand and held Maddox in contempt. The Justice Department had asked for a contempt fine of $1,000, but Judge Hooper assessed a different penalty. There would be no fine for past contempt, he ruled, but any future act of contempt would be penalized at a rate of $200 a day. Furthermore, the fine would be assessed from the date of his order, Hooper noted, regardless of when the actual act of contempt took place. If blacks were denied service on the tenth day, for example, Maddox would owe $2,000; if blacks were turned away on the thirtieth day, he would owe $6,000.[45]

The next day, Lester Maddox surprised the city by announcing he would abide by the ruling. In a quaking voice, Maddox stood outside his restaurant and read yet another prepared statement to reporters. The Civil Rights Act had caused "more hate, prejudice, violence, death and property destruction than any other law," he charged. But he would obey it. "I have been bound by things I think unjust," Maddox said sadly, "but I must obey the law." Appealing to a higher power, he invoked the Book of Mark: "No man can enter into a strong man's house and spoil his goods, except he will first bind the strong man; and then he will spoil his house." During the next day's Sunday lunch, a forty-nine-year-old black tailor named Jack Googer showed up at the cafeteria's door. "You got any fried chicken in here today?" he asked an employee. As the man ran off to find Maddox, a small group of whites crowded around the tailor. "Don't you push me, nigger," one snarled. "I didn't push you," Googer replied. "You're just trying to make trouble." Minutes later, Maddox posted a sign in the door: "Closed. Out of business resulting from act passed by the U.S. Congress, signed by Pres. Johnson and inspired and supported by deadly and bloody communism." But even this defiance was short-lived. After a week, Maddox leased the restaurant to two of his employees, who reopened it as the Gateway Cafeteria. "All orderly individuals and groups" would be welcome, they announced. On February 23, 1965, Googer returned for another try. He passed through the serving line, picked out a meal of fish, string beans, pie and milk, and dined without incident. As Googer ate, Lester Maddox drove by the building twice but never entered. The Pickrick had finally integrated.[46]

THE REPERCUSSIONS OF FEDERAL INTERVENTION

Most observers, in Atlanta and the nation, interpreted the integration of the Pickrick as a sign that the Civil Rights Act had succeeded. There had been a showdown between the federal government and the last remaining segregationists, and the government had won. In truth, however, the Civil Rights Act did not significantly weaken the power of segregationists. By making manifest their darkest predictions about the supposedly coercive nature of liberal politics and the "tyranny" of a national government riding roughshod over the rights of individual businessmen, the enactment and enforcement of the Civil Rights Act of 1964 paradoxically strengthened the politics of white resistance throughout the South. This fact was perhaps made clearest in Georgia, where the first governor elected after its enactment was none other than Lester Maddox.

Maddox reached the governor's mansion through an unlikely combination of good luck, bad competition, and hard-nosed campaigning. When he announced his candidacy for the 1966 Democratic nomination, he was quickly dismissed as the dark horse in a field of six candidates. When the frontrunner withdrew with health problems and others stumbled on the campaign trail, however, Maddox emerged with a solid second-place finish in the Democratic primary. In the run-off, Maddox faced former Governor Ellis Arnall. A once popular and progressive figure in state politics, Arnall now seemed out of touch. In a crucial gaffe, he failed to understand the depths of white anger over the national Democratic Party's embrace of civil rights. As other southern Democrats finessed the issue, Arnall simply announced that he was a Georgia Democrat and a national Democrat—and anyone who didn't like it "could go to Hell." Meanwhile, Maddox had a visceral appeal for the average voter. "He's a folk hero," one Georgian noted. "People look at him and understand exactly what he stands for and it's what they stand for." When the runoff votes in the Democratic primary were counted, a stunned state learned that Maddox had crushed Arnall, 430,000 to 360,000.[47]

No one was more surprised—or disgusted—than the state's moderates. Mayor Ivan Allen Jr. dashed off a bitter statement. "It is deplorable that the combined forces of ignorance, prejudice, reactionism, and the duplicity of many Republican voters have thrust upon the State of Georgia Lester Maddox, a totally unqualified individual," Allen announced. "The seal of the great State of Georgia lies tarnished." The moderation which Atlanta had achieved must not, the mayor warned, "be surrendered to the rabble of prejudice, extremism, buffoonery, and incompetency." ("If you think that was a strong statement," a friend told the *New York Times*, "you should have seen what he was going to say before we toned him down.") Congressman Charles Weltner went even further than the mayor. In the midst of his own reelection campaign, Weltner had signed a normally perfunctory oath to support all of his party's candidates in the fall election. Rather than support Maddox, however, he resigned. "I cannot compromise with hate," he announced. "I cannot vote for Lester Maddox. I will give up my office before I give up my principles."[48]

In the fall election, Maddox faced Republican Howard "Bo" Callaway, a former Democrat and a staunch segregationist in his own right. In 1964, Callaway had ridden Barry Goldwater's coattails to become the first Republican congressman from Georgia since Reconstruction. Although Callaway came from a rather different background than Maddox—he was the young heir to a textile fortune—the two men were virtually indistinguishable in their politics. In a statement which could have easily come from his opponent, Callaway claimed that "God, the individual, and free enterprise" were the three ideals for which he stood. During his time in the House, the young Republican quickly became Georgia's most conservative congressman. He was the only one, for instance, to receive a "liberal" rating of zero from Americans for Democratic Action. As historian Numan Bartley noted, Callaway's ability to outflank his colleagues in their conservative politics was "a feat of no mean magnitude considering the ideological orientation of the Georgia congressional delegation." Much like the middle-class segregationists of Atlanta who learned to rid themselves of the appearance of radicalism and instead project an air of respectability, Bo Callaway had the sense to present his views in subtler terms. As a shrewd press aide to Lester Maddox acknowledged, the Goldwater Republican "represented old Southern Democrat segregationist ideals," but he smartly "presented these views in a vocabulary of couched euphemisms and respectable synonyms." Other observers agreed. Congressman Charles Weltner, for instance, issued a statement claiming that "Callaway is the same as Maddox on race, except in a slicker way. He uses code names such as 'property rights,' which means 'we ain't gonna serve no niggers.' "[49]

Indeed, the rise of southern Republicanism, in the person of Bo Callaway and others like him, was largely due to the white backlash against the Civil Rights Act. No one understood this fact more than President Lyndon Johnson. Upon signing the landmark legislation, he famously told an aide that he had just "delivered the South to the Republican Party for a long time to come." The proof of Johnson's prediction became clear in his reelection campaign that year, when he was pitted against Republican Senator Barry Goldwater, who had voted against the Civil Rights Act. Importantly, Goldwater claimed he opposed not integration itself, but federal intervention to achieve it. "It is wise and just for Negro children to attend the same schools as whites," he wrote in 1960, but "I am firmly convinced . . . that the Constitution does not permit any interference whatsoever by the federal government in the field of education." With Goldwater and Johnson moving their parties in different directions in terms of federal involvement in civil rights, voters came to see the parties as distinctly divided on these issues. As late as 1962, polls asking which political party was "more likely to see to it that Negroes get fair treatment in jobs and housing" showed that Americans saw virtually no difference between Democrats and Republicans. But in 1964, when asked the same question, 60 percent said Democrats and 7 percent said Republicans. Asked which party was more likely to support school integration, 56 percent pointed to the Democrats while 7 percent did so for the Republicans. In the South, such assumptions about the parties' racial policies led segregationist whites to rally around the Republican banner for the first time in a century. Not surprisingly, Barry Goldwater won every state in the Deep South.[50]

Although Goldwater failed to win the White House that year, his campaign had a transformative effect on southern Republicanism. To be sure, the party had won southern states in the presidential races of the postwar years, but such successes had little impact at the local level, in terms of either party identification or down-ticket victories. Indeed, for much of that era, the regional presence of the Republican Party had been laughable. "It scarcely deserves the name of party," noted political scientist V. O. Key Jr. in 1949. "It wavers somewhat between an esoteric cult on the order of a lodge and a conspiracy for plunder in accord with the accepted customs of our politics." In Georgia, as elsewhere, the state Republican Party had been a small collection of blacks who still held an allegiance to the "Party of Lincoln" and a few transplanted white moderates who failed to understand why they had to change parties simply because they had changed addresses. In Atlanta, for instance, there had been a few white Republicans, such as Judge Elbert Tuttle, and a slightly larger number of black Republicans, like John Welsey Dobbs. These Eisenhower Republicans not only took a fairly liberal stance on civil rights but looked favorably on the federal government as well. Indeed, as a judge of the U.S. circuit court and an employee of the U.S. Post Office, respectively, these two Republicans were themselves *part* of the federal government.[51]

The Civil Rights Act and the Goldwater insurgency brought into the Georgia Republican Party a rather different constituency, one that opposed both the goals of the civil rights movement and the means that the federal government used to reach them. Bo Callaway, of course, embodied this new group. When he became the first Georgia Republican elected to Congress since Reconstruction, the state party found itself forced to choose between the old constituency of Eisenhower moderates, who had been loyal to the party but ineffective, and the new group of Goldwater conservatives, who demonstrated success at the polls. In the state assembly elections of 1965, the Georgia GOP tried to please both branches by advancing moderate black candidates in urban districts and conservative white candidates in the suburbs. The black candidates all lost decisively, but the whites made impressive gains, taking in nine seats in Atlanta's suburbs and eight more in other metropolitan areas. Seeing their presence in the General Assembly soar from four seats to nineteen on the basis of its conservative appeals, the Georgia GOP understood where its future stood.[52]

The 1966 gubernatorial race demonstrated the newfound strength of Georgia's Republicans. In past years, the general election had been little more than a formality, since the Democratic nominee always won. In 1966, however, the Republican candidate not only made it a closely contested election, but actually secured more votes than his Democratic rival. When the final tallies were in, Callaway edged Maddox by a slim margin of less than 3,000 votes. Only the fact that Ellis Arnall had taken in some

50,000 votes in a write-in campaign prevented Callaway from claiming victory then and there. Because none of the candidates had the absolute majority required by law, the election was thrown to the Georgia General Assembly, which was empowered to choose from the top two candidates. On the night of January 10, 1967, the legislature convened in a special session to make its decision. In the end, confronted with the choice of Lester Maddox or what would have been the first Republican governor since Reconstruction, the overwhelmingly Democratic legislature swallowed hard and went with the Democrat, by a vote of 182 to 62.[53]

As Maddox was installed in the governor's mansion, many across the country reacted with horror. "Things here in Georgia are bad," Ralph McGill confided to President Lyndon Johnson. Maddox was a "psycho," he warned, and the thought of him in the governor's mansion was "something that makes you draw back in disbelief that such a thing could be possible. The very worst old ones in the state are attached to him like leeches—Marvin Griffin, Roy Harris, and that crowd—but maybe Georgia deserves it." Mayor Allen was just as despondent. "For eight years, this state has had its mind on important issues," he fumed off the record. "Now we go back to our old ways." There was simply one ugly, inescapable issue, he said: "You can't get away from the fact this man was elected partially by the third of the people of Georgia who hate Niggers." Of all the criticism pouring down on Maddox, the unkindest cut of all came from his own political hero. Speaking with Walter Cronkite of CBS, Barry Goldwater reflected on the vote just taken by the General Assembly. "Georgia was a most progressive Southern state," the senator noted, "and all of a sudden they have a fellow that belongs back in the Stone Age, and I think if the Legislature of Georgia were really true to their state's reputation, they'd see that Maddox went back to serving hot dogs." At this, Cronkite interrupted: "It was fried chicken." "Fried chicken," Goldwater mused, "is that right? And baseball bats."[54]

Although both Democrats and Republicans dismissed Maddox's election as an aberration and an embarrassment, the central themes of his political appeal, particularly his hostility to federal "interference" in local affairs, had firmly taken root in Georgia and, indeed, the rest of the South. In the 1966 election, both parties had run candidates who stood strongly opposed to the civil rights movement, the Great Society, and their intersection as federal intervention in local race relations. This was no accident. Southern Democrats had long understood the depths of white resentment to these issues and, now, in the wake of the Goldwater revolution, southern Republicans had learned the lesson too. In an ironic touch, the Civil Rights Act succeeded in eliminating the last legal vestiges of segregation in the South but, in so doing, etched the worldview of segregationists ever more firmly onto the political landscape.

CHAPTER NINE

City Limits:
Urban Separatism and Suburban Secession

BY THE END of the 1960s, the effects of white resistance to desegregation and white flight from it were apparent to all Atlantans. But how they appreciated the legacies of white flight depended largely on where they stood and where they looked. For those still inside the city limits, white flight represented the last gasp of segregationists. The black community, together with a scattering of white liberals and a moderate white elite undisturbed by the racial changes in the city, could only view the suburban exodus as the racists' retreat. For decades, the two sides had struggled over the racial terrain of the city, but now segregationists had finally abandoned the field. At long last, a new era of black power and empowerment would dawn inside cities like Atlanta. For those in the suburbs who looked back at the city, however, white flight represented not a closed chapter from the past but rather a current state of mind. The decision to leave the city had changed their outlook, and their arrival in the suburbs did nothing to change it back. Once settled in suburbia, these whites did not abandon the mind-set of white flight but instead carried it to its logical conclusion, what might be termed the "politics of suburban secession." During the 1970s, these suburbanites severed all local ties with the city and, once that was accomplished, made their presence felt on the national stage to ensure that the isolation they now enjoyed in the suburbs would never be disturbed.

A NEW ERA IN ATLANTA: "FULL PARTNERSHIP OR SEPARATISM"

White flight had, of course, brought dramatic changes to the city of Atlanta itself. The most obvious transformation came in the racial composition of the population. As late as 1960, Atlanta's white population stood at just over 300,000. Over the course of that decade, however, roughly 60,000 whites fled the city. During the 1970s, another 100,000 left. Naturally, as whites fled, the city's racial balance swiftly shifted from white to black. Blacks represented little more than a third of the city's residents in 1960, more than half by 1970, and a full two-thirds by 1980. The changes in population had a ripple effect throughout the rest of Atlanta.

The urban landscape had been altered in ways both big and small, with everything from the placement of massive projects such as interstate highways and public housing to the rezoning of individual neighborhoods hinging on the shifting demography of the city. Community institutions had come and gone, and the provision of public spaces and public services had been radically transformed as well, perhaps forever.[1]

As significant as all of the changes in Atlanta's physical landscape were, they paled in comparison to the changes white flight had wrought on the city's political landscape. "For nearly two decades," Ivan Allen Jr. later reflected, "the black community had been a silent partner in the election of city officials in Atlanta, generally going along with whatever moderate candidate the white business and civic fathers endorsed." But as it grew larger in size and more radical in its politics, the black population chafed at its "silent partner" role. Truthfully, the old relationship with the business establishment had been decaying for the better part of the 1960s. The student sit-ins had brought to the forefront new tensions at the dawn of the decade, tensions that erupted again when the national wave of urban unrest hit Atlanta during disturbances in Summerhill in 1966 and Dixie Hills in 1967. All the while, the older generation of black leaders slowly but steadily passed away, replaced by militant advocates of Black Power like Stokely Carmichael and H. Rap Brown. The new leaders had no patience for drawn-out negotiations, no trust in the white establishment. "Ivan Allen was a chump," Brown later recalled. "Like the rest of the chumps at that time. A dude who took advantage of the situation."[2]

As Atlanta's black militants rejected the white power structure, the establishment responded in kind. The dramatic shift in white moderates' attitude found countless avenues of expression, but the most telling change occurred in former Mayor Hartsfield. The old politician had long bragged about his pivotal role in the election of President John F. Kennedy, but by the decade's end he was commiserating with conservative Vice President Spiro Agnew about the "phony liberals and so-called intellectuals," whom Hartsfield claimed were "far more bigoted and intolerant than the old southern racists whom I used to denounce." Indeed, by the end of the 1960s, the mayor who had regularly bragged about the "city too busy to hate" found plenty of time to complain about civil rights activists and other liberals in his midst. "We have spent billions in welfare and in coddling racial agitators, only to see the blackened ruins of our principal cities," he groused in 1968. "Not a very pretty picture, but I sincerely hope that a wave of conservatism will sweep over the country before it is too late."[3]

With distrust and apprehension rising on all sides, the crumbling coalition of blacks and white businessmen finally collapsed in 1969. As Mayor Ivan Allen retired, the city searched for a replacement. The white elite settled on Rodney Cook, a white alderman and, in a notable departure from traditional politics, a Republican. Meanwhile, their black counterparts not only split away from the old coalition but also divided their vote again, between Sam Massell, the Jewish vice mayor, and Horace Tate, a black school board member. In the primary, Massell's middle-of-the-road identity won him the race. He split the black vote with Tate and took a fifth of the white vote from Cook. In the runoff election between Massell and Cook, Massell captured a staggering 92 percent of the black vote— even though Tate endorsed Cook—and, as a result, Massell won the election. The new strength of black Atlanta was underlined by the fact that the number of black aldermen jumped from one to five, out of a total of eighteen, and the city even elected its first black vice mayor.[4]

The new vice mayor, Maynard Jackson Jr., personified not just the new political strength of black Atlanta, but also the growing pains that came with it, such as the generational divide. As the grandson of John Wesley Dobbs, Jackson had deep, personal ties to the elder generation. But the thirty-one-year-old distanced himself from its watch. When Jackson announced his candidacy, the black establishment was completely caught off guard. The elders had planned to focus on races for the board of aldermen and board of education, but Jackson's unforeseen announcement upset their plans. Several were furious that he would go ahead without their blessing. (One asked angrily, "Who'd he *check* with?") Despite his brashness, Jackson demonstrated convincingly that it was finally time for blacks to reach for the city's highest offices. In his race for vice mayor, he snared 98 percent of the black vote and easily defeated a white opponent. Jackson immediately became an odds-on favorite for the next mayoral race, when the black vote would represent half the total.[5]

For members of the city's white elite, the political awakening of black Atlanta was sobering. After ruling the city's political scene for well over two decades, they had seen the supposedly weaker half of their coalition break away from them—and win. In 1971 the Atlanta Chamber of Commerce caught its breath and took stock of the changes unfolding around it. "The old marriage wherein City Hall and the Chamber were practically identical in character and goals is dead," noted its planning committee. "The 'junior partner' role of the black leadership in the last decade has been rejected by the black leaders. Full partnership or separatism are the two courses now open." Ultimately, however, the old white elite and new black political power forged yet another Atlanta compromise. Instead of choosing between "full partnership" or "separatism," they chose both. In the more occasional realm of politics and economics, the two groups would continue to work closely; but in their day-to-day life, the races would remain as separate as they had been during the Jim Crow era—if not more so.[6]

By the early 1970s the persistence of racial "separatism" inside Atlanta was undeniable. Despite the apparent triumphs of the civil rights movement in Atlanta, the city remained highly segregated. According to the segregation indices developed by sociologists Douglas Massey and Nancy Denton, Atlanta was actually more segregated in 1970 than it had been in 1940. Although white flight had opened up many individual neighborhoods to black residents for the first time, the phenomenon also heightened the concentration of blacks and whites in different, discrete sections of the city. There were exceptions to the rule, but blacks essentially occupied most of central and southern Atlanta, while the white population remained centered on the posh neighborhoods of the Northside. The two sides came together in municipal politics and economic issues, but they rarely interacted in any meaningful social sense. "Like the residents of old, divided Berlin," noted journalist Tamar Jacoby, "Atlantans lived in self-contained zones, not exactly antagonistic, but cut off and indifferent to each other."[7]

Buckhead, the traditional Northside home of the white elite, remained the most prized residential area for whites inside Atlanta. With its beautiful large homes, lush tree-lined streets and a general air of serenity and security, the region seemed an ideal slice of suburban life inside the city limits. Buckhead not only replicated the physical feel of a stereotypical suburb, but its racial and economic characteristics as well. In 1970, for instance, almost all of its census tracts had populations that were less than 1 percent black, a degree of racial homogeneity that surpassed even the whitest of Atlanta's northern suburbs. Not surprisingly, Buckhead remained home to the city's wealthiest and most powerful white families. The Allens and Woodruffs had long made their homes there, and now so did the new leaders of the white business elite. Even as they tried to pursue a new "partnership" with the ever-growing black community in city politics, the white businessmen of Buckhead would still have their own white city-within-a-city as their retreat. "It was as gracious—and segregated—a life as it had ever been," reflected one reporter. "In those north-side neighborhoods, it might as well still have been 1958."[8]

Confronted with the pervasiveness and persistence of residential segregation, Atlanta's civil rights leadership gave a strong signal in the early 1970s that the decades-long drive for desegregation would be relaxed. The key arena here was the same one that had long dominated the city's struggles over segregation, the public schools. Since 1961, Atlanta's school system had been technically desegregated under a "freedom of choice" plan. These plans seemed fair on paper, in that they supposedly allowed all parents to send their children to the schools of their choice. But a closer examination showed that, in practice, such plans parceled out the "freedom of choice" unevenly. Black parents had to petition for their children's transfer themselves and then overcome a complex series of bureaucratic obstacles. White parents, meanwhile, had a much easier time keeping their children in largely white schools. As a result, the "freedom of choice" scheme fostered little real integration in Atlanta, or in other cities for that matter. As late as the 1969—70 school year, only 20,000 students in Atlanta's system of over 100,000 pupils attended desegregated schools. The bar for considering schools "desegregated" had been set extremely low—a school merely needed a minimum of 10 percent of both blacks and whites in its student body—but, still, only 34 out of 117 public schools met the standard. While the "freedom of choice" plan did little to encourage integration, it certainly enabled white flight from the school system. By 1970 white enrollment in the public schools had plummeted to half what it had been at its peak in 1963. While whites and blacks had been evenly represented in the 1964–65 school year, black students outnumbered whites by margins of two-to-one in 1969 and three-to-one in 1971. Frustrated by white flight, school officials threw up their hands. "I don't know what you can do," shrugged Benjamin Mays, the black head of the school board, "to keep white folks from being scared if you move into their neighborhood."[9]

The continued segregation of Atlanta's public schools made it clear that the "freedom of choice" concept had been little different than the old segregationist trope of "freedom of association." To be sure, southern whites defended the new phrase with as much passion as the old. As an official with the Department of Health, Education and Welfare (HEW) later marveled, "One would find that freedom to choose one's own school was being talked about in the South in the same breath as the freedoms of speech and assembly under the First Amendment." Southern moderates understood the significance and sought to educate the nation about it. On February 4, 1969, Ralph McGill turned his column in the *Constitution* into an open letter to Robert Finch, who, as the incoming HEW secretary for the Nixon administration, would lead the federal government's enforcement of school desegregation. "There is all too often no freedom in the freedom of choice plan," McGill explained. "It too frequently is freedom in reverse. It offers a segregationist, racist-dominated community or board an opportunity to proclaim a free choice, while they covertly employ 'persuasions' to maintain segregation or meager tokenism." The "freedom of choice" approach, McGill warned, was simply segregation in a subtler form. "It will be the greatest tragedy with the most foreboding consequences if public school officials are allowed to perpetuate dual school systems," he warned Secretary Finch. "You may be assured, sir, that the freedom of choice plan is, in fact, neither freedom nor a choice. It is discrimination." This column from the Pulitzer Prize winner was made even more forceful by the fact that it was his last. The night before its publication, Ralph McGill passed away.[10]

As Atlantans found the "freedom of choice" approach unworkable, so too did the federal courts. In 1968 the U.S. Supreme Court indicated in *Green v. New Kent County, Virginia* that "freedom of choice" plans were no longer sufficient to fulfill the Court's desegregation mandate and had to be replaced with more aggressive approaches. Like many cities, Atlanta then shifted to a program of majority-to-minority student transfers as a way to create a greater racial balance in city schools. In 1971, the Court signaled in *Swann v. Charlotte-Mecklenburg County* that metropolitan busing programs could be used to aid and enlarge such an approach. While other cities adopted such plans, black leaders in Atlanta balked at the idea. "Massive busing would be counterproductive at this point," Benjamin Mays sighed. "We'd end up with no whites to bus." Lonnie King, the former sit-in organizer who then led the local NAACP, agreed with the school board president. "There were no white kids to bus," he mused later. "You'd be busing children from an 87 percent black school to another 87 percent black school."[11]

Instead of seeking a solution through wide-scale busing, the Atlanta school board and the local NAACP forged yet another of the city's negotiated settlements, an agreement that critics called the "Atlanta Compromise" of 1973. For its part, the school board promised to increase student transfers, to create a program of biracial magnet schools, to integrate school staffs further, and to make aggressive moves toward increasing the number of blacks in administrative positions. In exchange, the local NAACP branch agreed to drop its ongoing lawsuit against the school board and ease its demands for massive, metropolitan-wide busing. Although the settlement seemed the best solution to local parties, the national NAACP was outraged. As NAACP attorney Howard Moore put it, the Atlanta chapter had traded "the constitutional rights of Negro pupils for the constitutional rights of Negro administrators." After suspending Lonnie King and other local officials, the national organization sought to scuttle the settlement. But the district court approved the plan anyway, issuing a final decree in May 1974 and thus accepting the end of Atlanta's decades-long school desegregation suit.[12]

While the Atlanta Compromise ended the legal struggles over school segregation, it did nothing to stem the tide of white flight from the city's public schools. In fact, whites continued to abandon the city and its public school system at a staggering rate. In 1973 whites still made up 23 percent of the total enrollment. By 1985, however, that figure had fallen to just 6 percent. By 2002 the nearly completely black character of Atlanta's public school system was unmistakable. Of the city's 93 schools, 54 had just 1 or 2 white students enrolled, while another 21 had no white students at all. The massive drop in white enrollment was due not simply to the larger migration of whites to the suburbs, but to the fact that whites who stayed in the city generally opted for private schools instead. In 1985, for instance, the city's school system had only 7,000 white students out of a total enrollment of 110,000. Private academies, meanwhile, enrolled about 12,000 students, the vast majority of whom were white. Once again, Atlanta seemed split into two cities: a public one, officially "desegregated" but almost completely black, and a private one, nominally "integrated" but overwhelmingly white. Looking back on the Atlanta Compromise, many civil rights activists believed the settlement represented not simply the end of a decades-long drive to desegregate the city's schools but an abandonment of the civil rights struggle on a wide variety of fronts. "It was the end of integration in Atlanta," judged one activist. "The school deal killed whatever chances it might have had."[13]

Instead of opting for full integration, many black Atlantans rested their hopes on securing a greater degree of political power in the city. The same year the local NAACP worked to get black control of the local school system, the city also elected its first black mayor, Maynard Jackson Jr. Incumbent mayor Sam Massell had been a compromise candidate in 1969, precariously positioned between the black community and the white business elite, yet fully embraced by neither. As mayor, Massell initially tried to straddle the racial divide as Allen and Hartsfield had before him, but when it became apparent that he could not surpass his vice mayor's standing in the black community, he placed his reelection hopes in white hands. A desperate ad that illustrated Massell's new tactic cautioned voters that "Atlanta's Too Young To Die." Although Massell insisted that the slogan was simply about Jackson's lack of experience, many voters—white and black—understood it as a warning that a black mayor would destroy Atlanta. With racism injected into the election, the final vote was starkly segregated. 95 percent of black votes went to Jackson; 83 percent of white votes to Massell.[14]

While the city's election of a black mayor represented a revolution in southern politics, many Atlantans—including the new mayor—hoped that some practical elements of the old system could be preserved. Shortly after taking office, Jackson sought to repair the bridge between city hall and the Chamber of Commerce. "I don't need you guys to get elected," he told the head of Citizens & Southern Bank, "but I've learned that I certainly need you to govern." In spite of such overtures, Jackson and the business community never really warmed to each other. Dan Sweat, executive director of Central Atlanta Progress (CAP), a powerful organization of downtown businesses, remembered that his colleagues watched Jackson assume the mayoralty with "a great sense of apprehension, fear, . . . in some cases bordering on panic." A major point of contention came when the new mayor forcefully tried to "integrate the money" in Atlanta. He held up $400 million in airport construction until white businesses complied with a plan to allocate a fifth of construction contracts to minority firms and then threatened to remove another $450 million in city funds from white banks unless they likewise removed racial restrictions from their loan policies. Many white businesses recoiled from the moves. In 1974 CAP became so worried over the white flight of businesses from the city that Harold Brockey, chairman of both Rich's Department Store and CAP, sent the mayor a telling letter. Noting that some businesses "have moved and more are considering moving for other than economic or management reasons," CAP gave him a list of grievances, including a "perceived racial split in leadership, growing racial imbalance of the labor force, fear of crime, . . . schools [which] lack racial and income mix, . . . white flight from the city, perceived attitudes of the mayor as anti-white, [and] dilution of the partnership between government and business in Atlanta which [has] resulted in a major communications-action vacuum." The papers reported the letter, which they characterized as a strong "attack" on Jackson. The mayor downplayed the criticism and tried to calm the fears of businessmen, but he ultimately made little progress.[15]

Andrew Young, mayor from 1982 to 1990, had much more success in rebuilding the bridges between city hall and the Chamber of Commerce. After his election, he too met with white business leaders and repeated, almost verbatim, the words of Maynard Jackson. "I know none of you voted for me," he said. "That's over now. I can't do what I need to do without you. I need your help." While his predecessor had rarely backed up such words with deeds, Young quickly moved to win businessmen to his side. He eased the burden on property taxes, for instance, and cut the red tape for new construction projects, paving the way for approval of a record 20,000 projects in his first three years. As one critic later put it, "He never met a building permit he didn't like." For white businessmen, of course, that was a good thing. Years later, builder Bob Holder marveled how Andrew Young, the civil rights activist once considered so radical by the white elite, "turned out to be the best friend a business community ever had." In 1985, a reporter for *Esquire* magazine summed up the renewed relationship between the black mayor and the white establishment with praise that would have made the civil rights community cringe. "Andy Young," the reporter noted, "is doing for Atlanta what Reagan has done for America: he's making rich white people feel good again."[16]

As the business community rediscovered its old faith in city hall, the old combination of black political power and white economic might resurfaced, only with black mayors now serving as the balancing point. To be sure, Mayor Young consciously thought of himself as a conduit between the two groups. "My job," he told a reporter in 1985, "is to see

that whites get some of the power and blacks get some of the money."
Under his watch, the new relationship showed results. For five straight
years, from 1982 to 1987, metropolitan Atlanta led the nation in job
growth. Hartsfield International Airport soon carried 2,400 flights a day,
attracting new migrants and new businesses alike. Old stalwarts like
Coca-Cola were joined by new corporate giants, such as Delta Airlines,
BellSouth, Home Depot, United Parcel Service (UPS), and the Cable News
Network (CNN). To be sure, some members of this new business elite
lacked the civic-mindedness of their forbearers. After merging R. J. Reynolds with Nabisco and moving the corporate headquarters to Atlanta, for
instance, Ross Johnson made it clear to the Atlanta Rotary Club that he
would not be active in the city's philanthropy. "I told them that I can't
support every organization from the United Way to the Seven Jolly Girls
Athletic Club Beanbag competition," he told a reporter. "If it pisses them
off, I can't help that." But many in the new Chamber of Commerce kept
alive the boosterish spirit of their predecessors. Notably, Coca-Cola remained as involved under new CEO Roberto Goizueta as it had under its
old "Boss," Robert Woodruff. So did Ted Turner, founder of CNN and
owner of the Atlanta Braves and Atlanta Hawks. As a sign of the city's
renaissance, Atlanta soon began hosting such showcase events as the 1988
Democratic National Convention and the 1996 Centennial Olympic
Games.[17]

In the end, the new world of Atlanta looked very much like the old.
Together, black political power and white economic strength had once
again combined to create a boosterish, business-focused power structure.
Although the figureheads were now black, the essential relationship between the two groups seemed unchanged. But there was a noticeable difference in the new arrangement, since the coalition was, for the first time
since its founding, no longer confronted with the resistance of reactionary
whites. This was not, of course, because such segregationist whites
changed their minds; it was because they changed their addresses. In the
suburbs surrounding the city—away from Atlanta, away from the biracial
coalition, and away from blacks—whites created the Atlanta of which the
city's segregationists long dreamed.

THE LOCAL POLITICS OF SUBURBAN SECESSION

While the processes of white flight had wrought tremendous changes inside the city limits of Atlanta, those transformations were almost insignificant when compared with the massive changes in the suburbs surrounding it. The steady stream of white middle-class migrants to these
regions, first from inside Atlanta and then from other parts of the country,

launched an era of incredible population and economic growth. Despite the boosterish talk about the city's revival during the 1970s and 1980s, the vast majority of the "Atlanta boom" actually took place in the suburbs. "If you look at the statistics on a five-county metropolitan basis, Atlanta looks like the booming Sun Belt," the city's planning director noted in 1983. "But based on the city limits, we look like Newark. It's that simple." (In truth, Atlanta looked *worse*. Its population losses in the 1970s actually outpaced Newark's.) Despite the steady loss of Atlanta's residents, the total metropolitan population continued to rise. The surrounding suburbs more than doubled their population in the 1970s and continued to grow after that. During the 1980s, some 86 percent of Atlanta's metropolitan population growth occurred in the suburban ring, especially along the northern rim—Cobb County to the northwest, Gwinnett County to the northeast, and, between them, a small section of Fulton County north of the city limits. Of the ten fastest-growing counties in America during the 1980s, three stood situated outside Atlanta and one of them, Cobb County, took top honors as the fastest-growing in the nation. By 1999 Cobb and Gwinnett *each* had a population greater than that of the city of Atlanta.[18]

For those who had long taken pride in Atlanta's stature, the suburban surge came as a shock. As late as the mid-1960s Atlanta's political and business leaders were working toward a revitalized downtown, which they imagined would keep affluent residents close to the city's center and help fuel a booming economy. For instance, when Ben Massell, the largest individual landowner in the city, first learned of the plans for a perimeter highway around Atlanta, he assumed the new road would serve as a dividing line between a prestigious and prosperous central city and the backwards regions huddled around it. "Like the Chicago loop!" he shouted. "Everything on the inside, chicken salad! Everything on the outside, chicken shit!" In time, the Interstate-285 Perimeter would serve as a line of demarcation between an economy which boomed and one which had gone bust, but the relationship would be precisely the reverse of the one imagined by Massell. Indeed, by every economic indicator, Atlanta's suburbs swiftly outpaced the city. Between 1963 and 1972, for instance, Atlanta's share of retail sales in the metropolitan area fell from 66 to 44 percent, with the share of the once-booming central business district (CBD) bottoming out at just 7 percent. Jobs followed the general pattern, as employment in the CBD fell from 20 to 12 percent between 1960 and 1975. If old-guard members of the business elite, such as Coca-Cola and Georgia Power, had not remained fiercely loyal to downtown Atlanta, the decline would have been even more pronounced. Instead of opening offices in the city center, Atlanta's new corporate arrivals largely settled in the suburbs. Ben Massell had assumed the Perimeter would keep businesses in the central city, but I-285 actually emerged as a magnet for new suburban office parks. As early as 1973, forty such business centers dotted both sides of the highway. With the Perimeter region emerging as a new economic hub, Atlanta's businesses abandoned downtown. Back in 1960, central Atlanta had contained roughly 90 percent of the region's office space; by 1980, it held only 42 percent; by 1999, just 13 percent.[19]

The sudden surge in suburbanization around Atlanta and elsewhere had been sparked by a number of factors. As historian Kenneth Jackson has demonstrated, individual desires for larger homes, safer streets, and neighborhoods characterized by a homogeneity of race and class led postwar Americans to the suburbs, where both land and housing costs were comparatively cheaper. These market-driven solutions were amplified by government policies that strongly encouraged such decisions. Taken together, the government's approach on a variety of fronts—tax policies that benefited homeowners instead of renters, transportation plans that called for highway construction instead of mass transit, public housing programs that placed low-income projects in the central cities, and federal loan policies that favored the construction of new housing over the renovation of old—all combined to funnel middle-class Americans toward suburbia. "Because of public policies favoring the suburbs, only one possibility was economically feasible," Jackson concluded. "The result, if not the intent, of Washington programs has been to encourage decentralization."[20]

Of course, such suburbanization took place in starkly segregated terms. As several urban historians have demonstrated, discriminatory federal policies—especially the FHA and VA lending programs that served as the engine of postwar suburbanization—greatly favored whites over blacks and the middle class over the poor. This is not to suggest that working-class whites and racial minorities were completely shut out from suburbia. To the contrary, as recent studies have shown, both groups secured places for themselves in suburbs across the country. On the eastern edges of Atlanta, for instance, middle-class blacks carved out their own suburban refuges in DeKalb County during the 1980s. But the arrival of minority or working-class residents in suburbia did not mean that suburbs now had anything resembling racial or socioeconomic integration. As a rule, the place created by such groups was a place apart. Through the use of exclusionary zoning, real-estate steering, and discriminatory lending practices, many suburbs sealed themselves off from groups they deemed undesirable as neighbors. Even though suburbia was not the sole province of affluent whites, the suburbs to which such whites fled largely were.[21]

The northern suburbs of Atlanta illustrate that, in many places, the stereotypical image of suburbia was grounded in a good degree of truth. In terms of income, for instance, residents of these suburbs stood well above the Atlanta average. In 1970 median incomes in the suburbs of

Gwinnett, Cobb, and north Fulton Counties were 14, 32, and 45 percent larger, respectively, than that of the city. (If the elite neighborhood of Buckhead were factored out of the city's figures, the urban-suburban difference would have been even more pronounced.) In terms of racial isolation, meanwhile, the suburban stereotype stood even closer to the mark. Again, in 1970, Gwinnett County stood at 95 percent white; Cobb County, 96 percent white; and the suburban section of north Fulton County, an astonishing 99 percent white. If such suburbs seemed stereotypically "suburban" in terms of their race and class composition, it was because they were.[22]

Despite the overwhelming whiteness of these suburbs and the importance of white flight in their creation, it would be a distortion to assume that Atlanta's suburbs were populated *only* by self-styled "refugees" from the city. As urban historian Carl Abbott noted in 1981, "The new resident of a suburban ring is typically a migrant from the suburbs of another metropolis, not a refugee from the central city." The changing demography of metropolitan Atlanta bears out this observation. During the 1960s, for instance, some 60,000 white residents fled the city, while the counties encircling it added nearly 360,000 newcomers in all. Even considered separately, the northern arc—Cobb, Gwinnett, and north Fulton—added more than 153,000 whites during the 1960s, more than twice the number of whites fleeing the city during the same period. Furthermore, census data demonstrates that half of those new arrivals to the northern suburbs, roughly 67,000 in all, came from areas outside metropolitan Atlanta. Clearly, then, the suburbs were not populated solely, or even mostly, by people fleeing the city, but instead by a mix of whites arriving from across the state, region, and nation.[23]

Whether they had been involved in white flight or not, the new arrivals to southern suburbs like those around Atlanta came to understand and accept the politics born out of white flight all the same. The whites who made their homes in the suburbs of Cobb, Gwinnett, and north Fulton counties blended together not just spatially but ideologically. The transformation of segregationist rhetoric in the postwar era had led southern conservatives to reject the traditional appeals to populism and racism and instead embrace a new, middle-class rhetoric of rights and responsibilities. The change in language had made segregationist politics much more palatable to whites inside the city, and it remained attractive to those in the suburbs. Removed from their obviously racial origins, segregationist phrases, such as "freedom of choice" or "neighborhood schools," as well as segregationist identities, such as the angry taxpayer or concerned parent, could be easily shared by middle-class whites who had no connection to the segregationist past but who gladly took part in crafting the suburban future.

Regardless of their origins, those who made homes for themselves in the suburbs generally held a common indifference to the people and problems of the city. The typical suburban resident, Carl Abbott observed in 1981, "has no ties to the core city, no sense of responsibility for its problems, and little need for its services that are duplicated in the 'main street' of the regional shopping mall." In the end, "it seems clear that central cities are simply outside the daily orbit" of suburbanites. A decade later, such observations had become commonplace. In 1990, for instance, urban theorist Mike Davis decried the "suburban separatism" he saw in the affluent areas around Los Angeles, while in 1992 Thomas and Mary Edsall similarly noted the rising independence and isolation of such suburbs across the nation. In their study of the New Jersey suburb of Mount Laurel, David Kirp, John Dwyer, and Larry Rosenthal likewise argued that the search for "a better life" in suburbia entailed leaving the problems of the city behind. "Pointedly, [white suburbanites] have left the city as blacks have been moving in," the authors noted. "The very last thing they want to do is to assume responsibility for those whom they deliberately left behind."[24]

Taken together, the attitudes of such suburbanites amounted to a national phenomenon that liberal political economist Robert Reich dubbed the "secession of the successful." In 1991 Reich noted that the country's most affluent were "quietly seceding from the large and diverse publics of America into homogenous enclaves, within which their earnings need not be redistributed to people less fortunate than themselves." Reich would soon thereafter become a member of Bill Clinton's administration, but his observations were shared by those across the political spectrum. That same year, for instance, conservative social scientist Charles Murray warned that the continued economic success of the upper class would "make it tempting to bypass the problem [of the underclass] by treating the inner city as an urban analogue of the Indian reservation."[25]

In the 1990s the suburbs around northern Atlanta embodied the secessionist attitude as well as anywhere else. "People who can afford it," noted the *New York Times Magazine* in 1996, "have increasingly fled to the suburbs, pushing the borders of the booming Atlanta metropolitan region farther and farther out, and separating themselves not only more and more from the city's old downtown, but also from any sense of responsibility for its future. Paradoxically," the piece continued, "the area is full of people who eagerly describe themselves as coming from Atlanta when they are far from home; once back, however, they think of themselves as residents of Sandy Springs or Roswell, with barely more feeling of connection to Atlanta than to Savannah." ("We still say we're from Atlanta when we travel," a suburban lawyer told another reporter. "No one's ever heard of 'East Cobb County.' ") But back home, Atlanta's suburbs had little identification with the city or, for that matter, each other. The area that national observers confidently referred to as "metropolitan Atlanta" actually consisted of 53 distinctly separate and frequently hostile governments. "And instead of getting more cooperative," the *Wall Street Journal* noted, "many believe they are becoming more Balkanized."[26]

While the "secessionist" nature of suburbs only came to national attention in the 1990s, suburbanites around Atlanta had been thinking and speaking in precisely such terms for well over two decades. The whites who had fought hard to defend their "freedom of association" inside cities like Atlanta had made their dreams manifest in the spatially and socially removed lands of suburbia. Not surprisingly, they were as determined to preserve their "freedom of association" in their new environments as they had in the old, if not more so. As a state legislator from the Atlanta area put it in 1971, "The suburbanite says to himself, 'The reason I worked for so many years was to get away from pollution, bad schools and crime, and I'll be damned if I'll see it all follow me.'" Likewise, Joe Mack Wilson, later mayor of the Cobb County seat of Marietta, summed up the secessionist attitude in 1975 with an appropriate image. Pointing to the Chattahoochee River which runs between the county and city, he tried to explain to an outsider the worldview of his constituents. "They love that river down there," he said. "They want to keep it as a moat. They wish they could build forts across there to keep people from coming up here."[27]

White suburbanites' desire to remain apart from the city was made abundantly clear in their repeated resistance to all forms of annexation by or incorporation with Atlanta. Whites on the city's outskirts had seen neighboring areas incorporated under Atlanta's last annexation campaign, the 1952 Plan of Improvement, only to be "ruined" by the racial changes that came with the city. And so, in the mid-1960s, when Atlanta's white leaders once again worried about the increasing black population and considered annexation the answer, these suburbanites would have none of it. In 1965, for instance, former Mayor Bill Hartsfield championed the incorporation of several northern suburbs, especially Sandy Springs, "so as to preserve the proper white balance which is necessary for amicable relations between both races." He called for immediate action, warning that "we have only 5 or 6 more years until the racial balance is 50–50 and then on its way to further racial imbalance at an accelerated pace. What are we waiting on?" Whites inside Atlanta readily accepted the idea. The head of the Chamber of Commerce told Hartsfield, "your thinking and ours is the same." But suburban whites refused to go along. "We will NEVER agree to coming into Atlanta," warned spokesmen for Sandy Springs. Instead, they vowed to "build up a city separate from Atlanta and your Negroes and forbid any Negroes to buy, or own or live within our limits. You have forced this on us and we will fight to the finish."[28]

In "defending" Sandy Springs and other areas north of Atlanta, white suburbanites appropriated the language of segregationists inside the city. A 1966 booklet, *Save Sandy Springs*, reminded whites that "the City power structure bases its ability to stay in office on being able to satisfy a Negro bloc vote." If the suburban communities were annexed by the city, their political clout would be overwhelmed. "We would be drawn into this quagmire and swallowed up without even making a ripple." A second leaflet made the same point, in cruder terms. "Under the one-man/one-vote ruling, the lowest, least educated and most irresponsible biped has the same vote as does the educated, responsible, and conscientious taxpayer," it observed. "What kind of government will this give us in the melting pot of Atlanta?" These whites worried that annexation would hurt them not just politically but economically. The reason for the annexation plan was simple, one pamphlet warned: "Atlanta needs our taxes." The city promised that those taxes would go for public improvements, but these suburban segregationists, much like their urban predecessors, believed that any such improvements would be made pointless by desegregation. "Even if we did have public parks," the piece noted, "the citizens of Sandy Springs are well aware that the people who have rendered Atlanta's public parks virtually useless to its white citizens would soon monopolize new parks in Sandy Springs." Echoing the earlier tax-revolt rhetoric of whites inside the city limits, these whites believed that they would foot the bill for public spaces used solely by blacks and then be cast aside. "Atlanta couldn't care less about the welfare of our (already) out-voted white citizens," they asserted. "Sandy Springs needs Atlanta like a hole in the head." With white resistance so strong, the plan to annex Sandy Springs failed, as did several other annexation and consolidation plans of the late 1960s and early 1970s. By 1983, an Atlanta economist could declare with confidence, "Annexation is pretty much a dead issue."[29]

Suburban whites resisted not just official annexation by Atlanta but any sort of association whatsoever. This trend was evident in the stiff resistance they offered to all attempts to address the region's growing pains through "metropolitan" approaches that linked the city and suburbs together. By the mid-1960s, for instance, intense population growth in the suburbs had led to incredible congestion on all major roads, forcing suburbanites to suffer long daily commutes into the city and face slow traffic even inside their enclaves. In spite of the apparent need for mass transit, suburbanites waged a sustained campaign against the Metropolitan Atlanta Rapid Transit Authority (MARTA) from its inception. In the early stages, suburbanites worried that MARTA would draw their neighborhoods into a program of metropolitan-wide busing to desegregate the city's schools. Some suspected that bus and rail lines would be used to transport poor black students to lily-white suburban schools. Others worried that if the suburbs and city were jointly identified, even unofficially, as "metropolitan Atlanta," the courts would think of the two areas that way, too. As a result, suburban counties refused to take part. Cobb County rejected the system in a 1965 vote and never looked back. MARTA was so unpopular there that local politicians refused to be associated even with the planning phases of the project for fear that it would end their careers. Cobb County commissioner Emmett Burton endeared himself to many of his constituents when he promised to "stock the Chattahoochee with piranha" if that were necessary to keep MARTA away. In a similar vein, two other counties—Clayton County to the south and Gwinnett to the northeast—likewise rejected MARTA by massive 4-1 margins in 1971. As a result, MARTA became a "metropolitan" system in name only. The suburbs refused to take part, and thereby remained isolated from the poor and minority residents of the city for decades to come. "For an unemployed Atlantan without a car," noted the *New York Times* in 1988, "jobs in Cobb and Gwinnett counties might as well be in China." That, of course, was precisely the point.[30]

Suburban whites claimed that opposition to MARTA was rooted not in racism, but rather in concrete worries about the influx of criminals who would surely flow out of the city. In 1987, for instance, bumper stickers could be found in Cobb County with the slogan, "Share Atlanta Crime—Support MARTA." Likewise, a Gwinnett man claimed in 1993 that resistance to MARTA had nothing to do with race, although his arguments suggested otherwise. "All the 'white flight' people moved to Gwinnett," he said. "These people have been sensitized to public transportation and the population of the inner city and moved away from it. It boils down to personal security." Despite such protests to the contrary, many observers—white and black, urban and suburban—repeatedly identified racism as the key reason for the persistent resistance. "The people you hear opposing MARTA in Cobb and Gwinnett, they've been pretty open about it," noted Rev. Joseph Lowery, a civil rights activist who had been on the transit system's board since 1975. "They don't want black people coming into their areas. It's blind prejudice and fear." Likewise, David Chestnut, the white chairman of MARTA, noted dejectedly in 1987 that the opposition to public transit had been "90 percent a racial issue." ("I am very disturbed," he sighed, "when I hear young professionals tell me they are going to form NNIG—No Niggers in Gwinnett.") A white Republican legislator from Gwinnett agreed with these views in 1993. "Couple of years ago they had a vote on MARTA," noted Mike Barnett, "and you would be surprised what people will tell you. They will come up with 12 different ways of saying they are not racist in public. They try to be nice and tippy-toe around it. But you get them alone, behind a closed door and you see this old blatant racism that we have had here for quite some time."[31]

The resistance to MARTA—and the low-income blacks whom white suburbanites associated with it—was merely part of a larger trend of suburban resistance to metropolitan-wide solutions to urban problems in the early 1970s. When the city sought to build low-income housing in unincorporated suburban areas, for instance, local residents fought the measure as strongly as they could. In a cynical move, suburban governments promptly created their own housing agencies—not to address the housing shortage themselves but to claim authority over unincorporated lands and thereby prevent the Atlanta Housing Authority from constructing its own housing there. As journalist Reese Cleghorn noted in 1971, "not one of the five county governments has a 'workable program,' so that none may receive funds for public housing or urban renewal. This may be assumed to be a calculated policy." The resistance of these suburban counties extended beyond public housing to all low-income housing. In the early 1970s, for instance, Fulton County's commissioners happily rezoned an area for multifamily use on the expectation that the site would feature "executive apartments" of a "luxury" character. But when the builder revealed plans to construct low-income housing instead, the commissioners refused to issue a building permit. The controversy soon wound up in the U.S. District Court as the case of *Crow v. Brown*. In his decision, Judge Newell Edenfield determined that "the only objection the County authorities have . . . is that the apartments would be occupied by low-income, black tenants" from Atlanta. As a result, Edenfield ordered the county to work with city officials to disperse public housing throughout the metropolitan area.[32]

Not surprisingly, suburbanites reacted with considerable alarm. They were, once again, furious over the assertion that they bore responsibility for solving the problems of a city they had purposely left behind. But unlike the MARTA controversy, the suburban resistance to public housing was made all the fiercer because the calls for metropolitan solutions to "urban" problems were being made by the federal government. In escaping the city, suburban whites had sought to escape not just the problems they associated with blacks but the solutions imposed by federal officials. Confronted with both once again, suburbanites renewed their rebellion. "Middle America is losing control of its own country," complained Congressman Ben Blackburn of DeKalb County. "I am really afraid that we are going to end up with some federal bureaucrat telling people where they have to live and in what kind of house." In a sign of how far suburban whites would go to stop the federal dispersal of public housing, the leaders of six small towns around Atlanta's southern rim petitioned the state to have their region of 120,000 residents consolidated as the new city of "South Fulton." "If we incorporate all our own land," the mayor of East Point promised, "we could be immune from this public housing requirement." Faced with such fierce resistance from suburban forces and the refusal of elected politicians to stand against them, the federal drive for public housing dispersal soon stalled. In the end, even Judge Edenfield backed away from his potentially revolutionary ruling. "There's nothing I can do," he shrugged. "The court, by the nature of the institution, cannot go out and execute the laws. I can't build public housing or have it built. I can't appropriate the funds."[33]

By the early 1970s, the suburban counties around Atlanta had thus succeeded in isolating themselves from the city and all the problems they associated with it. The movement for official annexation of the suburbs had failed and, significantly, so had all attempts to link suburbanites with the city in unofficial ways. Standing against the dispersal of public housing, the spread of mass transit, and, most significantly, metropolitan approaches to school desegregation, suburbanites made their rejection of the city painfully clear. Taken together, these forms of suburban resistance served as a reminder to all that white flight represented a movement away from not just the city but from its people and problems as well.

THE NATIONAL POLITICS OF SUBURBAN SECESSION

No one understood the secessionist mentality of these suburbanites better than the new breed of politicians who represented them. Throughout the late 1960s and early 1970s, staunchly conservative politicians rose to "defend" the suburbs around Atlanta from federal interference in local affairs in general and liberal solutions to racial problems in particular. While their politics were nothing new to the South, their party was. Throughout the once-Democratic region, a new generation of conservative, suburban Republicans emerged, following the example of Bo Callaway. In his 1964 congressional campaign, Callaway had polled equally well in both the metropolitan regions of Columbus and the rural areas around it. In the 1966 gubernatorial race, however, Callaway abandoned the rural vote to Lester Maddox and shrewdly placed his hopes in the hands of suburban whites. The Republican candidate did extremely well in metropolitan areas, outpacing Maddox's totals there by an impressive 120,000 votes. In fourteen metropolitan counties, Callaway took in nearly twice the vote of his rival. Even in Atlanta, Maddox's hometown, Callaway beat the two-time mayoral contender by a 2-to-1 margin. If not for the write-in campaign of Ellis Arnall—which drew away 50,000 votes, largely from the same metropolitan sections where Callaway had an overwhelming edge over Maddox—Callaway's decision to focus on the affluent, metropolitan sections of the state would have succeeded in making him Georgia's first Republican governor since Reconstruction.[34]

Although Callaway's election was thwarted by the Democratic legislature in 1966, individual suburban districts succeeded in electing conservative Republicans. In fact, that same year, both of Atlanta's congressional districts—the Fifth, which encompassed the city and its Fulton County suburbs, and the Fourth, which covered DeKalb County—sent conservative suburban Republicans to Congress. In the Fifth District, insurance executive Fletcher Thompson secured the House seat vacated by liberal Democrat Charles Weltner; in the Fourth, attorney Ben Blackburn ousted Congressman James Mackay, another Democrat who supported civil rights measures. Staunchly conservative and keenly attuned to the desires of their suburban constituents, Thompson and Blackburn led a new group of Georgia Republicans who made strong gains on Callaway's beginnings. Indeed, by 1970 the state party had become so popular that it actually needed to hold a primary—its first in nearly a century—to decide who would be its gubernatorial candidate in a likely victory that year. In the end, Republican hopes were dashed when Callaway's handpicked successor stumbled badly. (Among several mistakes, he denounced Earth Day as a communist plot.) The eventual GOP nominee, a television newscaster with no political experience, was then beaten by an upstart Democratic candidate named Jimmy Carter. Still, the trend in Georgia politics was clear. That same year, for instance, the five most powerful officials in the statehouse—commonly known as the "capitol clique"—all switched their party allegiances to join the GOP. The number of Republicans in the state assembly had steadily been rising during the late 1960s, and redistricting in the wake of the 1970 census only added more suburban Republican seats to the legislature.[35]

The new suburban Republicans succeeded because they understood and articulated the secessionist attitude of their constituents. When it came to stopping Atlanta from spreading its public housing into the suburbs, for instance, Congressman Ben Blackburn stood at the forefront. "Suburbanites have invested their lives in their houses and they don't want to see them ruined," he argued. The heart of the problem was "the welfare mother with her numerous kids" coming out from the city. "People work their hearts out to move away from it," Blackburn explained, but "now they might be moved in next door." This opposition to dispersed public housing paled in comparison to their fierce resistance to the furtherance of school desegregation. Congressman Fletcher Thompson, for instance, constantly railed against the "catastrophe" of using busing to achieve a "forced racial balance" in metropolitan school systems. When the HEW Department tried to desegregate two schools in suburban

Fulton County—one black, one white, less than two blocks apart—
Thompson threatened to initiate impeachment proceedings against the
HEW secretary.[36]

But it was not simply local representatives who understood and appreciated the secessionist politics of suburbia. In his successful campaign
for the presidency, Richard Nixon relied on suburbs like those around
Atlanta's Northside as a predominant part of his "silent majority" coalition. The 1968 presidential election was the first in American history in
which votes from the suburbs outnumbered the votes of either rural or
urban areas, and the Republican Party did its best to capitalize on the
demographic changes. Perhaps the clearest signal made by the campaign
in its courtship of suburban voters was the selection of Spiro Agnew as
Nixon's running mate. As governor of Maryland, Agnew had gained fame
for his tough law-and-order response to rioting in Baltimore. Nixon introduced his running mate to the nation as an expert on "urban problems,"
but Agnew's real experience lay in the suburbs. He had begun his political
career as the chief executive officer of suburban Baltimore County, a
booming area that was less than 3 percent black by the decade's end.
Well versed in the politics of white flight, Agnew carried its lessons to the
national stage. As Garry Wills astutely noted, Agnew's main contribution
to the Nixon campaign was that he "early grasped and overcame what
white urbanites take to be their main city problem—how to escape the
city."[37]

As the Nixon campaign embraced the politics of white flight, many
assumed the Republicans were following a "southern strategy" focused
on the rural and working-class supporters of George Wallace. There were,
of course, links between the segregationist politics of the Old South and
the Republican campaign in the New South. The decision of Democratic
Senator Strom Thurmond, an archsegregationist who ran for president as
the Dixiecrat candidate in 1948, to switch to the GOP in 1964 and then
offer strong support for Nixon's candidacy was one notable instance. So
too was the way in which Republicans adopted George Wallace's rhetoric
in their own stump speeches. ("I wish I had copyrighted my speeches,"
Wallace complained in 1969. "I would be drawing immense royalties
from Mr. Nixon and especially Mr. Agnew.") Despite the strong imprints
of Old South segregationists on the 1968 campaign, Nixon's "southern
strategy" was not an appeal to the rural and working-class whites who
supported Wallace and Thurmond. It was, instead, an appeal to middle-
class suburbanites. Tellingly, Nixon's southern campaign manager was
not a fire-breathing segregationist but instead a man who embodied the
newer, more respectable suburban Republicanism—Bo Callaway. As journalist Robert Sherrill noted, Callaway was "Nixon's Man in Dixie," the

personification of the new politics that the Republicans hoped would take hold in the region, from the 1968 election on.[38]

Indeed, in the wake of their 1968 victory, Republican strategists understood that the southern suburbs had been their greatest source of strength. As political analyst Kevin Phillips recognized in his 1969 blueprint, *The Emerging Republican Majority*, "Nixon's only good showings in the Deep South came in the cities and suburbs." As Phillips understood, Nixon's "urban" support largely came from well-to-do sections like Buckhead, places that physically stood inside a city's limits but socially and politically seemed more like the stereotypical suburb. If the GOP wanted to craft a new political coalition in the region, it would need to build on the existing base of white middle-class conservatives in the suburbs and like-minded metropolitan sections. This, Phillips concluded, was wholly within their reach. "When new eras and alignments have evolved in American politics, the ascending party has ridden the economic and demographic wave of the future," he noted with a flourish. "Now it is Richard Nixon's turn to build a new era on the immense middle-class impetus of Sun Belt and suburbia." Naturally, the overlap of these constituencies— the Sunbelt suburbs, such as those around Atlanta—would stand at the core of the new Republican coalition. And Phillips knew how to reach such voters. "The whole secret of politics," he confided, was understanding "who hates who." Suburbanites hated the cities, so the conclusion was simple: the GOP should embrace the politics of suburban secession.[39]

While such politics played especially well in the Sunbelt suburbs, the president understood that the same appeals would attract suburban voters across the country. In October 1972, for instance, Nixon explained his campaign strategy to a top gathering of southern Republicans in Atlanta. Earlier in the day, the president had made a triumphant march down Peachtree Street, where he was welcomed by a blizzard of confetti and a crowd of more than half a million supporters. Now, Nixon explained how the successes Republicans had found in metropolitan areas like Atlanta would be repeated across the country. "It has been suggested that . . . I have a Southern strategy," he told the GOP gathering. "It is not a Southern strategy; it is an American strategy," he insisted. "That is what the South believes in and that is what America believes in." Taking measures that worked in southern suburbs and spreading them across the country, the Republicans would perfect a political strategy that some observers would mistakenly characterize simply as southern and not suburban. While the journalist John Egerton perhaps contributed to this misunderstanding by coining the term "the Southernization of American politics" in 1974, a closer reading of his own work shows that he understood the true roots of Nixon's politics. Unlike those who mistook the "southern strategy" as an appeal to the largely rural and openly racist

Wallace supporters, Egerton appreciated that Nixon's plan involved a rather different appeal, one that he could take nationwide. "In order to capture the white South," Egerton noted, the president had "promised it relief from the incursions of the black South, and he has extended that promise to the rest of white America: busing will not succeed; the suburbs will not be desegregated."[40]

During his presidency, Richard Nixon certainly kept that promise to white America. Through his policies and appointments, the president firmly cemented the politics of suburban secession and thereby ensured that suburbs across the country would remain isolated from urban problems and undisturbed by federal action. When suburban representatives like Ben Blackburn complained about federal policies designed to promote the racial and economic integration of their neighborhoods, for instance, Nixon put an end to the program. The president first made his allegiances known, announcing at a press conference: "I believe that forced integration in the suburbs is not in the national interest." When Housing and Urban Development (HUD) secretary George Romney persisted in speaking about suburban housing integration, Nixon replaced him with an appointee more attuned to suburban concerns. Likewise, after Bo Callaway and Fletcher Thompson repeatedly complained about federal intervention in school desegregation, Nixon forced out the HEW secretary and his liberal aides. When the new secretary seemed willing to support federal busing, Nixon came down on him hard. "*Knock off this Crap*," he told aides. "Do what the law requires and not *one bit more*."[41]

The most important personnel changes that Nixon made in the federal government, however, took place at the U.S. Supreme Court. As the president understood, his suburban supporters demanded nothing less. Bo Callaway put it best, in one of his frequent confrontations with HEW officials over school desegregation. "Nixon promised he would change the law, change the Supreme Court, and change this whole integration business," the Georgian shouted. "The time has come for Nixon to bite the bullet, with real changes." To the delight of suburbanites everywhere, the new president did just that. In just two years, he would appoint four new Justices to the bench. After installing Warren Burger as the new Chief Justice, Nixon wanted all future vacancies to be filled by judges who would defend the politics of suburban secession. "I'd say that our first requirement is [to] have a southerner," Nixon instructed Attorney General John Mitchell. "The second requirement, he must be a conservative southerner. . . . Third, within the definition of conservative, he must be against busing, and against forced housing integration. Beyond that, he can do what he pleases."[42]

As vacancies appeared on the Court, the president did his best to put this plan into action. Initially, he chose candidates who perhaps fit the bill *too* well. In his first nomination for associate justice, for instance, Nixon repeatedly ran into trouble. First, he nominated Clement Haynsworth of Greenville, South Carolina, a staunch conservative with a segregationist background. Revelations about a possible past conflict of interest killed Haynsworth's candidacy, so Nixon then nominated G. Harold Carswell from northern Florida. As press reports soon made clear, however, Carswell had been actively involved in the politics of white resistance and withdrawal for decades. As a U.S. attorney, he had arranged for the transfer of a public golf course to private hands in order to avoid its integration—precisely as segregationists had hoped to do in Atlanta—and later incorporated a "whites only" club. If such actions were not a clear enough signal of Carswell's segregationist beliefs, the judge had voiced them in no uncertain terms. "I believe that segregation of the races is proper and the only practical and correct way of life in our states," he told an American Legion group. "I yield to no man in the firm, vigorous belief in the principles of white supremacy." Only after Carswell followed Haynsworth to defeat did Nixon relent in his pursuit of a southern justice and nominate Harry Blackmun of Minnesota instead.[43]

When two more seats suddenly opened up in 1971, however, Nixon renewed his campaign to place defenders of suburban secession on the Court. Representative Fletcher Thompson from Atlanta's suburbs was reportedly among those considered for nomination, as was, in a fleeting moment, Vice President Agnew. But the eventual choices, Lewis Powell and William Rehnquist, were as attuned to the politics of the Sunbelt suburbs as anyone else. Powell, for his part, had led the Richmond school board until 1961. While he was certainly not a proponent of Virginia's massive resistance, neither did he do much to encourage integration. When Powell left the school board, only two black students in the entire system attended class with white children. Rehnquist, meanwhile, had grown up in an affluent suburb outside Milwaukee and settled in the Sunbelt city of Phoenix. There, he became active in the Goldwater wing of the Republican Party, frequently relying on a "freedom of choice" rationale to oppose civil rights legislation. In 1964, for instance, Rehnquist came out against the city's public accommodations law, defending the "historic right of the owner of a drug store, lunch counter or theater to choose his own customers." Likewise, in a 1967 defense of "neighborhood schools," he asserted that "we are no more dedicated to an 'integrated' society than we are to a 'segregated' society; . . . we are instead dedicated to a free society, . . . in which each man is accorded the maximum amount of freedom of choice in his individual activities." Finally, in 1970, as an assistant attorney general in the Nixon White House, Rehnquist had quietly composed a draft of, and a detailed justification for, a constitutional amendment that would have enshrined the "freedom of choice" rationale for segregated schools and barred the use of metropolitan busing to achieve racial balance. In placing Rehnquist and Powell on the bench, Richard Nixon finally succeeded in crafting a new conservative majority on the Supreme Court, one that interpreted the Constitution as the president's constituents in the suburban Sunbelt demanded.[44]

In the early 1970s this new "Nixon Court" did much to give legal approval to the politics of suburban secession. Together, the four Justices appointed by Richard Nixon—along with Potter Stewart, who had been appointed by Dwight Eisenhower when Nixon was vice president—formed a bare majority that was responsible for a series of pivotally important rulings that succeeded in sealing off white suburbanites from the city. First, in the 1973 case of *San Antonio Independent School District v. Rodriguez*, these Justices ruled in a 5–4 decision that affluent suburbs bore no responsibility to share their property-tax school funding with poorer districts in the city. In his ruling, Justice Powell readily acknowledged the "substantial disparities" in the two areas' educational spending, but claimed the federal courts had no role to play in solving the "chaotic and unjust" system. A year later, in the landmark ruling of *Milliken v. Bradley*, this same 5–4 majority ended the movement for metropolitan school desegregation. Speaking for the Court, Chief Justice Burger ruled that the suburbs of Detroit could not be made to take part in metropolitan remedies for the persistent segregation of the city's schools. Cross-district busing, perhaps *the* central concern for Nixon's constituents, was now a dead issue. As a coda, in yet another 5–4 decision in 1975, these same justices tossed aside complaints about exclusionary suburban zoning laws in the Rochester-area case of *Warth v. Seldin*. Together, these landmark decisions represented an abandonment of the integrationist ideal and a practical acceptance of the secession of American suburbs. In his impassioned dissent in *Milliken*, Justice Thurgood Marshall made clear the causes and consequences of the new suburban jurisprudence. "Today's holding, I fear, is more a reflection of a perceived public mood that we have gone far enough in enforcing the Constitution's guarantee of equal justice than it is the product of neutral principles of law," he warned. "In the short run, it may seem to be the easier course to allow our great metropolitan areas to be divided up each into two cities—one white, the other black—but it is a course, I predict, our people will ultimately regret."[45]

In the end, the intervention of the new Nixon Court served to cement the suburban secessionism that had been underway in local and national politics throughout the 1960s and early 1970s. Around cities like Atlanta—and, as the Supreme Court's docket made clear, cities across the country such as San Antonio, Detroit, and Rochester—suburbanites insisted that they bore no responsibility for the persistent segregation of modern America by both class and caste. Through either ignorance or apathy, suburbanites possessed a convenient, collective amnesia about the nation's troubling history of residential apartheid, school segregation, and economic discrimination. Refusing to recognize past patterns that had led to both the rise of suburbia and the decline of inner cities, they came to see their isolation as natural and innocuous. In the end, the ultimate success of white flight was the way in which it led whites away from responsibility for the problems they had done much to create.

Epilogue: The Legacies of White Flight

THE WHITE FLIGHT and suburban secession chronicled in these pages did not stop where this story does. Long after the 1970s, these movements continued to spread, gaining strength and speed as they went. Suburbs, which represented only a fourth of the country in 1950 and still just a third in 1960, encompassed more than half of America by 1990. To be sure, the "new suburban majority" was by no means monolithic. Suburbs came in countless varieties: white and black, old stock and new immigrant, working-class and wealthy, conformist and eclectic. And yet, if the archetype of the affluent, white, conservative suburb no longer held true for all suburbs at the century's end, it still did for many. During the 1980s and 1990s, a powerful new political philosophy took hold in these post-secession suburbs. Finally free to pursue a politics that accepted as its normative values an individualistic interpretation of "freedom of association," a fervent faith in free enterprise, and a fierce hostility to the federal government, a new suburban conservatism took the now-familiar themes of isolation, individualism, and privatization to unprecedented levels. On their own, individual decisions to abandon a city or seal off a suburb might have gone unnoticed on the national stage. But such local actions, repeated across the country again and again, had an aggregate effect, one that drastically changed the course of the nation. At the dawn of the twenty-first century, America found itself dominated by suburbs and those suburbs, in turn, dominated by the politics of white flight and suburban secession. Thus, long after the physical relocations of white flight had slowed, the political revolution sparked by it continued to spread.

By the 1990s, the political power of suburbs was evident across the country. "The third century of American history," political analyst William Schneider declared with confidence in 1992, "is shaping up to be the suburban century." Indeed, as postsecession suburbanites emerged from their isolation and took the lead in national life, they would shape the course of politics and reshape the country itself. The trend was evident across the country, but nowhere more so than in the suburbs around Atlanta. Indeed, for much of that decade, the city's northern suburbs were represented by some of the most influential conservative politicians in the nation. The northwestern expanse, which included western Cobb County and beyond, was represented by Congressman Bob Barr, an archconservative Republican who emerged as the earliest congressional advocate of President Bill Clinton's impeachment. The northeastern suburbs, meanwhile, elected Congressman John Linder, head of the Republican National Congressional Committee. While both were powerful representatives of the Sunbelt South and key figures in the Republican Party, they were surpassed on both counts by a colleague who represented the suburban enclave between their districts, Speaker of the House Newt Gingrich. More than anyone else in the 1990s, Newt Gingrich embodied the politics of the suburban Sunbelt, especially suburban conservatives' embrace of privatization, free enterprise, and local autonomy, as well as their antipathy to the federal government, public services, and the tax policies designed to support both.[1]

Gingrich's career served as a testament to the new political strength of the southern suburbs and their roots in the phenomena of white flight and suburban secession. Gingrich was not a native Georgian, a fact which made him more like his suburban constituents than not, but his political instincts had been honed during his years as a college student in Atlanta. Enrolled at Emory University between 1961 and 1965, Gingrich lived through the pivotal years of the city's civil rights confrontations and the tumultuous white flight that followed in its wake. While hundreds of his classmates walked the picket lines at Leb's and the Pickrick, Gingrich's inclinations had already turned in a different direction. "He was real active in local Republican politics," one of his professors later recalled. Indeed, Gingrich founded a Young Republican club at Emory and, as a sophomore, explained to fellow students that the Republican Party believed in the same things as most white, middle-class southerners: "personal freedom, limited government, the federal system, the law, and capitalism." During his college years, Gingrich tried to put his theories into practice. He managed an unsuccessful Republican congressional campaign and then went on to work hard for the gubernatorial campaign of Bo Callaway. Years later, Callaway returned the favor by becoming chairman of Gingrich's powerful GOP Action Committee (GOPAC) and helping develop what would become the "Contract with America" during the 1994 congressional elections.[2]

Like his political predecessors, Newt Gingrich understood the worldview of postsecession suburbanites with incredible clarity. Shortly before the 1994 elections that made him speaker of the House, the congressman explained to journalist Peter Applebome the concerns of his Cobb County constituents. "These people want safety, and they believe big cities have failed and are controlled by people who are incapable of delivering goods and services," Gingrich noted. "What they find here is a sort of Norman Rockwell world with fiber-optic computers and jet airplanes. But the values that would have been the *Saturday Evening Post* of the mid-fifties are the values of most of these people now." ("Soon he was on a roll," Applebome noted, "contrasting the pristine work ethic of

Cobb versus the 'welfare state' values of Atlanta.") Gingrich quickly rattled off a litany of white suburban fears about the inner city. "People in Cobb don't object to upper-middle-class neighbors who keep their lawn cut and move to the area to avoid crime," he said breezily. "What people worry about is the bus line gradually destroying one apartment complex after another, bringing people out for public housing who have no middle-class values and whose kids as they become teenagers often are centers of robbery and where the schools collapse because the parents that live in the apartment complexes don't care that the kids don't do well in school and the whole school collapses." In a single sentence, without ever mentioning race, Newt Gingrich had managed to tie together suburban concerns over public transportation, public housing, and public education just as whites around Atlanta had been doing for four decades.[3]

During the 1990s Gingrich and his allies relied on conservative suburbanites to find success at the polls, much as Nixon and Agnew had done a generation before. The 1968 presidential election had been the first in which the suburban vote surpassed the urban and rural votes in head-to-head counts, but the 1992 campaign was the first in which suburban votes outnumbered urban and rural votes combined. In order to appeal to the new "suburban nation," Gingrich and his colleagues formulated their "Contract with America." In many ways, the contract embodied the politics of the suburban Sunbelt. Of the ten pieces of legislation proposed in the platform, five called for major reductions in federal taxation, including cutting the capital gains tax in half, ending the "marriage penalty," and giving middle-class families tax credits for children or elderly dependents. Four of the remaining five focused on reducing the size and scope of the federal government and curtailing the powers of "Washington bureaucrats." Indeed, as conservative columnist Charles Krauthammer explained, the contract's whole point was to "limit the power, resources and reach of government" and embrace a vision of "re-limiting and, in some areas, de-legitimizing government" itself. For suburbanites who had long fought the "reach of government" and already limited and privatized government in their own towns, this sort of appeal had a natural resonance.[4]

In many ways, the "conservative revolution" that Gingrich led was as much a product of the suburban South as the "silent majority" had been a quarter century before. While the Republicans made staggering gains across the country in the 1994 elections, their greatest successes came in the South. Republican candidates for the House outpolled their Democratic challengers in every single state in the region, with the lone exception of Mississippi. (And, as the New York Times noted, Democrats in that state were so conservative they might as well have been Republicans.) The landslide was so severe it had aftershocks. The year after the elections, five southern Democrats in the House followed the general trend and switched party allegiances, raising to nineteen the number of southern seats the Republicans had added to their ranks. In 1990 the Georgia congressional delegation had consisted of nine Democrats and one Republican; in 1995 it was eight Republicans and three Democrats. In a sign of the two parties' cemented racial identities, all the Republicans were white and all the Democrats black.[5]

As the incoming House leadership made clear, the new strength of the Republican Party was not just southern but suburban as well. The installment of Cobb County's congressman as the new speaker of the House was a telling sign, of course, but the rest of the congressional leadership came from places almost indistinguishable from the suburbs around northern Atlanta. The new House majority leader, Dick Armey, came from a conservative, white, middle-class suburban district sandwiched between Dallas and Fort Worth. Tom DeLay, the new majority whip, represented an almost identical spot southwest of Houston. The chairmen of the two most powerful committees in the House came from similar southern suburbs. Congressman Bob Livingston, who now led the Appropriations Committee and who would nearly succeed Gingrich as speaker of the House, represented conservative white suburbanites in the area between Baton Rouge and New Orleans. Meanwhile, the new head of the Ways and Means Committee, Bill Archer, came to Congress from similar suburbs west of Houston. (He had represented the region since 1971, when he inherited the seat from a pioneering Republican congressman named George H. W. Bush.) In the ascendancy of this new Republican leadership, the suburban South had clearly come of age.[6]

Once in power, the House Republicans sought to push through the contract they had made with suburban voters. Dick Armey and Bill Archer, for instance, hoped to make radical reductions in federal taxation. They differed in their approaches—Armey preferred installing an extremely low flat tax, while Archer favored a consumption-based solution like a national sales tax—but their goal was the same: the end of the progressive income tax. Such a change would, of course, drastically reduce federal revenues and thereby help the GOP meet another of its goals, shrinking the size of government. Without doubt, the antigovernment animus of the suburban Sunbelt reached unprecedented heights with the new Republican leadership. "There is hardly a federal agency so obscure, a policy so benign, that it has not aroused its own aspiring executioner in the GOP," noted journalists Dan Balz and Ron Brownstein. And, not surprisingly, their hostility to the government was matched with a strong faith in free enterprise. "The market is rational," Armey argued, "and the government is dumb." Together, the two beliefs pushed the Republicans to embrace the politics of privatization that had already spread through their own suburban districts. While key programs such as Social Security and Medicare were left untouched, other aspects of the welfare state were targeted for privatization. "I believe in a social safety net," Gingrich noted, "but I think that it's better done by churches and by synagogues and by volunteers."[7]

On the surface, these policies seemingly had little or nothing to do with race. In an astute study of the role of race in the conservative counterrevolution, historian Dan Carter allowed that the Republican hostility to the welfare state could not be caricatured as a simple product of racism. "Class fears and moral outrage played a critical role in demonizing welfare mothers," he noted; "the hostility of middle- and upper-income taxpayers toward welfare recipients was far more complicated than a dressed-up version of the old southern demagogue's cry of 'nigger, nigger, nigger.'" Still, Carter argued, racial tensions were a factor. A longtime student of welfare reform agreed. The voters with whom the Republicans had made their contract were largely middle-class whites who believed the government was funneling their tax dollars to "inner-city substance-abusing blacks." In the past, the hostility to the federal government, the welfare state, and taxation had been driven by racial resentment, whether in the form of segregationists inside Atlanta or secessionist suburbanites outside it. In the 1990s the new generation of suburban Republicans simply took the politics of white flight to the national stage.[8]

And, to be sure, white flight itself had not come to rest. Indeed, as Gingrich and his allies pressed the course of suburban conservatism on the national stage, white flight continued to surge in their own districts. Over the course of the 1980s and 1990s, a steady stream of minorities moved into the suburbs around Atlanta, dramatically altering their racial composition. Mirroring the patterns of racial division inside the city, these new black suburbanites largely settled in counties to the east and south. Still, significant numbers ventured into the predominantly white northern counties as well. While Cobb and Gwinnett counties had been 96 and 95 percent white in 1970, for instance, their white majorities had thinned to 72 percent each by 2000. As had happened inside Atlanta, the suburbs found that small erosions in the general population's white majority were greatly amplified in the enrollment at public schools. The school system in DeKalb County, which had been 94 percent white as late as 1969, was less than 12 percent white three decades later. In parts of the county, white abandonment of the public schools was even starker. In 2003, for instance, the posh neighborhood of Avondale Estates was 89 percent white, yet the public Avondale High School had a student population which was just 5 percent white. Surrounding suburbs looked even worse, according to a report by the Civil Rights Project at Harvard University. Focusing on the country's largest school systems, the project measured the changes in racial composition in schools between 1986 and 2000. Of 239 school systems nationwide, three of the top four rates of resegregation were found in suburban counties around Atlanta. Clayton County's school system had the single fastest rate of school resegregation in the entire country, while Gwinnett and Cobb had the third- and fourth-fastest rates of resegregation, respectively.[9]

As had happened inside the city, suburban whites' abandonment of racially diverse schools signaled a new phase of white flight. This time around, whites fled from the inner-ring suburbs just outside the city to the outer-ring "exurbs" in the counties beyond. Migration to these regions mirrored not just the tone of earlier white flight, but the tempo as well. In the 1980s the white exodus from Atlanta had helped make Cobb and Gwinnett two of the nation's fastest-growing counties; in the 1990s white flight from Atlanta's suburbs did the same for three exurban counties. Forsyth County, north of Gwinnett, had a 123 percent increase in its population over the decade, making it the second fastest-growing county in the United States. Henry County, just south of DeKalb, was fourth in the nation, while Paulding County, west of Cobb, placed seventh. As with the initial surge in the suburban population, this new explosion of exurban population growth was almost completely white. Forsyth, for instance, stood at 95 percent white in 2000, just as Gwinnett had been in 1970, and only 0.7 percent black. Likewise, Paulding was 91 percent white, while Henry County stood at 81 percent white. (Henry adjoins south DeKalb, where the population had become overwhelmingly black, and thus this figure was still surprisingly high.) At the dawn of the twenty-first century, white flight had spread from the city through the suburbs to a new exurban frontier, with no signs of slowing down.[10]

As white flight picked up speed, the politics created by it kept pace. Taking stock of southern politics in 1996, journalists Dan Balz and Ron Brownstein noted, "Almost every new housing development rising in the suburban and exurban counties of the South represented another potential Republican enclave and a further nail in the Democrats' coffin." Likewise, when pollster Stanley Greenberg assessed the state of politics in 2004, he singled out "exurbia" and "the Deep South" as two persistent sources of Republican strength. With 54 percent of all American exurbs located in the South, it became clear that southern exurbs would be to twenty-first-century Republicans what the Sunbelt suburbs had been for them three decades before—an area in which key demographic groups overlapped and new political ideologies emerged. Indeed, when Michael Barone, lead author of the biannual *Almanac of American Politics*, looked for an area that represented the core voters of modern Republicanism, he pointed to the southern exurbs, specifically those around Atlanta. Forsyth County, for instance, voted for Republican candidates by overwhelming margins, giving 78 percent of its votes to George W. Bush in the 2000 presidential campaign and 77 percent to Saxby Chambliss in the 2002 senatorial race. "These edge counties are usually ignored by reporters and political scientists, who can't imagine living in such places," Barone observed, "but they are in many ways the cutting edge of America, the wave of the future."[11]

As such political demographers noted, President George W. Bush had long relied on southern suburban and exurban areas in his rise to power. His first success in politics, a challenge to Democratic governor Ann Richards of Texas, unfolded the same year as the Gingrich revolution and relied on the same constituency. Not surprisingly, the conservative suburban districts that repeatedly sent Republican representatives like Armey, DeLay, and Archer to Congress served as Bush's greatest source of strength. Residents in such suburbs, in the words of political strategist Karl Rove, were loyal "paint-me-red Republicans" who readily embraced the Bush campaign. Indeed, in the 1994 governor's race, the ten fastest-growing "collar counties" around Texas cities gave Bush solid majorities, ranging from 54 to 73 percent. Likewise, in his 2000 presidential campaign, Bush commanded strong pluralities in similar suburbs and exurbs across the Sunbelt.[12]

In George W. Bush's assumption of the presidency, the politics of the suburban and now exurban Sunbelt found its most powerful advocate yet. His "compassionate conservatism" shunned the coded racial appeals of earlier Republican campaigns, but the policies that remained were unmistakably products of suburban secession. The new president was a strong advocate of the privatization of public services, for instance, especially for select parts of the social safety net. During his tenure as governor of Texas, Bush made bold efforts to privatize the state's welfare system, which he proposed handing over to defense contractor Lockheed Martin. The domestic agenda of Bush's presidential campaign, meanwhile, centered on a proposed transfer of federal responsibility for welfare to private "faith-based institutions." His education policy likewise embraced the extension of tuition vouchers, which would allow individual parents to move their children (and their funding) from public to private schools. In his boldest move, Bush proposed the partial privatization of Social Security. Once in office, the president even privatized key parts of the military and national defense—long considered by conservatives to be the one realm of national work handled well by the federal government. Given his preference for privatization, it is not surprising that, as both candidate and president, President Bush wholeheartedly embraced the tax revolt as well. Indeed, in his first three years in office, he succeeded in securing the first and third largest tax cuts in American history and still clamored for more.[13]

Thus, at the start of the twenty-first century, the politics created by white flight are not simply still present; they are predominant. Despite its fundamental importance in contemporary political and social life, however, the roots of modern suburban conservatism remain largely obscured. On the surface, its policies appear to have little to do with the forgotten struggles over segregation. Upon closer examination, however, much of the modern suburban conservative agenda—the secessionist stance toward the cities, the individualistic outlook, the fervent faith in free enterprise, and the hostility to the federal government—was, in fact, first articulated and advanced in the resistance of southern whites to desegregation. No matter how sincere conservatives may be in insisting that their politics are "color-blind"—and, to be sure, a great number of them are sincere—a closer reading of the historical record shows that the politics of race and racism did inspire policies that now seem to have little to do with race. Recognizing the legacies of white flight would be a first step in reducing the steady tensions between the cities and suburbs and help bring together a nation that with every year seems ever more polarized by race, region, and class. Before that can happen, however, white Americans must stop running away from their past.

Abbreviations

ABP	Atlanta Bureau of Planning, Archives, Atlanta Historical Society, Atlanta
AC	*Atlanta Constitution*
ADW	*Atlanta Daily World*
AHS	Archives, Atlanta Historical Society, Atlanta
AI	*Atlanta Inquirer*
AJ	*Atlanta Journal*
AJC	*Atlanta Journal-Constitution*
APSA	Atlanta Public School Archives, Atlanta
AT	*Atlanta Times*
ATA	Atlanta Transit Authority, Archives, Atlanta Historical Society, Atlanta
ATW	Austin T. Walden Papers, Archives, Atlanta Historical Society, Atlanta
AUL	Atlanta Urban League Papers, Special Collections, Robert W. Woodruff Library, Atlanta University, Atlanta
CC	Calvin Craig Papers, Special Collections, Robert W. Woodruff Library, Emory University, Atlanta
EP	Eliza Paschall Papers, Special Collections, Robert W. Woodruff Library, Emory University, Atlanta
ESCRU	Episcopal Society for Cultural and Racial Unity Papers, Special Collections, Robert W. Woodruff Library, Emory University, Atlanta
FCSC	Records, Fulton County Superior Court, Atlanta
FFP	Frances Freeborn Pauley Papers, Special Collections, Robert W. Woodruff Library, Emory University, Atlanta
FH	Floyd Hunter Papers, Special Collections, Robert W. Woodruff Library, Emory University, Atlanta
GGDP	Georgia Government Documentation Program, Special Collections, William Russell Pullen Library, Georgia State University, Atlanta
GTH	Grace Towns Hamilton Papers, Archives, Atlanta Historical Society, Atlanta
HB	Helen Bullard Papers, Special Collections, Robert W. Woodruff Library, Emory University, Atlanta
HTJ	Herbert T. Jenkins Papers, Archives, Atlanta Historical Society, Atlanta

JAS	John A. Sibley Papers, Special Collections, Robert W. Woodruff Library, Emory University, Atlanta
JCD	General Correspondence Series, James C. Davis Papers, Special Collections, Robert W. Woodruff Library, Emory University, Atlanta
JCD-C	Campaign Series, James C. Davis Papers, Special Collections, Robert W. Woodruff Library, Emory University, Atlanta
JDC	Jim D. Cherry Papers, Special Collections, Robert W. Woodruff Library, Emory University, Atlanta
JHC	John H. Calhoun Papers, Special Collections, Robert W. Woodruff Library, Atlanta University, Atlanta
JMR	Jacob M. Rothschild Papers, Special Collections, Robert W. Woodruff Library, Emory University, Atlanta
JWM	James William May Papers, Special Collections, Robert W. Woodruff Library, Emory University, Atlanta
LRA	Long-Rucker-Aiken Family Papers, Archives, Atlanta Historical Society, Atlanta
MH	*Metropolitan Herald* (Atlanta)
MM	Mule to Marta Papers, Archives, Atlanta Historical Society, Atlanta
NA	Southeastern Depository, National Archives and Records Administration, East Point, Georgia
NAACP	National Association for the Advancement of Colored People Papers, Microfilm Edition
NAB	Newsweek, Atlanta Bureau Files, Special Collections, Robert W. Woodruff Library, Emory University, Atlanta
NN	*Northside News* (Atlanta)
NYT	*New York Times*
REM	Ralph Emerson McGill Papers, Special Collections, Robert W. Woodruff Library, Emory University, Atlanta
RHR	Richard H. Rich Papers, Special Collections, Robert W. Woodruff Library, Emory University, Atlanta
RWW	Robert W. Woodruff Papers, Special Collections, Robert W. Woodruff Library, Emory University, Atlanta
SRC	Southern Regional Council Papers, Microfilm Edition, Special Collections, Robert W. Woodruff Library, Atlanta University, Atlanta
SSN	*Southern School News*
WBH	William Berry Hartsfield Papers, Special Collections, Robert W. Woodruff Library, Emory University, Atlanta
WEE	*West End Eagle* (Atlanta)
WP	*Washington Post*
WSJ	*Wall Street Journal*

Notes

INTRODUCTION

1. For a sampling of Atlanta's positive press coverage, see *Christian Century*, 3 June 1953; *Saturday Evening Post*, 31 October 1953; *Newsweek*, 15 March 1954, 11 September 1961; *Reporter*, 11 July 1957, 15 September 1961; *NYT*, 31 August 1961; *U.S. News and World Report*, 11 September 1961; *Life*, 15 September 1961; *AJC*, 18 January 1970.

2. Telex report, [early 1963], box 1, NAB; Ivan Allen Jr. with Paul Hemphill, *Mayor: Notes on the Sixties* (New York: Simon and Schuster, 1971): 70–72; Alton Hornsby Jr., "The Negro in Atlanta Politics, 1961–1973," *Atlanta History Bulletin* 21 (Spring 1977): 14; *AJ*, 20 December 1962; Harold H. Martin, *William Berry Hartsfield: Mayor of Atlanta* (Athens: University of Georgia Press, 1978): 171–72.

3. *AC*, 20 December 1962; *City Directory, 1962* (Atlanta: Atlanta City Directory Company Publishing, 1962); telex report, [January 1963], box 1, NAB; memorandum, "List of Residents in Peyton Road Area," [1962], box 10, EP.

4. *AJ*, 8–9 January 1963; *ADW*, 10–11 January, 26 February 1963; telex report, 27 February 1963, box 1, NAB.

5. *AC*, 2 March 1963; *AJ*, 2, 26 March 1963; Allen, *Mayor*, 72; telex report, 29 July 1963, box 1, NAB.

6. Ivan Allen Jr., "1962 Annual Message," 7 January 1963, box 11, HTJ; Eliza Paschall, "Report on Housing Situation," 22 January 1963, box 3, EP; *MH*, 11 September 1963, 8 January 1964, copy in reel 110, pt. 11, SRC; U.S. Bureau of the Census, *U.S. Censuses of Population and Housing: 1960*, vol. 1, pt. 8, *Census Tracts: Atlanta, Ga., Standard Metropolitan Statistical Area* (Washington, D.C.: U.S. Government Printing Office, 1962), table P-1; U.S. Bureau of the Census, *1970 Census of Population and Housing*, vol. 1, pt. 14, *Census Tracts: Atlanta, Ga., Standard Metropolitan Area (and Adjacent Area)* (Washington, D.C.: U.S. Government Printing Office, 1972), table P-1; U.S. Bureau of the Census, *1980 Census of Population and Housing*, vol. 2, pt. 80, *Census Tracts: Atlanta, Ga. Standard Metropolitan Statistical Area* (Washington, D.C.: U.S. Government Printing Office, 1983), table P-2.

7. See Numan V. Bartley, *The Rise of Massive Resistance: Race and Politics in the South during the 1950's* (Baton Rouge: Louisiana State University Press, 1969); Neil R. McMillen, *The Citizens' Council: Organized Resistance to the Second Reconstruction, 1954–64* (Urbana: University of Illinois Press, 1971); Frances M. Wilhoit, *The Politics of Massive Resistance* (New York: Braziller, 1973).

8. Michael J. Klarman, "How *Brown* Changed Race Relations: The Backlash Thesis," *Journal of American History* 81 (June 1994): 81–118.

9. Bartley, *Rise of Massive Resistance*.

10. James W. Ely, *The Crisis of Conservative Virginia: The Byrd Organization and the Politics of Massive Resistance* (Knoxville: University of Tennessee Press, 1976); Nadine Cohodas, *Strom Thurmond and the Politics of Southern Change* (New York: Simon and Schuster, 1993); Stephan Lesher, *George Wallace: American Populist* (Reading, Mass.: Addison-Wesley, 1993); Dan T. Carter, *The Politics of Rage: George Wallace, the Origins of the New Conservatism, and the Transformation of American Politics* (Baton Rouge: Louisiana State University Press, 1995); Roy Reed, *Faubus: The Life and Times of an American Prodigal* (Fayetteville: University of Arkansas Press, 1997); Kari Frederickson, *The Dixiecrat Revolt and the End of the Solid South, 1932–1968* (Chapel Hill: University of North Carolina Press, 2001).

11. McMillen, *Citizens' Council*; David Chalmers, *Backfire: How the Ku Klux Klan Helped the Civil Rights Movement* (Lanham, Md.: Rowman and Littlefield, 2003).

12. Elizabeth Jacoway and C. Fred Williams, eds., *Understanding the Little Rock Crisis: An Exercise in Remembrance and Reconciliation* (Fayetteville: University of Arkansas Press, 1999); William Doyle, *An American Insurrection: The Battle of Oxford, Mississippi, 1962* (New York: Doubleday, 2001).

13. Carter, *Politics of Rage*, 133–55.

14. See, for instance, Jane Dailey, Glenda Gilmore, and Bryant Simon, eds., *Jumpin' Jim Crow: Southern Politics from Civil War to Civil Rights* (Princeton: Princeton University Press, 2000).

15. See, for example, Howell Raines, *My Soul Is Rested: The Story of the Civil Rights Movement in the Deep South* (New York: Putnam, 1977); Aldon Morris, *The Origins of the Civil Rights Movement* (New York: Free Press, 1986); Robin D. G. Kelley, *Race Rebels: Culture, Politics and the Black Working Class* (New York: Free Press, 1994); John Dittmer, *Local People: The Struggle for the Civil Rights Movement in Mississippi* (Urbana: University of Illinois Press, 1995); Charles M. Payne, *I've Got the Light of Freedom: The Organizing Tradition and the Mississippi Freedom Struggle* (Berkeley: University of California Press, 1995).

16. See, for instance, David L. Chappell, "The Divided Mind of Segregationists," *Georgia Historical Quarterly* 82, no. 1 (Spring 1998): 45–72; Matthew D. Lassiter and Andrew Lewis, eds., *The Moderates' Dilemma: Massive Resistance to School Desegregation in Virginia* (Charlottesville: University of Virginia Press, 1998); Pete Daniel, *Lost Revolutions: The South in the 1950s* (Chapel Hill: University of North Carolina Press, 2000).

17. See, for instance, Jonathan Rieder, *Canarsie: The Jews and Italians of Brooklyn against Liberalism* (Cambridge, Mass.: Harvard University Press, 1985); Ronald P. Formisano, *Boston against Busing: Race, Class and Ethnicity in the 1960s and 1970s* (Chapel Hill: University of North Carolina Press, 1991); Michael Kazin, "The Grass-Roots Right: New Histories of U.S. Conservatism in the Twentieth Century," *American Historical Review* 97 (February 1992): 136–55; Lisa McGirr, *Suburban Warriors: Origins of the New Right* (Princeton: Princeton University Press, 2002).

18. In stressing the rights-based ideology of segregationists, this study borrows from Alan Brinkley's analysis of "individualistic conservatism" writ large. Brinkley, "The Problem of American Conservatism," *American Historical Review* 99 (April 1994): 415–19.

19. Jean Hardisty, *Mobilizing Resentment: Conservative Resurgence from the John Birch Society to the Promise Keepers* (Boston: Beacon Press, 1999), 131.

20. See Numan V. Bartley, *From Thurmond to Wallace: Political Tendencies in Georgia, 1948–1968* (Baltimore: Johns Hopkins University Press, 1970); Jonathan Rieder, "The Rise of the 'Silent Majority'," in *The Rise and Fall of the New Deal Order*, ed. Steve Fraser and Gary Gerstle (Princeton: Princeton University Press, 1989), 243–68; Thomas Byrne Edsall with Mary Edsall, *Chain Reaction: The Impact of Race, Rights, and Taxes on American Politics* (New York: Norton, 1992); Earl Black and Merle Black, *The Vital South: How Presidents Are Elected* (Cambridge, Mass.: Harvard University Press, 1992); William C. Berman, *America's Right Turn: From Nixon to Bush* (Baltimore: Johns Hopkins University Press, 1994); Mary C. Brennan, *Turning Right in the Sixties: The Conservative Capture of the GOP* (Chapel Hill: University of North Carolina Press, 1995); Carter, *Politics of Rage*; Dan T. Carter, *From George Wallace to Newt Gingrich: Race in the Conservative Counterrevolution, 1963–1994* (Baton Rouge: Louisiana State University Press, 1996); Frederickson, *Dixiecrat Revolt*; Earl Black and Merle Black, *The Rise of Southern Republicans* (Cambridge, Mass.: Harvard University Press, 2002).

21. The phrase "Sun Belt" first appeared in Kevin Phillips, *The Emerging Republican Majority* (New Rochelle, N.Y.: Arlington House, 1969), esp. 437–43. See also Kirkpatrick Sale, *Power Shift: The Rise of the Southern Rim and Its Challenge to the Eastern Establishment* (New York: Random House, 1975); David C. Perry and Alfred J. Watkins, *The Rise of the Sunbelt Cities* (Beverly Hills, Calif.: Sage Publications, 1977); Carl Abbott, *The New Urban America: Growth and Politics in Sunbelt Cities* (Chapel Hill: University of North Carolina Press, 1987); Raymond Mohl, ed., *Searching for the Sunbelt: Historical Perspectives on a Region* (Knoxville: University of Tennessee Press, 1990); Bruce Schulman, *From Cotton Belt to Sunbelt: Federal Policy, Economic Development, and the Transformation of the South* (New York: Oxford University Press, 1991); Jack Bass and Walter DeVries, *The Transformation of Southern Politics: Social Change and Political Consequences since 1945* (Athens: University of Georgia Press, 1995); Numan V. Bartley, *The New South: 1945–1980* (Baton Rouge: Louisiana State University Press, 1995), 417–54.

22. See Robert Kuttner, *Revolt of the Haves* (New York: Simon and Schuster, 1980); Alvin Rabushka and Pauline Ryan, *The Tax Revolt* (Stanford, Calif.: Hoover Institution Press, 1982); David O. Sears and Jack Citrin, *Tax Revolt: Something for Nothing in California* (Cambridge, Mass.: Harvard University Press, 1982); Edsall, *Chain Reaction*; Bruce J. Schulman, *The Seventies: The Great Shift in American Culture, Society, and Politics* (New York: Free Press, 2001), 193–217; Robert O. Self, *American Babylon: Race and the Struggle for Postwar Oakland* (Princeton: Princeton University Press, 2003).

23. See Richard Louv, *America II* (New York: Penguin, 1983); Mike Davis, *City of Quartz: Excavating the Future in Los Angeles* (New York: Verso Books, 1990); Joel Garreau, *Edge City: Life on the New Frontier* (New York: Anchor Books, 1991); Edward J. Blakely and Mary Gail Snyder, *Fortress America: Gated Communities in the United States* (Washington, D.C.: Brookings Institution Press, 1999).

24. See Davis, *City of Quartz*; John D. Donahue, *The Privatization Decision: Public Ends, Private Means* (New York: Basic Books, 1989); Evan McKenzie, *Privatopia: Homeowner Associations and the Rise of Residential Private Government* (New Haven, Conn.: Yale University Press, 1994).

25. For a critique of "color-blind" conservatism, see Matthew D. Lassiter, *The Silent Majority: Suburban Politics in the Sunbelt South* (Princeton: Princeton University Press, forthcoming).

26. There are noted exceptions to this general rule. For excellent community-level studies, see William H. Chafe, *Civilities and Civil Rights: Greensboro, North Carolina, and the Black Struggle for Freedom* (New York: Oxford University Press, 1980); Timothy B. Tyson, *Radio Free Dixie: Robert F. Williams and the Roots of Black Power* (Chapel Hill: University of North Carolina Press, 1999), on Monroe, North Carolina.

27. The landmark works in this field are Arnold R. Hirsch, *Making the Second Ghetto: Race and Housing in Chicago, 1940–1960* (Chicago: University of Chicago Press, 1983), and Thomas J. Sugrue, *The Origins of the Urban Crisis: Race and Inequality in Postwar Detroit* (Princeton: Princeton University Press, 1996). Although these two works remain the most significant scholarship on postwar urban race relations, there is a broader body of scholarship that addresses the role of earlier racial conflict and negotiation in northern cities, largely focused, once again, on Chicago and Detroit. See St. Clair Drake and Horace R. Cayton, *Black Metropolis: A Study of Negro Life in a Northern City*, 2 vols. (New York: Harcourt, Brace, 1945); Allan H. Spear, *Black Chicago: The Making of a Negro Ghetto, 1890–1920* (Chicago: University of Chicago Press, 1967); David M. Katzman, *Before the Ghetto: Black Detroit in the Nineteenth Century* (Urbana: University of Illinois Press, 1973); Kenneth L. Kusmer, *A Ghetto Takes Shape: Black Cleveland, 1870–1930* (Urbana: University of Illinois Press, 1976); David Levine, *Internal Combustion: The Races in Detroit, 1915–1926* (Westport, Conn.: Greenwood Press, 1976); Joe W. Trotter Jr., *Black Milwaukee: The Making of an Industrial Proletariat, 1915–1945* (Urbana: University of Illinois Press, 1985); James R. Grossman, *Land of Hope: Chicago, Black Southerners and the Great Migration* (Chicago: University of Chicago Press, 1989); Lizabeth Cohen, *Making a New Deal: Industrial Workers in Chicago, 1919–1939* (New York: Cambridge University Press, 1990).

28. Ronald H. Bayor, *Race and the Shaping of Twentieth-Century Atlanta* (Chapel Hill: University of North Carolina Press, 1996): 7; Hirsch, *Making the Second Ghetto*, 17; Sugrue, *Origins of the Urban Crisis*, 23.

29. Heavily industrialized cities such as Birmingham, Alabama, and Winston-Salem, North Carolina, proved exceptions to the rule. There, the confluence of desegregation and deindustrialization produced a pattern that evoked both the North and South. See Glenn T. Eskew, *But for Birmingham: The Local and National Movements in the Civil Rights Struggle* (Chapel Hill: University of North Carolina Press, 1997); Robert Rodgers Korstad, *Civil Rights Unionism: Tobacco Workers and the Struggle for Democracy in the Mid-Twentieth-Century South* (Chapel Hill: University of North Carolina Press, 2003).

30. See, among others, David L. Lewis, *King: A Biography* (Urbana: University of Illinois Press, 1978); Clayborne Carson, *In Struggle: SNCC and the Black*

Awakening of the 1960s (Cambridge, Mass.: Harvard University Press, 1981); Adam Fairclough, *To Redeem the Soul of America: The Southern Christian Leadership Conference and Martin Luther King, Jr.* (Athens: University of Georgia Press, 1987); Taylor Branch, *Parting the Waters: America in the King Years, 1954–1963* (New York: Simon and Schuster, 1988); David Levering Lewis, *W. E. B. DuBois: Biography of a Race, 1868–1919* (New York: Holt, 1993); Harvard Sitkoff, *The Struggle for Black Equality, 1954–1992* (New York: Hill and Wang, 1994); Andrew Young, *An Easy Burden: The Civil Rights Movement and the Transformation of America* (New York: Harper Collins, 1996); John Lewis with Michael D'Orso, *Walking with the Wind: A Memoir of the Civil Rights Movement* (New York: Simon and Schuster, 1998); Stephen G. N. Tuck, *Beyond Atlanta: The Struggle for Racial Equality in Georgia, 1940–1960* (Athens: University of Georgia Press, 2001).

31. Mark Bauerlein, *Negrophobia: A Race Riot in Atlanta, 1906* (San Francisco: Encounter Books, 2001); Leonard Dinnerstein, *The Leo Frank Case* (New York: Columbia University Press, 1968); Nancy MacLean, "The Leo Frank Case Reconsidered: Gender and Sexual Politics in the Making of Reactionary Populism," in Daily et al., *Jumpin' Jim Crow*, 183–218; Nancy MacLean, *Behind the Mask of Chivalry: The Making of the Second Ku Klux Klan* (New York: Oxford, 1994); David M. Chalmers, *Hooded Americanism: The History of the Ku Klux Klan* (New York: New Viewpoints, 1981), for "holy city" quotation, see p. 3; Wyn Craig Wade, *The Fiery Cross: The Ku Klux Klan in America* (New York: Simon and Schuster, 1987); Melissa Faye Greene, *The Temple Bombing* (New York: Fawcett Columbine, 1996); Bartley, *Thurmond to Wallace*, 179–207; Richard C. Cortner, *Civil Rights and Public Accommodations: The* Heart of Atlanta Motel *and* McClung *Cases* (Lawrence: University Press of Kansas, 2001).

32. See Clifford M. Kuhn, Harlon E. Joye, and E. Bernard West, *Living Atlanta: An Oral History of the City, 1914–1948* (Athens: University of Georgia Press, 1990); Clifford M. Kuhn, *Contesting the New South Order: The 1914–1915 Strike at Atlanta's Fulton Mills* (Chapel Hill: University of North Carolina Press, 2001); Karen Ferguson, *Black Politics in New Deal Atlanta* (Chapel Hill: University of North Carolina Press, 2002).

33. Floyd Hunter, *Community Power Structure: A Study of Decision Makers* (Chapel Hill: University of North Carolina Press, 1953).

34. See, for instance, Allen, *Mayor*; Martin, *Hartsfield*; Floyd Hunter, *Community Power Succession: Atlanta's Policy-Makers Revisited* (Chapel Hill: University of North Carolina Press, 1980); Alton Hornsby Jr., "A City That Was Too Busy to Hate: Atlanta Businessmen and Desegregation," in *Southern Businessmen and Desegregation*, ed. Elizabeth Jacoway and David R. Colburn (Baton Rouge: Louisiana State University Press, 1982), 120–36; Clarence N. Stone, *Regime Politics: Governing Atlanta, 1946–1988* (Lawrence: University of Kansas Press, 1989).

35. Until recently, for instance, the only work of note on civil rights protests inside Atlanta was a collection of essays covering a single year of the student sit-in protests against segregated lunch counters. See David Garrow, ed., *Atlanta, Georgia, 1960–1961: Sit-Ins and Student Activism* (Brooklyn, N.Y.: Carlson Publishing, 1989). With the exception of one essay on the history of Atlanta's black upper class, this collection focuses solely on the early phase of the city's student

sit-ins. Even then, it fails to give that topic the detail and depth of discussion it deserves.

36. As the Olympics brought attention to Atlanta in 1996, the host city witnessed a sudden surge in popular histories. The best two of these accounts are Gary Pomerantz, *Where Peachtree Meets Sweet Auburn: A Saga of Race and Family* (New York: Scribner, 1996), and Frederick Allen, *Atlanta Rising: The Invention of an International City, 1946–1996* (Atlanta: Longstreet Press, 1996).

37. The best current work is Bayor, *Race and Atlanta*. This account does an excellent job of examining the evolution of black political and economic power in the city, chronicling the many ways in which the city sought to contain black expansion, not just politically or socially but also physically, in the application of zoning ordinances, routing of roads and highways, and placement of public housing. In this sense, Bayor's work provides an excellent examination of the intersection of race and public policy, detailing the interactions of civil rights leaders and the city's white establishment quite well. However, it fails to go any deeper. Bayor focuses solely on the top levels of society—the white political and economic establishment and the leaders of the black community. Working-class and middle-class whites are almost completely ignored.

CHAPTER ONE
"THE CITY TOO BUSY TO HATE": ATLANTA AND THE POLITICS OF PROGRESS

1. Floyd Hunter, "Process Recording of Interview: Atlanta Power Structure," box 16, FH.

2. Floyd Hunter to Gordon W. Blackwell, 27 November 1950, box 16, FH.

3. Hunter, "Process Recording," box 16, FH.

4. Numan V. Bartley, *The Creation of Modern Georgia* (Athens: University of Georgia Press, 1983), 147–53; John Dittmer, *Black Georgia in the Progressive Era, 1900–1920* (Urbana: University of Illinois Press, 1977), 90–104; Michael Perman, *Struggle for Mastery: Disfranchisement in the South, 1888–1908* (Chapel Hill: University of North Carolina Press, 2001), 281–97; Charles E. Wynes, "Civil Rights, 1890–1940," in *A History of Georgia*, gen. ed. Kenneth Coleman (Athens: University of Georgia Press, 1991), 277–80.

5. Jane Herndon, "The County Unit System in Georgia," *Atlanta Historical Journal* 22 (fall–winter 1978): 7–9; Joseph L. Bernd, *Grass Roots Politics in Georgia: The County Unit System and the Importance of the Individual Voting Community in Bi-Factional Elections, 1942–1954* (Atlanta: Emory University Research Committee, 1960), 30–32; V. O. Key Jr., *Southern Politics in State and Nation* (New York: Vintage, 1949), 106, 117–24.

6. Bartley, *Modern Georgia*, 192; Key, *Southern Politics*, 107–17; William Anderson, *The Wild Man from Sugar Creek: The Political Career of Eugene Talmadge* (Baton Rouge: Louisiana State University Press, 1975), 230; Bass and De Vries, *Transformation of Southern Politics*, 136–37; telex report, "More on Talmadge," [n.d.], box 16, NAB.

7. Numan V. Bartley, "Race Relations and the Quest for Equality" in Coleman, *History of Georgia*, 361; Bartley, *Rise of Massive Resistance*, 43; Key, *Southern Politics*, 106–12.

8. Harold Paulk Henderson, *The Politics of Change in Georgia: A Political Biography of Ellis Arnall* (Athens: University of Georgia Press, 1991), 89–92, 141–44; Thurgood Marshall, "The Rise and Collapse of the 'White Democratic Primary,' " *Journal of Negro Education* 36 (Summer 1957): 249–54; John Egerton, *Speak Now against the Day: The Generation before the Civil Rights Movement in the South* (Chapel Hill: University of North Carolina Press, 1994), 380–81; Paul Douglas Bolster, "Civil Rights Movements in Twentieth-Century Georgia" (Ph.D. diss., University of Georgia, 1972), 113–21; *AC*, 5 April 1946; Clarence A. Bacote, "The Negro Voter in Georgia Politics, Today," *Journal of Negro Education* 26 (Summer 1957): 307.

9. Bartley, *Modern Georgia*, 187; Bass and De Vries, *Transformation of Southern Politics*, 137; Joseph L. Bernd and Lynwood M. Holland, "Recent Restrictions upon Negro Suffrage: The Case of Georgia," *Journal of Politics* 21 (1959): 502; Calvin McLeod Logue, *Eugene Talmadge: Rhetoric and Response* (New York: Greenwood Press, 1989), 226; Stetson Kennedy, *The Klan Unmasked* (Boca Raton: Florida Atlantic University Press, 1990), 64; Floyd Hunter, manuscript draft with notes, "Regional City in Political Perspective," [1946], box 16, FFP.

10. Logue, *Talmadge*, 228; Langston Hughes, *Fight for Freedom: The Story of the NAACP* (New York: Norton, 1962), 112–13; Wallace H. Warren, " 'The Best People in Town Won't Talk': The Moore's Ford Lynching of 1946 and Its Cover-Up," in *Georgia in Black and White: Explorations in the Race Relations of a Southern State, 1865–1950*, ed. John C. Inscoe (Athens: University of Georgia Press, 1994), 266–83; Branch, *Parting the Waters*, 64.

11. Bartley, "Politics and Government in the Postwar Era," in Coleman, *History of Georgia*, 394–96.

12. Kuhn et al., *Living Atlanta*, 311–12; Stone, *Regime Politics*, 17.

13. Louis Williams, "William Berry Hartsfield and Atlanta Politics: The Formative Years of an Urban Reformer, 1920–1936," *Georgia Historical Quarterly* 84, no. 4 (Winter 2000): 651–76; Pomerantz, *Peachtree*, 130; Allen, *Atlanta Rising*, 20–33; Martin, *Hartsfield*, 12–36; Kuhn et al., *Living Atlanta*, 327–29.

14. Stone, *Regime Politics*, 27; Martin, *Hartsfield*, 24; Kuhn et al., *Living Atlanta*, 312–13.

15. Pomerantz, *Peachtree*, 133; *Saturday Evening Post*, 31 October 1953.

16. Allen, *Atlanta Rising*, 40–41; Mark Pendergrast, *For God, Country and Coca-Cola: The Unauthorized History of the Great American Soft Drink and the Company That Makes It* (New York: Scribner, 1993), 252; Hughes Spaulding, interview with Floyd Hunter, draft transcript, [1950], box 16, FH; Bass and De Vries, *Transformation of Southern Politics*, 138.

17. Martin, *Hartsfield*, 20–23; Allen, *Atlanta Rising*, 28–29, 41; Pendergrast, *God, Country and Coca-Cola*, 253.

18. Kuhn et al., *Living Atlanta*, 329; Allen, *Atlanta Rising*, 41; Hunter, *Community Power Structure*; Allen, *Mayor*, 30–31.

19. Lewis, *King*, 8–9; Pomerantz, *Peachtree*, 123–24; Kuhn et al., *Living Atlanta*, 39, 95, 100–102; Alexa Benson Henderson, *Atlanta Life Insurance Company: Guardian of Black Economic Dignity* (Tuscaloosa: University of Alabama Press, 1990), 20–42, 148–51, 168–88; Allen, *Atlanta Rising*, 36; August Meier and David Lewis, "History of the Negro Upper Class in Atlanta, Georgia, 1890–1950," in Garrow, *Atlanta*, 5–7.

20. Pomerantz, *Peachtree*, 116, 123–27, 180; Robert J. Alexander, "Negro Business in Atlanta," *Southern Economic Journal* (Winter 1951): 455–56.

21. Martin Luther King Sr. with Clayton Riley, *Daddy King: An Autobiography* (New York: Morrow, 1980), 91–94; James W. English, *Handyman of the Lord: The Life and Ministry of the Reverend William Holmes Borders* (New York: Meredith, 1967), 31–35; Branch, *Parting the Waters*, 34, 42–43, 54; Kuhn et al., *Living Atlanta*, 106.

22. Lewis, *Du Bois*, 213; Kuhn et al., *Living Atlanta*, 156–58.

23. Edgar A. Toppin, "Walter White and the Atlanta NAACP's Fight for Equal Schools, 1916–1917," *History of Education Quarterly* 7 (Spring 1967): 3–21; Stone, *Regime Politics*, 33; Lorraine Nelson Spritzer and Jean B. Bergmark, *Grace Towns Hamilton and the Politics of Southern Change* (Athens: University of Georgia Press, 1997), 89–143; Nancy J. Weiss, *The National Urban League, 1910–1940* (New York: Oxford University Press, 1974), 163–75; Nancy J. Weiss, *Whitney M. Young, Jr., and the Struggle for Civil Rights* (Princeton: Princeton University Press, 1989), 55–124.

24. Bayor, *Race and Atlanta*, 19.

25. Ferguson, *Black Politics in New Deal Atlanta*, 152–60; Douglas L. Smith, *The New Deal in the Urban South* (Baton Rouge: Louisiana State University Press, 1988), 254–55; Bayor, *Race and Atlanta*, 20; Jack L. Walker, "Protest and Negotiation: A Case Study of Negro Leadership in Atlanta, Georgia," *Midwest Journal of Political Science* 7 (May 1963): 114; Bayor, *Race and Atlanta*, 21.

26. Anna Holden, "Race and Politics: Congressional Elections in the Fifth District of Georgia, 1946 to 1952" (Ph.D. diss., University of North Carolina, 1955), 18–21; C. A. Bacote, "The Negro in Atlanta Politics," *Phylon* 16 (1955): 344; Lorraine Nelson Spritzer, *The Belle of Ashby Street: Helen Douglas Mankin and Georgia Politics* (Athens: University of Georgia Press, 1982); Bayor, *Race and Atlanta*, 21; Clarence A. Bacote, interview by Lorraine Nelson Spritzer, 23 July 1977, transcript, GGDP; *AJ*, 13 February 1946; *Newsweek* 27 (25 February 1946): 28; *Time* 47 (25 February 1946): 22.

27. Bolster, "Civil Rights Movements," 121–22; Bayor, *Race and Atlanta*, 24; Bacote, "The Negro in Atlanta Politics," 347–49; Ferguson, *Black Politics in New Deal Atlanta*, 253, 260, 264; Spritzer and Bergmark, *Grace Towns Hamilton*, 109–114. Black registration represented 27.2 percent of the total electorate in June 1946, compared to 8.3 percent in February and approximately 4.0 percent the year before. See Jack Walker, "Negro Voting in Atlanta, 1953–1961," *Phylon* 24 (Winter 1963): 380.

28. Louis Williams, "William Berry Hartsfield: The Reluctant Accommodationist and the Politics of Race in Atlanta, 1900–1961" (Ph.D. diss., Georgia State University, 1996), 187–91; Kuhn et al., *Living Atlanta*, 313; Bayor, *Race and Atlanta*, 25, 173–75.

29. Martin, *Hartsfield*, 51–52; Allen, *Atlanta Rising*, 35; Williams, "Hartsfield: Reluctant Accommodationist," 191–96.

30. Pomerantz, *Peachtree*, 184–88; Bacote, "The Negro in Atlanta Politics," 349; Bolster, "Civil Rights Movement," 123–24; Bacote, "Negro Voter in Georgia Politics," 311.

31. Atlanta Negro Voters League, endorsement list, 3 September 1946, box 10, WBH.

32. "Official Corrected List—September 6, 1946," box 10, WBH. Brown denied any involvement in the scheme, but the confusion over the list could only have benefited his campaign. For more on this episode and Brown's larger career in politics, see Charlie Brown, *Charlie Brown Remembers Atlanta: Memoirs of a Public Man as Told to James C. Bryant* (Columbia, S.C.: R. L. Bryan Company, 1982).

33. William B. Hartsfield, "Announcement," 7 September 1949, box 10, WBH.

34. Bayor, *Race and Atlanta*, 26; Williams, "Hartsfield: Reluctant Accommodationist," 219.

35. Martin, *Hartsfield*, 46, 87; Luther Spinks to William B. Hartsfield, 10 September 1951, box 5, WBH; J. T. Moseley to Herbert T. Jenkins, 2 January 1952, box 5, WBH; Moseley to Jenkins, 11 January 1952, box 5, WBH; Williams, "Hartsfield: Reluctant Accommodationist," 267–88.

36. *AJ*, 23 February 1971; Martin, *Hartsfield*, 68. For similar interpretations of Hartsfield's view of his black supporters, see Charles Garofalo, "A Study of the Interracial Coalition in Atlanta Politics" (M.A. thesis, Emory University, 1970), 7–11; Stephen Burman, "The Illusion of Progress: Race and Politics in Atlanta," *Ethnic and Racial Studies* 2 (October 1979): 443–444; Harry Holloway, *The Politics of the Southern Negro: From Exclusion to Big City Organization* (New York: Random House, 1969), 217–19.

37. Hunter, *Community Power Structure*, 138; Pomerantz, *Peachtree*, 317; John A. Sibley to Robert Woodruff, 9 August 1954, document case 253, RWW; John A. Sibley to Carl Vinson, 30 January 1956, box G11, JAS; Jeff Roche, *Restructured Resistance: The Sibley Commission and the Politics of Desegregation in Georgia* (Athens: University of Georgia Press, 1998).

38. King, *Daddy King*, 112.

39. Bayor, *Race and Atlanta*, 7, 85–87; Stone, *Regime Politics*, 30; William B. Hartsfield to "Gentlemen," 7 January 1943, box 9, WBH; Bradley R. Rice, "The Battle of Buckhead: The Plan of Improvement and Atlanta's Last Big Annexation," *Atlanta Historical Journal* 25 (Winter 1981): 9–13; Williams, "Hartsfield: Reluctant Accommodationist," 224–33; *AC*, 1 January 1952; *AJC*, 18 January 1970.

40. Rice, "Battle of Buckhead," 15–18; Allen, *Atlanta Rising*, 50; Abbott, *New Urban America*, 178.

41. Pomerantz, *Peachtree*, 186–88; Martin, *Hartsfield*, 100–101; Bayor, *Race and Atlanta*, 29.

42. Susan Margaret McGrath, "Great Expectations: The History of School Desegregation in Atlanta and Boston, 1954–1990" (Ph.D. diss., Emory University,

1992), 25, n. 31; *Nation*, 30 May 1953; Allen, *Atlanta Rising*, 51; Bacote, "Negro in Atlanta Politics," 349; Egerton, *Speak Now against the Day*, 604.

43. *Saturday Evening Post*, 22 September 1945; *Christian Century*, 3 June 1953; *Newsweek*, 15 March 1954; *Saturday Evening Post*, 31 October 1953; *AJC*, 18 January 1970; Martin, *Hartsfield*, 142.

44. Memorandum, "Ideas on the Mayoralty Campaign," [1953], box 12, WBH; Walker, "Negro Voting in Atlanta," 374–87; James Q. Wilson, "The Negro in Politics," in *The Black Revolt and Democratic Politics*, ed. Sandra Silverman (Lexington, Mass.: D. C. Heath, 1970), 27–32; M. Kent Jennings and Harmon Zeigler, "Class, Party, and Race in Four Types of Elections: The Case of Atlanta," *Journal of Politics* 28 (May 1966): 406.

CHAPTER TWO
FROM RADICALISM TO "RESPECTABILITY":
RACE, RESIDENCE, AND SEGREGATIONIST STRATEGY

1. Report and Columbians Pledge Card, 3 September 1946, box 51, REM; Kennedy, *Klan Unmasked*, 127–30.

2. Howard L. Preston, *Automobile Age Atlanta: The Making of a Southern Metropolis, 1900–1935* (Athens: University of Georgia Press, 1979), 103–7; Dana F. White, "The Black Sides of Atlanta: A Geography of Expansion and Containment, 1870–1970," *Atlanta Historical Journal* 26, nos. 2–3 (Summer–Fall 1982): 218; Samuel L. Adams, "Blueprint for Segregation: A Survey of Atlanta Housing," *New South* 22 (Spring 1967): 75; Spritzer, *Belle of Ashby Street*, 99.

3. Robert A. Thompson, Hylan Lewis, and Davis McEntire, "Atlanta and Birmingham: A Comparative Study in Negro Housing," in *Studies in Housing and Minority Groups*, ed. Nathan Glazer and Davis McEntire (Berkeley: University of California Press, 1960), 22–25; Atlanta Metropolitan Planning Commission, *A Factual Inventory: A Report Containing Texts and Maps on Georgia's Capital City* (Atlanta: Metropolitan Planning Commission, 1950), 40; Andrew Wiese, *Places of Their Own: African American Suburbanization in the Twentieth Century* (Chicago: University of Chicago Press, 2004), 174–96.

4. The Columbians, Petition for Incorporation, Fulton County Superior Court, 16 August 1946, cited in *The State of Georgia v. The Columbians, Incorporated*, Civil Case No. A-161937, FCSC (hereafter cited as *Georgia v. Columbians*); C. A. Browne, *The Story of Our National Anthems* (New York: Crowell, 1960); Greene, *Temple Bombing*, 35; Emory Burke to Ted Giles, 13 February 1943, box 51, REM; Kennedy, *Klan Unmasked*, 121.

5. Kennedy, *Klan Unmasked*, 125, 130; *Friends of Democracy's Battle* 4 (30 November 1946): 3; Testimony of Holt Gewinner, *Contested Election Case*, Helen Douglas Mankin v. James C. Davis, *Fifth District of Georgia, before the House of Representatives of the Eightieth Congress*, 80th Cong., 2d sess., 16 March 1948, House Unpublished Hearings Collection, 266, cited in Holden, "Race and Politics," 88; *AJ*, 3, 10 December 1946; J. Wayne Dudley, " 'Hate' Organizations of the 1940s: The Columbians, Inc.," 42 *Phylon* (September 1981): 267.

6. Holden, "Race and Politics," 87; Kennedy, *Klan Unmasked*, 120–22; Emory Burke, "Chain Ganged by the Jewish Gestapo," [1949], box 51, REM.

7. For excellent accounts of mill life in Atlanta specifically and Georgia generally, see Kuhn, *Contesting the New South Order*; and Douglas Flamming, *Creating the Modern South: Millhands and Managers in Dalton, Georgia, 1884–1984* (Chapel Hill: University of North Carolina Press, 1992).

8. Kennedy, *Klan Unmasked*, 127–29; report, 3 September 1946, box 51, REM; *AJ*, 3 November 1946.

9. George Harrison to Atlanta Housing Council, 19 June 1947, AUL; Holden, "Race and Politics," 89; *AJ*, 4 November 1946; *AC*, 30 October 1946.

10. *AJ*, 3 November 1946; Kennedy, *Klan Unmasked*, 151.

11. *ADW*, 30 October, 6 November 1946; Steven Weisenburger, "The Columbians, Inc.: A Chapter of Racial Hatred from the Post–World War II South," *Journal of Southern History* 69, no. 4 (November 2003): 824–26; Kennedy, *Klan Unmasked*, 148–51; Dudley, " 'Hate' Organizations," 269; *AJ*, 1, 3 November 1946.

12. *ADW*, 9 November 1946; Information in the Nature of Quo Warranto, 5 November 1946, *Georgia v. Columbians*; *AJ*, 5, 8 November 1946; confidential report, "Columbians," 8 November 1946, box 51, REM.

13. Response of the Defendant, 28 November 1946, *Georgia v. Columbians*; Egerton, *Speak Now against the Day*, 383; Chalmers, *Hooded Americanism*, 239.

14. Greene, *Temple Bombing*, 145; Kennedy, *Klan Unmasked*, 183.

15. Report, "Columbians," 8 November 1946, box 51, REM.

16. Exalted Cyclops to Klansmen, 22 April 1946, box 60, REM; Wade, *Fiery Cross*, 276–77.

17. This quotation referred specifically to textile workers in the vicinity of Columbus, Georgia, whom Green hoped to recruit for his organization. Confidential report, "Klavern No. 1, March 24, 1947," 1 April 1947, box 60, REM.

18. Notes, "Oakland City Post No. 297," [n.d., 1946], box 60, REM; "Notes on Talk with SK [Stetson Kennedy] May 11 [1946]," box 60, REM; Report, "Klavern No. 1," 1 April 1947, box 60, REM; Wade, *Fiery Cross*, 283; Kennedy, *Klan Unmasked*, 62.

19. Kennedy, *Klan Unmasked*, 151; Homer Loomis to Whom It May Concern, [n.d.], box 51, REM; Statement of Attorney Morgan Belser, trial transcript, *State of Georgia v. Knights of the Ku Klux Klan*, Civil Case No. A-159313, FCSC.

20. Reports, "Klavern No. 1," 28 April, 5 May 1947, box 60, REM; Kennedy, *Klan Unmasked*, 62–67.

21. Reports, "Klavern No. 1," 12 May, 2 June, 7 July 1947, box 60, REM.

22. Reports, "Klavern No. 1," 26 May, 30 June 1947, box 60, REM; Chalmers, *Hooded Americanism*, 329.

23. Kennedy, *Klan Unmasked*, 90–94; Chalmers, *Hooded Americanism*, 329–30; Wade, *Fiery Cross*, 283–84; Reports, "Klavern No. 1," 5 May, 21 April 1947, box 60, REM.

24. Samuel Green to Esteemed Klansmen, 23 June 1947, box 60, REM; Anti-Defamation League of B'nai B'rith, reports, 24 July, 31 August 1949, reel 131, SRC; *ADW*, 29 April 1949; *AC*, 29 June 1949; *AJ*, 19, 21 August 1949; Harold H. Martin, "It's Tougher Now for the Kluxers," [1950], box 60, REM.

25. Report, "West End Cooperative Corporation," 7 May 1947, box 240, AUL; *AC*, 27 May 1949; Kennedy, report, 24 March 1947, box 246, AUL; report, "Klavern No. 1," 14 April 1947, box 60, REM.

26. Kennedy, *Klan Unmasked*, 68.

27. Kennedy, *Klan Unmasked*, 68; Kennedy, report, 24 March 1947, box 246, AUL; report, "West End Cooperative Corporation," 7 May 1947, box 240, AUL.

28. Kennedy, report, 24 March 1947, box 246, AUL; Kennedy, *Klan Unmasked*, 68; report, "West End Cooperative Corporation," 7 May 1947, box 240, AUL.

29. *Shelley v. Kraemer*, 334 U.S. 1 (1948); report, "Meeting of 'Outraged White Georgians,' " 15 July 1948, box 240, AUL.

30. *WEE*, 8 April 1949; Statement of Petitioners, *The B-X Corporation et al. v. Joseph M. Wallace et al.*, Civil Case No. A-10564, FCSC.

31. *AJ*, 6 March 1949; statement of Rose Torrence, 8 March 1949, box 240, AUL; *AC*, 6 March 1949; *ADW*, 6 March 1949.

32. *WEE*, 8 April 1949.

33. Among other things, Atlantans have disagreed on the correct spelling of Mozley, writing it out as "Mozely," "Mosley," "Moseley," and "Mosely" from time to time. (Even a map of the city today still spells the park "Mozley" and the street running alongside it "Mozely.") For the purposes of this study, the "Mozley" spelling will be used; variations in quotations follow the original.

34. Thompson et al., "Atlanta and Birmingham," 27.

35. Dana F. White, "Landscaped Atlanta: The Romantic Tradition in Cemetery, Park, and Suburban Development," *Atlanta Historical Journal* 26 (Summer–Fall 1982): 102; Franklin M. Garrett, *Atlanta and Environs: A Chronicle of Its People and Events*, vol. 2 (New York: Lewis Historical Publishing Company, 1954), 71–72, 434; Timothy J. Crimmins, "West End: Metamorphosis from Suburban Town to Intown Neighborhood," *Atlanta Historical Journal* 26 (Summer–Fall 1982): 41; *AJ*, 21 August 1949; Gail Anne D'Avino, "Atlanta Municipal Parks, 1882–1917: Urban Boosterism, Urban Reform in a New South City" (Ph.D. diss., Emory University, 1988), 148–50; Charlayne Hunter-Gault, *In My Place* (New York: Farrar Straus Giroux, 1992), 82; Sanborn Map Company, *Insurance Maps of Atlanta, Georgia*, vol. 5, AHS.

36. Adams, "Blueprint for Segregation," 76; Thompson et al., "Atlanta and Birmingham," 27.

37. Preston, *Automobile Age Atlanta*, 102–3; Bayor, *Race and Atlanta*, 58; Thompson et al., "Atlanta and Birmingham," 28.

38. Charles S. Johnson and Herman H. Long, *People vs. Property: Restrictive Covenants in Housing* (Nashville: Fisk University Press, 1947), 71; Luigi Laurenti, *Property Values and Race: Studies in Seven Cities* (Berkeley: University of California Press, 1960), 24–25; Kenneth T. Jackson, "Race, Ethnicity and Real Estate Appraisal: The Home Owners' Loan Corporation and the Federal Housing Administration," *Journal of Urban History* 6, no. 4 (August 1980): 430–47; Kenneth T. Jackson, *Crabgrass Frontier: The Suburbanization of the United States* (New York: Oxford University Press, 1985), 190–218; Charles Abrams, *Forbidden Neighbors: A Study of Prejudice in Housing* (New York: Harper, 1955), 229.

39. Abrams, *Forbidden Neighbors*, 156; Johnson and Long, *People vs. Property*, 59.

40. Report, "Historical Trends in Negro Population Areas," box 1, ABP; U.S. Bureau of the Census, *U.S. Census of Housing: 1940*, vol. 3, *Supplement to the First Series: Housing Bulletin for Georgia: Atlanta: Block Statistics* (Washington,

D.C.: U.S. Government Printing Office, 1942), table 3, census tract F-40, blocks 18, 28, 29; U.S. Bureau of the Census, *U.S. Census of Housing: 1950*, vol. 5, *Block Statistics*, pt. 9 (Washington, D.C.: U.S. Government Printing Office, 1952), table 3, census tract F-40, blocks 8, 24, 25. There was a notable exception to the poor quality of black homes in the West End. Around the northeast of Atlanta University, west of Ashby Street and along Hunter Street, stood an impressive array of upper-class black residences, including the mansion of insurance magnate Alonzo Herndon. See Ann DeRosa Byrne and Dana F. White, "Atlanta University's 'Northeast Lot': Community Building for Black Atlanta's 'Talented Tenth,' " *Atlanta Historical Journal* 26 (Summer–Fall 1982): 155–75.

41. *City Directory, 1948–1949* (Atlanta: Atlanta City Directory Company Publishing, 1948).

42. Adams, "Blueprint for Segregation," 76, 80; Thompson et al., "Atlanta and Birmingham," 28; U.S. Bureau of the Census, *U.S. Census of Housing: 1950*, vol. 5, *Block Statistics*, pt. 9, table 3.

43. Other observers apparently agreed. The AUL, for instance, assumed in 1947 that an area bound by "Mosely Drive (to Chappell Road) and the A.B. and C. Railroad (to Gordon Road) and Gordon Road on the South . . . may be thought of as the main area for Negro expansion in the City of Atlanta." See report, "Proposed Expansion Areas for Negroes in Atlanta, Georgia," [n.d., 1947], box 243, AUL.

44. E. F. Turner, testimony, Hearing before Georgia Real Estate Commission, State Capitol, Atlanta, 10 March 1949, 109–10, copy located in *E. M. Smith, Investigator, Georgia Real Estate Commission, v. J. H. Calhoun*, Civil Case No. A-12007, FCSC (hereafter cited as GREC Hearing); Thompson et al., "Atlanta and Birmingham," 28; Frank Bearden, Testimony, GREC Hearing, 30.

45. [Robert Thompson], "Fr Chn Hearing," 10 March 1949, box 246, AUL; testimony, Maybelle Turner and Margaret Field Hall, GREC Hearing, 95, 22.

46. Testimony, R. A. Allen, Maybelle Turner, and E. F. Turner, GREC Hearing, 36, 89–90, 103.

47. Testimony, Maybelle Turner, GREC Hearing, 91.

48. Andrew Jackson, "The Case of J. H. Calhoun, Atlanta, Georgia Real-Estate Agent," box 255, AUL; testimony, W. W. Weatherspool, Mrs. Ernest Brooks, Geneva Allen, and Margaret Field Hall, GREC Hearing, 180, 11, 24; *AC*, 15 February, 11 March 1949; [Robert Thompson], typewritten notes on GREC Hearing, 10 March 1949, box 246, AUL; Thompson et al., "Atlanta and Birmingham," 29.

49. *AC*, 15, 16 February, 11, 18 March 1949; Carson Lee, "The Social Characteristics of Negroes Who Invaded a White Residential Area in the City of Atlanta" (M.A. thesis, Atlanta University, 1957), 9. See also Joe T. Darden, "Black Residential Segregation: Impact of State Licensing Laws," *Journal of Black Studies* 12, no. 4 (June 1982): 415–26; testimony of Geneva Allen and Wesley Allen, GREC Hearing, 10, 178; Jackson, "The Case of J. H. Calhoun," copy in box 255, AUL.

50. Sugrue, *Origins of the Urban Crisis*, 211; *AC*, 15 April 1949; *AJ*, 25 April 1949; *City Directory, 1948–1949*.

51. *AJ*, 22 April, 20 May 1949; *WEE*, 8 April 1949; *ADW*, 11 May 1949; Adams, "Blueprint for Segregation," 76.

52. [Robert A. Thompson], "Fr Chn Hearing," typewritten notes on GREC Hearing, 10 March 1949, box 246, AUL; J. R. Wilson to Jack Dilliard, 1484 Adele Avenue, 23 November 1949, box 240, AUL; Empire Real Estate Board, "History," *Annual Banquet Program*, 1955, box 6, ABP; Minutes, Empire Real Estate Board, 18 January 1950, box 254, AUL; Memorandum of West End Business Man's Association, 31 May 1950, box 8, LRA.

53. Report, "Recommendation: Mozley Park Home Owners Protective Association," [March 1950], box 8, LRA; *AC*, 28 April 1950; West End Business Man's Association to Hartsfield, 31 May 1950, box 8, LRA; R. A. Thompson and A. T. Walden to T. M. Alexander, 6 June 1950, box 234, AUL; Minutes, Empire Real Estate Board, 21 June 1950, box 254, AUL.

54. Minutes, Empire Real Estate Board, 13 March 1950, 22 September, 19 December 1951, box 254, AUL; Thompson et al., "Atlanta and Birmingham," 29; *ADW*, 19, 26 August, 2, 9, 16 September, 7 October 1951; Theodore Martin Alexander Sr., *Beyond the Timberline: The Trials and Triumphs of a Black Entrepreneur* (Edgewood, Md.: M. E. Duncan Publishers, 1992), 161.

55. R. A. Thompson to Lester Granger, Executive Director, National Urban League, 19 July 1954, box 236, AUL; W. O. DuVall, testimony, United States Commission on Civil Rights, *Hearings before United States Commission on Civil Rights: Hearing, Atlanta, Georgia, 10 April 1959* (Washington, D.C.: U.S. Government Printing Office, 1959), 521; Thompson et al., "Atlanta and Birmingham," 29.

56. Minutes, Empire Real Estate Board, 19 September 19 December 1951, 16 January 1952, box 254, AUL; typewritten notes, "Sutton," [Robert Thompson interview with R. O. Sutton], [August 1956], box 246, AUL.

57. *AC*, 7 May 1952; *City Directory, 1951–1952* (Atlanta: Atlanta City Directory Company Publishing, 1951).

58. Plaintiff's Petition, *Mr. and Mrs. Donald A. McLean v. A. J. Smith, et al.*, Civil Case No. A-30041, FCSC, (hereafter cited as *McLean v. Smith*).

59. Report, 24 March 1947, box 246, AUL; typewritten notes, "Sutton, " [Robert Thompson interview with R. O. Sutton], [August 1956], box 246, AUL.

60. Plaintiff's Petition, *McLean v. Smith*.

61. Response to Plaintiff's Petition [Gann Realty], 13 May 1952, and Response to Plaintiff's Petition [Wilson Realty, Wolfe Realty, Glass Realty, Bell Realty, N. D. Jones Realty, Alexander-Calloway Realty, and Williamson and Company], 14 May 1952, *McLean v. Smith*; *ADW*, 15 May 1952.

62. Minutes, Empire Real Estate Board, 20 August, 8 September 1952, and copy of EREB statement, 9 September 1952, box 254, AUL.

63. This interpretation borrows from an analysis of "civic associations" in Sugrue, *Origins of the Urban Crisis*, 211.

64. *ADW*, 14 October 1952; *AJ*, 13 October 1952, *AC*, 14 October 1952.

65. *ADW*, 7, 18 September, 10 December 1952; T. M. Alexander to Housing Committee Members, 10 September 1952, box 243, AUL; Robert A. Thompson, Draft, Statement before United States Commission on Civil Rights, [1959], box 244, AUL; Thompson et al., "Atlanta and Birmingham," 30.

66. Visitors Log, Hartsfield Campaign Headquarters, [8 May 1953 entry], box 12, Hartsfield Papers.

67. *ADW*, 31 May, 7 June 1953; Hunter-Gault, *In My Place*, 83; Robert C. Stuart to S. B. Avery, 10 June 1953, box 3, ABP; Stuart to Hartsfield, 7 August 1953, box 3, ABP; *AC*, 17 February 1954.

68. *City Directory, 1953* (Atlanta: Atlanta City Directory Company Publishing, 1953); Membership List, Mozley Park Civic Association, 1954–55, box 224, AUL; Lee, "Social Characteristics of Negroes," 24–30.

69. Lee, "Social Characteristics of Negroes," 24; Hunter-Gault, *In My Place*, 74; William B. Hartsfield to Clarke Donaldson, 6 August 1954, box 3, ABP; John Calhoun and Charles Bell to William Holmes Borders, 9 October 1959, box 2, ATW. Borders eventually secured a total compensation of $1,560. See Judgment in Fulton County Superior Court, Civil Case No. A-76053, and Edwin L. Sterne to A. T. Walden, 24 March 1961, box 2, ATW. On the value of similar homes, see U.S. Bureau of the Census, *U.S. Census of Housing: 1950*, vol. 5, *Block Statistics*, pt. 9, table 3, census tract F-40, block 38.

70. C. Adams, letter to the editor, *AC*, 12 June 1949.

71. A. T. Walden to Wyont Bean, 12 December 1952, box 240; R. A. Thompson to "Mr. and Mrs. Home Owner," 15 December 1952, box 243; Petition to the Members of the Municipal Planning Board and Board of Adjustment, December 1952, box 243, AUL.

72. *ADW*, 5 June 1952, 21 October 1954; Atlanta Urban League, "A Report on Parks and Public Recreational Facilities for the Negro Population of Atlanta, Georgia," [1954], box 5, GTH; Hunter-Gault, *In My Place*, 82; *AI*, 23 May, 3, 8 August 1964.

73. U.S. Bureau of the Census, *U.S. Census of Housing: 1950*, vol. 5, *Block Statistics*, pt. 9, table 3, census tract F-40; U.S. Bureau of the Census, *U.S. Census of Housing: 1960*, vol. 3, *City Blocks* (Washington, D.C.: U.S. Government Printing Office, 1961), table 2, census tract F-40; quotation from Jackson, *Crabgrass Frontier*, 198, describing the theories of Homer Hoyt and Robert Park. The Mozley Place blocks were numbered, in the 1950/1960 censuses respectively, 24/26, 15/14, 20/10, and 23/30. The southern blocks were 27, 28, and 29 in both censuses. For related observations in different cities, see Laurenti, *Property Values and Race*; William M. Ladd, "The Effect of Integration on Property Values," *American Economic Review* 52, no. 4 (September 1962): 801–8; Erdman Palmore, "Integration and Property Values in Washington, D.C.," *Phylon* 27 (1966): 15–19; and A. Thomas King and Peter Mieszkowski, "Racial Discrimination, Segregation, and the Price of Housing," *Journal of Political Economy* 81, no. 3 (May–June 1973): 590–606.

CHAPTER THREE
FROM COMMUNITY TO INDIVIDUALITY:
RACE, RESIDENCE, AND SEGREGATIONIST IDEOLOGY

1. William B. Hartsfield to W. H. Aiken, T. M. Alexander, S. B. Avery, Richard Florrid, E. A. Sewall, and A. T. Walden, 8 December 1952, box 3, ABP; *City Directory, 1953*.

2. WSMDC discussion draft, "Policy Proposal of the West Side Mutual Development Committee Regarding the Operation of the Real Estate Market with Respect to Race of Occupancy," 20 August 1958, box 3, ABP; Bayor, *Race and Atlanta*, 59–69.

3. WSMDC discussion draft, 20 August 1958, box 3, ABP; draft, "Testimony of Robert C. Stuart, Prepared for Public Hearing, Commission on Civil Rights, Atlanta, Georgia, April 10, 1959," 9 April 1959, box 1, ABP.

4. Alexander, *Beyond the Timberline*, 165; Douglass Cater, "Atlanta: Smart Politics and Good Race Relations," *Reporter* 17 (11 July 1957): 20.

5. Rice, "Battle of Buckhead," 19–20; *AC*, 1 January 1952; memorandum, Margaret C. Breland to Leon S. Eplan, "Social and Economic Conditions—Adamsville," 22 August 1955, box 5, ABP; Adamsville Civic Club, *Adamsville: Now . . . and Tomorrow*, [1955], box 5, ABP; WSMDC, map, "Collier Drive-Hightower Road Area," August 1955, box 3, ABP.

6. The similar dates and language of these pleas suggest a coordinated campaign of letter writing. See the various letters of Mrs. Fred D. Phillips, L. G. Weese, Mrs. W. E. Dunn, Mrs. F. E. Hamilton, Frank L. York, Mrs. Marvin L. Hoke, G. H. Stone and E. H. Harper, Rev. Rex Brown and W. E. McDavid to Robert Stuart, 22–23 November 1954, box 5, ABP.

7. Memorandum, "Residence of Delmar Lane Area," [n.d., 1955–56], box 5, ABP; *City Directory, 1956* (Atlanta: Atlanta City Directory Company Publishing, 1956); "Adamsville Petition," [January 1955], box 5, ABP; Robert C. Stuart to Adamsville Civic Representatives and the Executive Committee of the Empire Real Estate Board, [13 January 1955], box 5, ABP; Mrs. R. E. Mitchell to Robert C. Stuart, 25 January 1955, box 5, ABP.

8. Metropolitan Planning Commission, "Subject: Commission Work with Neighborhood Civic Groups," box 5, ABP; Adamsville Civic Club, *Adamsville: Now . . . and Tomorrow*, [1955], box 5, ABP.

9. WSMDC to "Dear Friend in the Delmar Lane Area," 8 November 1956, box 5, ABP; Del Mar Lane Residents to Governor Marvin Griffin, 19 November 1956, box 5, ABP; Mrs. E. E. Watson Jr. to Robert Stuart, 2 November 1956, box 3, ABP; Hartsfield to Stuart, 21 November 1956, box 5, ABP.

10. Del Mar Lane Residents to Governor Marvin Griffin, 19 November 1956, box 5, ABP.

11. Memorandum, Robert C. Stuart to C. R. Allen, "Adamsville Assignment," 26 November 1956, box 5, ABP; WSMDC to Real Estate Brokers and Home Mortgage Brokers, 4 January 1957, box 3, ABP; Del Mar Sales Contracts and Walter A. Stubbefield, Notarized Statement, 21 January 1957, box 1: Calhoun Personal, JHC; WSMDC to Real Estate Brokers and Home Mortgage Brokers, 4 January 1957, box 5 ABP; Charles Allen to Harold Dennis, 8 March 1957, box 5, ABP; Allen to Will Crawford, 29 May 1957, box 3, ABP; Allen to J. L. Wolfe, 12 June 1957, box 3, ABP.

12. Memorandum, Charles R. Allen to Robert C. Stuart, "Historical Sequence of Events on M. C. Jackson (Delmar Lane Situation)," 18 July 1957, box 3, ABP; Charles R. Allen to M. B. Satterfield, 17 July 1957, box 3, ABP; *AC*, 13 July 1957, 3; WSMDC to "Real Estate and Home Mortgage Brokers," 30 June 1957, box 3, ABP.

13. Robert C. Stuart to Hartsfield, 29 July 1958, box 3, ABP; Stuart to "Dear Collier Drive Resident," 23 July 1958; "Statement of Policy of Fairburn Road Residents," [July 1958], box 3, ABP; form letter, "Attention: Owner and Manager," [July 1958], box 3, ABP; memorandum, Burt Sparer to Bob Stuart, "Notes on Telephone Conversation with Mr. Fuller of Fuller Realty and Insurance Company," 4 September 1958, box 3, ABP; Burton Sparer to L. J. Fuller, 17 September 1958, box 3, ABP; [Thomas M. Parham Jr.], "Report on Adamsville Transition Area," 26 August 1960, box 5, ABP.

14. WSMDC discussion draft, "Policy Proposal of the West Side Mutual Development Committee Regarding the Operation of the Real Estate Market with Respect to Race of Occupancy," 20 August 1958, box 3, ABP; draft, "Testimony of Robert C. Stuart, Prepared for Public Hearing, Commission on Civil Rights, Atlanta, Georgia, April 10, 1959," 9 April 1959, box 1, ABP.

15. WSMDC, Moreland Heights Survey Report, [October 1957], box 3, ABP; Kirkwood Survey Responses, 61, 68, 72 Anniston Avenue, 105, 111 Montgomery Avenue, and 1415, 1492 Woodbine Avenue, box 5, ABP; *City Directory, 1957* (Atlanta: Atlanta City Directory Company Publishing, 1957); *City Directory, 1960* (Atlanta: Atlanta City Directory Company Publishing, 1960); U.S. Bureau of the Census, *U.S. Census of Housing: 1950*, vol. 5, *Block Statistics*, pt. 9, table 3, census tract F-31, blocks 7, 18, 21, 22; census tract F-32, blocks 1, 15, 17, 19, 20; and census tract D-6, blocks 1, 3, 6 -10, 13–17.

16. Petition to Honorable Lee Evans, acting mayor, 2 December 1954, box 5, ABP; Sara S. Livingston, 105 Montgomery Street, to Hartsfield, 8 August 1956, box 3, ABP; Mason L. Chaffin, 1052 Manigault Street, Moreland Heights Survey Response, 9 October 1957, box 5, ABP; Robert C. Stuart to E. A. Gilliam, 6 February 1957, box 5, ABP.

17. WSMDC to "Dear Resident," 2 October 1957, box 5, ABP; handwritten notes, "W.S.M.D.C. Meeting, 9–16–57," box 5, ABP; WSMDC, Moreland Heights Survey Report, [October 1957], box 3, ABP; J. T. Edward Thompson, 1129 Kirkwood Avenue, Moreland Heights Survey Response, 9 October 1957, box 5, ABP.

18. West Side Mutual Development Committee, Moreland Heights Survey Report, [October 1957], box 3, ABP. No residents reported attending area synagogues, and only one (a tenant) reported attending the Catholic Immaculate Conception Cathedral, located outside the neighborhood on Hunter Street. See Moreland Heights Survey Responses, October 1957, box 5, ABP.

19. Rev. William R. Ridgeway of McKendree Methodist (1321 Boulevard), Rev. Guy Rainwater of Moreland Avenue Baptist Church (226 Wilburn Avenue), Rev. Evan B. Shivers of Inman Park Baptist (450 Claire), Rev. Wendell Wellman of the First Church of the Nazarene (1180 Cloverdale), and Rev. Sylvester Fields of Calvary Baptist (1206 Merlin Avenue). *City Directory, 1958* (Atlanta: Atlanta City Directory Company Publishing, 1958).

20. Carl L. Cooper to Burt Sparer, WSMDC, 6 November 1957, box 5, ABP; Sparer to "Dear Sir or Madam," 15 November 1957, box 5, ABP; Stuart to J. A. Alston, 21 February 1958, box 3, ABP; [Thomas M. Parham Jr.], "Report on Southeast Kirkwood Transition Area," 26 August 1960, box 5, ABP; U.S. Bureau of the Census, *U.S. Census of Housing: 1960: Block Statistics*, series HC (3)-118

(Washington, D.C.: U.S. Government Printing Office, 1962), table 2, census tract F-31, blocks 4, 6–17, 19, 22, 27–29, 41; "List of Churches in Moreland Heights Area," [1960], box 5, ABP.

21. U.S. Bureau of the Census, *U.S. Census of Housing: 1960: Block Statistics*, series HC (3)-118, table 2, census tract F-31, blocks 4, 6–17, 19, 22, 27–29, 41; census tract D-5, blocks 1, 5, 6, 11; and census tract D-6, blocks 4, 5, 7–14, 24–28. D. C. Vinson, 72 Anniston Avenue, Kirkwood Survey Response, [June 1960], box 5, ABP; *City Directory, 1960*; [Thomas M. Parham Jr.], handwritten notes, "Analysis of Fire at 1408 Woodbine, June 1960," box 5, ABP; *AJ*, 9, 17 June 1960; *AC*, 10, 17 June 1960; *ADW*, 10, 11 June 1960.

22. The term "hidden violence" appears in Hirsch, *Making the Second Ghetto*, esp. 40–67. For accounts of violence inspired by racial residential transition, see Arnold R. Hirsch, "Massive Resistance in the Urban North: Trumbull Park, Chicago, 1953," *Journal of American History* 82 (September 1995): 522–50; Thomas J. Sugrue, "Crabgrass-Roots Politics: Race, Rights, and the Reaction against Liberalism in the Urban North, 1940–1964," *Journal of American History* 82 (September 1995): 551–78; and Eskew, *But for Birmingham*, 53–83.

23. [Anon. #1] Woodbine Circle; C. S. Englett, 1520 Woodbine Avenue; [Anon. #2] Woodbine Circle; Lillie Ivie, 1492 Woodbine Avenue; Watson J. Holland, 100 Montgomery Street; Daisy K. Johnson, 1415 Woodbine Avenue; H. T. Avery, 52 Montgomery Street; and D. C. Vinson, 72 Anniston Avenue, Kirkwood Survey Responses, [June 1960], box 5, ABP. For examples of those who claimed they were financially or physically unable to move, see Kirkwood Survey Responses, 61, 68, 72 Anniston Avenue, 105, 111 Montgomery Avenue, and 1415, 1418, 1432, 1470 Woodbine Avenue, box 5, ABP.

24. H. T. Avery, 52 Montgomery Street, Kirkwood Survey Response, [June 1960], box 5, ABP. For a similar warnings, see the anonymous letters from Boulevard Drive and Vinson Drive, Kirkwood Survey Response, [June 1960], box 5, ABP.

25. *AC*, 24 February 1961; [Thomas M. Parham Jr.], "Report on Southeast Kirkwood Transition Area," 26 August 1960, box 5, ABP; [Sid Avery], handwritten notes, "Feb 7 1961 Kirkwood Methodist Church," box 5, ABP; draft report, "South Kirkwood Area," [7 February 1961], box 5, ABP; report, "South Kirkwood Area," [14 February 1961], box 5, ABP; *AJ*, 28 October 1960. On the similar role played by Jewish religious institutions in white flight, see Wendell Pritchett, *Brownsville, Brooklyn: Blacks, Jews and the Changing Face of the Ghetto* (Chicago: University of Chicago Press, 2002).

26. *AC*, 9 July 1960; report, "Kirkwood Churches Committee," [20 February 1961]; Minutes, Kirkwood Community Committee, 21 February 1961, box 5, ABP; notes, "Strategy Meeting—Eastern Atlanta Civic & Kirkwood Community," 3 March 1961, box 5, ABP; notes, "Meeting of March 10, 1961," box 5, ABP; "Notes for Meeting with Empire Real Estate Board Committee, Subject: Moreland-Kirkwood Areas," [March 1961], box 5, ABP; "Notes for Aldermen for Meet with Empire," [10 March 1961], box 5, ABP; draft, form letter, "The Kirkwood Community Committee," box 5, ABP.

27. Mrs. Sammye Coan and Louise Sims to Robert A. Thompson, 6 September 1961, box 244, AUL; program book, Annual Meeting of the Council on Human Relations of Greater Atlanta, 30 November 1964, box 5, EP.

28. Memorandum, Jim Parham to Hartsfield, "Fletcher-Mayland Circle Area," 6 October 1959, box 5, ABP; Sara Snead, Fletcher-Mayland Circle Questionnaire Response, [1959], box 5, ABP; confidental report, "Mayor's Committee on Stewart, University, and Mayland Neighborhood," [September 1959], box 3, ABP.

29. H. G. Bennett Sr. to Hope-Mayland Panel, 20 October 1955, box 3, ABP; Adair Park Civic Club, "To Whom It May Concern," 6 October 1955, box 3, ABP; and Adair Park Civic Club, "Special Notice," October 1955, box 3, ABP.

30. Letters of John Pirkle, Myrtle Marshall, Mrs. Arthur H. Puckett, Myrtle Wheeling, Mr. and Mrs. W. M. Allen, Mr. and Mrs. R. E. Nichols, Camille Denton, E. B. Hazelrig, and Odessa Stanley to Hope-Mayland Panel, 11–12, 14, 18, 20 October 1955, box 3, ABP; *City Directory, 1956* (Atlanta: Atlanta City Directory Company Publishing, 1956); handwritten petition, Dewey Street and Arthur Street Residents, 29 June 1956, box 3, ABP; memorandum, Jim Parham to Hartsfield, "Fletcher-Mayland Circle Area," 6 October 1959, box 5, ABP.

31. Burt Sparer to Property Owners on Mayland Circle and Mayland Avenue, 22 September 1958, box 3, ABP; memorandum, Jim Parham to Hartsfield, "Fletcher-Mayland Circle Area," 6 October 1959, box 5, ABP; Ollie Reeves, Pres., Southwest Development Company, Inc., Flyer, [September 1959], box 5, ABP; Adair Park Civic Club, Report, 24 September 1959, box 5, ABP; and Adair Park Civic Club, "Last Call" Flyer, [October 1959], box 5, ABP.

32. Adair Park Civic Club, "Last Call" flyer, [October 1959], box 5, ABP; Adair Park Civic Club, Report, 24 September 1959, box 5, ABP; Ollie Reeves, flyer, [September 1959]; [Thomas M. Parham Jr.], "Report on Adair Park Transition Area," 26 August 1960, box 5, ABP. Mike Davis has outlined a similar confusion over "community" boundaries and identities in *City of Quartz*, 153–56.

33. Sara J. Snead, Fletcher-Mayland Circle Community Questionnaire, [September 1959], box 5, ABP; memorandum, "Confidential: Mayor's Committee on Mayland Circle, Stewart Avenue, University Avenue," [September 1959], box 3, ABP; *City Directory, 1958–1959* (Atlanta: Atlanta City Directory Company Publishing, 1958); Mr. and Mrs. R. E. Nichols to Hope-Mayland Panel, [18 October 1955], box 3, ABP; R. E. Nichols, Fletcher-Mayland Circle Community Questionnaire, [September 1959], box 5, ABP; 1074, 1078, 1087, 1091 Hobson Street, Fletcher-Mayland Circle Community Questionnaires, [September 1959]; Mrs. R. J. [Mary] Edge, Fletcher-Mayland Circle Community Questionnaire, 8 October 1959; [Thomas M. Parham Jr.], "Report on Adair Park Transition Area," 26 August 1960; and Mrs. A. E. Latimer to Hartsfield, 15 June 1960, box 5, ABP.

34. J. R. Wilson Jr. to Adair Park Civic Association, Inc., 2 October 1959; J. R. Wilson Jr. to Ollie D. Reeves, Adair Park Civic Club, 29 February 1960; memorandum, Jim Parham to Mayor Hartsfield, "Fletcher-Mayland Circle Area," 6 October 1959; and [Thomas M. Parham Jr.], "Report on Adair Park Transition Area," 26 August 1960, box 5, ABP; Residents of 552, 574 Fletcher Street, 1082, 1087, 1088, 1104, 1106 Hobson Street, and 553, 562, 576 Mayland Avenue, to Georgia Securities Investment Corporation, Atlanta Federal Savings and Loan Association, Fulton County Federal Savings and Loan Association, Standard Fed-

eral Savings and Loan Association, and Georgia Savings Bank and Trust Company, 18 March 1960, box 5, ABP.

35. Al Kuettner, "Problem of Negro Housing Solved Peacefully in Atlanta," [n.d., 1957], box 158, AUL.

36. Collier Heights Civic Club, "Committee Report," 15 January 1954, box 3, ABP; Al Kuettner, "Problem of Negro Housing Solved Peacefully in Atlanta," [n.d., 1957], box 158, AUL; Collier Heights Civic Club, Report, 21 January 1954, box 3, ABP; Sid Avery to [Collier Heights Residents], 28 January 1954, box 3, ABP.

37. Collier Heights Civic Club, "Committee Report," 15 January 1954; Joint Agreement of Southwest Citizens Association, Inc., Collier Heights Civic Club, Metropolitan Planning Council, Mayors Bi Racial Housing Committee and National Development Company, 18 February 1954; Sid Avery to [Collier Heights Residents], 28 January 1954, box 3, ABP. For more on the access road proposal, see Bayor, *Race and Atlanta*, 63–65; Ronald H. Bayor, "Roads to Racial Segregation: Atlanta in the Twentieth Century," *Journal of Urban History* 15 (November 1988): 9–12.

38. Meeting Minutes, Empire Real Estate Board, 20 January 1954, box 254, AUL; WSMDC and Advisory Panel on Collier Heights, Grove Park, Center Hill, and Bolton, to "Dear Collier Heights Resident," 11 February 1954, box 3, ABP; Stephens Mitchell to Robert Stuart, 17 February 1954, box 3, ABP; WSMDC and Advisory Panel, "February 1954 Survey: Final Summary," box 3, ABP; Mrs. E. L. [Jane] Russell (356 Hightower Road), J. C. Hudgins (435 Forest Ridge Drive), F. J. Goss (2654 Baker Ridge Dr.), [Baker Road residents], and Samuel J. Martin (410 Forest Ridge Drive), Collier Heights Survey Responses, [24 February 1954], box 3, ABP; *City Directory, 1954* (Atlanta: Atlanta City Directory Company Publishing, 1954).

39. WSMDC and Advisory Panel to "Dear Collier Heights Resident," 5 March 1954, and WSMDC and Advisory Panel, "February 1954 Survey: Final Summary," box 3, ABP.

40. Al Kuettner, "Problem of Negro Housing Solved Peacefully in Atlanta," [n.d., 1957], box 158, AUL.

41. Philip Hammer to S. B. Avery et al., 15 December 1952, box 3, ABP; *City Directory, 1953*; WSMDC and Advisory Panel on Collier Heights, Grove Park, Center Hill, and Bolton, to "Dear Collier Heights Resident," 11 February 1954, box 3, ABP; Hartsfield to Clarke Donaldson, 20 March 1954, box 3, ABP.

42. Meeting Minutes, Empire Real Estate Board, 15 September 1954, box 254, AUL; notes, "Commercial Ave. (Confidential)," [November 1955], box 5, ABP; resolution, Atlanta Baptist Ministers Union, [1954], box 255, AUL; Bayor, *Race and Atlanta*, 64.

43. Notes, "Commercial Ave. (Confidential), Conversation with Col. Pitts, a Realtor with Alexander-Calloway," [November 1955], box 5, ABP; report, "Minutes of a Meeting of a Special Committee of the Atlanta Negro Voters League to Investigate Tensions in Grove Park Area, Atlanta, Ga., Butler Street YMCA, April 27, 1956," box 33, ATW.

44. Notes, "Commercial Ave. (Confidential), Conversation with Col. Pitts, a Realtor with Alexander-Calloway" and "Commercial Ave. (Confidential), Con-

versation with Mr. Dodgins (ACL RR)," [November 1955], box 5, ABP; *AC*, 7 November 1955, 27 February, 1 March 1956; *ADW*, 28 February 1956; *AJ*, 1 March 1956.

45. WSMDC to Mervin Overstreet, President, West Side Corporation, 12 March 1956, box 3, ABP. The WSMDC also encouraged local residents to support the repurchasing program. See Robert C. Stuart to Property Owner, 12 March 1956, and Robert C. Stuart to Property Owner On: Hood Avenue, Commercial Avenue, Robert Street, Hightower Road, Oldknow Drive, Baker Road, 20 March 1956, box 4, LRA; [Thomas M. Parham Jr.], "Report on Grove Park Transition Area," 26 August 1960, box 5, ABP; [Robert Thompson], typewritten notes, [1956], box 236, folder 22, AUL; Thompson et al., "Atlanta and Birmingham," 46–50.

46. [Thomas M. Parham Jr.], handwritten notes, "9–2–59" and "9–15–59"; G. R. Bilderback to D. C. Black Jr., 27 July 1960; Hartsfield to D. C. Black Jr., 20 May 1960; and Black to Hartsfield, 27 May 1960, box 5, ABP.

CHAPTER FOUR
THE ABANDONMENT OF PUBLIC SPACE:
DESEGREGATION, PRIVATIZATION, AND THE TAX REVOLT

1. Handbill, "The Plan of Improvement," [January 1959], box 6, WBH.

2. For broader investigations of this concept, see Rachel F. Moran, *Interracial Intimacy: The Regulation of Race and Romance* (Chicago: University of Chicago Press, 2001), and Randall Kennedy, *Interracial Intimacies: Sex, Marriage, Identity and Adoption* (New York: Pantheon, 2003).

3. See C. Vann Woodward, *The Strange Career of Jim Crow* (New York: Oxford University Press, 1955); Howard N. Rabinowitz, *Race Relations in the Urban South, 1865–1890* (New York: Oxford University Press, 1978); Don H. Doyle, *New Men, New Cities, New South: Atlanta, Nashville, Charleston, Mobile, 1860–1910* (Chapel Hill: University of North Carolina Press, 1990); David R. Goldfield, *Black, White and Southern: Race, Relations and Southern Culture, 1940 to the Present* (Baton Rouge: Louisiana State University Press, 1990).

4. Leon F. Litwack, *Trouble in Mind: Black Southerners in the Age of Jim Crow* (New York: Vintage, 1998); 245; Ray Stannard Baker, *Following the Color Line: An Account of Negro Citizenship in the American Democracy* (repr., Williamstown, Mass.: Corner House, 1973), 34.

5. A. C. Wilson to Preston Arkwright, President, Georgia Railway and Power Company, 31 December 1920, box 6, MM; "Petition to the Honorable Board of R. R. Commissioners," 1 December 1926, box 6, MM.

6. P. S. Arkwright to W. R. Pollard, 30 March 1943, box 116, MM; Floyd Hunter, manuscript draft, box 16, FFP; Hunter, *Community Power Structure*, 145–46.

7. *ADW*, 3, 11, 12, 19 April, 17 October 1946; *AJ*, 11 April 1946.

8. *AJ*, 11 April 1946; *ADW*, 19 April, 17 October 1946; Manager, Transportation Department, to 1st Lt. William P. Jones, 23 April 1946, box 116, MM.

9. Vester M. Ownby, letter to the editor, *AC*, 17 April 1946; flyer, Atlanta's Political and Civic League, "Big Mass Meeting!" [April 1946], box 116, MM; *ADW*, 18 April 1946.

10. James L. Delk to Georgia Power Company, 24 July 1948, box 116, MM; typewritten note and newsclipping, "An Ex-Transit Rider Gives Reason for 'Ex,' " [September 1953], box 6, MM; resolution, Atlanta Methodist Ministers Conference, "Complaint against Policy of Unfair Treatment of the Negro People," 28 January 1952, box 116, MM.

11. Bayor, *Race and Atlanta*, 189; Thompson et al., "Atlanta and Birmingham," 33; Stone, *Regime Politics*, 35; M. M. Melson to William B. Hartsfield, 15 October 1958, box 6, WBH.

12. C. L. Harper, "Annual Report of the President—Dec. 13, 1949," part 26, series A, reel 9, NAACP; E. E. Moore to Robert L. Sommerville, 31 May 1956, and Sommerville to Moore, 15 June 1956, box 35, MM; Minute Books, 1954–56, box 1, ATA; memorandum, "ATS—Segregation of Passengers," 28 October 1954, box 35, MM.

13. Branch, *Parting the Waters*, 143–68, 173–205; Sitkoff, *Struggle for Black Equality*, 37–56; Lewis, *King*, 46–80; Plaintiff's Petition, *Reverend Samuel W. Williams and Reverend John T. Porter v. Georgia Public Service Commission, et al.*, Civil Action No. 6067, U. S. District Court, Northern District of Georgia (hereafter cited as *Williams v. GPSC*), copy in box 116, MM.

14. *Browder v. Gayle*, 352 U. S. 903; Catherine A. Barnes, *Journey from Jim Crow: The Desegregation of Southern Transit* (New York: Columbia University Press, 1983), 120–26; typewritten draft, Atlanta Transit System, box 35, MM; Robert L. Sommerville to A. T. Walden, draft of letter, 8 January 1957, box 35, MM; Williams, "Hartsfield: Reluctant Accommodationist," 74, 264–65; English, *Handyman of the Lord*, 90.

15. *ADW*, 8–10 January 1957; *AJ*, 9 January 1957; Affadavit, Ganis V. Daniel, driver, Atlanta Transit System, 14 January 1957, box 35, MM; Plaintiff's Petition, *Williams v. GPSC*; Cater, "Atlanta: Smart Politics," 18.

16. H. T. Jenkins to Paul Webb, solicitor, Atlanta Judicial Circuit, Fulton County Court House, 10 January 1957, box 18, HTJ; Herbert T. Jenkins, *Forty Years on the Force: 1932–1972* (Atlanta: Center for Research in Social Change, 1973), 108; Pomerantz, *Peachtree*, 217; Martin, *Hartsfield*, 119; Herbert T. Jenkins, *Keeping the Peace: A Police Chief Looks at His Job* (New York: Harper, 1970), 39; *ADW*, 11 January 1957; English, *Handyman of the Lord*, 93; Cater, "Atlanta: Smart Politics," 18.

17. *AJ*, 9, 10 January 1957; *AC*, 11 January 1957; Cater, "Atlanta: Smart Politics," 18–21.

18. English, *Handyman of the Lord*, 90, 97; *MH*, 20 June 1956; *AJ*, 9, 11 January 1957; William T. Bodenhamer, press release, 9 January 1957, box 32, JCD; A. L. Ellis to James C. Davis, 28 January 1959, box 38, JCD; L. B. Parrish, Detroit, to Herbert Jenkins, 29 December 1956, HTJ.

19. Minutes, Atlanta Transit System, directors meetings, 26 June, 27 November, 18 December 1957, box 2, MM; Bolster, "Civil Rights," 172–73; Herman

Randolph Phillips, "Patterns of Racial Segregation on City Buses in Atlanta, Georgia," (M.A. thesis, Atlanta University, 1957), 36–38.

20. Bolster, "Civil Rights," 172–73; *AJ*, 19 January 1959; *AC*, 20 January 1959; Fenton M. Dancy to James C. Davis, 21 March 1959, box 38, JCD; U.S. Bureau of the Census, *U.S. Censuses of Population and Housing: 1960*, Final Report PHC(1)-8, *Census Tracts: Atlanta, Ga.* (Washington, D.C.: U.S. Government Printing Office, 1961), tables P-1 and P-3, census tracts, F-47, F-48, F-49, F-50; Bayor, *Race and Atlanta*, 191.

21. D'Avino, "Atlanta Municipal Parks"; White, "Landscaped Atlanta," 104; Atlanta Urban League, "A Report on Parks and Public Recreational Facilities for the Negro Population of Atlanta, Georgia," [1954], box 5, GTH.

22. Calvin Trillin, *An Education in Georgia: Charlayne Hunter, Hamilton Holmes, and the Integration of the University of Georgia* (Athens: University of Georgia Press, 1991), 15; Williams, "Hartsfield: Reluctant Accommodationist," 234; *ADW*, 20 July 1951; *AC*, 24 December 1955; W. W. Law, interview by Cliff Kuhn and Tim Crimmins, 15, 16 November 1990, transcript, GGDP; Atlanta Urban League, "A Report on Parks and Public Recreational Facilities for the Negro Population of Atlanta, Georgia," [1954], box 5, GTH; *AJ*, 8 July 1954.

23. *ADW*, 27 June 1953, 9 July 1954; *AJ*, 8–9 July 1954, 8 November 1955; *AC*, 25 May, 9 July 1954, 8 November 1955; *AJC*, 11 July 1954; Williams, "Hartsfield: Reluctant Accommodationist," 259–60; *Holmes v. City of Atlanta*, 350 U.S. 879 (1955). Shortly after *Brown*, the Fourth Circuit Court of Appeals had ruled that the city of Baltimore could no longer segregate its public beaches. *Dawson v. Mayor*, 220 F. 2d 386 (1955). The city appealed the ruling, but the Supreme Court unanimously affirmed the decision on 8 November 1955. *Mayor v. Dawson*, 350 U.S. 877 (1955). That same day, the Court applied its affirmation of the Baltimore case as a governing precedent for the Atlanta golf course case. See Richard Kluger, *Simple Justice: The History of* Brown v. Board of Education *and Black America's Struggle for Equality* (New York: Vintage, 1975), 750; Bernard Schwartz, *Super Chief: Earl Warren and His Supreme Court: A Judicial Biography* (New York: New York University Press, 1983), 126; Mark V. Tushnet, *Making Civil Rights Law: Thurgood Marshall and the Supreme Court, 1936–1961* (New York: Oxford University Press, 1994), 301.

24. Herman E. Talmadge, *You and Segregation* (Birmingham, Ala.: Vulcan Press, 1955), 29; *AC*, 9 November 1955.

25. *AJ*, 8 November 1955; Cater, "Atlanta: Smart Politics," 19.

26. *AJ*, 8 July 1954, 9 November, 23 December 1955; *AC*, 10 November 1955; William B. Hartsfield, "Cities and Racial Minorities: Atlanta's Approach" (Washington, D.C.: National League of Cities, n.d.; reprinted from Marshall-Wythe Symposium, College of William and Mary, 1964), 57; Jenkins, *Keeping the Peace*, 34, 37; Williams, "Hartsfield: Reluctant Accommodationist," 262.

27. *AJ*, 23–24 December 1955; *AC*, 23 December 1955; Fred Powledge, "Black Man, Go South," *Esquire*, August 1965, 75; Cater, "Atlanta: Smart Politics," 19; *AJC*, 25 December 1955.

28. *NN*, 16 November 1955.

29. *NN*, 29 December 1955.

30. *NN*, 29 December 1955, 4 January 1956.

31. George Brownlee to editor, *Jacksonville Journal*, 10 October 1959, box 38, JCD; *AJC*, 11 October 1959.

32. Bayor, *Race and Atlanta*, 151; "A Second Look: The Negro Citizen in Atlanta," Atlanta Committee for Cooperative Action, January 1960, copy in box 116, MM; *AJ*, 26 June, 25 July, 21, 28 August 1961.

33. *AJ*, 25 July, 21, 24 August 1961, 28 August 1962; Eliza K. Paschall, *It Must Have Rained* (Atlanta: Center for Research in Social Change, Emory University, 1975), 54–55.

34. Jenkins, *Forty Years on the Force*, 115; *AJ*, 12 June 1963; Eliza Paschall to Mayor Ivan Allen Jr., 17 June 1963, box 3, EP; telex report, 25 June 1963, box 1, NAB.

35. Eliza Paschall to Mayor Ivan Allen Jr., 17 June 1963, box 3, EP; Ernest D. Key to Ralph McGill, 15 June 1963, box 24, REM; Mrs. William E. Reynolds to Ralph McGill, 6 June 1963, box 24, REM; telex report, 25 June 1963, box 1, NAB; Thomas McPherson Jr. to Ernest Lent, 13 June 1963, box 3, EP. During the Great Depression, white Atlanta experienced a similar panic over the supposed connections between blacks and syphilis in the city. See Ferguson, *Black Politics in New Deal Atlanta*, 112–15, 128–30.

36. Jenkins, *Forty Years on the Force*, 115; *AJ*, 13 June 1963.

37. *AJ*, 5 June 1964; *AC*, 19 July 1963; Rabbi Jacob Rothschild to Robert Sommerville, President, Atlanta Transit System, 23 September 1966, box 7, JMR.

38. *AJC*, 25 June 1961; Allen, *Atlanta Rising*, 122.

39. Edward Norton to Ralph McGill, 12 June 1963, box 24, REM; Pomerantz, *Peachtree*, 515, 547; James O. Smith to McGill and Eugene Patterson, 3 July 1963, box 24, REM.

40. A. W. McBerry to President Dwight D. Eisenhower, 10 December 1958, box 38, JCD; Mrs. W. C. Todd to Ralph McGill, 30 September 1957, box 24, REM; flyer, "Act for God and Country—Help Defeat Communism," [1960], box 56, REM.

41. Anonymous [Atlanta] to Ralph McGill and Eugene Patterson, 26 September 1966, box 25, REM; E. A. Rogers to Edward D. Staples, 11 June 1956, box 31, JCD; "N.A.A.C.P. Application," [1957], box 31, JCD; "The Black Spangled Banner," [c. 1963], box 25, REM; flyer, "Act for God and Country—Help Defeat Communism," [1960], box 56, REM.

42. Abrams, *Forbidden Neighbors*, 181; flyer, Fourth Ward Zoning Committee, "UNITED WE STAND!" [May 1958], box 24, AUL; Lawrence W. Neff, pamphlet, "Jesus: Master Segregationist," [April 1958], box 38, JCD.

43. "An Atlantan" to William Hartsfield, 1 May 1957, box 13, WBH; Mrs. J. T. McKibben, letter to the editor, *AJ*, 13 March 1957; Joe Prendergast to William Hartsfield, 31 March 1953, box 11, WBH.

44. *AJ*, 3 August 1962; handbill, United Klans, [n.d., 1962], box 30, WBH; White, "Landscaped Atlanta," 102–4; Allen, *Mayor*, 70.

45. Martin, *Hartsfield*, 181; *AJ*, 3, 6 August, 28 September 1962, 10, 29 March, 4 April, 9, 10, 13, 16, 17 May 1963; *AJC*, 12 May 1963; mimeographed letter, Mayor Ivan Allen Jr. to Dr. C. Miles Smith, [1963], box 3, JW.

CHAPTER FIVE
THE "SECOND BATTLE OF ATLANTA":
MASSIVE RESISTANCE AND THE DIVIDED MIDDLE CLASS

1. Herman E. Talmadge with Mark Royden Winchell, *Talmadge: A Politician's Legacy, A Politician's Life* (Atlanta: Peachtree Publishers, 1987), 154–55; telex report, [17 May 1954], box 16, NAB; Talmadge, interview by Harold Paulk Henderson, transcript, 26 June, 17 July 1987, GGDP; *AC*, 18 May 1954; Allen, *Atlanta Rising*, 53–54.

2. *AC*, 18 May 1954; Bartley, *Rise of Massive Resistance*, 116–17.

3. *SSN*, September 1954, February, March 1956; *AJ*, 6 February 1956.

4. For more on the hollowness of massive-resistance movements, see Kevin M. Kruse, "The Paradox of Massive Resistance: Political Conformity and Chaos in the Aftermath of *Brown v. Board of Education*," *Saint Louis University Law Journal* 48, no. 3 (Spring 2004): 1009–35.

5. Talmadge, *Talmadge*, 101; Chappell, "Divided Mind," 46; *SSN*, June 1956.

6. Edgar A. Toppin, "Walter White and the Atlanta NAACP's Fight for Equal Schools, 1916–1917," *History of Education Quarterly* 7, no. 1 (Spring 1967): 3–21; Bayor, *Race and Atlanta*, 197–220; J. H. Calhoun, "Annual Report of the Executive Secretary, Atlanta Branch, NAACP, 1950," December 1950, pt. 26, series A, reel 9, NAACP; NAACP Newsletter, "Atlanta Branch Ripples," October 1950, box 6, GTH; Herbert T. Jenkins, *Presidents, Politics, and Policing: Oral History Interviews on Law Enforcement and a Career in Public Life Spanning Fifty Years* (Atlanta: Center for Research in Social Change, Emory, 1980): 68; *AC*, 18 May 1954; *AJC*, 12 January 1958; *SSN*, February 1958; *Vivian Calhoun et al. v. A. C. Latimer et al.*, Civil Action No. 6298, United States District Court for the Northern District of Georgia, Atlanta Division, copy of record in group V, series B, pt. 23, NAACP (hereafter cited as *Calhoun v. Latimer*).

7. *AJ*, 13 January 1958; *AC*, 19, 21 November, 10 December 1958; *SSN*, December 1958.

8. *SSN*, October, November 1958; *Cooper v. Aaron*, 358 U.S. 1; *Aaron v. McKinley*, 173 F. Supp. 944; *James v. Almond*, 170 F. Supp. 331; James T. Patterson, *Brown v. Board of Education: A Civil Rights Milestone and Its Troubled Legacy* (New York: Oxford University Press, 2001), 109–17; J. Harvie Wilkinson, *From Brown to Bakke: The Supreme Court and School Integration, 1954–1978* (New York: Oxford University Press, 1979), 88–102; Paul E. Mertz, " 'Mind Changing Time All over Georgia': HOPE, Inc., and School Desegregation, 1958–1961," *Georgia Historical Quarterly* 76, no. 1 (spring 1993): 44, n. 6.

9. J. W. Peltason, *Fifty-eight Lonely Men: Southern Federal Judges and School Desegregation* (New York: Harcourt, Brace and World, 1961), 130; Orders, 5 June, 16 June 1959, *Calhoun v. Latimer*; *AC*, 5, 6, 17 June 1959.

10. *AC*, 6 June 1959; Ray McCain, "Speaking on School Desegregation by Atlanta Ministers," *Southern Speech Journal* 29, no. 3 (Spring 1964): 257; *AJC*, 27 October, 3 November 1957; Greene, *Temple Bombing*, 1–2, 166–268; Janice Rothschild Brumberg, *One Voice: Rabbi Jacob M. Rothschild and the Troubled*

South (Mercer: Mercer University Press, 1985), 73–74, 111–12; Rabbi Jacob Rothschild to [Rabbi] Norman [Goldberg], 27 March 1958, box 3, JMR.

11. Report, "The Beginning of HOPE," reel 213, SRC; Mertz, "Mind Changing Time," 41, 49; Kathryn L. Nasstrom, "Women, the Civil Rights Movement, and the Politics of Historical Memory" (Ph.D. diss., University of North Carolina, Chapel Hill, 1993): 139; Kathryn L. Nasstrom, *Everybody's Grandmother and Nobody's Fool: Frances Freeborn Pauley and the Struggle for Social Justice* (Ithaca, N.Y.: Cornell University Press, 2000), 54–61; Susan Margaret McGrath, "Great Expectations: The History of School Desegregation in Atlanta and Boston, 1954–1990" (Ph.D. diss., Emory University, 1992), 121; Frances Pauley to Dr. Phyllis J. O'Neal, 12 March 1959, box 7, FFP; Gordon L. Jacobson and Edwin B. Davidge to Mrs. [?] Harris, [1960], reel 212, SRC.

12. Bartley, *Thurmond to Wallace*, 41; Walter E. Taylor Jr. to Hope, 8 June 1959, and K. E. Edwards Jr. to HOPE, 24 February 1959, reel 212, SRC.

13. E. A. Spencer to Frances Pauley, [1959], box 7, FFP; George C. Dean to Ed Hughes, 19 November 1958, box 38, JCD.

14. Alton P. Ewing to James C. Davis, 30 January 1959, box 38, JCD; HOPE Newsletter, "Hope's Outlook," 1 June 1959, box 8, FFP; CBS Reports, "Who Speaks for the South?" (original broadcast date, 27 May 1960); *AJ*, 19 November 1960.

15. *AC*, 12, 26, 29 January, 2 February, 6 April 1960; *AJ*, 11–12 January, 2 February, 6 April 1960.

16. Griffin Bell, interview by Cliff Kuhn and William L. Bost, transcript, 12 June 1990, GGDP.

17. *AC*, 29 January, 3, 18, 27 February, 24 March 1960; *SSN*, March 1960; Nan Pendergrast, interview by Kathryn Nasstrom and Cliff Kuhn, transcript, 24 June 1992, GGDP.

18. Mertz, "Mind Changing Time," 53; *AC*, 22, 24 March 1960; *SSN*, April 1960; Jim Cherry and A. C. Latimer, testimony, General Assembly Committee on Schools, Hearing in Atlanta, Georgia, 23 March 1960, box G8, JAS (hereafter GACS Hearing); Rev. William Holmes Borders, GACS Hearing; Roche, *Restructured Resistance*, 145–52.

19. Ernest Lazarus, Rev. R. B. Montgomery, and Jack Dorsey, GACS Hearing.

20. Thomas J. Wesley, GACS Hearing; *AC*, 24 March 1960.

21. According to official GACS notes, "54 Witnesses, representing 8,505 people," opted for "open schools" at the first day's session, while "67 Witnesses, representing 14,155 people," favored closing schools rather than integrating them. Report, GACS, "Summary of Hearings, by District," [May 1960], box G11, JAS.

22. *AJ*, 28 April 1960; *AC*, 1, 29 April, 10 May 1960; *SSN*, May 1960.

23. *AC*, 11 July 1959, 7–10 January 1961; *AJ*, 19 November 1960, 7–10 January 1961; *SSN*, February 1961; Thomas G. Dyer, *The University of Georgia: A Bicentennial History, 1785–1985* (Athens: University of Georgia Press, 1985), 324–29; Bolster, "Civil Rights," 165–66; Judge Elbert Tuttle, interview by Cliff Kuhn, 21 September 1992, transcript, GGDP.

24. Hunter-Gault, *In My Place*, 74–86; Trillin, *An Education in Georgia*, 15, 20; W. C. Cowart, Georgia Council on Human Relations Bulletin, 27 July 1959, box 10, EP.

25. Robert Cohen, " 'Two, Four, Six, Eight, We Don't Want to Integrate': White Student Attitudes toward the University of Georgia's Desegregation," *Georgia Historical Quarterly* 80, no. 3 (Fall 1996): 617–18; Trillin, *An Education in Georgia*, 52–53; Dyer, *University of Georgia*, 329–34; *AC*, 7, 12, 13, 14 January 1961; *AJ*, 11, 12, 15 January 1961; telex report, 9 January 1961, NAB; Peltason, *Fifty-eight Lonely Men*, 177–78.

26. Ernest Vandiver, interview by Charles Pyles, 20 March, 28 July 1986, GGDP; Alton Hornsby Jr., "Black Public Education in Atlanta, Georgia, 1954–1973: From Segregation to Segregation," *Journal of Negro History* 76 (1991): 23; *AC*, 7–11, 19, 20 January 1961; *AJ*, 10 January 1961; Allen, *Atlanta Rising*, 105; Ernest Vandiver to Garland Byrd and George L. Smith II, 9 January 1961, copy in *SSN*, February 1961.

27. Patterson, Brown, 109–13; Daniel, *Lost Revolutions*, 251–83; David L. Chappell, *Inside Agitators: White Southerners in the Civil Rights Movement* (Baltimore: Johns Hopkins University Press, 1994), 97–121; Bartley, *Rise of Massive Resistance*, 251–69; John A. Kirk, *Redefining the Color Line: Black Activism in Little Rock, Arkansas, 1940–1970* (Gainesville: University of Florida Press, 2002).

28. Patterson, Brown, 107–9; Adam Fairclough, *Race and Democracy: The Civil Rights Struggle in Louisiana, 1915–1972* (Athens: University of Georgia Press, 1995), 234–64 (Steinbeck quotation from p. 248); Morton Inger, "The New Orleans School Crisis of 1960," in Jacoway and Colburn, *Southern Businessmen and Desegregation*, 82–97.

29. Jenkins, *Presidents, Politics, and Policing*, 72; Raines, *My Soul Is Rested*, 410; George B. Leonard Jr., "The Second Battle of Atlanta," *Look Magazine*, 25 April 1961, 34.

30. Martin, *Hartsfield*, 144; Inger, "New Orleans," 97; Chappell, *Inside Agitators*, 117; James C. Cobb, *The Selling of the South: The Southern Crusade for Industrial Development, 1936–1990* (Urbana: University of Illinois Press, 1993), 125–26; HOPE Newsletter, "Hope-Ful Outlook," 15 March 1959, box 8, FFP; Citizenship Committee of the United Church Women of Georgia, leaflet, "No Use Hiding Our Heads," [late 1950s], box 1, JWM.

31. William B. Hartsfield to Burke Marshall, 30 July 1961, box 18, HTJ.

32. *AC*, 12–16 December 1960; *AJ*, 12 December 1960.

33. Cobb, *Selling of the South*, 128; telex report, 4 September 1961, box 12, NAB; Pomerantz, *Peachtree*, 259–60; *AJ*, 27 August 1961; Virginia H. Hein, "The Image of 'A City Too Busy to Hate': Atlanta in the 1960s," *Phylon* 33, no. 3 (Fall 1972): 206.

34. Betty M. Harris, report, "History of OASIS (Organizations Assisting Schools in September)," 12 June 1961, SRC; Mertz, "Mind Changing Time," 60; *AC*, 17 May 1961; Hein, "Image," 206; Eliza Paschall to Ernie [Lent] and Harry [Boyte], 29 May 1961, box 1, EP.

35. Boyd Taylor, "Letson's Brainwash," *Separate Schools* 2, no. 4 (April 1961), copy in box 30, WBH; petition to Board of Education, Atlanta, box 57, REM;

AJ, 28 August 1961; *SSN*, September 1961; telex report, [September 1961], box 12, NAB.

36. Patterson, Brown, 100; resolution, Atlanta Board of Education, 30 November 1959 (amended 4 and 18 January 1960), box 14, EP; *AC*, 27 October 1959, 4, 6, 24, 25 November, 1, 2, 15, 31 December 1959, 2, 5, 21, 22 January 1960, 30 March 1961; *SSN*, May 1961.

37. *AC*, 2, 4, 5, 9 May 1961; *SSN*, June 1961; Bayor, *Race and Atlanta*, 224–25; Patterson, Brown, 86–117.

38. *SSN*, June, July, September 1961; *AJ*, 13 December 1960, 21 April 1961; Minutes, Atlanta Board of Education, 14 December 1959, 25 April 1960, 8 May 1961, APSA; Bayor, *Race and Atlanta*, 226; Susan M. McGrath, "From Tokenism to Community Control: Political Symbolism in the Desegregation of Atlanta's Public Schools," *Georgia Historical Quarterly* 79, no. 4 (Winter 1995): 853; Patterson, Brown, 104–5.

39. *SSN*, August 1961; Jenkins, *Presidents, Politics, and Policing*, 45; Jenkins, *Keeping the Peace*, 53–54; Hein, "Image," 207; Capt. R. E. Little, bulletin, 28 August 1961, box 18, HTJ; Stone, *Regime Politics*, 48.

40. Statement of Dr. John W. Letson, *Fourth Annual Education Conference on Problems of Segregation and Desegregation in Public Schools, United States Commission on Civil Rights, 3–4 May 1962* (Washington, D.C.: U.S. Government Printing Office, 1962); Allen, *Atlanta Rising*, 109–10; Detective Claude Dixon II, memorandum on Northside High, August 1961, box 18, HTJ; interviews with Damaris Jeanette Allen and Martha Ann Holmes, August 1961, box 18, HTJ; *SSN*, September 1961; Jenkins, "Special Notice and Assignments," 1 August 1961, reel 213, SRC; Jenkins to School Squad Leaders, 21 August 1961, box 18, HTJ.

41. Hein, "Image," 206; Hartsfield to Burke Marshall, 30 July 1961, box 18, HTJ; Jane Hammer to Members of the Co-Ordinating Committee and the Contingency Planning Committee, 8 August 1961, reel 213, SRC; *Newsweek*, 11 September 1961.

42. Telex report, [30 August 1961], NAB; Paschall, typewritten notes, [August 1961], box 1, EP; *AJ*, 30 August 1961.

43. *AJC*, 27 August 1961; *AJ*, 30–31 August, 1 September 1961; telex report, [September 1961], NAB; *AC*, 31 August 1961.

44. Telex reports, 30 August 1961, [September 1961], and 4 September 1961, NAB; *AJ*, 30 August 1961; Raines, *My Soul Is Rested*, 410.

45. Hein, "Image," 207; *NYT*, 31 August 1961; *Newsweek*, 11 September 1961, 31; *U.S. News and World Report*, 11 September 1961, 72; *Reporter*, 15 September 1961, 14; Leonard, "The Second Battle of Atlanta," 31; George McMillan, "Atlanta's Peaceful Blow for Justice: With the Police on an Integration Job," *Life*, 15 September 1961, 35–36; Hein, "Image," 207; Hornsby, "Too Busy to Hate," 120–21.

46. Detective H. H. Hooks, memorandum on Murphy High School, transportation route, [summer 1961], box 18, HTJ; "Analysis of Fire at 1408 Woodbine, June 1960," box 5, ABP; *ADW*, 21, 24 May, 10–11 June 1960; interview with Martha Ann Holmes, [1961], box 18, HTJ; Atlanta Police Department, Daily Bulletin #14–206, 29 August 1961, box 18, HTJ.

47. *AJ*, 27 October 1961; *SSN*, November 1961; Paschall to Judy [?], 22 May 1962, box 2, EP; Gerald Walker, "The Price of the Picture," *Progressive* (May 1963): 26–27.

48. Paschall, *It Must Have Rained*, 43; report, Greater Atlanta Council on Human Relations, "Tabulated Survey of Transfer Students," [1962], box 10, EP; *AJ*, 13 June 1962; *SSN*, November 1961.

49. *AJC*, 11 August 1963; Robert Coles, *The Desegregation of Southern Schools: A Psychiatric Study* (New York: Anti-Defamation League of B'nai B'rith, 1963), 9–14.

50. Robert Coles, "How Do the Teachers Feel?" *Saturday Review*, 16 May 1964, 89; Paschall to Jon Johnston, 29 May 1964, box 4, EP; Mrs. Charles C. Perkins Jr. to Rual Stephens, 21 February 1963, box 3, EP; Mark Chesler, "What Happened after You Desegregated the White School?" *New South* 22, no. 1 (Winter 1967): 12.

51. Minutes, Executive Board Meeting, Greater Atlanta Council on Human Relations, 11 October 1961, box 1, EP; Paschall to Eunice Bronson, Executive Secretary, YWCA, 23 October 1961, box 1, EP; *AJ*, 27 October 1961; *SSN*, November 1961; Coles, *Desegregation of Southern Schools*, 11; Paschall to Elmo Holt, 3 April 1963, box 3, EP; Mrs. Charles C. Perkins Jr. to Rual Stephens, 21 February 1963, box 3, EP; Paschall to Jon Johnston, 29 May 1964, box 4, EP.

52. Alvin S. Davis to Paschall, 29 May 1962, box 2, EP; *AJ*, 28 May 1962; Paschall to Judy [?], 22 May 1962, box 2, EP; Paschall to Morris Abram, 7 May 1964, box 4, EP; Minutes, Atlanta Board of Education, 10 June 1963, APSA; Paschall to Dr. Roy O. McClain, 23 May 1962, box 2, EP.

53. Paschall, typewritten notes, 30 August 1961, box 1, EP.

CHAPTER SIX
THE FIGHT FOR "FREEDOM OF ASSOCIATION":
SCHOOL DESEGREGATION AND WHITE WITHDRAWAL

1. *AJ*, 16 May, 7, 11 August 1961; *AC*, 17, 19 May 1961; *SSN*, June 1961; *City Directory, 1962*.

2. *AJC*, 2 July 1961; *AJ*, 16 May, 9, 23 June, 7–11 July 1961; *AC*, 17–19 May, 29 June 1961; *SSN*, June, August 1961; Minutes, Atlanta Board of Education, 14 August 1961, APSA.

3. *AJ*, 7–9, 15 August 1961; *AC*, 8, 15 August 1961; Paschall, notes, 8 August 1961, box 1, EP.

4. Minutes, Atlanta Board of Education, 14 August 1961, APSA; *AC*, 16, 17 August 1961; *AJ*, 16, 17 August, 13, 20 December 1961; *AJC*, 20 August 1961; transcript, Hearing in Motion for Further Relief, *Calhoun v. Latimer*, copy in box 27, ATW; *SSN*, January 1962.

5. James W. Tarpley to James C. Davis, March 1956, box 31, JCD; E. A. Veale to Ralph McGill, September 1957, box 24, REM; *AJ*, 19 November 1960, 8 August 1961; *SSN*, March 1961; Benjamin Muse, *Ten Years of Prelude: The Story of Integration since the Supreme Court's 1954 Decision* (New York: Viking, 1964), 224.

6. Anonymous to James C. Davis, 30 September 1957, box 32, JCD.

7. List, "Transfer Students—1962," box 18, HTJ; list, "Transfer Students, 1963–1964," box 18, HTJ.

8. Minutes, Atlanta Board of Education, 25 April 1960, 12 February 1962, APSA; Bayor, *Race and Atlanta*, 226–30; *AJ*, 13 December 1961; *SSN*, July 1961.

9. *AC*, 15 November 1960; *SSN*, July 1961; *AJ*, 14 August 1961; Atlanta Public Schools, *Statistical Report, 1964–1965*, APSA; School Reclassification List (June 1961–September 1971), file folder, APSA; Bayor, *Race and Atlanta*, 236.

10. Minutes, Atlanta Board of Education, 8–9 July 1962, APSA; Sara Mitchell Parsons, *From Southern Wrongs to Civil Rights: The Memoir of a White Civil Rights Activist* (Tuscaloosa: University of Alabama Press, 2000), 85–86; *AJ*, 10 July 1962; *AC*, 10 July 1962; *ADW*, 11 July 1962; *City Directory, 1962*.

11. Grant Park Civic Association, advertisement, 7 August 1962, box 159, AUL; *AJ*, 14 August 1962; *MH*, 10 June 1964, copy in reel 110, pt. 11, SRC.

12. *AJ*, 21 August, 20, 22 November 1963; 7, 12, 27, 30 March, 25 May, 24 June, 14, 29 July, 11 August 1964; *AC*, 7 April, 14, 29–30 July 1964; *AT*, 29 July 1964; Bayor, *Race and Atlanta*, 230–31; *MH*, 10 June 1964, copy in reel 110, pt. 11, SRC; Minutes, Atlanta Board of Education, 13 July 1964, APSA.

13. Report, "Summary of Evaluation at West Fulton," 20 March 1957, APSA; list, "Transfer Students—1962," box 18, HTJ; list, "Transfer Students, 1963–1964," box 18, HTJ; Statistical Report, 1964–1965, APSA; *AJ*, 4 June, 8 September 1964; Officer R. B. Moore to Supt. C. Chafin and Capt. W. L. Duncan, 8 September 1964, box 18, HTJ; *AC*, 9 September 1964; Minutes, Atlanta Board of Education, 14 September 1964, APSA; Parsons, *Southern Wrongs*, 109–10; Bayor, *Race and Atlanta*, 234; *AT*, 15, 27 September 1964.

14. *AJ*, 28, 31 August, 1, 22 September, 16 December 1964, 26 January 1965; Parsons, *Southern Wrongs*, 83; Bayor, *Race and Atlanta*, 230–34; *SSN*, September, October 1964; flyer, [22 September 1964], box 18, HTJ; McGrath, "From Tokenism to Community Control," 856–57; *AC*, 26 January 1965.

15. *SSN*, October, November 1959; *AC*, 15 January 1959; Lt. Col. Troy B. Browne to Jim Cherry, 14 July 1959, box 1, JDC.

16. *AC*, 8 January, 27 April 1960; *SSN*, January 1959, February 1960.

17. Moreton Rolleston Jr., interview with author, 17 May 1999; *Patrick Henry Schools, Inc., v. Dixon Oxford, Revenue Commissioner of the State of Georgia*, Civil Case No. A-74491, FCSC; *SSN*, August, October, November 1959.

18. *AJ*, 13–15, 20–24 November 1961, 29 May 1962; *SSN*, December 1961, January, June 1962; Minutes, Atlanta Board of Education, 13 August 1962, APSA.

19. *SSN*, March, April, November 1962, March 1963; *AJ*, 6, 19 December 1961, 16, 19 October 1962, 6, 13, 15, 18, 20 February, 25, 29 April, 2, 7 May, 23 August 1963; *AC*, 19 January 1959; Trillin, *An Education in Georgia*, 47–48.

20. In the landmark *Everson* ruling of 1947, the Court required a high wall of separation between state funding and religious schooling. That standard continued in its later rulings on the public funding of private segregated schools. In the 1958 Little Rock case, *Cooper v. Aaron*, the Court undermined the basic premise of tuition grants, holding that "the Fourteenth Amendment forbids States to use their governmental powers to bar children on racial grounds from attending

schools where there is state participation through any arrangement, management, *funds or property*" (italics added). Then, in the 1964 Prince Edward County, Virginia, case of *Griffin v. County School Board*, the Court supported a lower court ruling that directly barred the use of both tuition grants and tax credits. Thereafter, tuition grants continued to be used in several localities, until the late 1960s, when federal courts applied the Prince Edward precedent directly. See 330 U.S. 1; 358 U.S. 4; 377 U.S. 233; Wilkinson, *From* Brown *to* Bakke, 78–127; John C. Jeffries Jr. and James E. Ryan, "A Political History of the Establishment Clause," *Michigan Law Review* 100 (November 2001): 330–34.

21. *AC*, 23 November 1955; *AJC*, 17 September 1961; *SSN*, November 1961; *AJ*, 13 June, 16 October 1962.

22. Indeed, in a leading account of Atlanta's struggles with segregation, the only private schools mentioned were ones used by black Atlantans to escape segregated public schools, and not the other way around. See Bayor, *Race and Atlanta*, 11, 199, 205, 251.

23. *AC*, 23 November 1955; *AJC*, 20, 27 October, 10, 17 November, 8, 15, 22 December 1957.

24. Muse, *Ten Years of Prelude*, 229; *SSN*, July, August 1962.

25. Paschall, *It Must Have Rained*, 87, 150; Paschall to Robert Erkman, 22 April 1963, box 3, EP; Young, *An Easy Burden*, 197; Paschall to Dr. William Pressly, 30 May 1962, box 2, EP; typewritten draft report, [n.d., 1961], box 12, NAB; Paschall to Kay Hocking et al., 20 February 1963, box 3, EP.

26. Telex report, [n.d., 1961], box 12, NAB; James M. Sibley to Joseph Cumming, 14 October 1963, box 8, NAB.

27. *AC*, 4 August 1955; *AJC*, 27 October, 3 November 1957; *Diocesan Record: News of the Episcopal Church in the Diocese of Atlanta* 34, no. 2 (February 1956), copy in box 8, FFP; newsclipping, "Church Unit Asks Anti-Wall Voice," [n.d., 1963], box 1, NAB; Joseph A. Pelham, "Memorandum on Lovett School," 8 April 1963, box 61, REM.

28. In the summer of 1959, Rev. Morris had helped found the Episcopal Society for Cultural and Racial Unity (ESCRU) "to promote increased acceptance and demonstration of the Church's policies of racial inclusiveness in its own life, as well as its role of providing leadership in the community and nation." In the 1960s, ESCRU emerged as the church's unofficial conscience on racial matters. Morris to Harold Fleming, Southern Regional Council, 6 July 1959, and Morris, "A Proposal: Formation in the Episcopal Church of a Church Society for Racial Unity," [n.d., July 1959], reel 22, SRC; *AC*, 29 December 1959; Morris, ESCRU Newsletter, 6 August 1963, box 1, ESCRU.

29. Morris, ESCRU Newsletter, 6 August 1963, box 1, ESCRU; Dean Alfred Hardman to Ralph McGill, 29 June 1963, box 50, REM; Joseph Pelham, "Memorandum on Lovett School," 8 April 1963, box 61, REM.

30. *AJ*, 16 March 1963; Joseph Pelham, "Memorandum on Lovett School," 8 April 1963, box 61, REM; McGill to Dean Alfred Hardman, 1 July 1963, box 50, REM; Rev. John B. Morris to Society Members and Others in the Atlanta Area, 16 July 1963, reel 22, SRC; "History of the Lovett School," The Lovett School, Atlanta, Georgia, http://lions.lovett.org/about/history.htm, consulted 15 February 2002.

31. *AJC*, 16 June, 4 July 1963; *AC*, 3 July 1963; Morris to Claiborne, 11 November 1963, reel 22, SRC.

32. Morris to Society Members et al., 16 July 1963, reel 22, SRC; McGill to Dean Alfred Hardman, 1 July, 16 September 1963, box 50, REM; McGill to Henry Troutman, 22 October 1963, box 50, REM.

33. *AC*, 5 July, 18 September 1963; Morris to Society Members et al., 16 July 1963, reel 22, SRC; Morris to Claiborne, 11 November 1963, reel 22, SRC; *AJ*, 2 October 1963; *NYT*, 3 October 1963; *Time*, 15 November 1963; telex report, [1963], box 8, NAB.

34. Boyd Taylor to Fellow Communicant, [March 1963], box 6, JMR; *Time*, 15 November 1963.

35. Rev. Albert R. Dreisbach Jr. to Lovett School Parents, 27 May 1966, box 1, ESCRU; Rev. John B. Morris to Atlanta Members of ESCRU, 1 June 1966; transcript, "Dr. King's Comments at the Cathedral of St. Philip, Atlanta," 4 June 1966, box 1, ESCRU.

CHAPTER SEVEN
COLLAPSE OF THE COALITION:
SIT-INS AND THE BUSINESS REBELLION

1. *AC*, 9 March 1960.

2. Chafe, *Civilities and Civil Rights*, 71–101; Branch, *Parting the Waters*, 266–78; Julian Bond, interview by Vincent Fort, 10 April 1979, transcript, GGDP. The facts were largely taken from *A Second Look: The Negro Citizen in Atlanta*, published in February 1960 by the Atlanta Committee for Cooperative Action (ACCA). A political club of young black professionals, ACCA had hoped to inject a more militant tone into the city's discussions over civil rights and prepared *A Second Look* as proof of Atlanta's inequalities. ACCA's members included Carl Holman, an English professor at Clark University, who edited the publication; Jesse Hill, chief actuary and later president of Atlanta Life Insurance Company, which funded the report; Whitney Young, dean of the Atlanta University School of Social Work and later the executive director of the National Urban League; Clarence Coleman, a deputy director of the National Urban League; and Samuel Westerfield, dean of the Atlanta University School of Business. See David Andrew Harmon, *Beneath the Image of the Civil Rights Movement and Race Relations: Atlanta, Georgia, 1946–1981* (New York: Garland Publishing, 1996), 91–93; Jack L. Walker, "Sit-Ins in Atlanta: A Study in the Negro Revolt," in *Atlanta, Georgia, 1960–61: Sit-Ins and Student Activism*, ed. David J. Garrow (Brooklyn, N.Y.: Carlson Publ., 1989), 65.

3. Pomerantz, *Peachtree*, 253; Allen, *Atlanta Rising*, 90; *AC*, 10 March 1960.

4. *AC*, 10 March 1960; William B. Hartsfield, interview by Charles T. Morrisey, John F. Kennedy Presidential Library Oral History Project, 6 January 1966, transcript, box 31, WBH; Bayor, *Race and Atlanta*, 33.

5. *AC*, 16, 17 March 1960; John Neary, *Julian Bond: Black Rebel* (New York: Morrow, 1971): 55; Walker, "Sit-Ins in Atlanta," 69–70.

6. Neary, *Bond*, 55; *AC*, 23 April 1960; Jack L. Walker, "Functions of Disunity: Negro Leadership in a Southern City," *Journal of Negro Education* 23 (Summer 1963): 228; Celestine Sibley, *Dear Store: An Affectionate Portrait of Rich's* (Garden City, N.Y.: Doubleday, 1967); Raines, *My Soul Is Rested*, 87; Allen, *Atlanta Rising*, 95; *AJ*, 19 October 1960.

7. Pomerantz, *Peachtree*, 252–54; Branch, *Parting the Waters*, 286–87.

8. Walker, "Sit-Ins in Atlanta," 75; *AC*, 26 March, 28 June 1960; Raines, *My Soul Is Rested*, 87–88; Bayor, *Race and Atlanta*, 34.

9. Allen, *Atlanta Rising*, 94; Pomerantz, *Peachtree*, 257; Jewel Simpson and Margaret Young to Richard Rich, 14 April 1958, box 37, RHR; Richard Rich to Maxine Webb, 27 March 1958, box 37, RHR. For similar complaints about segregated facilities, see letters to Rich from Delores M. Robinson, 11 April 1958; Jesse Hill Jr., 10 March 1958; Maxine T. Webb, 24 March 1958; Mrs. J. S. Flipper and Mrs. M. L. Wingfield, 19 June 1958; and Jesse Hill Jr., 24 June 1958, box 37, RHR.

10. Richard Rich to Mrs. George H. Slappy, 13 April 1960, box 35, RHR; Morris B. Abram, *The Day Is Short: An Autobiography* (New York: Harcourt Brace Jovanovich, 1982), 127–28; Walker, "Sit-Ins in Atlanta," 80–81; Nan Pendergrast, interview by Kathryn Nasstrom and Cliff Kuhn, transcript, 24 June 1992, GGDP.

11. Abram, *Day Is Short*, 127–28; Allen, *Atlanta Rising*, 95–96; Allen, *Mayor*, 35–36; Griffin Bell, interview by Cliff Kuhn and William L. Bost, 19 September 1990, transcript, GGDP; Pomerantz, *Peachtree*, 258.

12. Benjamin Mays, interview by Vincent Fort, 29 November 1978, transcript, GGDP; John Wesley Dobbs to Rich's, Inc., 16 September 1960, and Frank H. Neely to John Wesley Dobbs, 21 September 1960, box 37, RHR; John V. Petrof, "The Effect of Student Boycotts upon the Purchasing Habits of Negro Families in Atlanta, Georgia," *Phylon* 24 (Fall 1963): 266–70.

13. Walker, "Sit-Ins in Atlanta," 75–76; Raines, *My Soul Is Rested*, 88; Judge Elbert Tuttle, interview by Cliff Kuhn, 21 September 1992, GGDP.

14. *AJ*, 19, 20 October 1960; *AC*, 20 October 1960; Raines, *My Soul Is Rested*, 87–90; Lewis, *Walking with the Wind*, 126.

15. *AC*, 20–22 October 1960; Coretta Scott King, *My Life with Martin Luther King, Jr.* (New York: Avon Books, 1970), 174; *AJ*, 20–22 October 1960; *AJC*, 23 October 1960.

16. *AJ*, 22 October 1960; *AJC*, 23 October 1960; *AC*, 24 October 1960; Pomerantz, *Peachtree*, 261; Walker, "The Functions of Disunity," 229; Branch, *Parting the Waters*, 356. For details of the truce agreement, see Lonnie King, William Holmes Borders, Otis Moss, Jesse Hill, and A. T. Walden to William B. Hartsfield, 1 November 1960, box 37, RHR.

17. William B. Hartsfield, interview by Charles T. Morrisey, John F. Kennedy Presidential Library Oral History Project, 6 January 1966, transcript, box 31, WBH; William B. Hartsfield to Paul Tillet, 7 April 1964, box 30, WBH; Abram, *Day Is Short*, 127–28; Branch, *Parting the Waters*, 353–70, 373–78; Pomerantz, *Peachtree*, 261–64; Henry Hampton and Steve Fayer, *Voices of Freedom: An Oral History of the Civil Rights Movement from the 1950s through the 1980s* (New York: Bantam, 1991), 68–71; Lewis, *King*, 121, 126–30; *AC*, 24–27 October

1960; *AJ*, 24–26 October 1960. For a thorough analysis of the King arrest, see Clifford M. Kuhn, " 'There's a Footnote to History!': Memory and the History of Martin Luther King's October 1960 Arrest and Its Aftermath," *Journal of American History* 84, no. 2 (September 1997): 583–95.

18. William B. Hartsfield to Rev. Otis Moss Jr., 2 November 1960, box 37, RHR; Walker, "Sit-Ins in Atlanta," 79; William B. Hartsfield to John A. Sibley, 16 November 1960, document case 123, RWW; Helen Bullard to Marian [?], [late 1960], box 1, HB.

19. *AC*, 26, 29–30 November 1960; *AJ*, 28–30 November, 1–2 December 1960; Rich to Jesse Hill, 1 September 1960, box 37, RHR; Eliza Paschall to Rich, 21 December 1960, box 37, RHR; *AJC*, 4 December 1960.

20. Petition, Georgians Unwilling to Surrender, [n.d.], box 1, ABP; *AC*, 3, 15, 26 November, 7, 17 December 1960; *AJ*, 15 November, 7 December 1960; telegram, J. H. Clark to Elmer H. Etling, [November 1960], box 37, RHR.

21. *AJ*, 22, 26 November, 9 December 1960; *AJC*, 27 November 1960; *The Rebel*, 12 December 1960, copy in box 11, NAB.

22. Allen, *Mayor*, 38; Pomerantz, *Peachtree*, 265–67.

23. Pomerantz, *Peachtree*, 267–68; press release, 7 March 1961, box 37, RHR.

24. Bayor, *Race and Atlanta*, 34–35; Pomerantz, *Peachtree*, 270–71; Allen, *Mayor*, 40–42.

25. Pomerantz, *Peachtree*, 272; *AC*, 29 September 1961; *AJ*, 29 September 1961.

26. Lester Maddox, *Prelude to One of a Kind* (Marietta, Ga.: n.p., 1994), 4–8; Bruce Galphin, *The Riddle of Lester Maddox* (Atlanta: Camelot Publishing, 1968), 8–9, 15–19; Lester G. Maddox, *Speaking Out: The Autobiography of Lester Garfield Maddox* (New York: Doubleday, 1975), 11, 27–28; Lester Maddox, interview by John Allen, 22 November 1988, 26 July 1989, GGDP.

27. Bob Short, *Everything Is Pickrick: The Life of Lester Maddox* (Macon, Ga.: Mercer University Press, 1999), 33–40; *AC*, 6 December 1958, 5 September 1959, 27 August 1960.

28. John Carlton Huie Jr., "The Dream of Lester Maddox" (M.A. thesis, Emory University, 1966), 58.

29. Maddox, *Speaking Out*, 54; *AC*, 14 July 1962.

30. Lester Maddox, interview with author, 12 May 1999; *AC*, 29 October, 2, 26 November, 7 December 1960; *AJ*, 2, 15 November, 7 December 1960.

31. *AJ*, 15 November, 7 December 1960; *AC*, 26 November, 7, 17 December 1960.

32. *AC*, 11, 18 March, 29 April 1961; flyer, "Race-Mixers, Inc.," [April 1961], box 37, RHR; United Klans, "Don't Be Fooled Again," [1961], box 37, RHR; flyer, Committee on Human Rights for White People, [1961], box 30, WBH.

33. Lester Maddox, interview with author, 12 May 1999; Huie, "The Dream of Lester Maddox," 20; Maddox, *Speaking Out*, 38; Galphin, *Maddox*, 29; Lester Maddox, interview by John Allen, 22 November 1988, 26 July 1989, GGDP; Martin, *Hartsfield*, 128–29; *AC*, 4–5 December 1957; Bartley, *Thurmond to Wallace*, 47; George Goodwin to William B. Hartsfield, 9 October 1959, box 6, WBH.

34. *AC*, 7, 9 June 1961; *AJ*, 7 June 1961.

35. *AJ*, 11 August, 11 September 1961; Allen, *Mayor*, 23–26, 30–31.

36. Allen, *Mayor,* 52; *AC,* 27 June 1961; *AJ,* 25 August 1961.

37. *AJ,* 3 July, 12 September 1961.

38. *AJ,* 3 July, 7, 8 September 1961.

39. *AC,* 16 September 1961; *AJ,* 18, 19, 21 September 1961.

40. Telex report, [October 1961], box 1, NAB; *AC,* 19, 21 September 1961; Pomerantz, *Peachtree,* 299; *AJ,* 18, 21 September 1961.

41. *AJ,* 18–21 September 1961; telex report, [October 1961], box 1, NAB.

42. *AJ,* 23, 29 September 1961; Hornsby, "Negro in Atlanta Politics," 11; Walker, "Negro Voting in Atlanta: 1953–1961," 381; Bartley, *Thurmond to Wallace,* 47.

CHAPTER EIGHT
"THE LAW OF THE LAND":
FEDERAL INTERVENTION AND THE CIVIL RIGHTS ACT

1. Pomerantz, *Peachtree,* 320–21 (Cooke quotation from p. 32); Testimony of Mayor Ivan Allen Jr., of Atlanta, July 26, 1963, *Hearings before the Committee on Commerce, United States Senate,* 88th Cong., 1st sess. (Washington, D.C.: U.S. Government Printing Office, 1963), 861–83; *AC,* 27 July 1963.

2. *AC,* 27 July 1963; *AJ,* 26 July 1963; Pomerantz, *Peachtree,* 322–23.

3. *AJ,* 8 March 1962.

4. Harry Boyte to Dean Rusk, 17 March 1961, box 1, EP; Minutes, Executive Board Meeting of the Greater Atlanta Council on Human Relations, 11 April 1961, box 1, EP; *AJ,* 22 May, 29 June 1962; flyer, "STOP! THE NAACP DARES YOU ...," [1962], box 30, WBH; flyer, "Live Like Martin Luther King and Harry Belafonte," [1962], box 57, REM.

5. *AJ,* 29 June 1962; Moreton Rolleston Jr. to "Customer," 19 June 1962, box 1, CC.

6. *AJ,* 2–3, 6–7 July 1962; *AC,* 3 July 1962; *AJC,* 4 July 1962.

7. Records, *Eugene T. Reed v. Jay J. Sarno and Stanley A. Mallin,* Civil Action No. 7982, United States District Court, Northern District of Georgia, Atlanta Division, copy in group V, series B, pt. 23, NAACP; *AC,* 6 July 1962; Eugene T. Reed to Bob [Carter], 25 June 1962, group V, series B, pt. 23, NAACP; *AJ,* 6 August 1962; Isabel Gates Webster to Robert Carter, 1 October 1963, group V, series B, pt. 23, NAACP.

8. *AJC,* 21 April 1963; *AJ,* 22 April 1963; Allen, *Atlanta Rising,* 126; Allen, *Mayor,* 103–4.

9. Eskew, *But for Birmingham,* 259–332; Carter, *Politics of Rage,* 133–55.

10. James N. Giglio, *The Presidency of John F. Kennedy* (Lawrence: University Press of Kansas, 1991), 177–78; Richard Reeves, *President Kennedy: Profile of Power* (New York: Simon and Schuster, 1993), 521–23; Carter, *Politics of Rage,* 151; Robert Mann, *The Walls of Jericho: Lyndon Johnson, Hubert Humphrey, Richard Russell, and the Struggle for Civil Rights* (San Diego: Harcourt, 1996), 364–66; Branch, *Parting the Waters,* 823–24.

11. Carter, *Politics of Rage,* 153; Branch, *Parting the Waters,* 824–25.

12. Anonymous to McGill, 18 June 1963, box 24, REM; anonymous to McGill, 10 July 1963, box 25, REM; J. A. Vandeen to Eugene Patterson, 13 June 1963, box 24, REM; George L. Booth to McGill, 26 June 1963, box 24, REM.

13. Pomerantz, *Peachtree*, 315–19; Allen, *Mayor*, 108.

14. Eliza Paschall to Staige Blackford, 30 August 1963, box 3, EP; Greater Atlanta Council on Human Relations, "Report of Telephone Conversations with Restaurants" and "Report of Telephone Conversations with Hotels," 20 August 1963, box 3, EP.

15. Telex report, November 1963, box 2, NAB; Mrs. Montez G. Albright to Ellen G. Sax, 7, 31 October 1963, reel 110, SRC.

16. Eliza Paschall, memorandum, 11 September 1963, box 3, EP.

17. *AJC*, 20 October, 3, 10 November 1963; Bayor, *Race and Atlanta*, 40–41; Greater Atlanta Council on Human Relations, draft, internal report, [March 1964], box 5, EP.

18. Lester Maddox, "Letter to Atlantans," 14 November 1963, box 2, NAB; telex report, November 1963, box 2, NAB; PASS press release, June 1963, box 57, REM; PASS letter to Atlanta Business and Civic Leaders, June 1963, document case 35, RWW; mimeographed list, "Integrated Hotels, Motels, Restaurants and Cafeterias," [1963], box 10, EP.

19. Telex report, 22 November 1963, box 2, NAB; *AJC*, 15 December 1963; Council on Human Relations of Greater Atlanta, draft, internal report, [March 1964], box 5, EP.

20. Council on Human Relations of Greater Atlanta, report, "Atlanta: Protests and Progress," 27 March 1964, box 6, EP; Council on Human Relations of Greater Atlanta, report, "What Happened in Atlanta," [February 1964], box 5, EP.

21. Telex report, 30 January 1964, box 2, NAB; transcript, Morris Abram Oral History Interview II, 3 May 1984, by Michael L. Gillette, 6–8. See www.lbjlib .utexas.edu/johnson/archives.hom/oralhistory.hom/Citing–Guide.asp.

22. Council on Human Relations of Greater Atlanta, Report, "What Happened in Atlanta," [February 1964], box 5, EP; telex report, 30 January 1964, Box 2, NAB; *AJC*, 26 January 1964; newsclipping, Reese Cleghorn, "Kommemorating an Anniversary," [1966], box 60, REM; *AJ*, 29 January 1964.

23. Newsclipping, "Was Atlanta's Image Too Good to Be True?" *National Observer*, 3 February 1964, reel 110, SRC; William B. Hartsfield to Prentiss Walker, 22 April 1965, box 7, WBH.

24. Lewis, *Walking with the Wind*, 233; telex report, 30 January 1964, box 2, NAB; *AJ*, 30 January 1964; Council on Human Relations of Greater Atlanta, draft, internal report, [March 1964], box 5, EP; Council on Human Relations of Greater Atlanta, report, "Atlanta: Protests and Progress," 27 March 1964, box 6, EP.

25. *AJ*, 27, 30 January 1964; telex report, 30 January 1964, box 2, NAB; Council on Human Relations of Greater Atlanta, draft, internal report, [March 1964], box 5, EP.

26. Lyndon B. Johnson, address before a Joint Session of the Congress, 27 November 1963, reprinted in Bruce Schulman, *Lyndon B. Johnson and American Liberalism: A Brief History with Documents* (Boston: Bedford Books of St. Mar-

tin's Press, 1995), 169–73; Mann, *Walls of Jericho*, 388–90; Merle Miller, *Lyndon: An Oral Biography* (New York: Ballantine, 1980), 446–48.

27. *AJ*, 13 February 1964; Gilbert C. Fite, *Richard B. Russell, Jr.: Senator from Georgia* (Chapel Hill: University of North Carolina Press, 1991), 409; Robert D. Loevy, *To End All Segregation: The Politics of the Passage of the Civil Rights Act* (Lanham, Md.: University Press of America, 1990), 153–66; Charles Whalen and Barbara Whalen, *The Longest Debate: A Legislative History of the 1964 Civil Rights Act* (Washington, D.C.: Seven Locks Press, 1985), 124–217, 239–42; Timothy N. Thurber, *The Politics of Equality: Hubert H. Humphrey and the African American Freedom Struggle* (New York: Columbia University Press, 1999), 127–48; John G. Stewart, "The Civil Rights Act of 1964: Strategy," in *The Civil Rights Act of 1964: The Passage of the Law That Ended Racial Segregation*, ed. by Robert D. Loevy (Albany: State University of New York Press, 1997), 167–209; Mann, *The Walls of Jericho*, 390–428, 513–15; Alexander M. Bickel, "The Civil Rights Act of 1964," *Commentary* 38 (August 1964): 36–38.

28. Moreton Rolleston, telephone interview with author, 17 May 1999; *AT*, 3, 6 July 1964; *AJ*, 6–7 July 1964; *AC*, 7 July 1964; Maddox, *Speaking Out*, 52–54; Lester Maddox, interview with author, 12 May 1999; telex reports, 26–27 August 1964, box 9, NAB; report, Sgt. M. G. Redding to H. T. Jenkins, 3 July 1964, box 18, HTJ; *AJC*, 4 July 1964.

29. Handbill, American Patriots Rally, [July 1964], box 2, NAB; Carter, *Politics of Rage*, 216; *AJC*, 5 July 1964; *AT*, 5 July 1964; *AJ*, 6, 8 July 1964; *AC*, 7 July 1964.

30. *AT*, 4 July 1964; Carter, *Politics of Rage*, 216–17; telex report, 17 July 1964, box 9, NAB.

31. Carter, *Politics of Rage*, 216–17; Calvin Craig to Esteemed Klanspeople, 2 July 1964, box 1, CC.

32. The record sold at the Pickrick for $2.98. On the jacket, Maddox was pictured against a red, white, and blue background. The flip side paired quotations from Nathan Hale ("I regret that I have but one life to give for my country") and Maddox ("While I do live, let me have not just a country, but a free country"). See Huie, "Dream of Lester Maddox," 74, n. 31; Galphin, *Maddox*, 64; *AJ*, 11 July 1964.

33. Lester Maddox, "If I Go to Jail," cited in Huie, "Dream of Lester Maddox," 71–74.

34. Galphin, *Maddox*, 63, 67; *AJ*, 10, 13, 15 July 1964; *AC*, 10, 14–18 July 1964.

35. *AJ*, 17 July 1964.

36. Telex report, 17 July 1964, box 9, NAB; transcript, 17 July 1964, *Heart of Atlanta Motel, Inc. v. United States of America and Robert F. Kennedy*, United States District Court, Northern Division of Georgia, Civil Action No. 9017, Record Group 21, NA (hereafter cited as "*Heart of Atlanta Motel v. U.S.*"); Moreton Rolleston, telephone interview with author, 17 May 1999; Cortner, *Civil Rights and Public Accommodations*, 39–62.

37. Telex report, 17 July 1964, box 9, NAB; transcript of proceedings, 17 July 1964, *George Willis Jr., Woodrow T. Lewis, and Albert L. Dunn, plaintiffs; United States of America, by Robert F. Kennedy, Attorney General, intervenor; v. The Pickrick Restaurant, a corporation, and Lester G. Maddox, defendants*; Civil

Action No. 9028, United States District Court, Northern District of Georgia (hereafter cited as *Willis v. Pickrick*), box 491, Record Group 21, NA.

38. Depositions for *Willis v. Pickrick*, box 490, Record Group 21, NA; testimony of Barbara Brandt, transcript of proceedings, 17 July 1964, *Willis v. Pickrick*, box 491, Record Group 21, NA; telex report, 23 July 1964, box 9, NAB; *AC*, 20–21 July 1964; *AJ*, 20 July 1964; *AT*, 20 July 1964.

39. Transcript of proceedings, 20 July 1964, *Willis v. Pickrick*, box 491, Record Group 21, NA.

40. *AJ*, 23 July, 11 August 1964; *AT*, 23 July, 11 August 1964; Judge Elbert Tuttle, Opinion, 22 July 1964, *Willis v. Pickrick*, box 491, Record Group 21, NA; Judge Elbert Tuttle, Opinion, 22 July 1964, *Heart of Atlanta Motel v. U.S.*; Galphin, *Maddox*, 68; telex report, 12 August 1964, box 9, NAB.

41. Telex report, [late August 1964], box 9, NAB; Galphin, *Maddox*, 74–76; *AJC*, 16 August 1964; Huie, "Dream of Lester Maddox," 39; *AT*, 21 September 1964.

42. *AJ*, 24, 28–29 September, 11 November 1964; *AJC*, 27 September 1964; *AT*, 27, 29 September 1964; Huie, "Dream of Lester Maddox," 41; Galphin, *Maddox*, 77.

43. Oral Arguments in *Heart of Atlanta Motel v. United States*, 379 U.S. 241, in Peter Irons and Stephanie Guitton, eds., *May It Please the Court: The Most Significant Oral Arguments Made before the Supreme Court since 1955* (New York: New Press, 1993), 265–71; Cortner, *Civil Rights and Public Accommodations*, 90–118.

44. 379 U.S. 242–62; *AJ*, 14 December 1964.

45. Galphin, *Maddox*, 77–79; transcript of proceedings, *Willis v. Pickrick*, 1 February 1965, box 492, Record Group 21, NA; *AJ*, 1–6 February 1965.

46. *AJC*, 7 February 1965; *AJ*, 8, 23 February 1965; Galphin, *Maddox*, 79–80.

47. Bartley, *Thurmond to Wallace*, 68; Arlie Schardt, "Lester Maddox and the Mad Democrats," *Reporter* 35 (20 October 1966): 29; Numan V. Bartley, "Moderation in Maddox Country?" *Georgia Historical Quarterly* 8 (Fall 1974): 343–44; telex report, 30 September 1966, box 9, NAB.

48. Pomerantz, *Peachtree*, 351; Allen, *Atlanta Rising*, 149; Joseph H. Dimon VI, "Charles Weltner and Civil Rights," *Atlanta Historical Journal* 24 (1986): 17.

49. *WP*, 3 January 1965; Short, *Pickrick*, 84–85; Bartley, *Thurmond to Wallace*, 76; Bartley, *Modern Georgia*, 206; *NYT*, 15 September 1968.

50. Robert Dallek, *Flawed Giant: Lyndon Johnson and His Times, 1961–1973* (New York: Oxford University Press, 1998), 120; Key, *Southern Politics*, 277; Dan Balz and Ronald Brownstein, *Storming the Gates: Protest Politics and the Republican Revival* (Boston: Little, Brown, 1996), 209–17; Edsall, *Chain Reaction*, 35–36.

51. Key, *Southern Politics*, 277.

52. *WP*, 3 January 1965; *NYT*, 17 June 1965; Short, *Pickrick*, 97.

53. Short, *Pickrick*, 83–100; Bartley, *Thurmond to Wallace*, 67–81; Bartley, "Moderation in Maddox Country?" 344; *NYT*, 11 January 1967.

54. Schardt, "Maddox and the Mad Democrats," 29–30; Allen, *Atlanta Rising*, 150; telex report, [January 1967], box 9, NAB; Galphin, *Maddox*, 164.

CHAPTER NINE
CITY LIMITS: URBAN SEPARATISM AND SUBURBAN SECESSION

1. U.S. Bureau of the Census, *U.S. Censuses of Population and Housing: 1960*, vol. 1, pt. 8, *Census Tracts: Atlanta, Ga., Standard Metropolitan Statistical Area*, table P-1; U.S. Bureau of the Census, *1970 Census of Population and Housing*, vol. 1, pt. 14, *Census Tracts: Atlanta, Ga., Standard Metropolitan Area (and Adjacent Area)*, table P-1; U.S. Bureau of the Census, *1980 Census of Population and Housing*, vol. 2, pt. 80, *Census Tracts: Atlanta, Ga. Standard Metropolitan Statistical Area*, table P-2.

2. Allen, *Mayor*, 222; Bayor, *Race and Atlanta*, 7, 83–84; James Holloway, "The Paradigm of Dixie Hills," *New South* (Summer 1967): 75–81; Pomerantz, *Peachtree*, 348.

3. Hartsfield to Spiro Agnew, 31 October 1969, box 7, WBH; Hartsfield to James Pope, 9 February 1968, box 7, WBH.

4. Richard M. Scammon and Ben J. Wattenberg, *The Real Majority: An Extraordinary Examination of the American Electorate* (New York: Coward-McCann, 1970), 269–72; Bayor, *Race and Atlanta*, 42–44; Stone, *Regime Politics*, 78–79.

5. Allen, *Atlanta Rising*, 173–74; Pomerantz, *Peachtree*, 383.

6. Report, Long Range Planning Committee to Atlanta Chamber of Commerce, 20 September 1971, cited in Bayor, *Race and Atlanta*, 44.

7. Douglas S. Massey and Nancy Denton, *American Apartheid: Segregation and the Making of the Underclass* (Cambridge, Mass.: Harvard University Press, 1993): 47, 76; Tamar Jacoby, *Someone Else's House: America's Unfinished Struggle for Integration* (New York: Free Press, 1998), 503–4.

8. U.S. Bureau of the Census, *1970 Census of Population and Housing*, vol. 1, pt. 14, *Census Tracts: Atlanta, Ga., Standard Metropolitan Area (and Adjacent Area)*, table P-1; Jacoby, *Someone Else's House*, 371–72.

9. Patterson, Brown, 100–101; Stone, *Regime Politics*, 103; Allen, *Atlanta Rising*, 176.

10. Wilkinson, *From Brown to Bakke*, 109; AC, 4 February 1969; Leon E. Panetta and Peter Gall, *Bring Us Together: The Nixon Team and the Civil Rights Retreat* (New York: Lippincott, 1971), 79.

11. Peter Irons, *Jim Crow's Children: The Broken Promise of the Brown Decision* (New York: Viking, 2002), 199–233; Wilkinson, *From Brown to Bakke*, 116–18, 136–39; Stone, *Regime Politics*, 103; Bayor, *Race and Atlanta*, 247.

12. John Egerton, *The Americanization of Dixie: The Southernization of America* (New York: Harpers, 1974), 89–93; Bayor, *Race and Atlanta*, 247–51; Stone, *Regime Politics*, 104–6; Tomiko Brown-Nagin, "Race as Identity Caricature: A Local Legal History Lesson in the Salience of Intraracial Difference," *University of Pennsylvania Law Review* 151 (June 2003): 6.

13. NYT, 6 May 1985; AJC, 10 August 2002; Jacoby, *Someone Else's House*, 368–69.

14. Bayor, *Race and Atlanta*, 47–48; Pomerantz, *Peachtree*, 408–21.

15. Allen, *Atlanta Rising*, 192; *Esquire*, June 1985; Ronald H. Bayor, "African-American Mayors and Governance in Atlanta," in *African-American Mayors:*

Race, Politics, and the American City, ed. David R. Colburn and Jeffrey S. Adler (Urbana: University of Illinois Press, 2001), 184; M. Dale Henson and James King, "The Atlanta Public-Private Romance: An Abrupt Transformation," in *Public-Private Partnerships in American Cities*, ed. R. Scott Fosler and Renee A. Berger (Lexington, Mass.: Lexington Books, 1982), 331–35.

16. Allen, *Atlanta Rising*, 232; Stone, *Regime Politics*, 136; Jacoby, *Someone Else's House*, 405–9; Pomerantz, *Peachtree*, 489; *Esquire*, June 1985; Bryan Burroughs and John Helyar, *Barbarians at the Gate: The Fall of RJR-Nabisco* (New York: Harper Business, 2003), 85.

17. *Esquire*, June 1985; Allen, *Atlanta Rising*, 222–23, 227–30, 235–36.

18. Brookings Institution, report, *Moving beyond Sprawl: The Challenge for Metropolitan Atlanta*, copy in author's possession; *WSJ*, 8 March 1983; *NYT*, 14 July 1988; Allen, *Atlanta Rising*, 247; William Schneider, "The Suburban Century Begins," *Atlantic Monthly*, July 1992, 33.

19. Allen, *Atlanta Rising*, 136; Abbott, *New Urban America*, 186–87; Larry Keating, *Atlanta: Race, Class, and Urban Expansion* (Philadelphia: Temple University Press, 2001), 15.

20. Jackson, *Crabgrass Frontier*, 283–96.

21. Jackson, *Crabgrass Frontier*, 190–230; Arnold Hirsch, " 'Containment' on the Home Front: Race and Federal Housing Policy from the New Deal to the Cold War," *Journal of Urban History* 26, no. 2 (2000): 158–89; Lizabeth Cohen, *A Consumers' Republic: The Politics of Mass Consumption in Postwar America* (New York: Knopf, 2003), 194–256; Wiese, *Places of Their Own*; Becky M. Nicolaides, *My Blue Heaven: Life and Politics in the Working-Class Suburbs of Los Angeles, 1920–1965* (Chicago: University of Chicago Press, 2002).

22. *AJC*, 3 May 1987; Peter Applebome, *Dixie Rising: How the South Is Shaping American Values, Politics, and Culture* (San Diego: Harcourt Brace, 1996), 34; U.S. Bureau of the Census, *1970 Census of Population and Housing*, vol. 1, pt. 14, *Census Tracts: Atlanta, Ga., Standard Metropolitan Statistical Area (and Adjacent Area*, tables P-1, P-4; Jacoby, *Someone Else's House*, 370.

23. Abbott, *New Urban America*, 184–85; Pomerantz, *Peachtree*, 379; U.S. Bureau of the Census, *U.S. Census of Population and Housing: 1960*, vol. 1, pt. 8, *Census Tracts: Atlanta, Ga., Standard Metropolitan Statistical Area*, table P-1; U.S. Bureau of the Census, *1970 Census of Population and Housing*, vol. 1, pt. 14, *Census Tracts: Atlanta, Ga., Standard Metropolitan Statistical Area (and Adjacent Area)*, tables P-1, P-2.

24. Davis, *City of Quartz*, 165–69; Edsall, *Chain Reaction*, 29, 227–31; David L. Kirp, John P. Dwyer, and Larry A. Rosenthal, *Our Town: Race, Housing and the Soul of Suburbia* (New Brunswick, N.J.: Rutgers University Press, 1997), 6.

25. Robert B. Reich, "Secession of the Successful," *NYT Magazine*, 20 January 1991, 16–17, 42–45; Robert Reich, *The Work of Nations: Preparing Ourselves for 21st Century Capitalism* (New York: Vintage, 1992), 268–69; Charles Murray, "Millennial Thoughts," *National Review*, 8 July 1991, 31–32.

26. *NYT Magazine*, 23 June 1996, 55; *WP*, 17 July 1988; *WSJ*, 26 March 1987.

27. *NYT*, 2 June 1971; Applebome, *Dixie Rising*, 35.

28. *AJ*, 13 December 1963, 6–7 January, 26 March, 14 August 1964, 19 February 1965; William B. Hartsfield to Pollard Turman, 22 February 1965, and Turman to Hartsfield, 1 March 1965, box 7, WBH; A. P. Hendrickson and Sarah Bendicks to Hartsfield, 21 February 1965, box 29, WBH.

29. Booklet, "Save Sandy Springs," [1966], box 29, WBH; booklet, "A Few Reasons Why Sandy Springs Should Vote against Annexation," 7 March 1966, box 29, WBH; Bayor, *Race and Atlanta*, 88–92; Abbott, *New Urban America*, 194; *WSJ*, 8 March 1983.

30. *AJC*, 26 July 1999; Keating, *Atlanta: Race, Class, and Urban Expansion*, 113–41; Abbott, *New Urban America*, 193; Stone, *Regime Politics*, 98–100; Bayor, *Race and Atlanta*, 194–95; Allen, *Atlanta Rising*, 198–200; Applebome, *Dixie Rising*, 35; *AJC*, 4 August 1985; *NYT*, 7 February, 14 July 1988.

31. *AJC*, 3 July 1987, 1 October 1990, 17–18 January 1993; *NYT*, 22 July 1987, 7 February, 14 July 1988, 13 August 1989.

32. Michael N. Danielson, *The Politics of Exclusion* (New York: Columbia University Press, 1976), 94, 98, 178, 185, 193; Reese Cleghorn, "A Closer Look: Atlanta," *City* 5 (January–February 1971): 36–37; *Crow v. Brown*, 332 F. Supp. 389 (1971); Abbott, *New Urban America*, 193.

33. Danielson, *Politics of Exclusion*, 161, 197; *NYT*, 2 June 1971; William Lilley III, "Housing Report: Courts Lead Revolutionary Trend toward Desegregation of Residential Areas," *National Journal*, 27 November 1971, 2336–48. As the *Crow* litigation crumbled, proponents of low-income suburban housing found greater success in New Jersey in the landmark *Mount Laurel* cases. See Kirp et al., *Our Town*.

34. Bartley, *Thurmond to Wallace*, 61–62, 75–81.

35. Reg Murphy and Hal Gulliver, *The Southern Strategy* (New York: Scribner's, 1971), 174–75, 194–95, 269; Bartley, *Thurmond to Wallace*, 75, 93; *NYT*, 17 June 1965, 10 November 1966, 15 October 1970; *AC*, 9 October 1971.

36. Lilley, "Housing Report," 2342; Cleghorn, "A Closer Look," 37; Murphy and Gulliver, *Southern Strategy*, 174–75; Panetta and Gall, *Bring Us Together*, 92–93, 106–9, 181, 287–88, 316; Danielson, *Politics of Exclusion*, 161, 197; Black and Black, *Rise of Southern Republicans*, 120–22.

37. Scammon and Wattenberg, *Real Majority*, 67–68; Kenneth D. Durr, *Behind the Backlash: White Working-Class Politics in Baltimore, 1940–1980* (Chapel Hill: University of North Carolina Press, 2003), 112–76; Jackson, *Crabgrass Frontier*, 283; Garry Wills, *Nixon Agonistes: The Crisis of the Self-Made Man*, 2nd ed. (New York: Mariner, 2002), 278.

38. *NYT*, 7 December 1969; Matthew D. Lassiter, "Suburban Strategies: The Volatile Center in Postwar American Politics," in *The Democratic Experiment: New Directions in American Political History*, ed. Meg Jacobs, William J. Novak, and Julian E. Zelizer (Princeton: Princeton University Press, 2003), 327–49.

39. Phillips, *Emerging Republican Majority*, 474, n. 207; Wills, *Nixon Agonistes*, 264–65.

40. Egerton, *Americanization of Dixie*, 126–29, 138. For a fuller and more nuanced explanation of the ways in which Nixon followed a "suburban strategy" rather than a "Southern strategy," see Lassiter, *Silent Majority*.

41. *NYT*, 11 December 1970; Panetta and Gall, *Bring Us Together*, 1–3, 368–72; Carter, *Wallace to Gingrich*, 45.

42. Panetta and Gall, *Bring Us Together*, 92; John W. Dean, *The Rehnquist Choice: The Untold Story of the Nixon Appointment That Redefined the Supreme Court* (New York: Free Press, 2001): 47.

43. Dean, *Rehnquist Choice*, 14–28.

44. *NYT*, 17 October 1971, 17 March 1972; Patterson, Brown, 150; Irons, *Jim Crow's Children*, 241–42; U.S. Congress, *Hearings Before the Committee on the Judiciary, U.S. Senate*, 92nd Cong., 1st sess., *Nominations of William H. Rehnquist, of Arizona, and Lewis F. Powell, Jr., of Virginia, to Be Associate Justices of the Supreme Court of the United States* (Washington, D.C.: U.S. Government Printing Office, 1971), 305–11; Donald E. Boles, *Mr. Justice Rehnquist, Judicial Activist: The Early Years* (Ames: Iowa State University Press, 1987), 75–77, 90–94.

45. 411 U.S. 1 (1973); 418 U.S. 717 (1974); 422 U.S. 490 (1975); 418 U.S. 814 (1974); Peter Irons, *The Courage of Their Convictions: Sixteen Americans Who Fought Their Way to the Supreme Court* (New York: Penguin, 1990), 283–303; Wilkinson, *From* Brown *to* Bakke, 216–49; Patterson, Brown, 177–83.

EPILOGUE
THE LEGACIES OF WHITE FLIGHT

1. William Schneider, "The Suburban Century Begins," *Atlantic Monthly* (July 1992): 33–44; Newt Gingrich, *To Renew America* (New York: HarperCollins, 1995), 23; Lee Edwards, *The Conservative Revolution: The Movement That Remade America* (New York: Free Press, 1999), 275–78.

2. Mel Steely, *The Gentleman from Georgia: The Biography of Newt Gingrich* (Macon, Ga.: Mercer University Press, 2000), 19–22; Edwards, *Conservative Revolution*, 274–75; *AJC*, 11 January 2003.

3. Applebome, *Dixie Rising*, 43–44.

4. Schneider, "Suburban Century," 33–44; Edwards, *Conservative Revolution*, 293–321 (Krauthammer quotation from p. 299); Contract with America, *http://www.house.gov/house/Contract/CONTRACT.html*, accessed 30 July 2004; WP, 11 November 1994.

5. Edwards, *Conservative Revolution*, 300–302 (*New York Times* from p. 301); Balz and Brownstein, *Storming the Gates*, 206.

6. Steely, *Gentleman from Georgia*, 288; Black and Black, *Rise of Southern Republicans*, 5–6, 231–33, 337–38, 394–95; Balz and Brownstein, *Storming the Gates*, 203–9; Carter, *Wallace to Gingrich*, 106–8, 118–20.

7. Balz and Brownstein, *Storming the Gates*, 296–98.

8. Carter, *Wallace to Gingrich*, 110–11.

9. U.S. Bureau of the Census, *1970 Census of Population and Housing*, vol. 1, pt. 14, *Census Tracts: Atlanta, Ga., Standard Metropolitan Statistical Area (and Adjacent Area)*, tables P-1, P-2; *AJC*, 30 September 1999; 10 August 2002; 22 June 2003.

10. *AJC*, 10 August 2002; U.S. Census Bureau, State and County QuickFacts, *http://quickfacts.census.gov*, accessed 3 February 2004; U.S. Census Bureau, Census 2000 (PHC-T-4), Ranking Tables for Counties: 1990 and 2000, table 4: Counties Ranked by Percent Change in Population: 1990 to 2000, *http://www.census .gov/population/www/cen2000/phc-t4.html*, accessed 3 February 2004; Myron Orfield, *American Metropolitics: The New Suburban Reality* (Washington, D.C.: Brookings Institution Press, 2002), maps 1-1, 1-2, 1-13, 1-14.

11. Balz and Brownstein, *Storming the Gates*, 211; Stanley B. Greenberg, *The Two Americas: Our Current Political Deadlock and How to Break It* (New York: St. Martin's Press, 2004), 95–116; Michael Barone, "Introduction: The 49 Percent Nation," in *Almanac of American Politics, 2002* (Washington, D.C.: National Journal, 2001), 21–45.

12. Balz and Brownstein, *Storming the Gates*, 238–39; John Milton Cooper Jr., "The Election of 2000 at the Bar of History," in *The Unfinished Election of 2000*, ed. Jack Rakove (New York: Basic Books, 2001), 24–25.

13. George W. Bush, *A Charge to Keep* (New York: Morrow, 1999): 234–36; David Frum, *The Right Man: The Surprise Presidency of George W. Bush* (New York: Random House, 2003), 5–6, 33–34, 41–42, 49–52, 273–74; Molly Ivins and Lou Dubose, *Shrub: The Short but Happy Political Life of George W. Bush* (New York: Vintage, 2000), 89–93; David Aikman, *A Man of Faith: The Spiritual Journey of George W. Bush* (Nashville: W Publishing Group, 2004), 99–103, 136–37, 143–46; James C. Moore and Wayne Slater, *Bush's Brain: How Karl Rove Made George W. Bush Presidential* (Hoboken, N.J.: Wiley, 2003): 222; Michael Lind, *Made in Texas: George W. Bush and the Southern Takeover of American Politics* (New York: Basic Books, 2003), 118–22; Kevin Phillips, *American Dynasty: Aristocracy, Fortune, and the Politics of Deceit in the House of Bush* (New York: Viking, 2004), 173–77.

Index

Page numbers in italics refer to illustrations.

Hartsfield, William B. (*cont.*)
movement and, 148; coalition leaders
and, 25–28; fire department desegregation and, 38; golf course desegregation
and, 119–21; mayoral elections and, 35,
39, 40–41, 197; NAACP and, 36; Plan
of Improvement and, 38, 105, 247; private racial attitudes of, 35–36; public relations advice of, 4; residential transition
and, 64, 70–71, 72–74, 78, 84, 101,
103; school desegregation and, 135–36,
138, 141, 147–49, 153–55; sit-ins and,
181–82, 188–91; on student protests,
217; tax revolts and, 127–28
Hatch, Alfred, 177
Haverty, Rawson, 218
Haynsworth, Clement, 256
Heart of Atlanta Motel, 208, 220
Heart of Atlanta Motel v. U. S., 223–25,
227–28
Help Our Public Education, Inc. (HOPE),
138–39, 141–43
Henry County, 264
Henry Grady Hotel, 207
Herndon, Alonzo, 29
Herren's Restaurant, 218
Hightower Road, 101–2
highway construction: in Adamsville, 86;
in Collier Heights, 99; interstate, 86,
243–44; in Mozley Park, 59–60, 71, 74.
See also street closings
Hilton Hotel (airport location), 208–9
Hines, Clifford, 48
Hobson Street, 96–97
HOLC (Home Owners' Loan Corpora-
tion), 60
Holder, Bob, 241
Holiday Inn, 213
Holly Street, 103
Holmes, Alfred, 117–20
Holmes, Dr. Hamilton, 117–20
Holmes, Hamilton (grandson of Dr. Hamil-
ton Holmes), 145
Holmes, Martha Ann, 156–57, 159
home loans. *See* lending practices, discrimi-
nation in
homeowners' associations, 12; Adair Park
Civic Club, 94–97; Adamsville Civic
Club, 82–84; assertion of "rights" by,
44, 127, 164; Collier Heights Civic
Club, 98–99; Grant Park Civic Associa-
tion, 166–67; Grove Park Civic Associa-
tion, 101; Grove Park Civic League,

103; Mozley Park Home Owners' Protec-
tive Assoc., 64–66, 68, 77; Southwest
Citizens Assoc., 4, 71, 77, 83–85, 98–
99; tactics of, 58, 183; violence against
blacks and, 56–57, 85, 102–3; West End
Cooperative Corp., 44, 54–58, 65; West
Manor Civic Club, 82
Home Owners' Loan Corporation
(HOLC), 60
Hooper, Frank A., 136–37, 141, 144, 162–
64, 223, 227–29
HOPE. *See* Help Our Public Education,
Inc.
Hope, John, 30
Hope Street, 94–95
hotel desegregation, 207–10, 212–13, 220,
223–25, 227–28
House Committee on Un-American Activi-
ties, 36, 39, 49
Housing Authority (Atlanta), 71–72
Howell Mill Road, 51
Huggins, B. M., 91
human rights, 84, 180–81, 196
Hunter, Charlayne, 73, 145
Hunter, Floyd, 19–20, 36
Hunter Street, 62
Hurley, Ruby, 207

individual rights/individualization, 8–9, 57,
195–96; Civil Rights Act and, 227–28;
"freedom of association" and, 164; modern conservatism and, 259; public accommodations desegregation and, 218; residential transition and, 80–81, 104;
suburbs and, 8; white supremacist
groups on, 44
"interracial intimacy," 48; bus services
and, 108, 115–16; golf courses and,
118–19; public spaces desegregation
and, 106; residential transition and, 88;
school desegregation and, 139, 141,
159; swimming pools and, 123
Interstate Highway 20, 86
Interstate Highway 285, 243–44
intrawhite hostility, 63, 90, 96–99

J. L. Wolfe Realty, 67
Jackson, James, 166
Jackson, Kenneth, 244
Jackson, M. C., 85
Jackson, Maynard, Jr., 29, 236, 240–41
Jacoby, Tamar, 237
Jefferson, Lawrence, 154

*Pocketbook Politics: Economic Citizenship
in Twentieth-Century America* by Meg Jacobs

*Taken Hostage: The Iran Hostage Crisis and America's
First Encounter with Radical Islam* by David Farber

*Morning in America: How Ronald Reagan
Invented the 1980s* by Gil Troy

*Phyllis Schlafly and Grassroots Conservatism:
A Woman's Crusade* by Donald T. Crichtlow

*White Flight: Atlanta and the Making
of Modern Conservatism* by Kevin M. Kruse